EARLY SCREENWRITING TEACHERS

1910–1922

Origins, Contribution and Legacy

Stephen Charles Curran

First published in 2019 by Accelerated Education Publications Ltd

Based on a thesis submitted for the degree of Doctor of Philosophy, Department of Media Studies, Brunel University London, United Kingdom, September 2015.

ISBN: 978-1910106-00-6

The vast number of screenwriting manuals has its precursors in the pre-studio era. These early screenwriting teachers are almost forgotten. It is Stephen Curran's merit to bring them back to our attention.

He delivers a meticulously researched, in-depth analysis of early screenwriting teaching and thus makes not only an important contribution to the study of screenwriting history, but delivers a welcome starting point for discussing the discourse about screenwriting and its influence on the industry in historical as well as in recent contexts.

CLAUS TIEBER, PhD, Head of Several Research Projects,
University of Vienna.

Early Screenwriting Teachers offers much needed insight and understanding of the genesis of screenwriting practices as a driving controlling factor in the emergence, development and eventual success of the Hollywood studio system.

Curran illuminates this overlooked area of inquiry by examining and unpacking elements and techniques adapted and honed from literary and theatrical traditions first; and then by focusing on the historical relevance of key teachers and their contributions to capture the complexity and fluid nature of training for the profession in the industry since its early days.

Richly illustrated and providing a wealth of vital references to fascinating primary sources, the book is a welcome addition to the current scholarship of screenwriting studies.

PAOLO RUSSO, PhD, Senior Lecturer in Film Studies
Oxford Brookes University.

CONTENTS

LIST OF FIGURES

PREFACE

Early Screenwriting Teachers 1910–1922: Origins, Contribution and Legacy is an historical study that reveals the previously unacknowledged contribution that early screenwriting teachers have made to the development of the Hollywood film industry.

Drawing on an extensive range of primary materials, including manuals and columns written for the fan and trade press, this book shows the significant role five key screenwriting teachers played in translating playwriting theory and theatrical tradition into writing for film. It demonstrates how these early teachers contributed to forming and codifying a set of foundational writing techniques specific to the film medium, as well as examining the legacy they have left in the context of the role and function of contemporary screenwriting gurus.

This book fills an important gap in the historiography of screenwriting in Hollywood. As well as giving due credit to a body of work that has previously received only passing consideration, it highlights the role of early screenwriting teachers, which has been understated if not ignored.

ACKNOWLEDGMENTS

I thank the following individuals who have been a source of encouragement and advice. I am grateful to Dr Ian W. Macdonald, Visiting Associate Professor in Screenwriting Research of the School of Media and Communication, University of Leeds, and Founder of The Screenwriting Research Network for his guidance on early UK screenwriting manuals and for urging me to examine the late nineteenth-century playwriting manuals for probable links. I am also grateful for the assistance of Associate Professor Steven Maras, Associate Professor of the School of Social Sciences, University of Western Australia, in sharing valuable primary source material, and for our helpful and constructive discussions about screenwriting manuals. His extensive knowledge and scholarship in this area of film studies has been greatly appreciated. I would also like to thank both J.J. Murphy, Hamel Family Distinguished Chair in Communication Arts, and David Bordwell, the Jacques Ledoux Professor of Film Studies of the Department of Communication Arts, University of Wisconsin-Madison, for their interest and support for the project. I am also grateful to all the many members of the Screenwriting Research Network for their support and encouragement.

Special thanks are due to Eric Hoyt, Associate Professor of Media and Cultural Studies of the Department of Communication Arts, University of Wisconsin-Madison and Co-Director of the Media History Digital Library, and all those who help provide this invaluable resource, without which this project would have involved spending months in the USA. I am especially grateful to Eric for responding to requests to scan and digitise particular US library holdings that I needed to access. I am similarly thankful to David Pierce, the Founder and Emeritus Director of the Media History Digital Library, for providing important background source information on fan and trade press circulation figures.

Most of all, I am thankful to Geoff King, Professor of Film and TV Studies, Brunel University, for seeing the potential of the project and giving me the opportunity to carry out the necessary research to fulfil it. I am appreciative of his great attention to detail, academic rigour and wisdom, as well as of the sound advice he has given, which has made it possible to complete the thesis on which this book is based.

INTRODUCTION

INTRODUCTION

Academic film historians divide up the periods of Hollywood history in various ways, but, in essence, most analyses are based on three broad phases of history, corresponding to the structure and development of the industry in each period. These are: the 'silent' period up to the 1920s; the studio period (1920s–1950/60s); and the package unit system or independent production period (1950/60s to the present). Generally, historians who have focused specifically on screenwriting history acknowledge the same broad phases of film history.[1]

These basic historical delineations are important for this study, as at the end of each of these periods a major shift in organisation occurred that had direct effects on the level and type of activity in which screenwriting teachers were engaged. My study will focus on the work of screenwriting teachers up to the first major shift in organisation: the establishment of the studio system in the 1920s. This early period coincided with a period of intense activity by screenwriting teachers, which then tailed off in the early 1920s as the studio system took hold.

Research Objectives

The aim of this project is to give an account of the origins, contribution and legacy of screenwriting teachers during the 12 years of the silent period when they were most active in the American film industry (1910–1922). 'Screenwriting teachers' are defined as those who gave written advice on screenwriting and gained a significant following or traction with the general public or in the film industry during this period. Given screenwriting teachers have been involved in the American film industry for more than a century, an investigation of their activity in this early period is of particular interest, as it

---

1 Tom Stempel identifies the first period as 'Silent Beginnings' (1894–1920), the second as 'The Studio Period' (1920–1950) and the third as 'Independent Production' from the 1950s onwards. See Tom Stempel, *Framework: A History of Screenwriting in the American Film*, 3rd ed. (New York: Syracuse, 2000), 3–48.

Marc Norman recognises the early period as distinct by describing the activities of screenwriters up to the early 1920s in the first two parts of his book, 3–109; the following section titled 'Control,' 113–286, refers to the growing power of the studios; and then 'Freelance' covers the 1950s onwards, 289–485. See Marc Norman, *What Happens Next: A History of American Screenwriting* (London: Aurum, 2008).

Janet Staiger identifies the process of cinematic development by changes in the modes of production over six stages. The first four of these occur up to 1931, roughly equating to the silent period. The next stage, the 'producer-unit system' (1931–1955), refers to the studio period; and the final stage, the 'package unit system' (1955–1960), to the period of independent production. See David Bordwell, Janet Staiger and Kristin Thompson, *The Classical Hollywood Cinema: Film Style and Mode of Production to 1960* (New York: Columbia, 1985), 85–153, 309–364.

Bordwell and Thompson identify five stages: early cinema (to about 1919), the late silent era (1919–1929), sound cinema (1926–1945), post-war cinema (1946–1960s) and the 1960s to the present; but if the first four periods are paired up, three broad phases of history can still be detected. See Kristin Thompson and David Bordwell, *Film History: An Introduction*, 3rd ed. (New York: McGraw Hill, 2010), xv.

permits an assessment of how their role was originally shaped and defined. This analysis also improves understanding of their role in the Hollywood industry today.

The intense activity of screenwriting teachers during this early period requires further investigation. Where it has been studied at all, this issue has only been examined in a fragmentary way in the context of work with a different focus, rather than in its own right. Film historians have presented it within the general context of film history or subsumed it within screenwriting historiography. While these historians frequently acknowledge and comment on the increased level of activity of screenwriting teachers at this time, this phenomenon has never been the focus of a full and systematic academic enquiry.

This lack of detailed research is further exacerbated by the fact that many early film histories were written with a particular bias and were closely linked to vested interests. They offer a less than objective or scholarly viewpoint of early Hollywood, and record next to nothing about screenwriting teachers of the period. The journalist Terry Ramsaye famously delivered a 12-week course of lectures in 1926 at the New School for Social Research in New York on the history of film, which would form the basis of his book, *A Million and One Nights*.[2] This book espoused a populist, biased and anecdotal view of Hollywood history that focused on 'great men' such as D. W. Griffith.[3] Dana Polan records that Ramsaye devoted only one lecture out of 12 to the history of the screenplay, and in this lecture Griffith was cast as one of the influential 'magicians' who made it happen.[4] This unscholarly version of Hollywood history not only ignored economic factors, but also minimised the role of screenwriting teachers:

> The history of film criticism and scholarship that emerged during the early years of the twentieth century fits into [a] historical discourse that stitches together artist-and-masterpiece theories in order to signal film's stake in the realm of the so-called high arts.[5]

---

2 Traditional film history of this kind was narrow in approach, focusing on films that had been canonised and lauding their creators as pioneers and adventurers. Thomas Edison even commissioned Ramsaye's book. See Terry Ramsaye, *A Million and One Nights: A History of the Motion Picture through 1925* (New York: Simon and Schuster, 1926), ix. This approach can still be detected in modern historians such as David A. Cook, who privileges some films as '"masterpieces" of the medium'. See James Chapman, Mark Glancy and Sue Harper, 'Introduction', in *The New Film History: Sources, Methods and Approaches*, eds., Chapman, Glancy and Harper (Basingstoke: Palgrave MacMillan, 2007), 2, and David A. Cook, *A History of Narrative Film* (New York: Norton, 1981), 73.

3 Quotes in this book reflect the language of the time, when the use of 'man' and male pronouns to represent both genders was commonplace and unquestioned. For simplicity, and to reflect the character of the era, this language remains unedited, and terms that were standard at that time such as 'cameraman' are retained.

4 Dana Polan, *Scenes of Instruction: The Beginnings of the U.S. Study of Film* (London: University of California, 2007), 98 and 90–112.

5 David A. Gerstner, 'The Practices of Authorship' in *Authorship and Film*, eds. Gerstner and Staiger (London: Routledge, 2003), 5.

More recent histories, written over the last 30 years, offer a more objective and balanced approach by examining cinematic development within a wider context. This new revisionist history of cinema, Robert Allen and Douglas Gomery explain, involves recognising film as:

> a complex historical phenomenon (an art form, economic institution, technology, cultural product) which, since its inception, has participated in many networks of relationships.[6]

More specifically, Janet Staiger's scholarly examination of the Hollywood mode of production indicates that:

> the production of meaning is not separate from its economic mode of production, nor from the instruments and techniques which individuals use to form materials.[7]

The role of the early screenwriting teacher has largely been left out of this re-evaluation. Yet to assess the contribution of the early screenwriting teachers, it is important to understand how they related to, and interacted with, this economic process and how they operated within the broader cultural context.

The Academic Debate

Screenwriting has been in existence for just over a century, producing a considerable body of work. As a result, Bordwell notes that:

> In the 1970s screenwriting became an academic enterprise – not only because it was studied in colleges, but also because, like nineteenth-century salon painting, it was characterized by rigid rules and a widely accepted canon.[8]

However, even the film academics have largely ignored the role of the early screenwriting teacher in the development of the Hollywood film industry. The activity of these teachers still tends only to be remarked upon insofar as it contributes to arguments on other topics.

Bordwell refers to screenwriting teachers both past and present in his narrative about story and style, *The Way Hollywood Tells It*. In observing the output of modern screenwriting teachers, he notes that 'the best manuals offer useful insights into the mechanics of movies'.[9] But he also acknowledges that most of these writers owe much of their understanding to their forebears; he asserts that, in essence, their manuals are

---

6   Robert C. Allen and Douglas Gomery, *Film History: Theory and Practice* (New York: McGraw-Hill, 1985), 16.

7   Bordwell, Staiger and Thompson, *Classical Hollywood Cinema*, 87.

8   David Bordwell, *The Way Hollywood Tells It: Story and Style in Modern Movies* (London: University of California, 2006), 34.

9   Ibid., 35.

simply a rehearsal and summation of 'principles [that] have been reiterated in screenplay handbooks since the 1910s'.[10] He elaborates on the current manual writers:

> the dozens of screenplay manuals pouring from the presses have demanded tight plot construction and a careful coordination of emotional appeals […] but their consolidation of studio-era principles nicely exemplifies how modern American moviemaking pays its tribute to tradition.[11]

It is thus clear that Bordwell accepts to some extent the debt that modern screenwriting teachers and the development of Hollywood narrative style owe to these early pioneers. He continues:

> In formal design, today's Hollywood cinema is largely continuous with yesterday's […and any] changes stand out against a backdrop of conventions that are as powerful today as they were in 1960, or 1940, or 1920.[12]

Bordwell also regularly quotes from early screenwriting manuals in support of his extensive analysis of what he terms 'classical Hollywood style'. For example, in his chapter on 'Story Causality and Motivation', he quotes Frances Taylor Patterson's 1920 manual, where 'plot' is defined as the:

> careful and logical working out of the laws of cause and effect. The mere sequence of events will not make a plot. Emphasis must be laid upon causality and the action and reaction of the human will.[13]

This underpins Bordwell's understanding of what constitutes classical narrative in Hollywood films: 'narrative causality' is synonymous with, and subordinated to, 'psychological causality' and is necessarily rooted in the actions and reactions of the main character as the 'prime causal agent'. This is in sharp contrast to the Soviet cinema of the 1920s, where, for example, 'causality could also be conceived as social – a causality of institutions and group processes' or 'impersonal determinism', where 'coincidence and chance leave the individual little freedom of personal action'.[14] Bordwell points out that, in Hollywood classical narrative, although 'impersonal causes' may begin a line of story action, the narrative will ultimately be driven by 'personal causes':

---

10   Ibid., 28.

11   Ibid., 27.

12   Ibid., 35.

13   Frances Taylor Patterson, *Cinema Craftsmanship: A Book for Photoplaywrights* (1920; repr., Charleston: Bibliolife, 2013), 5; cited in Bordwell, Staiger and Thompson, *Classical Hollywood Cinema*, 13.

14   Bordwell, Staiger and Thompson, *Classical Hollywood Cinema*, 13.

Hollywood rule-books insist upon confining coincidence to the initial situation. Boy and girl may meet by accident, but they cannot rely upon chance to keep their acquaintance alive.[15]

It necessarily follows that, if the main character is the 'primal agent', then this character must act consistently and according to the qualities and traits they have been assigned. This view is verified by '[s]creenplay manuals [that] demand that a character's traits be clearly identified and consistent with one another'.[16]

When discussing how characters become agents of that causality in Hollywood cinema, Bordwell refers to Frederick Palmer's 1924 definition of a character's action: 'the outward expression of inner feelings', which he notes is the 'litmus test of character consistency'.[17] The opinions of other manual writers such as John Emerson, Anita Loos and Tamar Lane[18] are mentioned as well and quoted in support of Bordwell's understanding of Hollywood story construction as:

causality, consequence, psychological motivations, the drive toward overcoming obstacles and achieving goals. Character-centred i.e., personal or psychological – causality is the armature of the classical story.[19]

However, Bordwell offers little or no analysis or in-depth explanation of why or how any manual writer's contribution might be significant in this debate. To the contrary, in numerous quotes from a number of other manuals he omits to even name their writers in his essay, although they are referenced. Among these writers is Henry Albert Phillips, one of the key screenwriting teachers examined in this study.[20]

The omission is perhaps unintentional, but it may be indicative of the overall lack of recognition or value that Bordwell and other film historians accord these writers for their contribution.

---

15 Ibid., 13.

16 Ibid., 13.

17 Frederick Palmer, *Technique of the Photoplay* (Los Angeles: Palmer Institute of Authorship, 1924), 67–68; cited in Bordwell, Staiger and Thompson, *Classical Hollywood Cinema*, 15.

18 John Emerson and Anita Loos, *How to Write Photoplays* (Philadelphia: Jacobs, 1920) and Tamar Lane, *The New Technique of Screen Writing* (New York: Whittlesey House, 1936); cited in Bordwell, Staiger and Thompson, *Classical Hollywood Cinema*, 28, 36, 44, 47–49.

19 Bordwell, Staiger and Thompson, *Classical Hollywood Cinema*, 13.

20 Bordwell, Staiger and Thompson, *Classical Hollywood Cinema*, 39–49. Early screenwriting teachers quoted by Bordwell without being named include Howard T. Dimick, *Modern Photoplay Writing* (Ohio: James Knapp Reeve, 1922) and Henry Albert Phillips, *The Photodrama* (1914; repr., Charleston: Bibliolife, 2013) and a later contributor Eugene Vale, *The Technique of Screenplay Writing* (1944; repr., London: Souvenir Press, 1973).

In her part of the extensive discourse on the Hollywood mode of production, Staiger similarly makes observations on early screenwriting teachers, but they appear among a whole range of comments about other influences that contributed to the establishment of Hollywood practices:

> The sites of the distribution of these practices were material: labor, professional, and trade associations, advertising materials, *handbooks,* film reviews. These institutions and their discourses were mechanisms to formalize and disperse descriptive and prescriptive analyses of the most efficient production practices, the newest technologies, and best look and sound for the films [emphasis added].[21]

Staiger extends this list of possible influences at another point, but makes small beer of the role of screenwriting handbooks:

> Other mechanisms for standardization included ones somewhat connected to the industry – trade publications and critics and *'how to' books* – and ones external to the industry – college courses, newspaper reviewing, theoretical writing, and museum exhibitions [emphasis added].[22]

Among her general assertions are some more specific comments about the contribution of manual writers to the development of style:

> While these mechanisms presented themselves as educational and informative, they were also prescriptive. A how-to-write-a-movie script book advised not only how it was done but how it ought to be done to ensure a sale.[23]

With regard to the continuity script, which had become standard practice by 1914, Staiger posits that 'trade papers and "how-to" handbooks helped to standardize its format'.[24] She does make some limited reference to the trade paper discourse and cites in full a lengthy sample from *The Nickelodeon* (1909) by Archer McMackin to indicate the type of material that appeared. However, although this is an interesting observation, the actual relevance of this kind of material, and how or why it shaped this discourse, is largely unexplored.[25] No real evidence is put forward to show to what extent manual writers influenced this development. In fact, her whole discourse makes little mention of these writers, except for an occasional reference to Epes Winthrop Sargent, who wrote a weekly column for the trade press publication *Moving Picture World* from 1911 until

---

21   Bordwell, Staiger and Thompson, *Classical Hollywood Cinema*, 89.

22   Ibid., 106.

23   Ibid., 106.

24   Ibid., 138.

25   Archer McMackin, 'How moving picture plays are written', *Nickelodeon*, December 1909, 171–73; cited in Staiger in Bordwell, Staiger and Thompson, *Classical Hollywood Cinema*, 107.

1919. The column, she acknowledges, formed the basis of his manual, *The Technique of the Photoplay,* which first appeared in 1912 and quickly 'became a classic'.[26]

Kristin Thompson is another who refers to the work of early screenwriting teachers but, again, only as part of her extensive narrative on the formulation of classical narrative style. In *The Classical Hollywood Cinema,* she comments that:

> trade journals, handbooks, and reviews disseminated and developed the norms of the classical model while standardized studio organization was putting those norms into effect.[27]

It is noteworthy that these are cited amid other influences rather than singled out for discussion. In support of her arguments, Thompson also refers periodically to the work of a number of manual writers; she usefully points out that they were part of a larger discourse on the development of classical film style, along with the contributions of writers of popular fiction and short stories, playwriting and theatrical manuals, drama critics and theorists and vaudeville writers and filmmakers. Thompson establishes some connections that were made, in the process of this discourse, between the content of screenwriting manuals and these materials. Among the more prominent manual writers mentioned are all five of the important screenwriting teachers in this study: Sargent, Phillips, Leslie Tufnell Peacocke, William Lord Wright and Eustace Hale Ball. John Nelson and Frederick Palmer are others included, although, as later chapters will show, their influence was limited. Like Bordwell, Thomson frequently does not directly credit these individuals in her text.[28] In contrast, the aim of this book is to consider how classical style developed with specific reference to the work of key screenwriting teachers.

All these historians refer to the screenwriting teachers only as forming part of a larger discourse on screenwriting history, rather than investigating their particular and explicit value to this discourse. Perhaps the one exception lies in Thompson's more detailed discussion of the development of the concept of continuity, where she states, 'Initially it occurred in the scenario columns and books.'[29] After that, she gives samples of the specific advice offered by a number of handbook writers, such as Nelson, Phillips, Sargent and Peacocke.[30] She also hints at their greater significance by discussing their role in the industry:

---

26 Bordwell, Staiger and Thompson, *Classical Hollywood Cinema,* 106.

27 Ibid., 157–158.

28 Ibid., 157–240.

29 Ibid., 195.

30 Ibid., 194–213.

> Some of these advisors were themselves scenario editors for the production
> companies: their guidelines would help determine the kinds of material accepted
> for filming.[31]

In her work on classical narrative technique, *Storytelling in the New Hollywood,*
Thompson again mentions early screenwriting manuals, albeit fleetingly, with regard to
the principles of storytelling and structure:

> we can get some help from screenwriting manuals. Such manuals date back to the
> 1910s, when the burgeoning studios still depended heavily on freelance submissions
> of scripts and stories.[32]

Thompson extends her work on the development of classical style with some further
research published in an anthology marking the centenary of cinema. However, the focus
of this work is limited to establishing whether the way modern screenwriting gurus advise
writers on 'narrative divisions and proportions' is similar to the instruction given by early
screenwriting teachers, which might also show 'rough versions of these divisions within
the narrative'. To test this hypothesis, Thompson examines 'about two dozen of the early
manuals' and the structure of some films from the early period, and compares them with
a number of the most popular manuals of modern screenwriting gurus and with films that
she assumes to have been influenced by their ideas.[33] Her conclusion is that the modern
gurus' emphasis on the three-act structure and the timing of the various proportions of a
film can clearly be detected in the teachings of the earliest screenwriting teachers, even
if these techniques were described differently. She points out that:

> The timing of each part [...] has remained fairly consistent between the two periods
> in question [and these] narrative principles [...] are simply one more instance of the
> remarkable stability of classical Hollywood filmmaking.[34]

In summary, Bordwell, Staiger and Thompson share a common approach, in that they
all make fairly frequent reference to manual writers in support of their work on the
development of classical Hollywood style. However, they only recognise those writers'
contribution among a range of other influences and factors. What is lacking is specific
and detailed comment on how exactly these early screenwriting teachers fit into the
overall picture of screenwriting development.

---

31 Ibid., 195.

32 Kristin Thompson, *Storytelling in the New Hollywood: Understanding Classical Narrative Technique*
(London: Harvard University, 1999), 11 and 21.

33 Kristin Thompson, 'Narrative Structure in Early Classical Cinema' in *Celebrating 1895: The Centenary
of Cinema*, ed. John Fullerton (Sydney: Libbey, 1998), 225–238.

34 Ibid., 237.

Another branch of historical writing that should be considered briefly is the work concerned with the antecedents of film, and how these interplayed with, and influenced, the advice contained in early screenwriting manuals. In discussing screenplay development, some authors have traced how filmic ideas developed from the theatrical practices of vaudeville, melodrama and 'the well-made play', and more serious theatrical endeavour. Nicholas Vardac, in his treatise *Stage to Screen: Theatrical Method from Garrick to Griffith,* links early photoplay content with romantic melodrama, burlesque and farce, trick effects and realistic spectacle in late nineteenth-century theatre. However, he makes no mention of how these ideas may have impacted the thinking and writings of screenwriting teachers.[35] In his anthology, *Theatre and Film,* Robert Knopf considers the complex historical, cultural and aesthetic relationship between theatre and film, and the effect that each had on the development of the other, but again he does not consider the role of the screenwriting teacher in this process.[36]

Nonetheless, some film historians of this ilk have given some thought to the writings of screenwriting teachers in this debate. Ben Brewster and Lea Jacobs, for example, while discussing the Aristotelian model of plot in nineteenth-century dramaturgy in *Theatre to Cinema,* refer to various screenwriting manuals alongside playwriting manuals of the period. However, while they make some limited comparisons between the various materials, they offer no extensive discussion of the link between theatrical traditions or ideas and what was contained in screenwriting manuals.[37]

Although a detailed analysis of all these various affinities and how they ultimately came to influence the early screenwriting teachers is beyond the scope of this present work, it is possible to draw some conclusions from the available evidence. Given that many screenwriting manuals make regular reference to theatrical and other sources of their ideas and inspiration, this at least provides a starting point for my discussion.

Tom Stempel's *A History of Screenwriting in the American Film* (2000) is, he claims, about 'the history of the process of screenwriting'. Namely, in it he relates 'how screenwriting is part of the process of making films', which 'involves everything from the selection of material through to the editing, rewriting and reshooting of material in post-production'.[38] However, Stempel's history of screenwriting is mainly descriptive rather than analytical or interpretive. It concentrates on the individual history of each screenwriter within the studio context and their particular contribution to screenwriting

---

35 A. Nicholas Vardac, *Stage to Screen: Theatrical Method from Garrick to Griffith* (Cambridge, Harvard University, 1949), 180–233.

36 Robert Knopf, 'Introduction', in *Theater and Film: A Comparative Anthology*, ed. Robert Knopf (London, Yale University, 2005), 1–20.

37 Ben Brewster and Lea Jacobs, *Theatre to Cinema: Stage Pictorialism and the Early Film* (Oxford: OUP, 1997), 18–32.

38 Stempel, *Framework*, xiii.

development. More detailed discussion of screenwriting teachers only appears if they have also been successful scenario writers – and then it appears only in a limited manner.

In his unpublished doctoral dissertation, 'The Theory, History and Practice of Screenwriting, 1897–1920' (1980), Edward Azlant surveys works of theory, criticism and production history from this period of screenwriting. To identify and define the nature and structure of the early screenplay and its role in film production, he critically examines the work of one leading screenwriting teacher, Sargent, and in particular Sargent's *Technique of the Photoplay* – a work he regards as 'exemplary' and representative of the 'best of its kind' for the period.[39] He then tests Sargent's views by applying them in the critical analysis of what he considers to be an excellent screenplay of the time, *Selfish Yates* (1918) by C. Gardner Sullivan, which went into production under Thomas H. Ince (1917).[40] Aside from the absence of any evidence that Sullivan ever consulted Sargent's manual, Azlant concedes that focusing on one exemplary and even revered practitioner from the period has its limitations:

> Such use of a single authority presents problems, including questions of whether such a testimony is representative, competent or objective. Hopefully, these problems will be moderated through investigation of the writer's background and some comparison with screenwriting manuals from the same period.[41]

As Azlant's focus is on the history of screenwriting practice and not on screenwriting teachers, his concentration on one screenwriting teacher to illustrate his findings does not necessarily damage his assertions.

Significantly, Azlant points out that the number of textbooks and manuals available from this period 'is perhaps the largest body of craft instruction within the materials of film study, with over ninety books on screenwriting published in English through 1920'. Most importantly, he suggests that it is also 'the largest *unexamined* body of craft instruction [emphasis added]'.[42] Azlant claims he has made 'a careful reading of over fifty screenwriting manuals',[43] but the supportive evidence that he cites in a supposed 'comparison' of Sargent's work 'with screenwriting manuals from the same period' is largely confined to endnotes on his text. These mention the views various screenwriting teachers held on topics such as scenario design, segmentation and continuity; but their inclusion as endnotes or summative statements means that they function merely as a contrast to Sargent's views. They do not really justify or support Azlant's decision to

---

39   Edward Azlant, 'The Theory, History and Practice of Screenwriting, 1897–1920' (PhD diss., Wisconsin University, 1980), 8–9. ProQuest (UMI 8111443).

40   Ibid., 12.

41   Ibid., 10–11.

42   Ibid., 209.

43   Ibid., 212.

adopt Sargent as the locus of his research in preference to other important screenwriting teachers of the period.[44] In contrast, this book considers extensively other key screenwriting teachers to whom Azlant pays scant attention.

In addition, to test Azlant's assertion that Sargent's views are representative of screenwriting teachers of the period, this book re-examines Sargent's work alongside a more detailed analysis of the extant body of material produced by other important screenwriting teachers. This more thorough examination of a wider body of work tells us more about the significance of the role of these teachers in the early screenwriting discourse. Given the apparently cursory nature of Azlant's treatment of other screenwriting teachers' material of the period, a more detailed investigation of these sources may indicate that his choice of Sargent as 'representative, competent or objective' is not necessarily justified.[45] It may also raise the profile and value accorded to some of these other teachers, who have remained more obscure and perhaps failed to receive the recognition they deserve.

Another scholar who has discussed the role of one particular screenwriting teacher is Anne Morey. In her book *Hollywood Outsiders,* Morey investigates how the Hollywood film industry interacted with the general public in the 1910s and 1920s and in particular how 'Hollywood outsiders could become members of the industry'.[46] Part of her study examines the Palmer Photoplay Corporation's correspondence school of screenwriting, which was one of the largest and most successful of these schools. However, she gives only limited consideration to the particular advice that this school gave about screenwriting and its value or otherwise in the Hollywood screenwriting discourse. Morey's main focus is on what the participants gained through personal development and how these types of self-improvement ideas fitted into American cultural history. Although it is of interest, such a discussion of the activities of just one advisor on screenwriting, who may or may not have been central, is far from sufficient in providing the information needed to assess early screenwriting teachers' overall contribution to and impact on the Hollywood film industry.[47]

---

44 In his endnotes, Azlant refers to Phillips, *Photodrama*; Eustace Hale Ball, *Photoplay Scenarios: How to Write and Sell Them* (1915; repr., Eastbourne: Wildside, 2013); Emerson and Loos, *How to Write Photoplays;* J. Berg Esenwein and Arthur Leeds, *Writing the Photoplay* (1913; repr., London: Dodo, 2007), Arthur W. Thomas, *How to Write a Photoplay* (Chicago: Photoplaywrights' Association of America, 1914); Catherine Carr, *The Art of Photoplay Writing* (1914; repr., Charleston: Nabu, 2013), Leslie Tufnell Peacocke, *Hints on Photoplay Writing* (1916; repr., Charleston: BiblioBazaar, 2012) and Dimick, *Modern Photoplay Writing.* Azlant, 'Theory, History and Practice of Screenwriting', 270–275.

45 Azlant, 'Theory, History and Practice of Screenwriting', 11.

46 Anne Morey, *Hollywood Outsiders: The Adaptation of the Film Industry 1913–1934* (Minneapolis: University of Minnesota, 2003), 1.

47 Anne Morey, '"Have You the Power?" The Palmer Photoplay Corporation and the film viewer/author in the 1920s', *Film History 9* (1997): 300–319 and *Hollywood Outsiders*, 70–111.

Among other accounts, Marc Norman's *What Happens Next: A History of American Screenwriting* (2008) highlights the plight of the oft-forgotten screenwriter who provided the foundations upon which careers of directors, stars and studio bosses were built. However, this work is biographical and anecdotal, lacking in academic rigour, and contains little information on and only incidental comment about the role of early screenwriting teachers.

Of more relevance to this study is the work of Steven Maras on screenwriting history, which charts how the written screenplay came to be understood, in industry terms, as the 'blueprint for production'. More importantly, Maras argues that 'scripting' is much broader than just the authoring of a screenplay, which is usually understood to be a separate part of the filmmaking process.[48] Maras challenges 'the logic of separating conception and execution'.[49] For him, the idea of the script as a 'blueprint for production' is merely one element that interacts with the whole dynamic process of filmmaking. His narrative on 'scripting' or screenwriting history, past and present, is pluralistic. Among the gamut of related activities it embraces are: the application of screenwriting theory learnt through practice and historical precedent; an acknowledgement of the role of directors and auteurs, editors and story-boarders; and more recently the contribution of new digital and interactive media.[50]

Some debate about the role of screenwriting teachers and their involvement in developing this broader process features in Maras's work. However, he limits this discussion to how screenwriting handbooks aided the professionalisation of writing for the screen and how this fits into his interpretation of the 'scripting' process. The history Maras provides is contextual rather than chronological, attempting to present a clear analysis of exactly what it means to write for the screen. In this regard, and so far as it is relevant to his argument about the process of 'scripting', Maras examines the development of writing for the screen in early handbooks, and accords particular value to the works of Sargent, Howard T. Dimick and Patterson. He also quotes Wright, Peacocke, Ball and Phillips in support of his contentions, although he does not assess the value of their contributions.[51]

This study embraces the views of Maras. Of particular note is his observation that in recent times scholars have taken a renewed interest in actual screenwriting manuals:

> Film scholars and historians have become adept at looking beyond the film as text
> and appreciating industrial and production conditions as well as technological and

---

48   Maras states that one of his aims is 'to create a bridge between scholarly work in film, media and screenwriting studies and practitioner-orientated discussions of craft and industry issues', in Steven Maras, *Screenwriting: History, Theory and Practice* (London: Wallflower, 2009), 1–8.

49   Maras, *Screenwriting*, 170.

50   Ibid., 185–186.

51   Ibid., 89–92, 130–153 and 157–169.

trade discourses [...] supporting film practice. They have even begun to talk about screenwriting manuals [52]

Maras gives clear hints that he also regards early screenwriting manuals as helping to shape industry standards and an understanding of what it means to write for the screen. In particular, he suggests that 'how-to' books aimed at novices helped:

> to define the shape of what qualifies, or does not, as industrial practice, as well as legitimate screenwriting; in other words, it regulates who can speak with authority and who cannot.[53]

However, despite these assertions, Maras's research is primarily concerned with other issues and he does not investigate this process thoroughly. He readily admits that this area of screenwriting history has not yet been fully understood or investigated. He also suggests that a 'comprehensive account of this output is [...] of special interest because it is a key place in which screen writing, and its industrial context, is explained to the wider public'.[54] Such an investigation, focused on the early period, is undertaken in this study.

As Bridget Conor envisages it in her research, screenwriting is a 'form of creative labor' within what has been termed the 'new cultural economy' or the current understanding of the industry context. She usefully draws attention to the 'long and particular history of professional practice' and how this 'problematizes notions of creativity, craft and authorship as they are practiced and experienced',[55] a subject that this book also considers. As part of her study, Conor briefly surveys early screenwriting history, the role the first screenwriting teachers played in the how-to discourse, and how this was 'central in the circulation and maintenance of standards and conventions'.[56] However, she largely draws on the conclusions of Azlant and Maras as a basis for her claim that 'the codes and conventions of the form, the elements of visuality that writing for the screen required, were carved out and legitimized' in this period by these individuals.[57] Her reliance on these scholars is understandable, as this subject is not the focus of Conor's research; however, her agreement with them further underlines the importance of carrying out a full and systematic historical investigation, which will both probe and uncover more precisely the role that early screenwriting teachers played in this process.

Based on thorough research, Torey Liepa explores the role of the intertitle in silent film in providing exposition and dialogue and advancing the storytelling possibilities of the

---

52 Ibid., 19.

53 Ibid., 25.

54 Ibid., 144.

55 Bridget Conor, *Screenwriting: Creative Labor and Professional Practice* (Oxon: Routledge, 2014), 1.

56 Ibid., 15–17 and 81–82.

57 Ibid., 17.

medium. Although he accords manual writers an important position in this history, this recognition is mostly only insofar as their work affects the development of intertitling. 'For roughly twelve years, from about 1910 until around 1922,' Liepa asserts, 'these screenwriting, or "photoplay" manuals negotiated the proper and ideal intertitle protocol.'[58] In his doctoral dissertation, Liepa quotes Sargent extensively, noting that he began discussing the use of intertitles in his column as early as February 1912.[59] His research, which covers the views of the other key screenwriting teachers as well, will be considered by this study.

In a more recent article about the popular writing movement in the early 1900s, Liepa follows up on the work of Maras. The interface between the development of screenwriting practice and the burgeoning early film industry is one aspect of his discussion. In this respect, he makes some interesting comments about a wider range of early screenwriting manuals:

> Given the diverse authorship of these volumes, taken collectively they often produced vague, contradictory and at times superficial suggestions and one should be cautious of simple confusion and charlatanism. Despite this caveat, however, the synthesis of the diverse advice found in manuals and trade journals presents a complex discourse that offers more than simply an example of journalistic opportunism, but rather a window into a chaotic moment in American cultural production.[60]

The 'complex discourse' referred to by Liepa, and interrogated to some extent by Maras and other eminent scholars, requires further scrutiny through a far closer examination of these manuals and the industry context in which they operated as a subject in its own right.

Possible Reasons for the Lack of Previous Research

Within a decade of the beginning of narrative cinema, controversy arose about the activities of some of those who were offering screenwriting guidance that was of little worth. Particular scorn was reserved for the many screenwriting schools that sprang up in the first few years of the industry. Many of their advertisements in popular fan magazines wildly exaggerated the potential opportunities for outsiders with claims such

---

58 Torey Liepa, 'The Sound of Silents: Representations of Speech in Silent Film', MiT4: The Work of Stories, New York University, May 7, 2005, 9, *Learning Ace*, accessed March 3, 2014, http://www.learningace.com/doc/68479/d904421577ff2a31aba0874760e184fb/liepa

59 Liepa, 'Figures of Silent Speech: Silent Film Dialogue and the American Vernacular, 1909–1916' (PhD diss., New York University, 2008), 148. ProQuest (UMI 3320809).

60 Liepa, 'Entertaining the Public Option: The popular film writing movement and the emergence of writing for the American Silent Cinema', in *Analyzing the Screenplay*, ed. Jill Nelmes (Oxon: Routledge, 2011), 18.

Figure 1: Advertisement for amateur playwrights' contest
Source: *Photoplay* November 1914, 2.

United Photo-Plays Company

Suite 148 28 South La Salle Street

Chicago August 11th 1914

Mr Elbert Moore
Chicago,
Illinois.

Dear Mr. Moore:-

We are in the market for an IDEA - an idea that can be made into a two-reel or three-reel photoplay of genuine Originality and Punch.

We receive many photoplays from amateur writers all over the country; but most of these writers are untrain-ed, and the plays they submit are not in acceptable form. Of course our own staff writers are producing good photo-plays for us; but we want something different, something that has never been thought of before - something of which we can make a big feature. In short, we want to produce a photoplay that will fill to the doors all the theatres in which it appears.

Are you willing to turn your pupils loose on this problem? We believe, that among all the new writers you are developing there are at least a few who can produce this photoplay. We are willing to pay $200 for the photoplay, (written by any one of your students between now and Decem-ber 31st), which in you judgement comes nearest to meeting our requirements.

We will also pay $50.00 for the second best photo-play and $10.00 each for the next five $300.00 in all

Trusting that this offer will interest you and your students, we are,

Yours very truly,

UNITED PHOTO-PLAYS COMPANY.

Vice President.

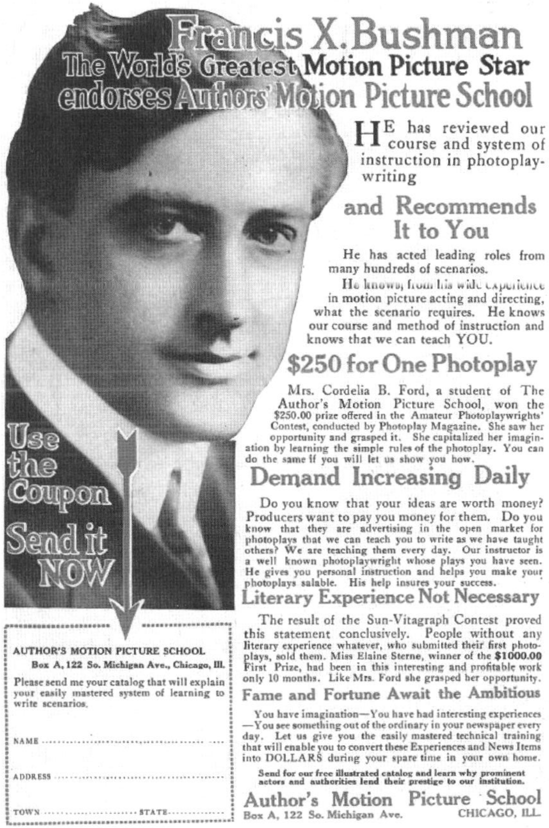

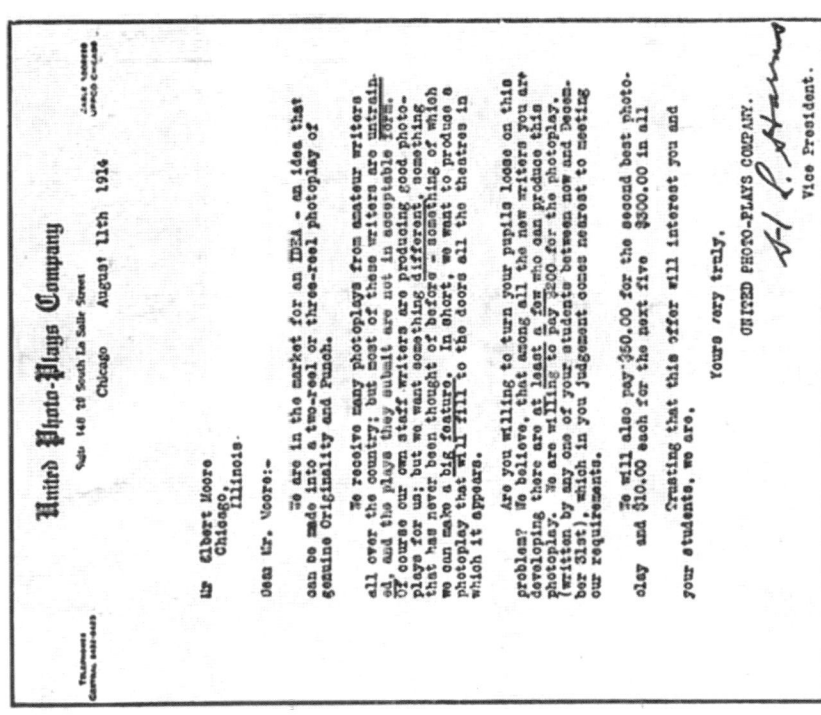

Figure 2: United Photo-Plays Company advertisement
Source: *Photoplay*, November 1914, 187.

as 'Fame and Fortune await the ambitious' (see Figures 1 and 2)[61] and 'You can earn big money writing photo-plays' (see Figure 3).[62] *Photoplay* was so concerned about what it considered to be the bogus nature of many of these schools that it announced in an article on advertising in 1915 (see Figure 4) that it had:

> decided to investigate the merits of the so-called motion picture schools [and] clearing houses [...]. As a result of this investigation it was decided to entirely eliminate this class of advertising.[63]

Notably this policy soon began to slip; within a month, advertising of a different kind began to appear in *Photoplay*. It still claimed to teach photoplay writing, but its rhetoric was somewhat toned down. One school altered its heading to read 'correspondence course is not required', no doubt to get around the ban on advertising (see Figure 5).[64] Even in 1917, apparently exaggerated claims such as 'Hundreds of people make BIG MONEY writing photoplays, stories, articles [capitals in original]' were still commonplace, although the scope had been broadened to include other forms of writing (see Figure 6).[65]

Such schools sparked further disapproval from among the ranks of fellow and more respectable screenwriting teachers and manual writers. For example, Sargent describes those who 'profess to teach the art of photoplay writing in from six to ten lessons' as 'incompetents'.[66] It seems that the poor offerings of some so-called screenwriting teachers of the time may have shrouded the more serious and substantial work of figures such as Sargent and his contemporaries.

Harsh, negative comments from scholars about early handbooks were very common in later years. Take, for example, the offhand remarks in a *General Bibliography of the Motion Pictures* (1953):

> [They] have the pretension of being guides to brilliant film careers and end up by being slightly ridiculous. These are often old books, dating back to a period anterior even to the phenomenon of stardom and the myths of the cinema.

---

61   An advertisement from The Authors' Motion Picture School claimed that as much as $250 could be paid for one photoplay and that one of their students had won the *Photoplay* Amateur Photoplaywrights' Contest. Another advertisement for Elbert Moore's school displayed a letter addressed to him from United Photoplays Company, claiming it was clamouring for new ideas, for which it would offer his students from $10 to $500 cash. See *Photoplay*, November 1914, 2 and 186–187.

62   A claim made by the Chicago Photoplay-wright College. See *MPM*, July 1914, 168.

63   'Scenario School Advertising Barred by Photoplay Magazine,' *Photoplay*, April 1915, 114.

64   The Atlas Publishing Company regularly advertised its wares on 'How to Write Moving Picture Plays' in a more moderate tone and in book form. See *Photoplay*, May 1915, 164.

65   This text is from The Writers' Service, New York in *MPM*, December 1917, 156.

66   Sargent, 'Progress in Photoplay Writing,' in *Motion Picture Annual and Yearbook for 1912* (New York: MPW, 1913), 18.

YOU
can earn
BIG MONEY

WRITING PHOTO=PLAYS

Great demand. We teach only **sure** method of **writing** and **selling** photo-plays. No experience or literary ability required. Our students are **selling** their plays. Send for free book of valuable information and **Special Prize Offer.**

CHICAGO PHOTO-PLAYWRIGHT COLLEGE
Key 278-O. T., Chicago

Figure 3: Chicago Photo-Playwright College advertisement
Source: *MPM*, July 1914.

Scenario "School" Advertising

PHOTOPLAY MAGAZINE has decided to eliminate motion picture school advertising.

This action has been taken only after careful investigation of the merits of these schools, and is the result of a determination that no advertising, to which the least suspicion is attached, shall be allowed space in this publication.

The scenario editors of the leading moving picture producing companies of the country seem to be unanimous in the opinion that these schools do not give value received, and many cases have come to our attention where people who could ill-afford the tuition charges answered these advertisements and enrolled in the schools only to meet with disappointment when they attempted to sell their writings.

> "I was a staff writer with the Universal Company for two years, and while I was there no scenario was ever accepted from a so-called school or clearing house."
>
> LESLIE T. PEACOCKE,
> World Film Corporation.

and authoritative publication in its field, and to permit no advertiser, whose claims the magazine cannot guarantee, to have access to its advertising columns.

One of the first acts of the new management was to investigate the merits of the so-called motion picture schools, clearing-houses, and correspondence schools of photoplay acting. As a result of this investigation it was decided to entirely eliminate this class of advertising.

The scenario editors of the motion p i c t u r e companies are the persons best fitted to decide the benefit that students have actually derived from these schools. These men are recognized as the leaders in their profession. They constitute the court of last resort for ambitious scenario writers, and therefore their words should carry great weight.

Figure 4: *Photoplay* announces its ban on scenario school advertising
Source: *Photoplay*, April 1915, 114.

HOW TO WRITE
MOVING PICTURE PLAYS

This is the title of a book which treats upon every feature of this fascinating work. Tells kind of plays wanted by film producing companies, kind **NOT** wanted, how to choose plots, how to write synopsis and scenario, how to introduce characters, how to begin story, importance of first scene, climax, continuity of scenes, all about inserts and leaders, what is wanted for two and three reel plays, how to submit manuscripts to insure attention, prices payed for plays, and dozens of other import ant points necessary to success; includes a complete sample play, showing just how it should be prepared and written, and a full list of all film producing companies wanting and buying plays, telling the kind of plays each one wants.

Correspondence Course is Not Required

This book, a few sheets of paper, envelopes and a few postage stamps are the "tools of your profession." There is nothing more to buy. Producers pay from $5.00 to $100.00 for each play accepted. Many ask if we guarantee success. NO, success is for YOU to acquire it cannot be bought. Our book merely offers the proper technical training and places clearly before you

The Methods by Which Others Are Succeeding

We have on our files hundreds of testimonials from satisfied purchasers. Send us P. O. Order, Express Order or Bank Draft for THREE DOLLARS today, keep book for five days, and then if not satisfied return it to us at once and money will be refunded immediately.

You run no risk. Send order today and we will let you be the judge. If not satisfied, send it back.

ATLAS PUBLISHING CO. 994 Atlas Bldg. CINCINNATI, O.

Figure 5: Atlas Publishing Company advertisement
Source: *Photoplay*, May 1915, 164.

Figure 6: Writer's Service advertising
Source: *MPM*, December 1917, 156.

> We have included them more as a curiosity than for reasons of scrupulous precision.[67]

Such comments, Azlant suggests, are typical of the attitudes that scholars have displayed towards screenwriting manuals:

> They are regarded with indifference, as ostensibly lacking precise information on screenwriting and promoting specious fantasies of a glamorous career [... and such] attitudes are questionable, even uninformed, but have nonetheless acquired the status of truism in the absence of detailed examination of the manuals.[68]

The way screenwriting manuals were viewed is also probably linked to the lack of recognition and credit that early writers received for writing screenplays. Azlant argues that 'the roots of the screenplay's neglect in film study' could be traced to limitations in early film theory. His analysis begins with Hugo Münsterberg's 1916 work, *The Photoplay: A Psychological Study*, which is generally acknowledged to be the first major work in this field.[69] Münsterberg asserts that, because film is fundamentally a visual medium, it cannot be conveyed through words on a page. He even regards the use of intertitles in the film for the purposes of dialogue or clarification as unacceptable.[70] For Münsterberg, it is only the act of collaboration that can transform the photoplay into its proper manifestation, the realm of visual imagery. This perspective necessarily demotes the value of literary content in such works and, by implication, that of those offering advice on how to write:

> the work which the scenario writer creates is in itself still entirely imperfect and becomes a complete work of art only through the action of the producer [... who] really must show himself a creative artist.[71]

Another forerunner in contributing to theory was William Morgan Hannon, scenario editor for the Nola Film Company. In an academic essay in 1915 about the relationship between film and art, Hannon exhibits a similar, though less severe, prejudice about the role of the writer:

---

67   Carl Vincent, Ricardo Redi and Franco Venturini, eds., *General Bibliography of the Motion Pictures* (1953; repr., New York: Arno, 1972), 115; quoted in Azlant, 'Theory, History and Practice of Screenwriting', 208.

68   Azlant, 'Theory, History and Practice of Screenwriting', 209.

69   Ibid., 18.

70   Ibid., 22.

71   Hugo Münsterberg, *The Photoplay: A Psychological Study* (1916; repr., Charleston: BiblioBazaar, 2007), 103.

the function of the director is by far the greatest [… it] is half 'the show' –
the author, the actors, the scenic artists, and so on, the other half.[72]

Support for this diminished view of writing for film came from Erwin Panofsky, another
early film theorist, who claimed 'that the screenplay, in contrast to the theater play,
has no aesthetic existence independent of its performance'.[73] This downgrading of the
scenario as a means of conveying visual ideas in a literary form had ramifications for the
way screenwriters and ultimately screenwriting teachers were viewed. The devaluing of
the writer meant that the pursuit of literary excellence in screenwriting became a fallacy
and the craft promoted by screenwriting teachers was not taken seriously. This attitude
emerged even though in reality screenwriting teachers were offering important advice to
writers on how to write in a visual form.

Similarly dismissive of the more conventional work of the screenwriter is Vachel Lindsay,
who pioneered work on film aesthetics. In *The Art of the Moving Picture*, written in 1915
and revised in 1922, he offers a theoretical outline of motion picture art as an essentially
visual medium. Film writing, Lindsay proposes, is conducted in a pictorial landscape
rather than a place of verbal explanations. He advises the screenwriter that '[h]e can
construct the outlines of his scenarios by placing […] little pictures in rows'.[74]

In Azlant's view, the tendency of film theorists to look unfavourably upon a language-
based process of design for a largely visual medium belittled the legitimacy of the
screenplay as a narrative form.[75] Azlant maintains that both Lindsay's and Münsterberg's
approach fed into the idea that only the completed narrative film or 'its final effects, or
the manner in which it is perceived or experienced by its audience' were of any value.[76]

The pedagogical efforts of the serious scenario teachers have received a re-evaluation
from Polan, with a focus on those who set out to promote film instruction in institutions
of higher learning between 1915 and 1935. He observes how past historical accounts
of screenwriting development readily acknowledge the 'often wacky ramblings' of
Lindsay, whom he terms a folk poet and at best a theoretician and academic, but not
a practitioner. This assessment is based on a comparison with theorists and teachers
who had a more direct involvement in the development of screenwriting practice,
such as Victor O. Freeburg and Patterson, who ran screenwriting courses at Columbia
University, and Sargent. Polan hints that the reason for this may be that Freeburg and

---

72 William Morgan Hannon, *The Photodrama: Its Place Among the Fine Arts* (1915; repr., Charleston:
BiblioBazaar, 2013), 24–25.

73 Erwin Panofsky, 'Style and Medium in the Motion Pictures (1934)', in *Film Theory and Criticism*,
4th ed. Gerald Mast, Marshall Cohen and Leo Braudy, eds. (Oxford: OUP, 1992), 243.

74 Ibid., 172.

75 Azlant, 'Theory, History and Practice of Screenwriting', 335.

76 Ibid., 39.

Patterson, the first teachers of a university course, and Sargent were focusing on the more practical matter of actually helping people to succeed as photoplay writers and, as a result, 'their practical textbooks do not raise foundational questions in as systematic or explicit a fashion'. Ironically, according to Polan, it is Lindsay's book that becomes more formative and representative of the discipline for the period.[77]

Screenwriters in the silent era garnered little respect from the artistic and literary community and in many cases they were not even credited for their work. In fact, as Maras points out, there was an overall lack of recognition of the role of the screenplay writer in the period before talking pictures were established. He notes that, in 1935, the successful Hollywood screenwriter Ernest Pascal dated screenwriting from the advent of the talking picture. Of the silent cinema, he states that 'stories were bought, but pictures were not written'.[78] This view has persisted, as the following 2003 account from Ceplair and Englund illustrates:

> The screenwriter came to Hollywood along with 'mike' booms and the Great Depression. The advent of the 'talkie' not only capped an evolution in production methods and imposed the need for a producer to standardize moviemaking; it also created a permanent need for professional writers who could turn out shootable, full-length scripts with dialogue.[79]

Azlant is another to observe that the negative attitude toward screenwriting manuals has perhaps meant that 'the impressive qualifications of many' of these authors have been overlooked.[80] As my study shows, many manual writers were successful journalists, and short story and scenario writers with impressive lists of credits. Significantly, Azlant goes on to observe that many of these scholars appear to have a 'seeming distance from their materials [which even suggests] the authors have not examined the books they so cavalierly dismiss'.[81] Later, this lack of recognition was further entrenched by the rise of the notion of the director as 'auteur' filmmaker, an approach that grew in influence from the 1960s and remains significant today, despite its shortcomings.

It is possible that the scorn some modern academics express for the plethora of modern screenwriting manuals may have also influenced views of this earlier material. Comments from most leading academics about modern screenwriting handbooks tend to be evaluative in nature. They are critical of a rather simplistic approach to classical structure

---

77 Polan, *Scenes of Instruction*, 19–20.

78 Ernest Pascal, 'The Author of the Piece,' *The Screen Guilds' Magazine* 2, August 8 (1935): 8; quoted in Maras, *Screenwriting*, 131–132.

79 Larry Ceplair and Steven Englund, *The Inquisition in Hollywood: Politics in the Film Community, 1930–1960* (Chicago, University of Illinois, 2003), 2.

80 Azlant, 'Theory, History and Practice of Screenwriting', 210.

81 Ibid., 268.

and its supposed negative effect on the industry. For example, Bordwell criticises what he considers the formulaic content of modern manuals:

> Few screenplay manuals inspire confidence. If you want proof that contemporary Hollywood is formula-ridden, look no further than Syd Field's 'Paradigm,' with turning points absolutely required on script pages 25–27 and 85–90.[82]

Similarly unenthusiastic about their role, Thompson believes their influence has been quite damaging in recent years:

> The manuals usefully point up the basic techniques of classical storytelling – or at least what Hollywood practitioners think those techniques are. And these manuals have had an impact on recent classical filmmaking. Indeed, there is some evidence that by the mid-1990s some of the more formulaic advice of such manuals was actually having a negative effect on the films coming out of Hollywood.[83]

Although Thompson claims 'some evidence' indicates that manuals were encouraging 'formulaic' output from Hollywood, it is very difficult to specifically link the activities of particular screenwriting gurus with this output. She does give some examples of writers who claim to have been influenced in varying degrees by screenwriting manuals.[84] However, similar types of films, dubbed 'formulaic', may have emerged from Hollywood for many other reasons, as has arguably always been the case. Thompson admits that she has 'not attempted to survey such handbooks systematically since they often repeat the same information with minor variations'.[85] A thorough survey of the material would at least have provided a foundation for making these strong assertions.

A more sympathetic examination of the work of early screenwriting teachers should yield a more balanced and even-handed understanding, not only of the content of their manuals, but also of the contribution they made to the development of early screenwriting practice and the wider Hollywood film industry. In the light of these findings, it may also be possible to offer some preliminary observations about the recent spate of screenwriting manuals and their value or otherwise to the industry.

---

82   Bordwell, *The Way Hollywood Tells It*, 27.

83   Thompson, *Storytelling in the New Hollywood*, 11.

84   The most extreme example Thompson gives is Hamilton Phelan, screenwriter of *Mask* (1985) and *Gorillas in the Mist* (1988), who claims she has virtually memorised *Screenplay* by Syd Field. From an interview in William Froug, *The New Screenwriter Looks at the New Screenwriter* (Los Angeles: Silman-James, 1991), 20; quoted in Thompson, *Storytelling in the New Hollywood*, 23–25.

85   Ibid., 11.

Research Methodology

Historians with a particular interest in screenwriting history have tended to concentrate on the process of how screenwriting itself began and developed. No one has conducted any extensive or more specific research on what led to, or what adequately explains, the phenomenon of the early screenwriting teacher within this process. This project is the first comprehensive investigation of the activity of screenwriting teachers during this early period of screenwriting history. It explores the causal factors that led to their existence, or encouraged them to thrive or otherwise; their connections with the infant film industry; and the importance of their function and role within that industry as it developed. It also assesses what they bequeathed to the industry in terms of the development of the screenplay form and the process of educating screenwriters.

To make this possible, it has been necessary to construct a critical history of the early screenwriting teachers by extracting and distilling information from respected and available past and modern film history sources.

In reaching a more detailed understanding of their role, one potential line of enquiry would have been to examine the possible influence of these screenwriting teachers on specific examples of screenwriting practice at the time. This area, as Stempel points out, is under-researched. He wants to know the result of the 'influence of the study of screenwriting on screenwriting is as it is actually practiced'.[86] However, the effectiveness, or otherwise, of screenwriting teachers in shaping or influencing the thinking of screenwriters on specific film projects is very difficult to assess in earlier periods, just as much as it would be today. It is not possible to analyse accurately the degree to which screenwriting teachers have influenced screenwriters directly, as too many complexities and variables are involved in the creative process. Nor would either examining the films screenwriters have written or contacting them directly (even if that were possible) necessarily provide accurate information on this subject. Moreover, for the early period in particular, uncovering any valid opinions would be difficult, as all those involved have long since passed away and documentary evidence of this nature seems to be in short supply. To mitigate this limited access to direct links between screenwriting teachers and industry practice, this book sets out a broader contextual study of the historical evidence as it presents itself. This will provide the basis for a more fruitful line of research.

In objectively studying and uncovering the history of these screenwriting teachers and attempting to account for their work, it may be possible to illuminate more extensively the avenues and spheres of influence in which they operated. This will in turn help to contextualise their work and perhaps permit a more reasoned, although not definitive, analysis of their role in the development of screenwriting practice.

---

86 Stempel, *Framework*, 263.

Therefore, this book focuses on the factors that led to the existence of screenwriting teachers in the early period of screenwriting history and the role they played in, or in relation to, the industry. It does not enter into an evaluative debate about whether one screenwriting teacher offered more valuable writing solutions than another, as that is not directly relevant to an objective examination of the role of the early screenwriting teacher. Nevertheless, it does not necessarily exclude consideration of the reasons why one particular manual or body of instruction may have had more appeal or been more successful than another, if likely reasons can be determined from the historical evidence and the wider cultural factors operating at the time.

In the light of more recent public interest in learning how to write screenplays and the numerous screenwriting gurus available to teach them, it may also be possible to draw some interesting parallels between the experience of would-be screenwriters of today and their counterparts in the fledgling Hollywood film industry a century ago. Although this is not the primary purpose of this study, some interesting links between these two periods are considered and some limited comparison does, I believe, furnish greater understanding of the role and contribution of screenwriting teachers in a broader context.

Hence, this study pursues the three areas of investigation expressed in the title of the book: the origins, contribution and legacy of early screenwriting teachers.

First, in investigating the origins of early screenwriting teachers, it examines the theoretical sources from which they drew, the industrial context from which they emerged and the causes of the 'scenario fever' that initiated their appearance.

The contribution of early screenwriting teachers, as the second focus area, is explored by tracing the appearance of the first screenwriting teachers, with reference to criteria that distinguish between peripheral teachers and those key screenwriting teachers who are likely to have played a more central role in the industry. Then the book critically examines the advice that the key screenwriting teachers gave on how to train for, write for and sell to the industry, as well as assessing their overall contribution to the industry.

Finally, the review of the legacy of early screenwriting teachers considers their equivalence to modern screenwriting 'gurus', their involvement in the evolution of the screenplay and their links to the roots of the education of the more recent screenwriter.

My study is based on detailed primary research and scrutiny of fan and trade press journals, handbooks and trade publications from the period. The screenwriting manuals of five screenwriting teachers, whose work can be justifiably demonstrated to be representative of, and of key significance to, the period, are analysed in detail. Other relevant manuals are also considered, where they take a significantly different approach.

This process helps to identify the main ideas that were prevalent during the period and to show why, and in what way, they were important to the industry at the time. It also indicates whether those ideas substantially changed, or remained more or less constant throughout the period, and why either trend might occur.

This research provides a deeper understanding of how screenwriting teachers interacted with the industry during the period under study and explores whether they had a central or more marginal role within it. It is also an opportunity to consider what these manuals argue and, broadly, where this material came from. Addressing these questions involves examining more proximate sources and concrete models from which these manuals drew, such as ancient and modern dramatic theory, theatre, vaudeville, journalistic and short fiction, photography and early film theorists.

The evidence this book presents suggests that the key screenwriting teachers it features played a significant part in the developing discourse about early screenwriting practice – a part that is likely to have shaped that practice itself. Their presence and roles within and around the industry gave their ideas important currency, not just generally, but at a key formative moment in the shaping of that practice (a period, therefore, in which the presence of their advice at the heart of the industry was more likely than at other times to be able to influence the direction of practice). This evidence provides a reasonable basis for arguing that they performed a more central role in this on-going process, rather than occupying the peripheral or insignificant position that others have often claimed in the past. Their substantial influence exists, this book argues, even though it remains impossible to prove a direct one-to-one link between any specific teacher and particular screenwriters or individual films, for reasons that will be explained.

This project offers a more in-depth picture of the history of key early screenwriting teachers and their role in the development of screenwriting than has previously been available. It includes a more detailed explanation of why screenwriting teachers existed, their likely level of influence and their apparent function in this early period of screenwriting history. This is achieved by investigating the sources of their main ideas and how these interacted with, and evolved within, the industry. The result is a more balanced and context-bound understanding of the origins, contribution and legacy of the early screenwriting teachers in the development of screenwriting and of the nascent Hollywood film industry.

PART ONE
ORIGINS

PART ONE: ORIGINS

Until relatively recently, historical accounts of the birth of the Hollywood film industry have tended to tell this story from the perspective of individual innovators or movie moguls, crediting them as the key agents of change. Over the last three decades, however, some film historians have challenged this earlier bias, putting forward instead a New Film History. As they have demonstrated, commercial drive and economic forces were important influences and provide a stronger contextual framework for understanding the roles of the key participants, traditionally understood to be studio heads, film producers and directors.[1]

One film historian to offer this more balanced perspective is Charles Musser, who claims that 'the history of early cinema cannot be a history of its films alone' and that 'Fitting the film product […] into this larger practice has required extensive research and a new approach.'[2] The main driver, Musser argues, was corporate power, rather than the maverick entrepreneur:

> The motion-picture industry exemplified a general trend toward larger commercial units and a hierarchical structure [… and] the very dynamics of change that favored consolidation and rationalization frequently worked against those in a dominant position.[3]

Taking a similar approach, Eileen Bowser notes that entrepreneurial activity increased greatly in just a few years. Innovation in every field was inspired by opportunity, and the potential market value was enormous for those who succeeded:

> [T]he film business itself changed from a hand-crafted amusement enterprise and sideshow to a gigantic entertainment industry and the first mass communication medium.[4]

These film historians, therefore, have highlighted how this success in America was both individually and collectively inspired, and a balance must be struck between the two. Certainly proper recognition is due to those individuals who, through their subjective motives and conscious actions, brought about change. However, as sociologists remind

---

1 The first recorded use of the term 'New Film History' was in a 1985 article, in which Thomas Elsaesser noted 'the tendency of recent scholarly works to move beyond film history as just the history of films and to consider how film style and aesthetics were influenced, even determined, by economic, industrial and technological factors'. See Chapman, Glancy and Harper, 'Introduction', in *The New Film History*, 5–6. This new approach is typified in Bordwell, Thompson and Staiger, *Classical Hollywood Cinema* and Allen and Gomery, *Film History*, both published in 1985.

2 Charles Musser, *The Emergence of Cinema: The American Screen to 1907* (London: University of California, 1994), 495.

3 Ibid., 492.

4 Eileen Bowser, *The Transformation of Cinema: 1907–1915* (London: University of California, 1990), xi.

us, collective forces in society that are expressed through culture, ideology, power structures, religious sentiment and stratification also effect change.[5] The New Film History paradigm not only takes industrial and technological factors into account, but also considers the impact of external agencies such as censors and funders and all the collaborative efforts of the individuals who contribute to filmmaking.[6] This broader approach must likewise be adopted when considering the history of screenwriting: it was from this maelstrom of rapid economic activity, cultural development and intellectual capital that the craft of writing for the screen was born and that the screenwriting teacher first emerged.

Both early scenarists and early screenwriting teachers are worthy of consideration as potential key participants in these developments. Despite their historical reassessment, revisionist film historians have still tended to ignore the role of the early scenarist in this process and, as a concomitant, the early screenwriting teacher has suffered a similar fate. Azlant's research on screenwriting before 1920 has done much to address this oversight. He dubs the early screenwriters 'forgotten pioneers' and rightly credits the early scenarist with a greater role.[7] Restoring the status of these early writers also opens up the prospect of raising the profile of those who supported and nurtured their talent. As already discussed, Azlant has added some credence to the role of screenwriting teachers by using the work of Sargent to illuminate the status of the screenplay and how it had developed up until 1920. However, much remains to be done to accord Sargent and other important early screenwriting teachers their correct role in the development of writing for the screen.

---

5 Sociologist Malcolm Waters argues that social theory must embrace both the actions of the individual and the collective forces that exist in a society. Individuals are motivated by 'agency' (subjective meanings or reasons) and 'rationality' (the accomplishment of specific conscious objectives). The collective forces of culture, ideology, power structures, religion and stratification are variously argued to exist in the collective unconscious mind, in symbolic relationships of myth and language and, significantly for this research, in the 'integrated wholes' or 'systems' in society. See Malcolm Waters, *Modern Sociological Theory* (London: Sage, 1994), 11–12.

6 Allen and Gomery 'identify four approaches to film history – aesthetic, technological, economic and social', which are all-embracing. See Chapman, Glancy and Harper, 'Introduction', *The New Film History*, 6.

7 Azlant notes that earlier film historians, such as Kevin Brownlow and David Robinson, virtually write off the role of early scenario writers. He quotes Brownlow as stating that early films were 'shot in a couple of days by directors who had a rough idea of the story and who improvised as they went along'. See Kevin Brownlow, *The Parade's Gone By* (London: Columbus, 1968), 270. He exposes Robinson's simplistic comments about Ince, who 'is credited with introduction of the film scenario'. See David Robinson, *The History of World Cinema* (New York: Stein and Day, 1974), 71. Azlant demonstrates that screenwriting proper began much earlier in Azlant, 'Screenwriting for the Early Silent Film: Forgotten Pioneers, 1897–1911', *Film History* 9 (1997): 228–256.

With this context in mind, it is important to recognise that screenwriting teachers were both victims and beneficiaries of the individualism prevalent at the time and of its subsequent historical interpretation. During the period in which they operated, they became minor celebrities and were seen as pioneers in their own right. However, when the teleological version of film history that ensued tended to credit successful movie moguls with the creation of the film industry, it sidelined writers and, as a consequence, the achievements of screenwriting teachers were also overshadowed. The revisionist version of film history that takes into account the corporate nature of the film industry now needs to widen its embrace to include them. First, it is important to correct the historical record and recognise the individual achievements of these teachers, which up until now have been overlooked. Second, in the spirit of the New Film History, any retelling of the history of these teachers must properly examine them within the context in which they operated, which also in large part accounts for their existence.

Probing for 'origins', according to Maras, 'can have the tendency to "fix" the landscape in particular ways, leading to a reductive view of the development […] of screenwriting'.[8] It is undoubtedly important to carefully guard against this inclination. However, by way of balance, Steven Price has pointed out, again in relation to the history of the screenplay, that 'posing the question can [… also] function as a worthwhile heuristic device, a means of opening up […] more substantial questions'.[9] Similarly, if we search for the origins of screenwriting teachers – an investigation closely related to the history of screenplay development – without exercising some degree of caution, we face the risk that nothing worthwhile will result. After all, trying to find the origins of anything is a complex process. However, if the approach to discovering the origins of the screenwriting teacher is narrowly focused on searching for literary and theatrical connections, and on examining the industrial context they emerged from and the phenomenon of 'scenario fever' they were caught up in, it could offer valuable insights and be a means of unlocking this important subject area within the history of screenwriting. That is the approach taken in this part.

---

8 Maras, *Screenwriting*, 29.

9 Steven Price, *A History of the Screenplay* (Basingstoke: Palgrave Macmillan, 2013), 22.

1. Literary and Theatrical Legacy

Early screenwriters, and those who instructed them, drew from multifarious sources and were mindful of the prevailing forms of entertainment of the period. They were subject to the influence of pantomime, masques and pageants, vaudeville, stage drama, music (even though film was silent), painting, sculpture, comic strips, novels and short stories, architecture, the illustrated lecture and photography. Early film theorist Freeburg suggests that the 'new art' of the 'motion picture play' inherited characteristics from most of these sources. In his words, 'a photoplay is a very complicated thing, involving many elements of expression and many principles of composition'.[1]

Recent scholars such as Azlant and Thompson likewise point out that film writing emerged from a fusion of various elements:

> Early screenwriting borrows much in concept, practice, personnel and instruction from the theatre [...], from literature, the graphic arts, vaudeville and [...] journalism.[2]

> [M]odels for structuring a film came, not from drama and fiction in general, but specifically from late nineteenth-century norms of those forms [...] which lingered on in popular stories, plays and novels.[3]

My aim in this section is to trace some of these specific influences more directly, as an important part of the context of early screenwriting and of those who taught it.

A great deal of evidence indicates that there was a cross-fertilisation of the propagation of various literary skills. For example, some screenwriting teachers also wrote story-writing manuals. As well as authoring *Writing the Photoplay* with Arthur Leeds, Joseph Berg Esenwein was editor of *The Writers' Monthly* and wrote manuals on short story writing, public speaking and children's stories. Esenwein's manual *Writing the Short Story* was regularly advertised in photoplay journals along with his courses on the subject (see Figures 7 and 8).[4] It was recommended by Sargent, one of the key screenwriting teachers examined in this book, and by Charlton Andrews, author of *The Technique of*

---

1 Victor Oscar Freeburg, *The Art of Photoplay Making* (1918; repr., Forgotten Books, 2012), 4–5.

2 Azlant draws on Musser's research, which shows that early film was influenced by popular culture, including comic strips, dime novels, popular songs, the magic lantern, vaudeville and theatre. Azlant, 'Screenwriting for the Early Silent Film', 228–229.

3 Bordwell, Staiger and Thompson, *Classical Hollywood Cinema*, 172.

4 See advertisements for the Home Correspondence School in *Photoplay*, June 1916, 175 and *MPM*, June 1915, 5.

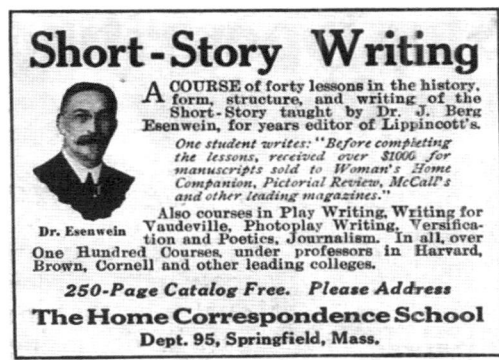

Figure 7: Advertisement for Esenwein's
Writing the Short Story
Source: *Photoplay,* June 1916, 175.

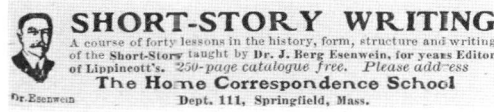

Figure 8: Advertisement for Esenwein's
Writing the Short Story
Source: *MPM,* June 1915, 5.

Figure 9: Endorsement by Sargent for
Esenwein's *Writing the Short Story* manual
Source: *MPW,* November 9, 1918, 660.

Play Writing, who saw it as an aid to the study of plot (see Figure 9).[5] Andrews makes further links across literary traditions in describing the process of preparing a theatrical scenario, which should 'set forth the gist of a drama to one who may possibly be interested in its production'. For the photoplay author, the one with this possible interest would have been the studio editor. Andrews claims that the scenario was like a one-act play or 'a condensed version of the longer play, partaking of the tabloid features of the playlet'.[6]

Much of the process of preparing scripts for the theatre transferred itself to cinema. The idea of the scenario had distinct similarities in drama and the photoplay, just as the full version of a play would have similarities to a film continuity script. Further indication of the level of crossover of disciplines comes from Phillips, another of the key screenwriting teachers in this book. His works *The Plot of the Short Story* (1912) and *Art in Short Story Narration* (1913) were advertised as 'A Valuable Aid to Successful Photoplaywriting' in the fan press and were again endorsed by Sargent as useful for photoplaywrights (see

---

5 Sargent, 'The Photoplaywright', *MPW*, November 9, 1918, 660 and Charlton Andrews, *The Technique of Play Writing* (1915; repr., Michigan: University of Michigan, 2013), 45.

6 Andrews, *Technique of Play Writing*, 201–211.

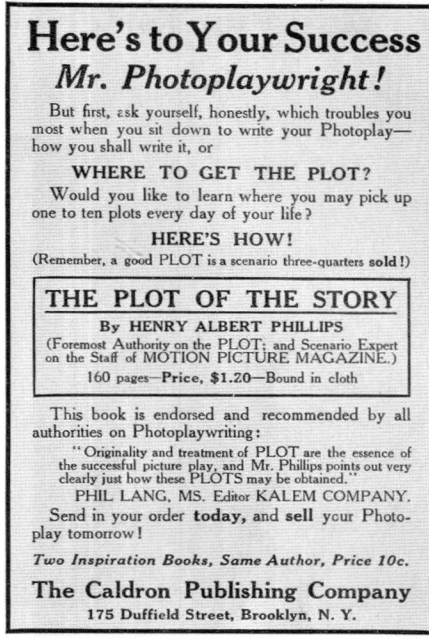

Figure 10: Advertisement for Phillips's
The Plot of the Story
Source: *MPSM*, July 1915, 155.

Figure 11: Advertisement for Phillips's
The Plot of the Short Story
Source: *The Photodrama*, 1914, 222.

Figures 10 and 11).[7] The playwright and critic Brander Matthews claimed of *The Plot of the Short Story* that he had 'read the book with continued interest'.[8] Thompson confirms the degree of crossover in noting that:

> The short story provided classical models upon which the early films could draw [… as] short films tended to follow the short story's pattern of a steadily rising action leading to a climax late in the plot.[9]

However, the evidence shows that by far the most powerful influence on the filmic process was theatrical practice. Patrick Loughney goes as far as to claim that the best way to understand the development of narrative film before 1915 is to see that the "theatrical writing" forms of the playscript and scenario […] evolved as the organizational elements essential to the production of all performing media decades before the advent of motion pictures'.[10] In other words, they were not unique to film, but were grounded in theatrical practice. The terminology that the industry used to describe film writing always included

7 Advertisement from Caldron Publishing, New York in *MPSM*, July 1913, 155 and Sargent, 'The Photoplaywright', *MPW*, February 7, 1914, 670.

8 Advertisement, in 'Art in Short Story Narration' in Phillips, *Photodrama*, 222.

9 Bordwell, Staiger and Thompson, *Classical Hollywood Cinema*, 167–168.

10 Patrick G. Loughney, 'In the Beginning Was the Word: Six Pre-Griffith Motion Picture Scenarios' in *Early Cinema: Space, Frame, Narrative*, eds. Thomas Elsaesser and Adam Barker (London: BFI, 1990), 211.

the word 'play': Maras lists the most common terms used as 'photoplaywright', 'photoplay writer', 'photoplay dramatist' or 'screen-playwright' as evidence of this connection.[11] The uses of the terms 'screen' and 'play' have fostered the idea of this link between theatre and film as a continuum, even today. Those who wrote in the trade press at the time certainly saw a strong connection between writing for the theatre and writing for film. As early as 1910, the writer Thomas Bedding makes this clear:

> A long course of theatergoing, and an apprenticeship to the moving picture development, has taught me [to] study the people around [me to] see what they like and why they like it. Then go home and write [the] play.[12]

Others not only saw the connection between theatre and film clearly, but also understood its potential. Carl Charlton, a play manual writer of the period, comments in 1916: 'With the advent of the moving pictures a new field in play-wrighting was opened up – and one in which there is increasing demand.'[13] Two years later, in *The Drama* magazine, writer Richard Sylvester similarly equates the work of the screenwriter with that of the playwright:

> The time is not far distant when the photo-dramatist will be the important individual in the studio. The director, the scenic artist, the actors, as well as the joiner, will then do his bidding. They will do all in their power to produce the playwright's play in the manner in which he intended it to be presented, just as is now done on the legitimate stage.[14]

The connection between theatre and film was strengthened by the flow of personnel between the two mediums. As John Tibbetts points out, 'theatrical entrepreneurs, from as early as 1896, actively worked with film personnel on all levels of movie making'.[15] Other prominent figures in the theatre were also beginning to see the possibilities of film narrative. In 1911 Clayton Hamilton, playwright, critic and author,[16] avers that 'the kinematograph [offers] many possibilities of narrative which lie far beyond the range of the restricted stage of the ordinary writer'.[17] Many actors, directors and writers with a theatrical background had entered the industry. Ted Nannicelli observes that William

---

11   Maras, *Screenwriting*, 82.

12   Thomas Bedding, 'The Dramatic Moment', *MPW*, March 12, 1910, 372.

13   Carl Charlton, *How to Write Photoplays* (1916; repr., Philadelphia: BiblioBazaar, 2012), 13.

14   Richard Sylvester, 'The New Art of the Photoplay-dramatist', *The Drama*, February 1918, 101.

15   John C. Tibbetts, *The American Theatrical Film* (Ohio: Bowling Green State University, 1985), 1.

16   Hamilton lectured at Columbia and worked for Goldwyn Studios as an editor. See *The New York Public Library Rare Books and Manuscripts Division: Accession Sheet 1955, Biographical Note*, http://archives. nypl.org/uploads/collection/pdf_finding_aid/hamiltonc.pdf

17   Clayton Hamilton, 'The Art of the Moving Picture Play', *Nickelodeon*, January 14, 1911, 51.

C. De Mille had begun his career in the theatre and saw writing for film as a kind of dramatic writing:

> De Mille [...] had transferred his scenario writing experience in the theater to scenario writing for films [... and] helped institute narrative norms for film writing that were based on principles of dramatic construction he had learned in the theater and from his study under Brander Matthews at Columbia University.[18]

In his enthusiasm for film, Matthews expanded the Columbia arts curriculum to pave the way for the university to teach photoplay courses under film theorist Freeburg.[19]

Many screenwriting teachers, including the key screenwriting teachers covered in this book, also had a strong theatrical pedigree and applied their theatrical understanding to the medium of film writing.

It is too simplistic to affirm the connection between playwriting for the theatre and early screenwriting teachers without unpacking the various strains of influence. An on-going scholarly debate, which has occupied the last few decades, concerns the interdependent relationship between theatrical practice and early film. Raffaele Chiarulli recognises that defining 'the relationship between the forms of theatre and those of cinema overall would mean to unravel a very complex pot of exchanges, connections and negotiations'.[20] Tracing the intricacy of this relationship and its precise history via the views of many scholars is beyond the reach of this study. However, the important issues that some have raised merit investigation, as they have some bearing on the understanding of the important role that screenwriting teachers played in contributing to the discourse on film writing. Most of these scholars fall into one of two camps, emphasising either the melodramatic or the classical elements in theatre as more influential. It is necessary to digress at this point to consider scholarly opinion on these influences, as it has implications for the instruction that early screenwriting teachers imparted.

Melodramatic Elements

A number of scholars have attempted to analyse the relationship between melodrama and film. However, what complicates this analysis is that, although they have moved towards some degree of consensus on what constitutes melodrama, some disagreement remains. Scholars tend to focus either on what they consider to be its plot or on its visual characteristics. Perhaps the most useful definition, as Steve Neale suggests, comes from Thomas Elsaesser. In his seminal 1972 article on the subject, Elsaesser draws

---

18   Ted Nannicelli, *The Philosophy of the Screenplay* (London: Routledge, 2013), 103–104.

19   Peter Decherney, *Hollywood and the Culture Elite: How the Movies Became American* (New York: Columbia University, 2005), 53.

20   Raffaele Chiarulli, 'Strong Curtains and Dramatic Punches: The Legacy of Playwriting and the Debate on the Three-act Model in the Screenwriting Manuals of the Studio Era', Screenwriting Research Network Conference, October 16–19, 2014, Potsdam, Berlin.

on the original definition of melodrama as 'a dramatic narrative in which the musical accompaniment marks the emotional effects', which means that melodramatic elements can:

> be seen as a system of punctuation, giving expressive colour and chromatic contrast to the storyline, by orchestrating the ups and downs of the intrigue.[21]

Neale summarises these melodramatic effects in terms of how the story is plotted. It will comprise an 'unequivocal dramatic conflict between good and evil' that results in the 'triumph' of the good. The principal characters will comprise a 'hero, heroine and villain' who will be drawn into a 'hyperbolic aesthetic' where 'motive, emotion and passion [are] laid bare'. In the 'episodic, formulaic and action packed plot', the 'initiation, development and resolution' are driven by the villain and many 'reversals and recognitions' will occur, which are dependent on 'fate, chance and coincidence'.[22]

Keeping the main focus on the plot, Koszarski agrees that '[m]elodrama continued to represent the dominant stylistic mode in Hollywood all through the silent period'.[23] Here Koszarski draws out its relevance for short films:

> the limited narrative capabilities of the silent short film severely restricted what might be accomplished in terms of characterization or thematic development. Early filmmakers inevitably turned to the melodramatic tradition for instant characterization of heroes and villains, simple dramatic confrontations that could be powerfully sketched in visual terms, and familiar thematic structures invoking traditional nineteenth-century ideals.[24]

Even a feature film such as *Birth of a Nation* (1914), Koszarski contends, was little 'more than a super-melodrama, offering the same heroes and villains, the same image of the family endangered, and the same inevitable victory of good over evil'.[25] He also points out that the characters do not ultimately change: 'Instead of psychological realism, what the film offers are characters who are true to type.'[26] Bordwell is another to recognise that Hollywood borrowed from 'melodrama's stock' character types that have 'sharply

21   Thomas Elsaesser, 'Tales of Sound and Fury: Observations on the Family Melodrama' in *Home is Where the Heart Is: Studies in Melodrama and the Women's Film*, ed. E. A Kaplar (London: BFI, 1987), 50; cited in Steve Neale, *Genre and Hollywood* (London: Routledge, 2000), 183. Melodrama originated from the early 19th-century French word *mélodrame*, which is derived from the Greek *melos* or music, and the French *drame* or drama (from Late Latin *drāma*, which in turn derives from the Greek *drān*, to do or perform).

22   Neale, *Genre and Hollywood*, 196.

23   Richard Koszarski, *An Evening's Entertainment: The Age of the Silent Feature Picture, 1915–1928* (London: University of California, 1994), 182.

24   Ibid., 181.

25   Ibid.

26   Ibid.

delineated and unambiguous traits' and the 'formula of hero versus villain' leading to 'two lines of action' of 'cause and effect' with characters 'defined by goals'.[27]

The scholars who have tended to concentrate more on the visual aspects include Vardac, who was the first to explore the close historical relationship between theatre and film. In *Stage to Screen* (1949), he argues that 'proto-cinematic' techniques were already evident in nineteenth-century theatre: 'The necessity for greater pictorial realism in the arts of theatre appears as the logical impetus to the invention of cinema.'[28] Theatrical pictorialism characterised Victorian melodrama, pantomime and Shakespearean productions:

> Pictorial mise-en-scène entailed elaborate scenery [...] vivid costumes and properties, spectacular scenic and lighting effects and the frequent use of tableaux vivants [living pictures].[29]

Vardac believed that the theatre was striving to create even greater spectacular effects without the appropriate technology – effects that would eventually be realised in cinema. Once this technology was in place, he claims, the 'motion picture finally made its appearance in response to the insistence of social pressure for a greater pictorial realism in the theatre'.[30] Although Vardac's interpretation is far-fetched, his observation that cinema was influenced by the pictorial elements of melodrama is important.

In a similar vein, John Fell believes that 'early films largely cannibalised the innards of the [previous] century's theatrical melodrama' for their visual material.[31] He claims that 'in the motion pictures there surfaced an entire tradition of narrative technique which had been developing unsystematically for a hundred years'. The melodramatic tradition was a conglomeration of many visual technologies that had been drawn from sources such as 'theater, print, optical amusements and "shows," and graphics (comics, engraving, lithography, photography, painting)'.[32]

The need to tell stories visually, Brewster and Jacobs contend, meant that film naturally leant towards the pictorialism that Vardac identifies in early film. They claim that after 1910, when the demand for longer films grew, filmmakers strove to be theatrical and readily assimilated pictorial realism.[33] According to Brewster and Jacobs, the nineteenth-

---

27   Bordwell, Staiger and Thompson, *Classical Hollywood Cinema*, 13–16.

28   Vardac, *Stage to Screen*, xx.

29   Richard Schoch, ed., *Great Shakespeareans: Macready, Booth, Irving, Terry* (London: Continuum, 2011), 4.

30   Vardac, *Stage to Screen*, xxv.

31   John Fell, *Film and the Narrative Tradition* (Oklahoma: University of Oklahoma, 1974), 12.

32   Ibid., xv.

33   See Brewster and Jacobs, *Theatre to Cinema*, 3–15.

century 'model of plot [was] a series of discrete moments called "situations"'. Each 'situation' was a particular conjunction of circumstances in which the characters were presented in a striking or exciting way through poses or tableaux. Thus, those involved in 'script construction for films […] made use of a conception of plot' that had been inherited from playwrights. As pictorial or visual representations, these 'situations' could be characterised in theatrical parlance as 'a deadlock, a temporary suspension of the action, a point of equilibrium among the forces that propel the narrative'.[34] Brewster and Jacobs point out that: 'The photoplay-writing manuals make similar definitions of the situation as that which precedes or delays action.'[35] The most common of these 'is in terms of suspense'.[36] Brewster and Jacobs argue that:

> pictorial effects developed along the lines of theatrical models were important because they provided ways of underscoring the dramatic action and punctuating the scene's duration.[37]

Photoplay manuals offer evidence in support of this view. In particular, the focus on plot taxonomy, which involved creating categorised lists of dramatic conundrums, was a sign of situational thinking that developed out of this more pictorial approach. As Brewster and Jacobs point out:

> this way of thinking of plot construction gives rise to attempts to derive a narrative lexicon – a comprehensive list of the situations of which all known plots, and all the as yet unwritten plots are comprised.[38]

Frederick Palmer's *The Photoplay Plot Encyclopedia* and Wycliffe A. Hill's *Ten Million Photoplay Plots* are evidence Brewster and Jacobs put forward to show how this approach had crept into screenwriting instruction.[39] Palmer summarised the meaning of the 'situation' as:

> when the characters are so brought together that their contrasts and conflicts are clear and dramatic, that the central character is placed in a dilemma in which he must make a choice, or in a predicament in which a change will be suffered, or is confronted with an obstacle to overcome.[40]

---

34   Ibid., 20–24.

35   Ibid., 23.

36   Ibid., 30.

37   Ibid., 29.

38   Ibid., 23.

39   Ibid., 23

40   Frederick Palmer, *Photoplay Plot Encyclopedia* (Los Angeles: Palmer Photoplay, 1922), 12; cited in Brewster and Jacobs, *Theatre to Cinema*, 25.

A significant contributor omitted from Brewster and Jacobs's work, however, is Phillips, one of the important screenwriting teachers examined in this study. The form of situational dramaturgy they describe can also be evidenced in his understanding of 'sequence', about which Phillips claims, 'The minor incidents of suspense [...] contribut[e] an element of suspense to the main theme that will be felt in the climax itself.'[41] Phillips' *The Universal Plot Catalogue* (1920) for screenwriters, containing countless lists of 'incidents', became widely available. His endorsement of this kind of approach lends validation to Brewster and Jacobs's observations.

Another noteworthy point from Brewster and Jacobs is that, rather than abandoning the narrative mode, screenwriting teachers attempted 'to reconcile an analysis of plot in terms of situation with the norms of narrative continuity and logic'. To avoid 'the kind of criticism that Aristotle makes of the episodic plot [..., close] attention to the motivation and resolution of situations [was] frequently recommended'.[42] 'Situations' were effectively embedded in a structure with a beginning, middle and end.

A challenge to Brewster and Jacobs's notion of 'situation' or 'arrested or suspended action' as the defining element of melodrama comes from Ben Singer. Viewing their idea as limiting, he claims that melodramas do not always involve shocking reversals, revelations or deadlocks and 'situations' are not always 'an intense, climactic plight that is crystallized in a flash and, after a moment of suspense, broken to allow another thrill to develop'.[43] By way of support for this argument, Neale challenges the situational model as inadequate because, although 'deadlocks' or 'a temporary suspension of the action' would seem to 'render the characters involved powerless, passive or vulnerable', the villains in melodrama 'are never characterized as powerless' but are constantly active.[44]

Pinning down the precise meaning of melodrama is difficult, Singer admits, so he defines it as a 'cluster concept', identifying its five key elements as: 'strong pathos' (powerful feelings of pity); 'overwrought emotion' (expressions of raw feeling); 'moral polarization' (extreme representations of good and evil); 'non-classical narrative structure' (implausibility and coincidence in plotting); and 'sensationalism' (thrilling spectacle).[45] This 'cluster concept', Neale acknowledges, is useful and he accepts that, with its:

---

41 Phillips, *Photodrama*, 163–164.

42 Brewster and Jacobs, *Theatre to Cinema*, 24.

43 Ben Singer, *Melodrama and Modernity: Early Sensational Cinema and Its Contexts* (New York: Columbia University Press, 2001), 43.

44 Neale, *Genre and Hollywood*, 197–198.

45 Singer, *Melodrama and Modernity*, 44–49.

distinct aesthetic features and traditions, all of which found their way into the cinema […] nineteenth-century melodrama, in all its guises, was both a fundamental progenitor of nearly all of Hollywood's non-comic genres, and a fundamental source of many of its cross-generic features, devices and conventions.[46]

Although no real agreement emerges, it is helpful that some scholars take a broader, more inclusive approach to the concept of melodrama. Indeed, as Bratton, Cook and Gledhill acknowledge, 'the protean nature of melodrama […] as it shifts between forms, cultures and decades' should be recognised alongside 'cinema's relation to its melodramatic inheritance'.[47] However, it is generally accepted today that melodrama was an important element in early film. Rick Altman indicates that the recognition of melodramatic influences is a necessary corrective because, he claims, Bordwell and Thompson have paid:

> little attention to the possible contribution of melodramatic material to the classical paradigm. This repression of popular theater has the effect of denying Hollywood cinema its fundamental connection to popular traditions and to their characteristic forms of spectacle and narrative.[48]

Underlining the reasons for and the importance of the connection to melodrama, Marc Norman draws attention to the insightful comments of Elmer Rice, a young playwright signed by Samuel Goldwyn:

> The absence of dialogue and rather limited aesthetic and intellectual capacity of the mass audience for whose entertainment films were designed necessitated a concentration upon scenes of action: melodramatic, comic, erotic. Wit and poetry were of course excluded.[49]

One result of such writing requirements was that melodramatic influences would form the backdrop of much of the instruction in early screenwriting manuals.

Classical Elements

The locus of John Tibbetts's research in 1982 was in showing how important 'theatrical film' was to early cinema. As the demand for story material grew, producers and writers increasingly turned to adapting plays and literature into scenarios. Challenging Vardac's ideas, Tibbetts claims that these writers went much further than simply imitating popular

---

46   Neale, *Genre and Hollywood*, 201–202.

47   Jacky Bratton, Jim Cook and Christine Gledhill, 'Introduction' in *Melodrama: Stage, Picture, Screen*, eds. Bratton, Cook and Gledhill (London: BFI, London, 1994), 1.

48   Rick Altman, 'Dickens, Griffith, and Film Theory Today' in *Classical Hollywood Narrative: The Paradigm Wars*, ed. Jane Gaines (Durham: Duke University, 1992), 25.

49   Norman, *What Happens Next*, 62. Norman quotes from Elmer Rice, *Minority Report: An Autobiography* (New York: Simon & Schuster, 1963), 173

theatre forms such as vaudeville and melodrama, to the extent that the narrative tradition of 'well-made plays as important models' should also be included.[50] He argues that these play structures formed the basis of the narrative that ultimately became a plank of Hollywood style.

The first narrative films attempted to replicate theatrical experience by just presenting parts of, or familiar scenes from, a play. The camera position was static, which 'preserved the illusion that the audience was watching players on a large stage from a fixed vantage point'.[51] By the early teens of the twentieth century, however, as Tibbetts points out, disillusionment with theatrical films was growing. In a growing chorus of disapproval, critics, commentators and even filmmakers, such as Griffith, objected to these closely imitative films. The 1913 comments of Robert Grau, the highly regarded impresario, theatrical manager and writer, typify this attitude: 'A majority of those who had seen these pictures on the screen would emphatically state they did not want to renew the experience.'[52] Theorists such as Münsterberg, Lindsay and the playwright and critic Luigi Pirandello developed the film aesthetic that a new approach was needed and 'that imitation was blocking original work in motion pictures'.[53] Pirandello's ingenious notebook, *Si Gara (Shoot!)* (1915), on the life of fictional camera operator Serafino Gubbio, illustrated the power and versatility of the camera.[54] Filmmakers realised that they had more options than just transferring plays to screen in the same way as they had appeared on the stage and treating the camera as if it were a spectator in the audience. As a consequence, they began to make careful choices about their use of the camera position to tell the central character's story from their point of view or vantage point.[55]

The ability to control point of view through the ubiquitous use of the camera would become one of the major differences between writing for the theatre and writing for the cinema. It was something that the key screenwriting teachers examined in this study would constantly emphasise. In a series of articles in the *New York Dramatic Mirror* entitled 'The Evolution of the Motion Picture', filmmaking professionals – including editors, directors and cameramen – explained how the motion picture differed from theatre. The final contributor was Peacocke, who is another of the screenwriting teachers considered in this study and who, Tibbetts notes:

---

50   John Tibbetts, 'The Stage/Screen Exchange: Patterns of Imitation in Art: 1896–1930' (PhD diss., Kansas University, 1982), 14. ProQuest (UMI 8301749).

51   Tibbetts, *American Theatrical Film*, 7.

52   Robert Grau, 'A Word About Celebrated Stars in Photoplays', *MPSM*, February 1913, 127; cited in Tibbetts, *American Theatrical Film*, 212.

53   Tibbetts, 'Stage/Screen Exchange', 394.

54   Lorenzo Princi, 'Review of Shoot! By Luigi Pirandello', *Blurb Hack*, August 21, 2010, http://blurbhack. com/reviews/review.php?recordID=80&type=book&code=shoot

55   Tibbetts, *American Theatrical Film*, 74.

admitted to substantial differences between the craft of playwriting and screenwriting. His remarks reveal recognition of the film medium as a unique form of expression.[56]

In the article, Peacocke points out that a film has shorter scenes and many more of them, and that they should not rely on dialogue.[57] As an aside, it is interesting to note that Tibbetts quotes from Peacocke because he was an editor and screenwriter rather than because he was a significant instructional voice in the industry.

Between 1912 and 1915, Tibbetts claims, filmmakers 'departed radically from the hitherto accepted idea that the artistic identity of motion pictures depended on how closely a film could simulate the illusion of a theatrical event'.[58] However, although the means of filming the material changed, the model of the 'well-made play' on which it was based would continue. As Tibbetts points out, the 'well-made play' was useful to early film, although melodramatic elements were also helpful, where immediate situation was more important than developing plot. Such elements offered opportunities for camera effects, illusions and visions, as 'melodrama did not emphasize the logic and rigor of plot construction'.[59]

The influence of classical narrative structure and character psychology embedded in what came to be known as the 'well-made play' traces its origins to Aristotelian thinking. Aristotle's *Poetics* contains four main components: dramatic action, unity of action, probability of action and the unified three-part dramatic structure.

A play, according to this prescription, begins with a protagonist who has a goal or need and the plot or dramatic action serves as a means of answering whether or not this goal or need is met. According to Aristotle, plot or action takes priority over characters and characters demonstrate who they are through their actions. *Poetics* asserts that a play:

> is not an imitation of persons, but of actions and of life [… and] people possess certain qualities in accordance with their character, but they achieve well-being or its opposite on the basis of how they fare […] so character is included [only …] on account of the actions.[60]

---

56   Frederick James Smith, 'The Evolution of the Motion Picture – VII. From the Standpoint of the Photoplaywright. An Interview with Captain Leslie T. Peacocke, special scenario writer with the Universal Company', *NYDM*, July 23, 1913, 25 and 31; cited in Tibbetts, 'Stage/Screen Exchange', 393.

57   Ibid., 393–394.

58   Tibbetts, *American Theatrical Film*, 219.

59   Ibid., 59.

60   Aristotle, *Poetics*, translated by Malcolm Heath (London: Penguin Books, 1996), 11.

According to Aristotle, the pattern of events (actions) of the plot must causally relate to one another and:

> should imitate a single, unified action – and one that is also a whole. So the structure of the various sections of the events must be such that the transposition or removal of any one section dislocates and changes the whole.[61]

By this reasoning, 'the arrangement of the incidents' must form a 'unity of action', whereby the incidents are structurally self-contained and bound together by internal necessity, each action leading to the next without a *deus ex machina* (divine intervention). The plot must have universal significance and meaning. The cause-and-effect chain leading from the incentive moment to the climax is the 'tying up' (*desis*) or complication. The more rapid cause-and-effect chain from the climax to the resolution is the 'unravelling' (*lusis*) or dénouement. Specific 'plot points' or moments when the character makes a moral choice must occur. At some point, too, the character will undergo a drastic change, which is only possible because the character has a 'tragic flaw' (*hamartia*) related to some great error or frailty in their nature. As a result, the pattern of events (actions) should accomplish some artistic or emotional effect. The end of all tragedy is *katharsis* or 'purging', the arousing of the emotions of 'pity and fear', which has a cleansing effect on the spectator.[62] According to Aryeh Kosman, this cathartic experience appears contradictory because 'the effect of witnessing tragedy is at once pleasurable and associated with the experience of fear and pity'. The reason for this effect is that the tragedy is a mimetic representation and spectators can experience these emotions in safety, unconnected to real life.[63]

These sets of actions relate to a single protagonist, who wages a conflict with an antagonist, which will lead to irreversible consequences. Moreover, 'anything that smacks of randomness or irrationality is part of the back-story [… and everything] that happens must have plausibility'.[64] Aristotle contends the actions must be necessary and probable:

---

61   Ibid., 15.

62   See Anthony Birch, 'Aristotle's Elements of Drama', http://www.mindtools.net/MindFilms/aristot.shtml and Barbara F. McManus, Outline of Aristotle's Theory of Tragedy in the Poetics, CLS 267 *Topics Page*, November 1999, http://www2.cnr.edu/home/bmcmanus/poetics.html and Aristotle's, The Poetics, Chapter 7; 'The Plot Must Be a Whole'; Chapter 8, 'The Plot Must Be a Unity and Chapter 9, 'Dramatic Unity', http://www.identitytheory.com/etexts/poetics.html

63   Aryeh Kosman, 'Acting: Drama as the Mimesis of Praxis' in *Essays on Aristotle's Poetics*, ed. Amélie Oksenberg Rorty (Princeton: Princeton University Press, 1992), 51–72.

64   David Wiles, 'Aristotle's Poetics and Ancient Dramatic Theory' in *The Cambridge Companion to Greek and Roman Theatre*, ed. Marianne McDonald and J. Michael Walton (Cambridge: CUP, 2007), 101.

> the function of the poet is not to say what has happened, but to say the kind of
> thing that would happen, i.e. what is possible in accordance with probability or
> necessity.[65]

According to Aristotle, these sets of actions should be expressed in a three-part unified
structure, meaning that a play should have a beginning, a middle and an end:

> A beginning is that which itself does not follow necessarily from anything else,
> but that some second thing naturally exists or occurs after it [...]. A middle is that
> which itself comes after something else and some other thing comes after it [...
> and an] end is that which does itself naturally follow from something else, either
> necessarily or in general, but there is nothing else after it.[66]

In her 'History of Three-act Structure', Jennine Lanouette observes that Horace of Rome
(65–8 B.C.) interpreted Aristotle's categories of prologue, *parados* (first song of the
chorus), episode, *stasimon* (second song of the chorus) and exodus more literally as five
acts. The neo-classicists of the sixteenth-century Italian Renaissance and the French
dramatists of the seventeenth century followed this structure rigidly. By the nineteenth
century, the idea of the 'well-made play' with five acts had evolved. However, as
Lanouette points out, three acts could still be detected in this five-act structure.[67]

The concept of the 'well-made play' had been distilled from the hundreds of plays
written by French dramatist Eugène Scribe (1791–1861) and was further popularised by
playwright Victorien Sardou (1831–1908). Scribe's formulaic plots operated strictly by
cause and effect. His ideas about structuring a play in five acts were reminiscent of the
construction of many of Shakespeare's plays. They often began with a misunderstanding
(a secret known to the audience but not the characters) set up by an inciting incident
in Act One. Rising action followed, interspersed with upsets and reversals in fortune
for the main character in Act Two. This eventually led to a climactic turning point that
determined the outcome in Act Three. The earlier complications were then worked out,
resulting in a final climax in Act Four. A dénouement followed in Act Five, where any
remaining tangles were unravelled and loose ends tied up and a happy ending usually
ensued.[68]

---

65 Aristotle, *Poetics*, 16.

66 Ibid., 13–14.

67 Lanouette describes the three acts as follows: 'the presentation in the first act of the sympathetic
character, background exposition and setting up of the situation […] in the second act, increasingly intense
action and a series of ups and downs in conflict with the adversary; the low point at the end of the second
act which comes from a reversal of fortune followed by a third act climax […]; which is in turn followed
by a dénouement.' See Jennine Lanouette, 'A History of Three-act Structure' in *Screentakes: Studies in
Screenwriting for Writers, Directors and Creative Professionals*, 3–12, December 24, 2012, 4–6, http://
www.screentakes.com/an-evolutionary-study-of-the-three-act-structure-model-in-drama/

68 Douglas Cardwell, 'The Well-made Play of Eugène Scribe', *The French Review* 56, May 1983, 876–
884, https://ibenglish2011.wikispaces.com/file/view/The+Well-Made+Play+of+Eugene+Scribe.pdf

A codification of this understanding came from Gustav Freytag, a German drama theorist and playwright. In his 1863 manual, *Technique of the Drama*, Freytag examined great works from different periods – by Sophocles, Shakespeare, Lessing, Goethe and Schiller – in an attempt to discover the fundamental laws of dramatic construction. On dramatic action, unity of action and probability of action, Freytag is largely consistent with Aristotle. He affirms that dramatic action must drive the story, as 'passion which leads to action is the business of dramatic art'.[69] Each piece of dramatic action must relate to that which comes before and after it, because 'the action must move forward with uniform consistency'.[70] As 'every spectator is a child of his time', probability of action must be in keeping with what is possible at that point in history, although more might become possible in the future.[71]

Another of Freytag's initiatives was to expand the three-part to a five-part structure, which he defines as exposition, rising action, climax, falling action and dénouement, using a 'pyramidal structure'. Within this structure he identifies three crises for the protagonist. Other interpretations of this structure commonly regard it as seven stages by dividing the action in another way, although it is fundamentally the same structure.[72]

Figure 12 shows how Freytag represented it diagrammatically.

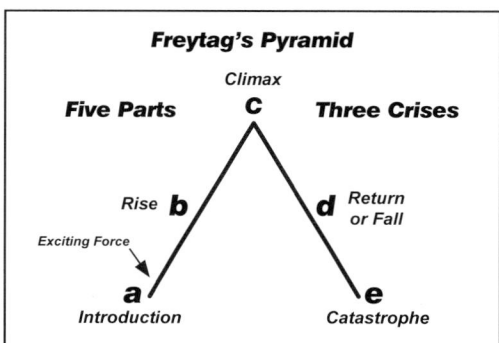

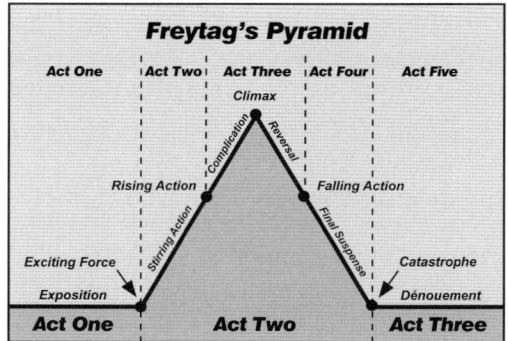

Figure 12: Freytag's pyramid structure of the five-act play
Source: Adapted from *archive.org/details/ freytagstechniqu00frey/page/115*.

Figure 13: Amending Freytag's pyramid to a three-act structure
Source: Adapted from *archive.org/details/ freytagstechniqu00frey/page/115*.

---

69 Gustav Freytag, *Technique of the Drama* (1895: repr., London: Forgotten Books, 2014), 19.

70 Ibid., 29.

71 Ibid., 51.

72 George Hartley understands the structure in seven stages: 1. Exposition of character and setting; 2. Inciting Incident that begins the conflict; 3. Rising Action building the story; 4. A Climax or tragic moment; 5. Falling Action signalling the story end; 6. A 'catastrophe' that resolves the conflict; 7. A Dénouement where character issues are resolved. See George Hartley, 'Analyzing a Story's Plot: Freytag's Pyramid' in English 250 Unit: *Freytag's Pyramid* (Ohio University), http://www.ohio.edu/people/hartleyg/ref/fiction/freytag.html

As Figure 13 indicates, amending Freytag's concept, the structure can still be understood as three parts or acts, with a beginning, middle and end. The wings of the diagram are sometimes extended to make this structure clearer.

In the three-act structure, the beginning (Act One) serves as an exposition to set the context and introduce the characters and situation. Thereafter, the 'exciting force' (inciting incident) occurs, 'where the counter-play resolves to use its lever to set the hero in motion'.[73] This means the characters or forces that oppose the hero will launch them into the quest. The middle (Act Two) consists of three separate parts: the rise, climax and return. The 'rise' means: 'The action has been started; the chief persons have shown what they are; the interest has been awakened.'[74] The climax of the drama that follows 'naturally forms the middle point of a group of forces, which darting in either direction, course upward and downward'.[75] The 'return' moves the hero towards a moment of truth where they have to make a stand and either accomplish their goal or fail; hence: 'The most difficult part of the drama is the sequence of scenes [in] the downward movement [where] dangers enter most.'[76] This leads to the final crisis or moment of truth, called 'the force of the final suspense', which is 'necessary, in good time to prepare the mind of the audience for the catastrophe'.[77] The end (Act Three) or 'catastrophe' of the drama is the closing action, 'which must present the logical "consequences of the action" and outcome for the characters and the 'more profound the strife [...] the more noble its purpose'. [78] In other words, the more conflict that occurs, the better the play. The drama is closed out by the dénouement or final situation for the hero. Later critics such as Ferdinand Brunetière (1849–1906) would seek to formulate 'the general "laws" of the theatre [and the] principles that provide a foundation for all drama in all times', which further encouraged standardisation.[79]

Plenty of evidence indicates that Aristotle's views were extant within the industry during the early period of film writing and were readily employed by screenwriting teachers. Drawing on Aristotle was common among column writers and those offering support to scenario writers. George Rockhill Craw, a less successful forerunner to Sargent, whom

---

73 Freytag, *Technique of the Drama*, 121.

74 Ibid., 125.

75 Ibid., 130.

76 Ibid., 133.

77 Ibid., 135.

78 Ibid., 137.

79 Marvin Carson, *Theories of the Theatre: A Historical and Critical Survey from the Greeks to the Present* (London: Cornell University Press, 1984), 298.

Sargent nevertheless calls a 'well known scenario writer',[80] claims in an article on structure that:

> Aristotle said [...] that drama has: first, an introduction; second, a climax or a clash; and third, a dénouement or a catastrophe.[81]

Similarly, Louis Reeves Harrison (regarded as more of a theoretician than a screenwriting teacher, as confirmed later in this study) claims, in his articles for *Moving Picture World*, that: 'Remarkably applicable are the three unities. They were propounded by Aristotle, 400 B.C. Unity of time, place and action.' Even though 'Harrison writes in high brow and we use more commonplace English', Sargent observes, he agrees with Harrison on most issues and he has had 'a profound respect' for him during their long association over many years.[82]

According to N. J. Lowe, the Aristotelian model was central then and endures today in storytelling for a compelling reason. He argues that the classical paradigm of plot stands outside:

> [the] West's own canonization of classical antiquity [... and] is teleological; it asserts the deep causality and intelligibility of its world even where it denies human access to direct apprehension or control [and therefore] is a uniquely powerful system for the narrative articulation of claims about the order of the world.[83]

In other words, it helps human beings to understand themselves and make sense of the chaotic, disordered and nonsensical occurrences they often experience in their lives. Lowe continues:

> Western classical plotting is not a purely cultural artefact; [...] much of its power resides in innate mechanisms of narrative processing that are part of our inheritance as occupants of human brains.[84]

Plot itself, or this particular form of plotting, could therefore be regarded as a 'label for a fundamental process in the way human minds decode and respond to narrative texts'.[85] Asking why this paradigm is 'so ubiquitous', John Yorke reaches a similar conclusion: it 'tells us much about perception, about narrative and about the workings of the human

---

80 Sargent, 'The Scenario Writer', *MPW*, December 16, 1911, 895.

81 George Rockhill Craw, 'The Technique of the Picture Play', *MPW*, January 28, 1911, 178.

82 Louis Reeves Harrison, 'The Law of the Drama', *MPW*, January 25, 1919, 485 and Sargent, 'The Photoplaywright', *MPW*, January 26, 1918, 514.

83 N. J. Lowe, *The Classical Plot and the Invention of Western Narrative* (Cambridge: CUP, 2000), 260.

84 Ibid., 261.

85 Ibid., 259.

mind'.[86] This insight may also explain why early screenwriting teachers readily adopted Aristotle's approach.

Another clear link, which Nannicelli acknowledges, is between early screenwriting and nineteenth century theatrical practice. The practice is typified in playwriting manuals, which espoused:

> the principles of the well-made play as conceived by Victorien Sardou and Eugene Scribe, theorized by Ferdinand Brunetière and Gustav Freytag, and propounded by American critics such as Brander Matthews, Clayton Hamilton [,...] William Archer [...] and W.T. Price.[87]

These manuals would also be a source of inspiration to screenwriting teachers of the period. Much of the language found in screenwriting manuals is reminiscent of that in playwriting manuals; sometimes the borrowing of ideas is acknowledged and sometimes not. Price's playwriting manual, and those of other leading dramaturges, such as Archer, Matthews, Andrews and Hamilton, were regularly advertised and discussed in the film fan and trade press (see Figure 14).[88] Hamilton, also a well-known drama critic, lecturer and playwright,[89] wrote in 1911 about the possibilities that film presented.[90] Both he and Andrews would also go on to write successful photoplays and Archer's plays would also be filmed.[91]

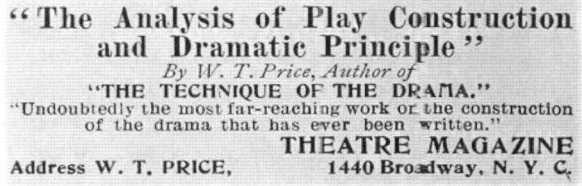

Figure 14: Advertisement for a publication by
W. T. Price, continuing to reference his influential
nineteenth-century playwriting manual
Source: *MPSM*, March 1912, 170.

---

86   John Yorke, *Into the Woods: A Five Act Journey Into Story* (London: Penguin, 2013), 23.

87   Nannicelli, *Philosophy of the Screenplay*, 100–101.

88   See advertisement in *MPSM*, March 1912, 170; Louis Reeves Harrison, 'Theatrical Plots', *MPW*, October 23, 1915, 586 and Palmer, 'Today and Tomorrow', *The Story World and the Photodramatist*, September 1923, 70–71.

89   He lectured at Columbia University and worked for Goldwyn Studios as an editor. He wrote *The Theory of the Theatre* (1910), *Studies in Stagecraft* (1914) and *The Problems of the Playwright* (1917). See Clayton Hamilton, *The New York Public Library Rare Books and Manuscripts Division: Accession Sheet 1955, Biographical Note,* http://archives.nypl.org/uploads/collection/pdf_finding_aid/hamiltonc.pdf

90   Hamilton, 'Mr. Hamilton on Photoplays', *The Nickelodeon*, January 14, 1911, 41–42.

91   See *IMDbPro*: on Clayton Hamilton, https://pro-labs.imdb.com/name/nm0357793/ and Andrews, https://pro-labs.imdb.com/name/nm0028602/. William Archer's *The Green Goddess* was filmed in 1923 and remade in 1930 and 1939. https://pro-labs.imdb.com/name/nm0033742/

A more conventional view comes from William T. Price, a theatrical impresario, teacher and critic.[92] His manual, *The Technique of the Drama* (1892), is, according to Price himself, a re-statement of the 'obvious and accepted principles as underlie the drama' or 'tricks of the trade'.[93] Accessible and explanatory rather than experimental in approach, it strongly reiterates Aristotle's ideas and advocates the five-act structure outlined by Freytag.[94]

While still making constant references to Aristotle's *Poetics* and drawing more generally on the literary tradition of playwriting back to the Greeks, Archer's *Play-making* manual (1912) is a more scholarly, critical work. He acknowledges Aristotle's requirements 'that a play should have a beginning, middle and end', but spends much of his manual discussing theatre's agitation and moving away from this model. Playwrights, he contends, 'are more than sufficiently apt to ignore or despise this rule'.[95] From this perspective, Archer examines the works of Shakespeare and of many nineteenth-century playwrights such as Ibsen and Pinero. The discussion covers all the theorists on drama, including even the relativistic ideas of Hegel.[96]

Freytag's pyramid, dividing a story into five parts and placing the climax in the middle of the action, features frequently. However, Archer modifies this idea to suggest that, once the 'tension sets in', it should not be relaxed until 'just before the fall of the curtain'.[97] He also criticises Freytag's pyramidal structure as too rigid and urges flexibility:

> In the days of the five-act dogma, each act was supposed to have its special and pre-ordained function. Freytag assigns to the second act, as a rule, the Steigerung or heightening – the working up, one might call it – of the interest. But the second act in modern plays, has often to do all the work of the three middle acts […]. For our present purposes, we may treat the interior section of a play as a unit, whether it consists of one, two or three acts.[98]

---

92   Price taught in the American School of Playwriting and worked as a critic for the *New York Star.* See J. E. Kleber, ed., *The Encyclopedia of Louisville* (Kentucky: University of Kentucky, 2001), 522.

93   William T. Price, *The Technique of the Drama* (1892: repr., Miami: Hard Press, 2013), iv.

94   Ibid., 65–111.

95   William Archer, *Play-making: A Manual of Craftsmanship* (1912: repr., London: Forgotten Books, 2012), 67.

96   Hegel, unlike Aristotle, claims that the conflict 'is not between good and evil but between goods that are each making too exclusive a claim'. This relativistic rather than absolutist approach sees the tragic hero as adhering to one ethical system that comes up against competing, equally justifiable ethical claims. See Mark W. Roche, 'Introduction to Hegel's Theory of Tragedy', http://aplangandcomp.blogs.rsu1.org/files/2011/03/hegelontragedy.pdf

97   Archer, *Play-making*, 148.

98   Ibid., 145.

In Archer's argument, the beginning, or what we must grasp in order to begin the action, is particularly important. It is the 'point of attack' that is a 'stirring episode' or Freytag's 'exciting force', 'calculated to arrest the spectator's attention and awaken his interest, while conveying to him little or no information', which is all that is needed to start the action.[99] This set-up necessarily leads to the 'obligatory scene' near the end, which is a scene 'an audience expects and ardently desires'.[100] This scene, derived from the theme of the work, serves as a resolution to the question that has been raised by the drama and completes the emotional journey of the spectator.

Archer seems to exhibit some ambivalence about whether the five-act or three-act model is preferable, but only because he does not want to impose arbitrary rules based on mere segmentation or the fall of the curtain. As Lanouette indicates, Archer sees the appropriate model as dependent on:

> the natural progression of a real life crisis, grounding his emerging model of dramatic structure in the rhythms of human nature [...] the rhythms of growth, culmination and solution.[101]

Nevertheless, Archer clearly affirms the usefulness of the three-act structure, because he senses that Aristotle saw this as a demarcation that arose from the natural pulse of the material rather than as an imposed paradigm:

> It was doubtless the necessity for marking this rhythm that Aristotle had in mind when he said that a dramatic action must have a beginning, middle and an end. Taken in its simplicity, this principle would indicate the three-act division as the ideal scheme for a play.[102]

Concurring that Archer proposes a more organic approach to the structural design of a play, Ian Macdonald describes the playwright in this approach as 'constructing a series of crises in a rhythm appropriate to the theme'.[103] Archer confirms that every:

> act ought to consist either of a minor crisis, carried to its temporary solution, or of a well-marked group of such crises; and there can be no rule as to the number of such crises which ought to present themselves to the development of a given theme.[104]

---

99   Ibid., 72.

100   Ibid., 173.

101   Lanouette, 'A History of Three-act Structure'.

102   Archer, *Play-making*, 107.

103   Ian W. Macdonald, 'Forming the Craft: Play-wrighting and Photoplay-writing in Britain in the 1910s' in *Early Popular Visual Culture*, 3.1 (2010): 83.

104   Archer, *Play-making*, 107.

Because 'Action ought to exist for the sake of character', he further asserts, structure is subservient to character – a view that is a departure from Aristotle.[105] Archer likens structure to a skeleton, which is necessary to prevent a human being from collapsing into 'an amorphous heap'; however, it is character that gives the human being life, just as:

> It is by his blood and nerve that he lives, not by his bones; and it is because his bones are, comparatively speaking, dead matter that they continue to exist when the flesh has fallen away from them.[106]

The dramatic theme, Archer believes, must also lead to 'a great crisis, bringing out the vivid manifestations of character'[107] and 'the highest order of drama should consist in the reaction of character to a series of crucial experiences'.[108] He again stresses that story structure must serve character development:

> The story which is independent of character – which can be carried through by a given number of ready-made puppets – is essentially a trivial thing. Unless, at an early stage of the organizing process, character begins to take the upper hand.[109]

Archer's influence is clear among those who wrote photoplays or offered instruction. Director, writer and film producer Clarence G. Badger (1880–1964), for example, refers to Archer's terminology of 'Point of Attack' in his short treatise on screenwriting. Like Archer, he recognises that the 'Point of Attack' must be a significant dramatic incident that draws the attention of the viewer, although in the case of screenwriting it cannot use dialogue. While making no specific reference to Archer, Badger links his own understanding of writing the photoplay to the writing of a stage play:

> The photoplaywright may be said to be a screen dramatist and he is bound by the restrictions similar to those governing the author of a stage play.[110]

One who readily admits that Archer is his source of inspiration is screenwriting teacher Howard T. Dimick. Archer, he claims, has come up with 'a newer formulation of the dramatic in terms of crisis', which refers to Archer's view of 'tension'. As support for this argument, he quotes Archer's definition: 'A play is more or less a rapidly-developing

---

105   Ibid., 19.

106   Ibid., 18.

107   Ibid., 33.

108   Ibid., 286.

109   Ibid., 17.

110   Clarence G. Badger, *The Point of Attack or How to Start the Photoplay* (Los Angeles: Palmer Photoplay Corporation, 1920), 6. Badger was a freelance worked for Lubin, Universal, Sennett-Paramount and Goldwyn Features.

crisis in destiny or circumstances.'[111] Notably too, Dimick lists most of the key playwriting manuals as source material in the appendix of his manual, *Modern Photoplay Writing*.[112]

A number of screenwriting teachers also refer to Price as a source. Leona Radnor quotes Price when discussing how to develop ideas for a plot: 'Every true play fashioned under a creative hand has its germ.'[113] In *The Technique of the Drama*, Price continues:

> This germ may be a pregnant and suggestive trait in some character, a happening;
> of personal knowledge in life, an incident in history, a paragraph in a newspaper –
> in short a dramatic idea from any source.[114]

Blatant examples of plagiarism are evident as well. Dimick defines the three problems facing the photoplaywright when adapting material for dramatic presentation as:

> The Moral Problem […] the object or significance of a play; The Aesthetic Problem
> […] the artistic value of the events […] from the vantage of taste and The Technical
> Problem […] of structure and dramatic effectiveness of the story.[115]

This has clearly been modelled on comments from Price's manual, *The Technique of the Drama*. The similarities are striking, as Price's version of the three problems demonstrates:

> The Ethical – The theme, with its facts and what is proved; […] The Aesthetic
> – The matter of taste is bound up in every drama [and] The Technical – […] the
> science and art of giving form to the dramatic material.[116]

Finally Frances Taylor Patterson reinforces the links between theatrical understanding and photoplay composition when discussing plot. In the space of just a few lines, she mentions five dramaturges, including Aristotle, Archer and Matthews.[117]

In summary, the strong connections between playwriting and screenwriting manuals clearly indicate that the tradition of the 'well-made play' provided a robust framework that helped shape the thinking of early screenwriting teachers.

---

111   Dimick, *Modern Photoplay Writing*, 94.

112   Dimick lists 10 playwriting manuals. He also cites, among others: Price, *Technique of the Drama;* Archer, *Play-making;* Brander Matthews, *The Principles of Play Making;* George Polti, *The Thirty Six Dramatic Situations;* and Hamilton, *Problems of the Playwright.* See ibid., 392.

113   Leona Radnor, *The Photoplay Writer* (1913; repr., New York: Nabu, 2013), 21.

114   Price, *Technique of the Drama*, 227.

115   Dimick, *Modern Photoplay Writing*, 33–34.

116   Price, *Technique of the Drama*, 29 and 39–40.

117   Patterson, *Cinema Craftsmanship*, 5–9.

Classical Melodrama

The perspective that the pictorial elements of melodrama are an important constituent of early film, as Vardac, Fell, and Brewster and Jacobs have observed, is valuable and forms the backdrop of screenwriting teachers' understanding of the importance of 'visualisation', which will be addressed later. Another contribution from Brewster and Jacobs, evidenced in screenwriting manuals, is that 'situations' were used as components of plot construction. Balancing this view, however, are the interpretations of melodrama (from Neale and Koszarski) that focus on its plot features – although early screenwriting teachers tended to resist one of these features, non-classical narrative structure.

Both the pictorial and plot-based interpretations are helpfully accommodated in Singer's definition of melodrama. Representing it as a 'cluster concept', Singer neatly categorises melodrama into five basic elements. Four of those elements, namely 'strong pathos', 'overwrought emotion', 'moral polarization' and 'sensationalism', were certainly common elements in early film and were influential in much of the instruction of early screenwriting teachers. Singer more clearly defines the fifth element of non-classical narrative structure as:

> outrageous coincidence, implausibility, convoluted plotting, deus ex machina resolutions, and episodic strings of action that stuff too many events together to be able to be kept in line by cause-and-effect chain of narrative progression.[118]

Early screenwriting teachers would have generally frowned upon the idea of 'non-classical narrative structure', as they tended to follow the regimen of the 'well-made play' with its strong notions of causality alluded to by scholars such as Tibbetts. However, as already identified, although this theatrical form could trace its origins back to the theatre of Shakespeare and Aristotelian thinking, it also exhibited many melodramatic elements because it had also developed from a dramatic understanding systematised in eighteenth- and nineteenth-century theatre. The tradition of the 'well-made play' had then been codified by Freytag and had been again reformulated in the manuals of Price and Archer, but was not without its melodramatic tendencies.

To summarise, screenwriting teachers were influenced by a fusion of melodramatic and classical elements, which I will term classical melodrama. Films such as *Birth of a Nation* demonstrate this strong link between the classical storytelling expressed in the feature film and the melodrama of popular theatre and literature. In confirming this link, Grieveson and Krämer allude to the views of Altman, who characterises such films as 'an amalgam of deformed, embedded melodramatic material and carefully elaborated

---

118   Singer, *Melodrama and Modernity*, 46.

narrative classicism'.[119] Patrick Keeting agrees that the two elements of classical storytelling and melodramatic spectacle 'can often cooperate to create an intensified emotional response'.[120] In other words, rather than the narrative being just a means of producing comprehension, it was also designed to elicit strong feelings. As will become clear, the early screenwriting teachers examined in this study drew on both these strains of dramatic tradition, as evidenced in their manuals and columns; and the fusion of classicism with melodrama, into what I have identified as classical melodrama, helped to frame their instruction.

---

119 Altman, 'Dickens, Griffith, and Film Theory Today' in *Classical Hollywood Narrative*, ed., Gaines, 41; cited in Lee Grieveson and Peter Krämer eds. 'Classical Hollywood Cinema' in *The Silent Cinema Reader* (London: Routledge, 2004), 274.

120 Patrick Keeting, 'Prologue: Emotional Curves and Linear Narratives' in *The Classical Hollywood Reader*, ed. Steven Neale (Oxford: Routledge, 2012), 7 and 18.

2. Industry Context

To explore how screenwriting teachers were drawn into the filmmaking process and interacted with it, it is important to see their work within the context of the industry as it grew. This involves examining three important issues: the growing importance of the script as a controlling factor in film production; the mounting pressure to produce films with clear and coherent narratives; and the difficulties that writers faced in dealing with laws on censorship, copyright restrictions and writing for stars.

The Script as a Controlling Factor

Filmmaking practices and narrative formulae were developed to facilitate production and, according to Koszarski, by the early teens of the twentieth century, '[s]ignificant economic and industrial forces now acted to standardize these procedures'.[1] Technical advances and the development of the film industry on an industrial scale would eventually demand advanced scripting practices. As Staiger has pointed out, the need to achieve continuous and regular production had convinced manufacturers to build factory-like studios and to use them efficiently and for maximum profit. This led to the advent, by 1909, of the scenario script, which generally included a fully numbered breakdown of action by events and a 'scene plot' listing these events by location.[2]

However, by the early teens it became clear that, for production purposes, even more precise governance would be needed. As Staiger observes, 'The solution was to pay more rigorous attention to preparing a script, which provided narrative continuity before shooting actually started.'[3] The continuity script that soon followed would act as a means of control that studios could use to manage output and costs through careful planning and budgeting. It featured many of the same elements as the scenario script, but in much greater detail: shooting dates, highly detailed descriptions of actions, shot footage estimates, budgeting data and information on release prints and distribution.[4]

Staiger's analysis of the changing modes of production in the film industry provides a useful framework for understanding how scripting developed up to and beyond 1920. Her categorisation of Hollywood's first four modes of production or management structures equates roughly to the silent period, before the first major shift in organisation when the studios took full control. These modes are: the cameraman system (1896–1907); the director system (1907–1909); the director unit system (1909–1914); and the central

---

1 Koszarski, *Evening's Entertainment*, 95.

2 Harry Aitken and Roy Aitken, 'The Continuity Script and the Rationalization of Film Production, *Wisconsin Center for Film & Television Research*, http://old.wcftr.commarts.wisc.edu/collections/featured/aitken/continuity/

3 Bordwell, Staiger and Thompson, *Classical Hollywood Cinema*, 126.

4 Aitken and Aitken, 'The Continuity Script and the Rationalization of Film Production', http://old.wcftr.commarts.wisc.edu/collections/featured/aitken/continuity/

producer system (1914–1931).[5] If certain aspects of each system of organisation are highlighted, an overall pattern emerges that is not dissimilar to the proposed structure of this study. Such changes in the division of labour and management systems had profound effects on the scripting process and helped to trigger the appearance of screenwriting teachers. These teachers would also interact with the industry and probably contributed to the development of advanced scriptwriting procedures.

Although the periodic divisions of this study cut across Staiger's choice of modes of production in the last stage (1914–1931), it is important to note that her interest lies in how production was organised generally, rather than in its specific effects on the writing process and the activity of screenwriting teachers. If the focus is shifted instead to establishing the idea of 'continuity' and classical-style filmmaking, the divisions selected for this study hold up. The principles of the continuity system (the matching of spatial and temporal relations from shot to shot in order to maintain continuous and clear narrative action)[6] were, according to Thompson, 'set forth and tested in the years up to 1917'.[7] Thompson and Bordwell confirm that, from this point on, a 'system of formal principles that were standard in American filmmaking [...that] has come to be called the classical Hollywood cinema'[8] had been established. These classical stylistic norms amounted to a set of recurring conventions where 'narrative logic is the dominant force', although how time and space are represented is also important.[9] In effect, it was very similar to the unity of action and the ideas of time and space that Aristotle had set out. These procedures dictated the use of cameras, film and equipment, enabling manufacturers and suppliers to 'assimilate technological change to [fit into] Hollywood's parameters'.[10] By the early 1920s, therefore – during the fourth stage of Staiger's modes (1914–1931) – the studios were set up to create a sustained output of movies for the next 40 years. The requirement of telling a story in this particular way would be the key factor that would lead aspiring writers to seek expert help from screenwriting teachers. A brief survey of the history of screenwriting up to this point will help to contextualise the appearance of screenwriting teachers.

---

5 See Introduction, footnote 1.

6 The continuity system is a highly standardised system of editing, now virtually universal in commercial film and television but originally associated with Hollywood cinema, Peter Donaldson, 'Film Editing Terms' from *Film Lexicon*, http://art3idea.psu.edu/locus/film_terms.pdf

7 Bordwell, Staiger and Thompson, *Classical Hollywood Cinema*, 195.

8 Thompson and Bordwell, *Film History*, 32.

9 Manchel explains that Bordwell's understanding of classicism comprises three elements: 'narrative logic' (definition of events, causal relations and parallelism between events); 'representation of time' (order, duration and repetition); and 'representation of space' (composition and orientation). See Frank Manchel, *Film Study: An Analytical Bibliography Vol. 1* (London: Associated University Press, 1990), 60.

10 Bordwell, Staiger and Thompson, *Classical Hollywood Cinema*, 367.

The earliest films had no formal scripting. According to Staiger's 'Cameraman System' (1896–1907), a single cameraman conceived an idea and filmed it without necessarily referring to a written plan. If writers were involved, it was merely to provide ideas and brief synopses. As early as 1897, the general public had been actively encouraged to submit ideas for films. For example, the American Mutoscope Company advertised a five dollar payment for '"suggestions for a good scene," preferably comic' in its bulletins.[11] However, public involvement remained limited at this point, while screenwriting teachers did not figure at all.

By the early 1900s it became clear that stories presented the best opportunity to turn a profit. Unlike 'topicals' (news or current affairs subjects), story films did not depend on unpredictable news events. Because they could be carefully planned in advance and created in or near a studio, it was possible to control them through scripting. However, the first story films clearly showed the problems created by the need to tell a story in 'continuity' or to ensure temporal and spatial coherency (that is, to make character traits, plot events, props and location details consistent).

In exploring narrative potential in *Le Voyage dans la Lune* (1902), for example, filmmaker Georges Méliès (1861–1938) repeats the moon landing in separate shots and two landings on the moon created a 'kind of overlapping continuity [that] clearly defines spatial relationships [but...] leaves temporal ones undeveloped'.[12] In other words, the idea of moving from one place to another was clearly represented but the film made no attempt to show that time had passed from one shot to the next. As Cook observes:

> Motion added the dimension of time, and the major problem for early filmmakers would soon become the establishment of linear continuity from one shot to the next.[13]

This shortcoming was not so problematic for early audiences, according to Cook. Accustomed to lantern slide shows and stereopticon presentations, audiences:

> understood a sequence of motion picture shots as a series of individual moving photographs, or 'attractions,' each of which was self-contained within its frame. If actions overlapped from shot to shot, it didn't matter since the temporal relationships between shots was assumed to be alinear – there was no assumption that time moved forward when cutting from one scene to the next.[14]

---

11   Azlant, 'Theory, History and Practice of Screenwriting', 104.

12   Cook, *History of Narrative Film*, 22.

13   Ibid., 22.

14   Ibid., 22.

Figure 15: Scene from *The Life of an American Fireman* (1903)
Source: *Wikimedia Commons*
commons.wikimedia.org/wiki/File:The_life_of_
an_american_fireman.webm.

Méliès' techniques significantly influenced Edwin S. Porter's *The Life of an American Fireman* (1903). The film combined real footage of firefighters on duty with a simple rescue drama. However, it still exhibited continuity problems from a classical perspective, by repeating the same rescue scene from two different viewpoints (see Figure 15).[15] According to Musser, from 1903–04 the industry made a transition to fiction films as its main product.[16] As the prevalence and complexity of these films increased, the issue of continuity was likely to arise more often.

The script for Porter's *The Great Train Robbery* (1905) could have been jotted down on the back of an envelope.[17] Nevertheless, this film is considered by many to be the first American film with a more sustained story, because according to Cook, Porter established narrative, spatial and temporal relationships and realised the art of telling a story in continuity form.[18] He asserts that *The Great Train Robbery* is:

> frequently credited with establishing the realistic narrative, as opposed to the Méliès-style fantasy, as the dominant cinematic form from Porter's day to our own. [… It also] probably did more than any film made before 1912 to convince investors that the cinema was a moneymaking proposition.[19]

---

15 Musser, 'The Early Cinema of Edwin S. Porter' in *The Wiley-Blackwell History of American Film*, eds. Cynthia Lucia, Roy Grundmann and Art Simon (Malden: Wiley-Blackwell, 2012), 39–86. Some claimed that *The Life of an American Fireman* was the first American story film. However, Musser has clearly shown that the version that was widely circulated in the 1940s had been re-edited to eliminate the problems of continuity in the earlier version.

16 Musser, *Emergence of Cinema*, 337.

17 The original scenario by Edwin S. Porter, from a story by Scott Marble, provides very brief descriptions of 14 scenes. *Screenplays for You*, http://sfy.ru/?script=great_train_robbery_1903

18 Cook, *History of Narrative Film*, 22–24.

19 Ibid., 25.

The success of *The Great Train Robbery* also played its part in helping 'with temporarily standardizing the length of that form to a single reel – 1,000 feet, or ten to sixteen minutes, depending on the speed of projection'.[20]

Between 1905 and 1907, as a result of a rapid expansion in demand for motion-picture entertainment of the narrative variety, a new type of playhouse (the nickelodeon) had to be created to accommodate the newcomers.[21] By 1907 these venues were so popular that they were drawing in over one million patrons across America a day, which would create a public demand for story films that forced the industry to rationalise production.[22] This short transitional period saw a substantive reorganisation that would ultimately lead to the scripting process becoming central to filmmaking and would prompt the appearance of the first screenwriting teachers. The role of the cameraman and the director became distinct, and the director began to wield considerable power. As already noted, Staiger calls this mode of operation 'the director system' (1907–1909). Cook confirms that job demarcation meant that '[b]y 1908 directing, acting, photographing, writing and laboratory work were separate crafts.'[23] Although camera work and editing were still the province of the director and cameraman, a number of important factors were to contribute to the need for a screenplay for the story.

The Drive for Narrative Clarity

Filmmakers were under pressure to produce coherent narratives of a particular kind within the standard distribution length of one or two reels, which Edison's Motion Picture Patents Company (MPPC) imposed.[24] Although this limitation had some advantages for filmmakers, many of its effects were negative. Films often had abrupt connections and sudden conclusions and character motivations were ambiguous or unexplained; unexpected changes in locale often left the spectator with no idea where the action was taking place. If an actor using elaborate pantomime failed to convey the meaning of a crucial action, the audience was left confused. A contemporary review of a 1906 Edison film indicates that audiences were often not able to understand the causal, spatial and temporal relations in many films of the time:

---

20 Ibid., 25.

21 Benjamin B. Hampton, *History of the American Film Industry from its Beginnings to 1931* (1931; repr., New York: Dover, 1970), 44.

22 Cook, *History of Narrative Film*, 25.

23 Ibid., 29–30

24 Thomas Edison joined others to form the MPPC in 1908 in an attempt to control the industry by hiring patented camera and projection equipment and by restricting the length of films to one or two reels as standard sold for one price. Tim Dirks, 'The History of Film – The Pre-1920s' *in Early Cinematic Origins and the Infancy of Film 3*, http://www.filmsite.org/pre20sintro3.html and J. A. Aberdeen, 'The Edison Movie Monopoly: The Motion Picture Patents Company vs. the Independent Outlaws', *Hollywood Renegades Archive – SIMPP Research Database*, http://www.cobbles.com/simpp_archive/edison_trust.htm

> A subject recently seen was very good photographically, and the plot also seemed
> to be good, but could not be understood by the audience.[25]

With stories growing more complex, if a film contained gaps in continuity or an unclear narrative, audiences needed sufficient intertextual or prior knowledge or, alternatively, lecturers present at the screening to interpret what was happening:

> There were complaints about the lack of clarity. One way in which the crisis
> manifested itself was in a renewed demand for someone talking along with the film
> to explain what was going on: the 'showman-narrator,' or lecturer.[26]

Ultimately, however, lecturers' explanations of the plot were not always satisfactory, due to variations in the quality and content of their delivery. The absence of clarity for audiences often led to some peculiar antics in theatres:

> Managers edited movies to fit their audiences' tastes. Sometimes projectionists
> would change the speed of the film and even run the film backwards for the
> amusement of the audience.[27]

It became clear that the film would need its own internal system of narrativity to make it understandable as a stand-alone product:

> The film lecturer could only serve as a short-term solution to narrative
> comprehensibility. The narrator system [where films could be understood through
> their own internal storytelling mechanisms] offered a more viable solution. It
> supplied narrative legibility along with diegetic coherence.[28]

Although stories remained relatively simple and scripting requirements were fairly straightforward, according to Bowser, audiences still wanted the 'illusion of reality' and to be able to 'suspend disbelief'.[29] One critic observed in 1908 that the audience seemed more engaged when the plot was sufficiently clear, even in the absence of a lecturer:

> As the spectators could follow the plot without the help of a lecturer, they were
> deeply interested and the different comments were highly favorable to the work.[30]

---

25   Quoted by Musser, *Before the Nickelodeon: Edwin S. Porter and the Edison Manufacturing Company* (Berkeley: University of California, 1991). 360; cited in Bordwell and Thompson, *Film History*, 32.

26   Bowser, *Transformation of Cinema*, 19.

27   Richard Butsch, 'The Making of American Audiences: From Stage to Television, 1750–1990', in *Movies and American Society*, ed., Steven J. Ross (Oxford: Blackwell, 2002), 23.

28   Tom Gunning, *D.W. Griffith and the Origins of Narrative Film: The Early Years at Biograph* (Chicago: University of Illinois, 1994), 93.

29   Bowser, *Transformation of Cinema*, 55.

30   'Comments on Film Subjects: "Saved by Love"', *MPW*, November 7, 1908, 358.

Connecting with the audience would be crucial for the spread to a wider market. Before the rise of the nickelodeon theatres (1905–06), films were exhibited in primarily middle-class environments: vaudeville theatres, summer parks, storefront theatres, lecture halls, churches, saloons and between the acts of plays of repertory companies touring the opera houses. Demand for nickelodeon-style entertainment, Thompson and Bordwell claim, 'was fuelled in part by the rising immigrant population and the shorter working hours gained by the increasingly militant labor-union movement'.[31] Shorter working weeks led to more time for leisure and the middle class also started to attend these shows:

> Within a few years just about everybody outside the large cities was going to the
> same theaters, seeing the same films, and sharing in the same communal experience;
> people of all classes, and the whole family.[32]

Staiger argues that filmmakers facilitated this growth by improving the continuity and clarity of narrative, which gave them more control and widened the appeal of their films:

> American film did not change its priorities to privilege a continuity narrative
> form after 1909, but … narrative continuity and clarity were dominant organizing
> principles from the beginning of filmmaking.[33]

In Staiger's view, the reason these principles were given prominence was not to woo the middle class into the nickelodeon, but rather to cater to the existing working-class immigrant clientele. For audiences with limited English, it was crucial to establish an internal logic to the film that did not rely on any exterior explanations:

> The textual continuity perceived by later historians is a result of the expansion
> of the audience to include the working class, immigrants, and rural audiences, to
> make moving pictures a mass medium rather than one accessible to just a privileged
> few.[34]

While the audience did widen for the reasons Staiger suggests, the concern with attracting the working class is perhaps overstated, as evidence indicates that filmmakers were attempting to extend their appeal to the better educated as well. Stories from celebrated literature or portrayals of important historical events were introduced to counterbalance popular slapstick chases and crime films. Along with this attempt to attract more refined audiences came changes to the places where films were shown. Although nickelodeons continued well into the 1910s, from 1908 onwards exhibitors began to build or convert larger theatres into movie 'palaces', which could hold thousands of patrons.

---

31 Thompson and Bordwell, *Film History*, 2.

32 Bowser, *Transformation of Cinema*, 8.

33 Janet Staiger, *Interpreting Films: Studies in the Historical Reception of American Cinema* (New Jersey: Princeton University, 1992), 102.

34 Ibid., 102.

Consequently, Bowser points out, 'Feature films showing in the big theatres were getting as much as two dollars, and were bringing in a higher class of people.'[35] This meant that filmmaking with some claims to higher cultural standards was now necessary, and writing opportunities expanded correspondingly. As Bowser suggests, 'There was a new emphasis on the need for a higher degree of art and intellect in keeping with this new audience.'[36] Cook agrees that:

> The feature film made motion pictures respectable for the middle class by providing a format analogous to that of the legitimate theatre and suitable for the adaptation of middle-class novels and plays.[37]

The wide appeal of cinema could perhaps be explained by the potential of film to absorb the viewer in a storyline, which was an experience that a culturally and ethnically diverse mass public could enjoy. As Patricia Bradley confirms, film entertainment 'was increasingly becoming an enclosed, privatized experience in which class values were incidental'.[38] In their manuals and columns, screenwriting teachers would continually address issues related to the quality of writing and constantly aspire to what were regarded as higher cultural standards, but would also encourage their students to write in a way that would satisfy the widest possible audience.

The requirements of early directors ranged from basic script outlines or brief causal scenarios with descriptions of each scene, to more formal documents that included character explanations, entrances and exits, stage directions and a few lines of dialogue.[39] These requirements were generally adopted as the norm, realising that continuity could only be achieved with rigorous preparation and careful, meticulous scripting. Continuity meant establishing an unbroken connection in the narrative throughout; it required a clear, coherent narrative with a beginning, middle and end. As Charlie Kiel records, there was a 'transformation at the hands of filmmakers experimenting with how to render narrative comprehensible'.[40] Bowser pinpoints a particular aspect of that transformation:

> The development of new ways to connect shots, or editing, was probably the most important change in film form to take place during the 1907–1909 period. Creating a spatiotemporal world, a kind of geography made of separate shots related to one another, was crucial in the construction of a complex narrative. The development

---

35   Bowser, *Transformation of Cinema*, 133.

36   Ibid., 255.

37   Cook, *History of Narrative Film*, 35.

38   Patricia Bradley, *Making American Culture: A Social History, 1900–1920* (New York: Palgrave Macmillan, 2009), 58.

39   Bordwell, Staiger and Thompson, *Classical Hollywood Cinema*, 119.

40   Charlie Kiel, *Early American Cinema in Transition: Story, Style, and Filmmaking 1907–1913* (London: University of Wisconsin, 2001), 3–4.

of new editing methods would also greatly increase the potential for enlisting the spectator's emotions in the film.[41]

At the same time, a gradual movement was occurring away from the 'cinema of attractions', a phrase Gunning coined to describe a cinema that:

> directly solicits spectator attention, inciting visual curiosity, and supplying pleasure through an exciting spectacle – a unique event, whether fictional or documentary, that is of interest in itself.[42]

Kiel's view of this transition, in support of which he cites Noël Burch, is that:

> The earliest films reinforce the 'exteriority' of the spectator's position, [but] eventually this gives way to the envelopment of the viewer within the diegesis. [...] Increased attention to character psychology and motivation [would...] maintain character as the driving force within the classical narrative.[43]

Representations of time would not always, or entirely, be linear from this point on: directors such as D. W. Griffith were already using parallel editing, which involved cutting away from a scene before it ended and into another one even if it had already begun. Gunning points out that 'by developing two trajectories of action at the same time and intercutting them, it complicates [...] simple linearity'.[44] This helped to build tension by delaying the resolution of each line of action. Subtle cues were needed to indicate that time was flowing without interruption, even across cuts, and other cues might suggest that time had passed. Filmmakers had to establish continuity between shots, even when cutting in for a closer view of details. In particular, they needed to:

> set up a chain of narrative causes and effects. One event would plainly lead to an effect, which would in turn cause another effect, and so on. [...An] event was [...] caused by a character's beliefs or desires. [Therefore] character psychology motivated actions. By following a series of characters' goals and resulting conflicts, the spectator would comprehend the action.[45]

Every aspect of silent film style could be used to enhance narrative clarity. Staging in depth could show special relationships among elements. Camera position, set design and lighting could imply time of day or the milieu of the action. The techniques of camera work, editing, acting and lighting were combined to clarify what was happening. Intertitles elucidated action and conveyed necessary explanations.

---

41 Bowser, *Transformation of Cinema*, 57–58.

42 Tom Gunning, 'The Cinema of Attractions: Early Film, Its Spectator, and the Avant-Garde' in *Theatre and Film*, ed. Robert Knopf (London: Yale University, 2005), 40.

43 Kiel, *Early American Cinema in Transition*, 9.

44 Gunning, *D.W. Griffith and the Origins of Narrative Film*, 103.

45 Thompson and Bordwell, *Film History*, 32.

The narrative mode, meaning films that conveyed some kind of fictional story to the audience, came to dominate almost completely. In 1900 it comprised only about 12 per cent of films copyrighted.[45] By 1903 comic films alone (which included gags – so were not purely narrative) comprised 30 per cent of those copyrighted, and by 1909 narrative (comedy and drama) had risen to an astounding 97 per cent of those registered.[47] Production schedules simply had to keep up with increasing consumer demand for films. The creation of scenarios and continuity scripts that could convey the complexities required by the industry was a challenge for the new writing fraternity. In order to meet it, they would increasingly need instruction.

The 'director unit system' (1909–14), in which directors worked in multiple units, required more than just a simple 'story outline'. The use of a scenario became standard, as it allowed for planning. Directors still had the flexibility to deviate from a scenario, but it was more limited than before. As story films developed, the screenwriter's task became more taxing, with characterisation and subplots beginning to creep into films around 1910. Trade literature described the scenario as 'a scene-by-scene account of the action including the intertitles and inserts'. It included a list of story settings for reasons of economy, so the script could be shot out of order in particular locations but still in accordance with the principles of continuity. A synopsis and cast of characters were also standard.[48]

Scripting did not, however, entirely solve issues of narrative comprehension. Problems persisted, as one critic's comment in early 1911 illustrates: 'when the student of moving pictures finds it difficult to sufficiently grasp the "plot", or see the "point" […,] the public is full of enquiries'.[49] Other factors aiding narrative comprehension included: intertextual understanding; the audience's knowledge of the plot or characters of a familiar story or classical play or book; a lecturer filling in the detail; and supplying information through textual material in fan magazines. The diverse factors helping to improve narrative comprehension support Singer's belief that '[c]inema's shift from primitive to Classical narrative was not an instantaneous and unproblematic metamorphosis'.[50] One important form of intertextual knowledge that he identifies is the 'fiction tie-in'. In his view, 'filmmakers and spectators alike might indeed have relied on tie-ins to compensate

46 Richard Arlo Sanderson, 'A Historical Study of the Development of American Motion Picture Content and Techniques Prior to 1904' (PhD diss., University of Southern California, 1961), 119. ProQuest (UMI 6102538); cited in Azlant, 'Theory, History and Practice of Screenwriting', 79.

47 Robert Allen, 'Vaudeville and Film 1895–1915: A Study in Media Interaction' (PhD diss., University of Iowa, 1977), 151 and 212. ProQuest (UMI 7728428).

48 Janet Staiger, 'Blueprints for Feature Films: Hollywood's Continuity Scripts' in *The American Film Industry*, ed. Tino Ballo (Madison: University of Wisconsin, 1985), 176–177. See also Sargent, 'Technique of the Photoplay', *MPW*, July 29, 1911, 197–198.

49 'The Ambiguous Picture – Some Causes', *MPW*, January 7, 1911, 14–15.

50 Ben Singer, 'Fiction tie-ins and narrative intelligibility 1911–1918', *Film History* 5 (1993): 489–490.

Figure 16: Early issue of *The Motion Picture Story Magazine*
Source: *MPSM*, February 1911, front cover and 10–11,
archive.org/details/motionpicturesto01moti.

for the limitations of cinematic storytelling.'[51] One source of such material was *The Motion Picture Story Magazine*, which was launched in 1911 as America's first movie fan magazine; 'each issue contained as many as twenty […] "photoplay stories", running about ten pages apiece including numerous movie-still illustrations' (see Figure 16).[52]

Despite these other contributions, however, the development of the scenario meant that the ideas of the writer had a significant and growing influence in the filmmaking process. Testimony to the tendency for producers around this time to require longer, more detailed scenarios comes from Sargent: 'The plot of action that is little more than a synopsis of the scenes is being replaced by the full script.'[53] This new reliance on scripting created a demand for written material and, in turn, the emergence of the first screenwriting teachers around 1909. The problems posed by writing in continuity were important factors that these teachers would address in great detail in their columns and manuals. They would also give extensive advice on the form of the scenario and the continuity script, and help writers to hone their craft by offering full training in all aspects of writing for film and marketing their product.

Important changes in market conditions also affected the length and complexity of films. Along with other independents, Carl Laemmle, who formed the Independent Moving Pictures Company (IMP), had refused to pay licence fees to the MPPC. He had both imported and made multi-reel films; and a group of independents, including IMP, had in effect become their own conglomerate. In 1912 the courts ruled against the MPPC and in 1915 the US government outlawed it for restrictive practices. As a result, Sargent reported in 1912, 'almost overnight the two, three and five-reel subject has come into its own'.[54] By 1914 feature films were extremely successful, the popularity of one- and two-reelers had waned and MPPC members that had advocated this restriction were virtually wiped out. The successful introduction of multiple reels and film times of 75 minutes, which were of similar length to films that had been imported from Europe, increased the potential profit.[55] A consequence that Cook notes is that:

> The advent of the feature [film…] opened up the possibility of more complicated narratives and offered filmmakers a form commensurate with serious artistic endeavor.[56]

Pre-production design was an inevitable requirement of the complexities created by longer films and developing production processes. This led to an even greater reliance

---

51 Ibid., 495.

52 Ibid., 492.

53 Azlant, 'Theory, History and Practice of Screenwriting', 125.

54 Sargent, 'Advertising for Exhibitors', *MPW*, February 24, 1912, 666.

55 See Dirks, 'The History of Film' and Aberdeen, 'The Edison Movie Monopoly'.

56 Cook, *History of Narrative Film*, 35.

on the screenplay as a 'blueprint' for the whole process, which further boosted the importance and reputation of those who offered instruction to writers. Important industry figures now recognised the primacy of the writer over the director in this process.

According to Staiger, after 1914 central planning became crucial to ensure quality control of the film product and the satisfaction of the audience consumers, which would maximise profit. This is Staiger's fourth mode of production, the 'central producer system' (1914–1931), whereby control of production was unified under a single producer who:

> used a very detailed shooting script, the continuity script, to plan and budget the entire film shot-by-shot before any major set construction, crew selection or shooting started.[57]

Continuity scripts allowed for extensive planning before filming and also aided in post-production. The process of filmmaking was increasingly divided among practitioners with expertise in different areas, including various kinds of writers. As Bordwell and Thompson indicate, 'There were separate scenario departments, for example, and a writer might specialize in plotting, dialogue or intertitles.'[58] In 1916 William Fox emphasises the paramount importance of the script in this process:

> The scenario is the basis of all good pictures. The creative brain that first conceives a story knows more about that story than anyone else can possibly know.[59]

Thomas Ince was one of the first to recognise that the script had to play a central role in production. After initially working for Laemmle at IMP in 1910, he signed for the New York Picture Company (NYPC) in 1911 and established studios on the West Coast that would eventually be known informally as 'Inceville'. In 1913, Staiger argues, Ince handed over to others the roles of directing and editing while he acted as 'Director-General'. This became the prototype for other Hollywood studios, with Lubin, Biograph, Edison and Vitagraph following suit later that year.[60] Ince is most famous for his collaborations with C. Gardner Sullivan, his most prolific and valuable screenwriter.[61] For Ince, the script was crucial, and it had to have a clear narrative structure by which the audience was caught up and propelled through the story. He relied on a very detailed 'continuity script' and a particular system of organising production.[62] Through the script, Ince sought to control every aspect of production, down to the last detail. Scripts, which

---

57   Bordwell, Staiger and Thompson, *Classical Hollywood Cinema*, 128.

58   Bordwell and Thompson, *Film History*, 56.

59   William Fox, 'The Scenario Makes the Picture', *Motography*, May 20, 1916, 1155.

60   Bordwell, Staiger and Thompson, *Classical Hollywood Cinema*, 136–137.

61   Sullivan was known for his Western scripts featuring actor William S. Hart as hero;. For more on his importance to Ince, see Azlant, 'Theory, History and Practice of Screenwriting', 172.

62   Stempel, *Framework*, 41.

were adhered to on the set, contained meticulous technical instructions about special effects and where intertitles were to be set.[63] As Azlant points out, Ince made his own notations on the scripts to improve narrative flow. Change included:

> further segmentation, condensation, or omission of actions, changes in plot development through cut-backs and changes in the language of leaders. [...To] construct a film plot [was] Ince's primary, and eventually his almost exclusive, concern.[64]

According to Stempel, Ince 'perfected the narrative style of filmmaking [...] that emphasized a smooth flowing continuity [...and] told stories clearly and cleanly'.[65] In effect, a 'blueprint' that was separate from the actual filming process and had the power to control the costs and logistics of production had finally emerged; and it would also significantly affect the kind of instruction that screenwriting teachers focused on.

The scenario or its more complex counterpart, the continuity script, became an increasingly important document for effecting such gains, because it allowed for the process of planning as films became longer and relatively more complex. Professionals in the trade press frequently discussed the importance of creating film continuity at the writing stage, which demonstrated the salience of this issue to the industry at the time. Pierre Key, the advertising and sales manager for Hoffman-Foursquare Pictures, comments:

> Ninety-nine picture fans in every hundred can instantly tell whether the continuity in a picture is good or bad [...]. They feel instinctively whether it is rhythmical or not; whether the scenes follow one another in proper sequence and whether the correct values of each to the other are maintained.[66]

Writers required a detailed and thorough understanding of how to construct scenarios that would meet these industry standards. The very problems of continuity – moving from place to place and the passage of time – that were encountered in the making of the earliest narrative films would present, if properly tackled, the greatest opportunity to the writer, as Hamilton indicated at the time:

> The main advantage of the moving picture play over the traditional types of drama is that the author is granted an immeasurably greater freedom in handling the categories of place and time.[67]

---

63   Bordwell, Staiger and Thompson, *Classical Hollywood Cinema*, 138–139.

64   Azlant, 'Theory, History and Practice of Screenwriting', 172.

65   Stempel, *Framework*, 47–48.

66   Pierre V. R. Key, 'Continuity Is Important Factor', *Motography*, November 17, 1917, 1033–1034.

67   Hamilton, 'The Art of the Moving Picture Play', 50–52.

By this time, the script had clearly become central to filmmaking, which would in turn increase the importance of the advice that screenwriting teachers gave to freelance writers at a time when these particular writers played a key role in the business. This state of affairs would continue up to around 1920. However, the focus on producing a highly developed script before production would also ultimately sound the death-knell for the amateur scenarist.

The development of the Hollywood studio system was to mark the take-over of the business by entrepreneurs who would help create a stable platform that increased the level of opportunity through investment and finance.[68] The film industry had assumed a structure that it would keep for the next four decades: vertically integrated monopolies controlling their own production, theatre chains and distributorships. Full studio control would signal the arrival of the professional screenwriter, who would be drawn mostly from the journalistic or writing fraternity.

Censorship, Copyright and Stardom

Three other issues also shaped the experiences of prospective writers and the type of instruction that screenwriting teachers would offer: the forbidden elements that were likely to be censored; the dangers of copyright infringement and the opportunities afforded by the demand for original material; and the problems and prospects associated with writing for the new stars of the screen.

Censorship

With cinema attendance increasing among all sectors of society at the cinema, new demands for censorship were soon voiced. The arch-antagonists of early cinema fell into two groups: organised religion and the political right. Many religious groups and social workers considered the nickel theatres to be sinister places where young people could be led astray, akin to training grounds for prostitution and robbery. Lurid subject matter, such as re-enacted executions and murders, was common fare in the early nickelodeon boom. The moralists denounced such leisure-time viewing as a threat to social control because of its often violent and erotic content. As George Mitchell points out, 'movie attendance' was condemned alongside other 'such diversions as dancing, gambling, novel reading, theatre going [and] drinking'.[69] To counter the moral condemnation, film theorist Münsterberg implied that film could actually be a means of social control. He supported 'film because of its ability to remove the viewer from the real world [and] its

---

68   Dirks, 'The History of Film' in *Early Cinematic Origins and the Infancy of Film 3*, http://www.filmsite. org/pre20sintro3.html and Aberdeen, 'The Edison Movie Monopoly', Hollywood Renegades Archive – SIMPP Research Database, http://www.cobbles.com/simpp_archive/edison_trust.htm

69   George Mitchell, 'The Movies and Münsterberg', *Jump Cut*, no. 27, July 1982, 57–60, http://www. ejumpcut.org/archive/onlinessays/JC27folder/Munsterberg.html

capacity to provide a vital interval of relaxation'.[70] Given the extent of the confusion and varying viewpoints, writers would need clear guidance on this issue.

The problem of censorship was a quagmire for the producers. In 1908 the Mayor of New York managed briefly to close down the entire city's nickelodeons, and local censorship boards were formed in many towns. By 1909 'it became obligatory in many parts of the country for ministers, businessmen and politicians to inveigh against the movies as a corrupter of youth and a threat to public morality'.[71] The real threat may have been more economic than ideological, as the substantial revenues of churches, saloons and vaudeville houses were under threat. In 1909 a group of New York citizens formed the National Board of Censorship of Motion Pictures, later known as the National Board of Review. This private body attempted to improve the movies and prevent the federal government from passing national censorship laws; it also reviewed films and provided a seal of approval to those that did not offend.[72] The MPPC supported this body, including financially; within a year, the National Board was reviewing 80 per cent of films. As Gregory Black points out, 'The only way industry leaders could fend off that eventuality [federal censorship laws] was to censor their own products [... so] self-censorship [...] was just good business.'[73] A series of legal challenges did follow, but a Supreme Court ruling in 1915 upheld the right of individual states to impose their own censorship on the movies.

In this context, prospective scenario writers needed a clear understanding of what was permissible and what was not. If restraint and self-censorship were necessary, they were best established at the scenario stage. As Azlant concludes, 'Censorship militated for pre-production control of story materials.'[74] Manufacturers had to insure themselves against the possibility that a film would be banned after they had laid out huge levels of expenditure on it. Screenwriting teachers commented extensively on this complex subject in their columns and manuals. Summing up their concerns and frustrations, Sargent states, '90 per cent of the various rulings of the various censors are childish and without foundation', but he did understand that public opinion was outraged by the irresponsibility of the few.[75] Freelance writers increasingly turned to screenwriting teachers in order to understand these forbidden elements and all the manuals responded to the demand by devoting considerable space to such issues, as will be evidenced later.

---

70   Ibid.

71   Cook, *History of Narrative Film*, 31.

72   Kenneth Macgowan, *Behind the Screen: The History and Technique of the Motion Picture* (New York: Delacorte, 1965), 350.

73   Gregory D. Black, *Hollywood Censored: Morality Codes, Catholics and the Movies* (Cambridge: CUP, 1994), 14–18.

74   Azlant, 'Theory, History and Practice of Screenwriting', 112.

75   Sargent, 'Another Censorship Angle', *MPW*, October 30, 1915, 806.

Filmmakers could not ignore the concerns of the moral uplift movement, even if it had more to do with respectability than morality. Such pressures would also contribute to the need for a narrative comprehension that reinforced morality, as it was perceived at the time:

> Producers were being urged to make films that would be morally improving and educational for the mass audience [...] The film [would have] to enlist the emotions of the spectator in a story [... and] carry a lesson or preach a sermon, and to do that it would have to learn to be expressive [...]. One could make moral and educational films and still lose the audience if they were dull or if the audience could not understand them.[76]

Screenwriting teachers would provide important, detailed instructions on how to write creatively within this strict moral framework.

Copyright

The demand for potential film topics had led producers to turn, even more than before, to adapting theatre and literature subjects into scenarios. The unauthorised use of extant material was widespread. In 1907 Gene Gauntier, who worked for Kalem, used all sorts of material as ideas for scenarios:

> a poem, a picture, a short story, a scene from a current play, a headline in a newspaper. All was grist that came to my mill. There was no copyright law to protect authors and I could, and did, infringe upon everything.[77]

When Gauntier prepared a 'working synopsis' for Kalem's one-reel production of *Ben Hur* (1907), she had failed to acquire any rights from the publisher of the novel. Subsequently Kalem was sued by the author's estate. Based on a 1908 court ruling, motion pictures were now subject to the same copyright restrictions as other dramatic productions, and in 1911 Kalem was forced to pay a $25,000 royalty under a Supreme Court ruling.[78] This judgment would have profound effects on screenwriting, as the supply of classic plays and novels available in the public domain was soon exhausted. This not only served as a warning to prospective writers against plagiarising, but left them fearing that others might plagiarise their own work. They would need assurances about this and encouragement in making the most of the opportunities presented by the explosion in demand for original stories as:

> Producers began aggressively soliciting the submission of original material, from known writers, the photoplay agencies and brokers that were springing up and the general public.[79]

---

76 Bowser, *Transformation of Cinema*, 54.

77 Gene Gauntier, 'Blazing the Trail', unpublished manuscript, 21; cited in Stempel, *Framework*, 8.

78 Ibid., 8.

79 Azlant, 'Theory, History and Practice of Screenwriting', 104.

Freelance writers would increasingly look to screenwriting teachers for guidance on what copyright infringement looked like, how to protect their own work and how to meet the challenge of creating original material for the market.

Stardom

The cinema had created stars and popular heroes, and screenwriting teachers would address the issue of how to write for these individuals. Theatre, opera and vaudeville already operated on the basis of the star system but, according to Staiger, the:

> industrialists who organised the film business did not take the star system into account. [...They] were manufacturing a product, trying their best to standardize it, and expecting the audience to ask for it by brand name.[80]

Once the film industry had been regularised through the nickelodeon boom and the MPPC in 1908, films were sold by brand name. Manufacturers hoped that audiences would associate a film they enjoyed with its studio, such as Edison, Vitagraph or Biograph. Filmmakers and actors at this point received no screen credit: their identities had been kept anonymous in order to give precedence to the film and to prevent performers from overvaluing themselves and demanding higher salaries. By 1909, however, filmgoers were clearly demonstrating interest in their favourite actors. Bradley points out that every member of the audience had equal access to a star when the camera moved in on a face, in 'the proportions they had only experienced in life in the most intimate setting' as a child, lover or under threat, and this experience drew on primal emotions.[81] By 1910 some companies were exploiting their popular actors for publicity purposes. For example, Kalem supplied theatres with photographs to display in their lobbies.

Laemmle, who had formed IMP, realised how much audiences wanted to know the names of the uncredited performers. After luring to IMP the previously unnamed but hugely popular 'Biograph Girl', Florence Lawrence, who had featured in Griffith films from the Biograph Studios, he revealed her name. Other studios soon followed his lead, creating their own stars by displaying lobby posters and film advertisements (see Figure 17).[82] Once the film companies began to name their stars, it led to a blitz of publicity in the form of photographs, posters and postcards. In 1911 the first fan press appeared – *The Motion Picture Story Magazine* – featuring the favourite stars. However, most films continued not to credit them until 1914.

---

80   Bowser, *Transformation of Cinema*, 106.

81   Bradley, *Making American Culture*, 59–60.

82   Dirks, 'The History of Film' in *Early Cinematic Origins and the Infancy of Film, 4,* http://www.filmsite.org/pre20sintro4.html

Figure 17: Poster advertising *Tillie's Punctured Romance* (1914)
by Keystone Film Company
Source: *Wikipedia Commons* en.wikipedia.org/wiki/Tillie%27s_
Punctured_Romance_(1914_film).

The public identification of players was to have its effect on screenwriting. Scenarists would become well aware of those aspects of character that a given player's personality generated. As Azlant points out, 'the star system would require screenplays [...] to serve as precise "vehicles" for pre-ordained characters in characteristic narrative patterns'.[83] Some film companies would also remind prospective writers in their own publicity that they should 'keep in mind the personalities of their top stars' when they wrote.[84] The development of the star system would prompt wide-ranging advice from screenwriting teachers on which stars to write for and how to write effectively for them.

---

83   Azlant, 'Theory, History and Practice of Screenwriting', 102.

84   Pamphlet on 'How to Write Motion Picture Plays' (New York, MOMA, 1912); cited in Stempel, *Framework*, 13.

3. Scenario Fever

By the early teens of the twentieth century, the demand for new material was so high that the film companies opened themselves up to outside ideas and submissions by advertising in the fan and trade press. They ran promotional campaigns and even made direct appeals to the general public. Poor overall organisation and the change to 'two week releases' (fortnightly programme changes) meant that directors no longer had time to devise their own scenarios and meet the level of demand. As early as 1909:

> The demand for screen stories was growing with the industry and rumors of easy money 'writing for the pictures' went through the gossip channels of the actor tribes, reaching the picture patrons as well. The beginning of the scenario writing craze was in sight.[1]

Most film companies were sending out free 'form sheets' or 'instruction sheets' on scenario formats to writers on request. The practice began with Vitagraph, but soon Essanay, Lubin and others were providing them too.[2] By 1909 the industry also began to mail out pamphlets on how and what to write. These were among the first written materials offering advice. Studios communicated the kind of stories they required according to their particular strengths; for example, a pamphlet from the Associated Motion Picture Schools[3] in about 1912, entitled 'How to Write Motion Picture Plays', allowed several story editors from various companies to detail 'What We Want' (see also Figure 18). Requested material ranged from problem stories contrasting the plights of rich and poor, and melodrama, to comedy, drama and Westerns.[4] Companies regularly made their requirements known through the trade press:

> ATTENTION SCENARIO WRITERS. The staff of the Scenario Department of the Universal Film Mfg. Co., Inc., will examine, edit and pass upon your scenarios, free of any charge whatsoever.[5] (Figure 19).

---

1 Ramsaye, *A Million and One Nights*, 512.

2 'Inquiries', *MPW*, November 11, 1911, 486; James O'Neill, 'Technique and the Tale', *MPW*, November 18, 1911, 541 and The Hermit, 'The Photoplaywright's Earnings', *Motography*, May 1911, 93.

3 E. F. McIntyre of Chicago founded Associated Motion Picture Schools, the first of the correspondence schools, in January 1911 with the backing of trade magazine *MPN*. It apparently received some encouragement from manufacturers and claimed its writers had successfully sold scenarios to them. See 'Associated M. P. Schools', *MPN*, 30 September 1911, 20 and 'Plots Wanted for Motion Picture Plays', advertisement that lists companies that have bought scenarios, *MPM*, August 1914, 164.

4 Pamphlet on 'How to Write Motion Picture Plays' (New York, MOMA, 1912); cited in Stempel, *Framework*, 13–14.

5 Advertisement in *MPW*, September 14, 1912, 1098.

Plots Wanted

: : FOR MOTION PICTURE PLAYS : :

You can write them.   We teach beginners in ten
easy lessons.   We have many successful graduates.
Here are a few of their plays:

"The Germ in the Kiss"	Universal
"The Lure of Vanity"	Vitagraph
"A Lively Affair"	Vitagraph
"The Amateur Playwright"	Kinemacolor
"A Soldier's Sacrifice"	Vitagraph
"No Dogs Allowed"	Vitagraph
"Captain Bill"	Universal
"Her Brother's Voice"	Selig
"The Little Stocking"	Imp
"A Motorcycle Elopement"	Biograph
"Downfall of Mr. Snoop"	Powers
"The Red Trail"	Biograph
"Insanity"	Lubin
"The Little Music Teacher"	Majestic
"Sally Ann's Strategy"	Edison
"Ma's Apron Strings"	Vitagraph
"A Cadet's Honor"	Universal
"Cupid's Victory"	Nestor
"A Good Turn"	Lubin
"His Tired Uncle"	Vitagraph
"The Swellest Wedding"	Essanay

If you go into this work go into it right. You
cannot learn the art of writing motion picture
plays by a mere reading of textbooks. Your actual
original work must be directed, criticised, analyzed
and corrected. This is the only school that delivers
such personal and individual service and the proof
of the correctness of our methods lies in the success
of our graduates. They are selling their plays.

Demand increasing. Particulars free.

Associated Motion Picture Schools
699 SHERIDAN ROAD, CHICAGO

Figure 18: Motion picture play plots
advertisement
Source: *MPM*, August 1914.

ATTENTION
SCENARIO WRITERS

THE Staff of the Scenario Department of the Universal
    Film Mfg. Co., Inc., will examine, edit and pass upon
your scenarios, free of any charge whatsoever.

Write to the Scenario Department for full information,
and you are guaranteed that if your offering can be put
into proper shape for picture purposes, same will be done
without any charge to you, and that you will be paid for
your scenarios as well.

Figure 19: 'Wanted' advertisement for
scenario writers
Source: *MPW*, September 1914, 1098.

Another example comes from The Photo Playwright. A monthly section called 'The Photoplay Mart' detailed what the various film companies were looking for, but what the requirement they invariably had in common was for 'original stories'.[6]

Mutually interested newspapers and magazines, film producers and journalists also collaborated to promote public excitement. The motion picture serial, a hybrid format between the short film and the multi-reel feature, was an ideal vehicle for launching screenwriting contests. In 1912 the Edison Company released *What Happened to Mary?*, an original scenario by Bannister and Ann Merwin, in a series of one-reel films simultaneously. The McClure magazine, *The Ladies' World*, published each short plot, with an offer of a $100 prize for anyone who could finish an episode. With this came the promise of film production for the winning story. The response was very strong, and circulation of the magazine increased (see Figure 20).[7]

---

6   'The Photoplay Mart', *Photo Playwright*, June 1912, 13–16.

7   Azlant, 'Theory, History and Practice of Screenwriting', 127–128.

Figure 20: Competition to finish an episode
of *What Happened to Mary?*
Source: *The Ladies' World*, August 1912.

The success of this initiative spurred other magazines and newspapers to adopt similar marketing strategies. The *Chicago Tribune* ran a contest for an original story, offering a $10,000 prize; it generated an impressive 19,003 entries and the winning story, *The Diamond from the Sky*, was written by Roy L. McCardell, a journalist who would go on to be a successful scenarist The explanation for this connection from Ramsaye, the then editor of the *Tribune*, was that it 'was the only professional offering in the contest. He had to win.'[8] His comment perhaps suggests that the competition was not such an open process as it appeared to be.

McCardell, Sargent claims, was 'the first man […] to be hired for no other purpose than to write pictures' for Biograph[9] His salary of $200 a week would soon draw other newspapermen, who were only earning around $25 a week, into the business. Possessing composite skills, McCardell brought his knowledge of comic strips, Broadway musicals and comedies, newspaper vignettes and serials, poetry, narrative, photography and popular fiction to the process of writing scenarios.[10] Sargent, who was also a journalist, would draw on his professional skills and interests derived from popular culture in a similar way. The other key screenwriting teachers examined in this study came from a comparable background. The initial involvement of someone of the calibre of McCardell was perhaps a sign of what was to come: the eventual exclusion of screenwriting submissions from the general public in favour of professional writers.

8　Ramsaye, *A Million and One Nights*, 668.

9　Sargent, 'The Literary Side of Pictures'. *MPW*, July 11, 1914, 199.

10　Stempel, *Framework*, 4–6.

However, in the early 1910s the lure of fame and fortune was drawing amateur writers to try their hand. Their enthusiasm was fuelled by high prices paid for some well-publicised story materials. In 1910, for example, Vitagraph paid scenarist Nell Shipman a substantial $100 (worth around $2,500 today[11]) a reel for an original scenario.[12] More commonly, prices ranged from $10 to $15 in 1911, with the rare price of $50 for exceptional work.[13] According to *Motography*, the average price paid for a scenario was around $25 and only in exceptional cases rose to $100.[14] Nevertheless, the trade literature indicated an ever-upward trend in prices that further stoked interest. By early 1912, the regular price had become $50 and by 1914, Sargent confirmed that this had potentially risen to $100.[15] Some screenwriters wrote articles that gave reason for some optimism. In *The Motion Picture Story Magazine* in 1912, for example, Wright recounts how a former farmer was now earning $2,500 a year and a carpenter who once earned only $2 a day had become a successful scenario writer. Yet even he recognised this was the exception rather than the rule, adding a note of caution that there are 'ten thousand writers in the Moving Picture scenario field and one in one hundred are fairly successful'.[16]

Many thousands of story ideas, synopses, scripts and scenarios were submitted. Story departments were set up to sift through these unsolicited manuscripts and, as early as 1909, *Moving Picture World* recorded that 'large numbers of scenarios are offered and very few of them accepted'.[17] A popular myth had developed that writing for film involved no literary skill and those who had only a basic education could succeed. This was fuelled initially by the belief among a number of the artistic community that film was not a real art. Even so, one of the fears of scenario writers was that their original work would be stolen. Although the manuals gave many assurances that ideas were rarely plagiarised and that scenario editors were honest, it was thought the sheer amount of material pouring into the studios could provide inspiration to staff writers. Arguing emphatically that such an experience was unlikely, Harrison, a regular columnist for Moving Picture World, insisted that producers were at great pains to avoid accepting any ideas from writers they could not vouch for. For those wanting to ensure that nobody else

---

11 For the changing value of money, see 'Inflation Calculator' in DaveManuel.com, http://www.davemanuel.com/inflation-calculator.php

12 Azlant, 'Theory, History and Practice of Screenwriting', 141.

13 'Letters to the Editor', *MPW*, July 22, 1911, 131 and The Hermit, 'The Photoplaywright's Earnings', 93.

14 The Hermit, 'The Photoplaywright's Earnings', 93.

15 Richard Spencer, 'Fifty Dollar Scenarios', *Photo Playwright*, November–October 1912, 5 and Sargent, 'The Photoplaywright', *MPW*, January 17, 1914, 282–283.

16 Wright, 'The Spark of Genius', *MPSM*, September 1912, 135–136.

17 Editorial, 'Old Wine in New Bottles', *MPW*, July 24, 1909, 115.

writes your story, Harrison advised that the best approach was to submit 'a scenario of masterly composition' rather than a synopsis.[18]

'Scenario fever' spread to the universities as well. In 1915 Famous Players-Lasky ran a competition for the best screen story, offering a $350 prize and a trip to Hollywood. The winner came from Columbia University and had attended one of the courses in 'Photoplay Composition' run by Freeburg.[19] This result further emphasised that succeeding required considerable literary skills and that, for the most part, such competitions gave the general public only the illusion of participation rather than anything more substantial.

Nationally advertised courses and schools also began to appear during this period. An industry directory published in 1915 listed 61 such scenario or photoplay schools throughout the country.[20] At first, a large number of these schools were scorned and criticised, and with justification, for many claimed they could teach the art of photoplay writing in just a few lessons. In 1915 The Photoplay Authors' League campaigned against them, with Sargent as its first president.[21] However, by the late teens some students of these courses had achieved considerable success and a number of those running them had courted the interest of some big studio names. For example, the Palmer Institute of Authorship, led by Frederick Palmer, who founded the Photoplay Correspondence School, could boast an eminent advisory council comprised of Ince and Sullivan.[22] The fact that one of their students was a life prisoner at Arizona State Penitentiary, who had sold a scenario to Universal for $500, was certainly trumpeted.[23]

This kind of school, Morey notes, could be another factor contributing to 'scenario fever'. Such schools promised access to scriptwriting and 'could offer men the recognition and wealth they craved'. Yet, as mentioned earlier, Morey indicates they were also part of a wider handbook culture of the time that offered 'self-cultivation' and 'self-improvement' and 'appeared to promise individual social rise through the mastery of some aspect of the film industry'.[24] According to Morey, it tapped into the wider sense of disenfranchisement on the part of those who felt excluded from the dominant culture of American society during this period.

---

18   Louis Reeves Harrison, 'Stealing Plays', *MPW*, June 24, 1916, 2208.

19   Patterson, *Cinema Craftmanship*, 184.

20   *The American Motion Picture Directory*, 1914–15 (Chicago: American Motion Picture Directory Co., 1915); 51, cited in Azlant, 'Theory, History and Practice of Screenwriting', 131–132.

21   Ibid., 132.

22   Brownlow, *Parade's Gone By*, 278.

23   Roy L. Manker, 'The New Way to Enter Motion Pictures', *Opportunities in the Motion Picture Industry* (1922, repr., Los Angeles: Nabu 2013), 7.

24   Morey, *Hollywood Outsiders*, 4–22.

The poor quality of many of the submissions led many to ask why the matter of 'How a scenario should be written' had received so little attention.[25] An editorial in *Moving Picture World* in March 1911, titled 'The Scenario School', expressed relief at the setting up of a 'school for scenario writers', while not giving the name of the school:

> Whether the school succeeds or not, depends upon the aptitude of the individuals requiring the necessary instruction [...] The school may accomplish some practical good if it will teach its students the formula or technique of scenario writing.[26]

Opening up companies to outside submissions eventually prompted successful scenarists and scenario editors to respond to this call and write in trade journals about how to write scenarios, which further spurred public interest. Many of these authors or screenwriting teachers in time published their ideas in the first screenwriting manuals, in part because doing so brought considerable commercial rewards, although they also appeared to be motivated by altruism or a genuine desire for improvement. For example, in 1911 Sargent, along with others, recognised that already the industry needed new blood. This would counteract, in his terms, the 'sameness of the films' that resulted from a naturally inbred company of directors who stifled the originality of authors.[27] The growth in instruction was phenomenal, with over 90 manuals published between 1910 and 1920.[28]

Stempel goes so far as to claim that such manuals and articles from screenwriting teachers actually created scenario fever.[29] Certainly it is likely that this literary response to public interest added to its rapid spread, particularly with the boom in trade and fan magazines, which would reach a combined circulation of several million by the early teens. However, Stempel probably overstates the case, given the many other factors contributing to this phenomenon as described above. Azlant sums up the situation in the early teens:

> [G]iven the advertisements for stories and writing talent, the distribution of scenario formats, the scenario writing contests, the nationally advertised schools and courses, the coverage of the craft, successful scenarists, and stellar literary figures in the burgeoning trade and fan magazines, and the tide of handbooks and manuals on screenwriting, it is understandable that screenwriting had, by the late teens, become a swollen public fantasy.[30]

---

25 R.V.S., 'Scenario Construction', *MPW*, February 11, 1911, 294.

26 'The Scenario School', *MPW*, March 18, 1911, 573–574.

27 Sargent, 'The Earmark on the Film', *MPW*, August 26, 1911, 521.

28 Azlant, 'Theory, History and Practice of Screenwriting', 134.

29 Stempel, *Framework*, 14–15.

30 Azlant, 'Theory, History and Practice of Screenwriting', 138.

4. Summary

The origins of early screenwriting teachers can be traced, first, to a complex array of literary traditions that delivered writing models they could draw upon. Second, economic factors in the film industry provided opportunities for new writers, who would in turn seek out instruction.

Early screenwriting teachers, including the key screenwriting teachers who form the subject of this study, were strongly influenced by theatrical practice. Some had worked as critics, directors, writers or actors in the theatre, but all had grown up in an era when this form of entertainment was one of the most powerful mediums of communication, before the advent of film. Notions of how to write for film had evolved mainly from a theatrical base, but were also influenced by literature and other forms of artistic expression. While this book cannot explore all the links that photoplay manuals shared with playwriting and story writing, it is clear those links are considerable and screenwriting teachers drew heavily on those sources, in particular theatrical tradition, to craft their own manuals.

Aspects of melodramatic tradition and the narrative conventions of the theatre influenced screenwriting teachers. Melodrama provided sharply delineated characters with few moral ambiguities, who could represent good or evil in the choices they made. The combination of music and silent imagery could be effective in eliciting strong emotions and pathos from spectators. Having inherited a sharp visual understanding of the pictorial elements of theatrical melodrama, screenwriting teachers understood the potential of film to outstrip it with photographic realism. However, their acceptance of the influence of these melodramatic elements did not, on the whole, extend to non-classical narrative structure along with its implausible and coincidence-laden plots. Screenwriting teachers preferred to draw mainly on the tried and tested theatrical narrative tradition that demanded tight plot construction and highly developed character psychology. Part Two, through its detailed analysis of the advice key screenwriting teachers gave, will make this preference clear. Screenwriting teachers were also aware of the many playwriting manuals that housed this tradition and freely accessed this material as a basis for their ideas.

Film had begun with novelty and spectacle, followed by simple story films and basic scripting and then developing through to complex feature films that required narrative clarity and detailed scenarios. The earliest films had a storyline laid out in the script, but the details of the action were left to the actors as 'business' to be worked out. As the production process and nature of films changed, the need emerged for more developed and sophisticated scenarios with narrative clarity, to ensure that people from all sectors of society could understand their content. Meeting this need saw the making of films move from informal to highly formal planning. The development of the scripting process was central to this change and ultimately the means of controlling it, which was important for commercial reasons. Mack Sennett, founder of Keystone, recollects the growing realisation of the centrality of the script:

> A new theory of motion-picture economics smote us pretty forcefully. It was this: the more money we spent on the script, on writing the story, the less money it cost us to shoot the pictures when we put the actors to work.[1]

Narrative film, with its clear structural norms, guaranteed a measure of control over the costs and logistics of production. The scenario or continuity script became an increasingly important document for effecting such gains, because it allowed filmmakers to plan. In that sense, screenwriting was a natural concomitant of more complex narrative film and the intricate production processes required to create it. As a result, it is likely that many of those who would create these scenarios would also seek the assistance of screenwriting teachers.

Rising levels of wealth increased social mobility and time for leisure activity, which drew rich and poor alike to the cinema. Large-scale attendance at film theatres led to increasing concern over the content of films; soon taking up the issue, social reformers and moralists demanded censorship. Manual writers offered extensive advice on what would be tolerated, as content issues were best resolved at the writing stage. As the ready supply of classic literature and plays dwindled, compounded by copyright issues, the industry faced a critical shortage of scenario material between 1908 and 1917. This massive growth in the need for synopses and scripts would spur those who aspired to write them to seek out screenwriting teachers for advice. Rapid expansion in film as a product would inevitably lead to the commodification of particular actors. New writers had to negotiate the difficulties presented by censorship, the opportunities afforded by copyright restrictions, and the challenge of how to write for these new film stars.

The evidence I will present in Part Two strongly suggests that inexperienced writers increasingly turned to screenwriting teachers to help them write scenarios. As a result, I argue, screenwriting teachers were at the heart of this development process and were also a product of it. America had become a nation of filmgoers and the demand for scenario material was insatiable. Screenwriting teachers would advise the industry and freelance writers on how to meet this challenge.

---

1 Mack Sennett, *The King of Comedy* (1954: repr., iuniverse.com, 2000), 126.

PART TWO
CONTRIBUTION

PART TWO: CONTRIBUTION

5. Screenwriting Teachers

Before closely examining how key screenwriting teachers have contributed to screenwriting and the filmmaking industry, it is necessary to consider the context in which the first screenwriting teachers emerged. A set of robust criteria then needs to be established to distinguish between screenwriting teachers who were on the periphery and those who played a key role in the early film industry and screenwriting development; these criteria will be applied to eliminate peripheral screenwriting teachers from the core study. The criteria will again be applied to corroborate why only five key screenwriting teachers should be considered as potentially making the greatest contribution to the discourse on early screenwriting.

The First Screenwriting Teachers

The debate about writing narrative film took place across a range of printed media and interest groups: journalists in the national press; studio heads and film directors; scenario editors and staff writers; actors of the emerging film companies; and the general public. Crucially, it took place in the fan and trade press and in the many screenwriting manuals that were produced by those who would come to be regarded as screenwriting teachers.

From 1910 onwards, articles began to appear in both the trade and fan press about the content and construction of scenarios, perhaps an indication of the increasing level of interest in writing for the screen. In one such article in *Moving Picture World*, Bedding was absolutely clear about what he considered to be the most important aspect in a scenario: 'I have no hesitation in saying it is what is called the dramatic moment. The climax of the story.'[1] He also points out the importance of emotionally engaging the audience because:

> moving picture audiences like other audiences are influenced very much by the mood of the moment [… and] the average audience responds to the moods or sentiment shown on the screen.[2]

Another 1910 article in *Moving Picture World* acknowledges the centrality of the scenario in the production process, but also laments the lack of recognition given to these writers:

> What is the first requisite in the manufacture of moving picture film? No one, understanding, will gainsay the assertion that it is the scenario. Who, filling a dominant requirement, is held in such complete obscurity as the writer of the scenario?[3]

---

1   Bedding, 'The Dramatic Moment', *MPW*, March 12, 1910, 372.

2   Ibid.

3   Emar, 'Concerning Scenarios', *MPW*, July 7, 1910, 76.

While recognising 'the writing of a scenario as a distinct profession', this same author is concerned that it was quite badly paid, which 'deters many from considering this new branch of literature'.[4] At this point, scenario writing was still considered the preserve of the professional writer, even though it was not a financially attractive option. However, this viewpoint was shifting, as Craw illustrates in one of his early articles for *Moving Picture World*: 'The picture play dramatist may be an amateur or a professional.'[5]

The overall lack of recognition for the writer as part of the film production process was a more persistent attitude. Critic and journalist Ada Barrett lauds this new form of silent drama as 'literature, drama and amusement, brought into the life of the poorest and most ignorant'.[6] However, she makes no mention of the role of the writer behind it, even though her article is supposed to be about 'the photoplay' – which it seems for her had become a way of referring to the finished film specifically. Others had more foresight about the potential for writing scenarios. In *The Motion Picture Story Magazine*, Grau comments on the growing respectability of picture plays and their potential profitability. Yet, in recognising the writing opportunity the industry would present, he also foretells the ultimate fate of the amateur writer: 'The Moving Pictures field is now emerging into an era […when] the world's greatest playwrights will provide the scenarios.'[7]

Open discussion in trade journals about what photoplaywrights might earn was beginning to make writing for films seem more financially viable. By May 1911 *Motography* was quoting between $10 and, in exceptional cases, $100 for a single scenario, although it admitted the upper limit was usually around $50.[8] The opportunity to make money also attracted more unscrupulous elements, and it was not long before fan press advertising sections were filled with all sorts of advertisements for film writing correspondence schools (see Figure 21). Some of these schools were no doubt run by charlatans touting their wares to a gullible public.

As well as appearing across the fan press from early 1911 onwards, such advertisements started to infiltrate the more conservative trade press. One advertisement from *The Motion Picture Story Magazine* in 1911 reads:

> PLOTS WANTED FOR MOTION PICTURE PLAYS. You can write them. We can teach you by mail in 10 easy lessons […]. No experience and only common school education necessary. Writers can earn $50 a week […]. Ass'd Motion Picture Schools.[9]

---

4 Ibid.

5 Craw, 'The Technique of the Picture Play', *MPW*, January 2, 1911, 126–127.

6 Ada Barrett, 'The Plea for the Photoplay', *MPSM*, July 1911, 115–116.

7 Robert Grau, 'The Potency of the Motion Picture', *MPSM*, November 1911, 118–119.

8 The Hermit, 'The Photoplaywright's Earnings', 93.

9 Advertisement in *MPSM*, April 1911, 130.

Associated Motion Picture Schools was the first of these correspondence schools and received recognition and backing from the trade magazine *Moving Picture News*, which carried similar advertisements from September 1911 (see Figure 22).[10] By December the following advertisement appeared in *Moving Picture World* (see also Figure 23):

> NEW FIELD, BIG MONEY, EASY WORK. Why don't you think up plots for motion picture plays? It's easy and pays well. We teach you by mail how to write and sell your plots. [..] Associated Motion Picture Schools.[11]

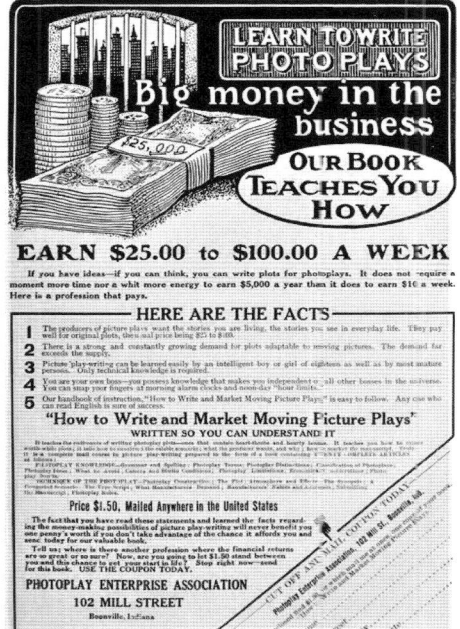

Figure 21: Advertisement for film writing correspondence school Photoplay Enterprise Association
Source: *MPSM*, April 1912, 169.

Figure 22: Associated Motion Picture Schools advertisement for motion picture plays
Source: *MPN*, September 30, 1911, 34.

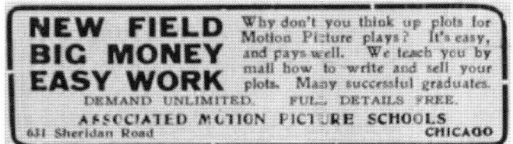

Figure 23: Associated Motion Picture Schools advertisement for plot creation for photoplays
Source: *MPW*, December 30, 1911, 1113.

---

10 'Associated M. P. Schools' advertisements in *MPN*, September 30, 1911, 34.

11 Advertisement in *MPW*, December 30, 1911, 1113.

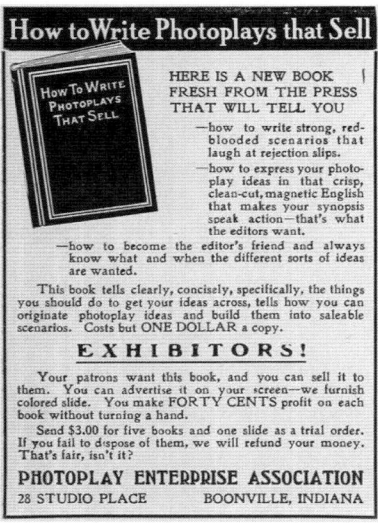

Cash for Picture-Play Scenarios

Demand practically unlimited. Writers earning $50 or more weekly. Literary excellence unnecessary. If you can read, write, and **think**, you need only **technical knowledge** to succeed in this pleasant, fascinating profession. We **must** have more play-wrights and we'll teach you the **technical secrets**. Send your name and address at once for Souvenir Booklet.

NATIONAL AUTHORS' INSTITUTE

36 Clinton Street   Newark, N. J.

Figure 24: National Authors' Institute advertisement offering cash for picture-play scenarios
Source: *MPSM*, August 1911, 157.

How to Write Photoplays that Sell

HERE IS A NEW BOOK FRESH FROM THE PRESS THAT WILL TELL YOU

—how to write strong, red-blooded scenarios that laugh at rejection slips.

—how to express your photoplay ideas in that crisp, clean-cut, magnetic English that makes your synopsis speak action—that's what the editors want.

—how to become the editor's friend and always know what and when the different sorts of ideas are wanted.

This book tells clearly, concisely, specifically, the things you should do to get your ideas across, tells how you can originate photoplay ideas and build them into saleable scenarios. Costs but ONE DOLLAR a copy.

EXHIBITORS!

Your patrons want this book, and you can sell it to them. You can advertise it on your screen—we furnish colored slide. You make FORTY CENTS profit on each book without turning a hand.

Send $3.00 for five books and one slide as a trial order. If you fail to dispose of them, we will refund your money. That's fair, isn't it?

PHOTOPLAY ENTERPRISE ASSOCIATION
28 STUDIO PLACE   BOONVILLE, INDIANA

Figure 25: Photoplay Enterprise Association advertisement for how to write photoplays that sell
Source: *MPN*, January 25 1913, 31.

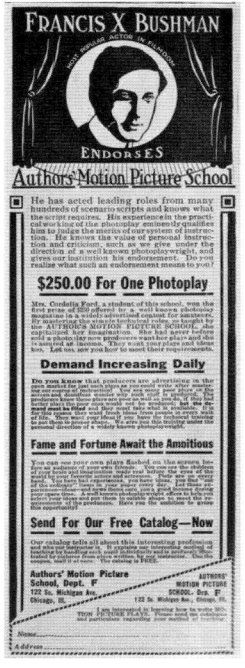

Figure 26: Francis X. Bushman's endorsement of Authors' Motion Picture School
Source: *MPM*, November 1914, 169.

Another of these schools was the National Authors' Institute, based in New Jersey. The draw in the advertisement was 'Cash for Picture-Play Scenarios', with its main claim: 'we'll teach you the technical secrets' (see Figure 24).[12] Similarly, the Photoplay Enterprise Association made claims in the fan press such as: 'Big money in the business. Our book teaches you how' (see Figure 21), although its advertisements were considerably toned down in the trade press (see Figure 25).[13]

---

12   Advertisement in *MPSM*, August 1911, 157.

13   Compare the advertisements in *MPSM*, March 1912, 159 and *MPN*, January 25, 1913, 31.

The Photoplay Enterprise Association published the monthly journal *The Photo Playwright*, with the successful scenarist Monte M. Katterjohn as editor and reputable contributors. Some of the key screenwriting teachers featured in this study wrote regularly for this journal, enhancing its legitimacy and, by implication, the reputation of its school too.[14]

It seems that such schools were initially tolerated, but eventually legitimate manual and column writers actively campaigned against them. Even in 1911, Grau had some misgivings about Associated Motion Picture Schools and the many others whose advertisements proliferated in the fan and trade press: 'The layman would be astonished were the vogue of these schools completely revealed.'[5] During the early teens, hundreds of similar advertisements appeared. A single edition of *The Motion Picture Story Magazine* in August 1913 carried no fewer than 10 advertisements for schools or photoplay brokerages.[16] By November 1914, The Authors' Motion Picture School had even managed to secure the endorsement of the film star Francis X. Bushman for its advertisements (see Figure 26).[17]

As the Introduction has stated, *Photoplay* finally decided to 'eliminate motion picture school advertising' in April 1915 and to replace it with a legitimate regular monthly column called 'Hints on Photoplay Writing' by Peacocke from May 1915 onwards.[18] For a short period, the most aggressive forms of advertising disappeared but within a month Atlas Publishing had returned.[19] Figure 27 shows its standard advertisement that appeared in *Photoplay*. To avoid the ban, it stressed that no correspondence course was required, although the promise of substantial financial rewards had crept back in.

---

14 *Photo Playwright* featured articles by Horace G. Plimpton, Studio Manager at Edison and the key screenwriting teachers Sargent, Wright and Ball. See *Photo Playwright*, April to December 1912 and the feature article on their work by Monte M. Katterjohn, 'The Photoplay Dramatist', *MPSM*, June 1912, 145–147.

15 Grau, 'The Picture Play', *MPN*, December 30, 1911, 9.

16 They included the Chicago Photo-playwright College, National Authors' Institute, Phillips Studio, Authors' Motion Picture School, United Play Brokerage, American School for Photoplaywriters, The United Correspondence College, The Photoplay Clearing House, Photo-play Syndicate and Associated Motion Picture Schools. See *MPSM*, August 1913, 143, 147, 159, 171 and 174–175.

17 Advertisements in *Photoplay*, November 1914, 2 and *MPM*, November 1914, 169.

18 In backing this decision, Peacocke describes his own experience as a staff writer with Universal: 'no scenario was ever accepted from a so-called school or clearing house'. See 'Scenario School Advertising Barred by Photoplay Magazine', *Photoplay*, April 1914, 114–117.

19 Atlas Publishing Co. advertised its materials under the guise of 'no correspondence course' and had toned down its rhetoric. See *Photoplay*, May 1915, 164.

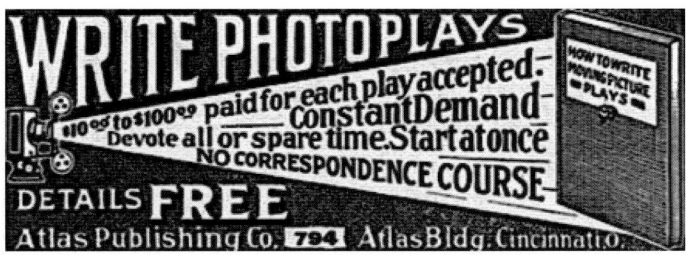

Figure 27: Advertisement for filmwriting school Atlas Publishing
Source: *Photoplay*, July 1915, 8.

Sargent's views about such institutions were clear. He probably had Associated Motion Picture Schools of Chicago in mind when he wrote about the many difficulties writers faced when trying to write scenarios:

> The fake correspondence school is the most vicious form of graft because it harms not alone those who take the course but also those who merely read the advertising with its specious and misleading statements about 'anyone' can learn to write plays, that no literary ability is required, that an income of at least $50 weekly is [e]nsured.[20]

In a 10-year review (1907–1917) of how far writing for film had developed, 'Photoplay Writing, Then and Now', Sargent refers to the first correspondence school based in Chicago. In his view, this course, 'poor as it was', formed the basis for innumerable other courses and those involved had made '[p]rofits of from $10,000 to $30,000 yearly […]. Literally thousands took the course, misled by the glowing promises.'[21]

In another article, Sargent recounts the problems that even genuine teachers were experiencing and the dubious connections some had to these schools. Apparently, another Chicago-based enterprise, the Photoplaywrights' Association of America, had in some way connected itself to Arthur Winfield Thomas (who had also worked as an editor of *Photoplay*) as a way of legitimising its activities (see Figure 28).[22] In its book titled *Wanted: More Photoplays*, the organisation claimed that 'Mr. Wm. Lord Wright […] has helped me' and was 'Consulting Editor'. The book also named Capt. Leslie T. Peacocke as an associate editor. The lure of financial gain seems to have dragged Thomas and Peacocke into the row, while Thomas and Wright fell out over the pending court action.[23]

---

20   Sargent, *Technique of the Photoplay,* 3rd ed. (New York: Moving Picture World, 1916), 351.

21   Sargent, 'Photoplay Writing, Then and Now', *MPW*, March 10, 1917, 1491–92. Sargent may have had in mind the same 'Chicago man [who] was the first to conceive the idea of a writing school course' as the Chicago firm featured in the advertisements, which was likely to be Associated Motion Picture Schools.

22   Advertisement in *Photoplay*, November 1914, 7.

23   See Sargent, 'The Photoplaywright', *MPW*, December 26, 1914, 1834 and February 6, 1915, 821. Thomas was voted 'Out' of the Photoplay Authors' League, presumably as a result of his suspected questionable activities.

Figure 28: Photoplaywrights'
Association of America advertisement
for photoplay writing
Source: *Photoplay*, November 1914, 7.

Figure 29: Phillips Studio advertisement
for successful photoplay writing
Source: *Photoplay*, November 1914, 181.

Phillips, another of the key screenwriting teachers of this study, even ran his own correspondence school, the Phillips Studio, although it appears to have been more legitimate than others at the time (see Figure 29).[24] Nevertheless, this brief survey reveals that the relationship between even the *bona fide* screenwriting teachers and correspondence schools was complex.

The role of the fan and trade press in disseminating information about how to write scenarios gradually grew in importance. Ultimately it would help popularise the work of a number of the emerging teachers of the screen.

Fan magazines had a much larger audience than the trade press, as they sought to engage the wider public. In addition, in offering readers portraits of their favourite stars and stories about their personal lives, they were an important promotional tool for the industry. According to Lewis Jacobs, initially:

> They only rarely ventured into criticism, but this restraint was not prolonged. *Photoplay* Magazine [...] set up new standards for fan journals by vigorously applauding the best pictures and staunchly condemning the mediocre.[25]

---

24 Advertisement in *Photoplay*, November 1914, 181.

25 Lewis Jacobs, *The Rise of the American Film: A Critical History* (1939: repr., New York: Teachers College Press, 1967), 134.

Confirming fan magazines made this change in direction, Koszarski observes that they attempted to promote critical judgment and to influence the viewing habits of their readers:

> For the most part, fan magazines [...] served a highly educative function [... and] did suggest various aesthetic bases for differentiating 'good' from 'bad' and supplied their readers with enough technical, social and economic background to help inform their decisions.[26]

To begin with, articles were mainly directed at the filmgoer, but they soon extended to instructing the public how to write scenarios. The industry's shortage of material, as Part One has described, drove this process and opened up new opportunities for the public. Column writers such as Peacocke, who wrote for *Photoplay*, tried to bridge the gap between the industry and freelance writers. Their position had a certain ambiguity, in that they were industry insiders, but were often addressing an enthusiastic public who had little idea their offerings would only be acceptable to the industry in rare cases. The concern of fan press editors, however, was not to launch the careers of scenario writers but to improve their sales figures. The most popular fan press magazines of the time were *Photoplay*, *The Motion Picture Story Magazine* (which became *Motion Picture Magazine* in 1914) and *Motion Picture Classic*.[27] Existing circulation figures for *Photoplay*, the most prominent of these publications, indicate its very wide readership.[28]

The audience for the trade press was far more select. These publications were initially geared to exhibitors and industry insiders only and all wanted to be able to tell their advertisers that they reached the most important buyers and people in the industry who mattered. For them, the priority was the quality rather than the quantity of readers. According to Koszarski, 'For those within the industry, information and opinion were shaped [by these] aggressive trade papers, each competing for the same limited number of subscribers.'[29]

The trade journals contained film reviews, summaries of the programmes of theatres across the nation, activities of regional exchanges in the cities and news of the major New York theatres. They also covered issues such as censorship and copyright. While the *New York Dramatic Mirror* and *Motion Picture News* were important, *Moving Picture World* was unrivalled from the early to mid-1910s, as it had the largest circulation of

---

26 Koszarski, *Evening's Entertainment*, 195.

27 Ibid., 193.

28 *Photoplay* was established in 1911 and based in Chicago; by 1915 it had a circulation of 100,000 and this had increased to 495,232 by 1925. These figures are courtesy of David Pierce and Eric Hoyt of the *Media History Digital Library* and were taken from N. W. Ayer and Sons' *Newspaper Annuals, 1900–1960*. Ayer & Son audited the circulation figures on behalf of advertisers. See *Media History Digital Library*, http://mediahistoryproject.org

29 Koszarski, *Evening's Entertainment*, 195.

any trade journal and saw itself as the leader in the discourse on writing for film. All of these publications ran regular columns, however. *Motion Picture News* was originally the voice for the independent, non-trust producers, but would soon come to speak for the whole industry. It would overtake *Moving Picture World* in popularity by the early 1920s and have a much larger circulation.[30] Both *Motion Picture News* and *Moving Picture World* would establish regular departments devoted to movie reviews and editorial criticism, eventually extending them to columns on how to write scenarios. The *New York Dramatic Mirror*, although primarily a theatrical journal, also became an important trade organ for film. It had run a column by Frank Woods since 1909 and prided itself on its even-handed approach: 'Photoplays were to be handled with the same respect, seriousness and freedom that have always characterised this publication's treatment of the stage productions.'[31]

According to Charlie Kiel, in terms of its level of industry access and linkage, and more directly its influence on film writing, the trade press:

> functioned as an arbiter of taste, emphasizing certain tenets of classicism that would be absorbed over time [… and] did provide expertise in particular realms (such as narrative construction) that helped establish certain norms. […W]riters and critics within industry journals helped map out some of the possible options for filmmakers and conveyed a mediated version of public response to developing formal tendencies.[32]

In other words, the trade press provided a useful forum for debate among the various interested parties about how films were constructed and to some extent this discourse helped consolidate practice within the industry. On the other hand, Liepa adds a note of caution for those who would make too many assumptions about this:

> One should be wary, however, of considering trade press discourse as indexically related to the film industry or film culture more generally. The film trade press

---

30 *Moving Picture World* was formed in 1907 and published in New York on a weekly basis. By 1915 the paper had a circulation of 17,200. In the 1920s it gradually lost ground to other trade papers and by 1925 circulation had fallen to 8,503. It ceased publication in 1927. The *Motion Picture News* was published from 1913 to 1930, following the 1913 merger of *Moving Picture News*, founded in 1908, and *The Exhibitors' Times*, founded in 1913. It was also published on a weekly basis. It was formed as a counterweight to the dominant *Moving Picture World*. By 1915 it had a circulation of 6,800. It became the leading trade journal of the 1920s and by 1925 its circulation had reached 10,000. These figures are courtesy of Pierce and Hoyt of the *Media History Digital Library* and were originally taken from Ayer and Sons' *Newspaper Annuals*, 1900–1960. See *Media History Digital Library*, http://mediahistoryproject.org

31 The *New York Dramatic Mirror* was founded in 1879 and had taken up the cudgels of film comment because, up until 1911, there was still 'no organized commentary concerning the motion picture'. See Tibbetts, *American Theatrical Film*, 6 and 56.

32 Kiel, *Early American Cinema in Transition*, 43.

addressed exhibitors, distributors and suppliers of exhibition materials and hardware, and tended to cater to their needs and interests.[33]

Supporting this view, Richard Abel argues that, from their establishment, the trade papers aggressively targeted the exhibitor and were almost exclusively focused on industry needs.[34] However, as Jordon Brower and Josh Glick point out, *Moving Picture World* also embraced the wider needs of the industry and served as a space for discourse, as:

> many of the paper's staff members were professional scenario writers, theater operators, or technicians [...and as such it] served as a forum for the film industry to speak to itself, about itself, but also mediated between the industry and the culture in which films were produced and viewed.[35]

At best, it seems, the trade press provided an inside view through which the American public could understand the various technological developments and the evolution of 'best practice' and could, to some extent, observe and gain access to the industry. In the role of interlocutor, it offered a forum for dialogue and discussion about all aspects of film production, exhibition and reception or the inner workings of the industry. A more nuanced role is also evident, Liepa claims, in that the trade press also mediated the relationship between industry outsider and insider:

> Trade journalists in the 1910s wrote ambiguously and simultaneously for interested amateurs, budding professionals and industry insiders. Perhaps even more so than films themselves, which, due to the nature of the medium retained an element of communicative unidirectionality, the trades served as an important forum [... of] negotiation [...], serving both popular and industrial interests.[36]

Taking a similar perspective, Santiago Hidalgo sums up the role of the trade press as a forum for discussion and a focus for the developing discourse:

> They mediated one of film's most intense periods of transformation – between roughly 1907–1914 – with the move from single reel to feature length films, and with significant changes to film aesthetics, narrative construction, production practices, exhibition conditions and audience spectatorship.[37]

---

33 Liepa, 'Entertaining the Public Option', 17.

34 Richard Abel, *The Red Rooster Scare: Making Cinema American, 1900–1910* (Berkeley: University of California, 1999), 80–86.

35 Jordon Brower and Josh Glick, 'The Art and Craft of the Screen: Louis Reeves Harrison and the Moving Picture World' in *Historical Journal of Film, Radio and Television*, 33:4 (2013): 535, http://dx.doi.org/10.1080/01439685.2013.847652

36 Liepa, 'Figures of Silent Speech', 122–123.

37 Santiago Hidalgo, 'Early American Film Publications' in *A Companion to Early Cinema*, eds. Andre Gaudreault, Nicholas Dulac and Santiago Hidalgo (Chichester: Wiley-Blackwell, 2012), 205.

It is a continuing point of debate as to how closely in touch with the mores of the industry the fan press and trade journals really were. Without going into this issue in detail, it seems likely that the fan and trade press did influence the development of screenwriting within the industry, although the extent of that influence is hard to measure.

Moreover, it appears likely that those among the general public who wished to familiarise themselves with studio and production company requirements and writing opportunities increasingly accessed the latest information from the trade press. Screenwriting manuals of the period regularly direct prospective amateur writers to the trade press as a source of current market information about the industry. Ball encouraged his readers to access trade papers, such as *Moving Picture World*, *Motography* and the *New York Dramatic Mirror*. Similarly, Wright urged his readers to study key trade journals, such as *Moving Picture World* and *Motion Picture News*.[38] In response to this level of interest, the trade press developed a significant discourse on film writing.

Sargent's columns in *Moving Picture World* and Wright's in the *New York Dramatic Mirror* are full of their responses to letters and questions from the general public about how to write and writing opportunities. They regularly provided information about what film companies were looking for. For example, in 1914 Sargent writes, 'Frontier is in the market for scripts, and is willing to pay top-notch prices for high-class stories',[39] while Wright advises that 'Civil War plots are not at a premium. The World Film Company is not buying at present.'[40] In an 'Inquiries' section in his column, Sargent printed comments from readers' letters about their successes and failures with various companies and identifying the ones that were best for pitching future scripts. Sometimes a writer's experiences are quoted at length:

> Here is part of a letter from an author whose success represents about the average writer who cannot devote his entire time to plays. [...] 'Had good business with the plots in November: sold four, one to _____ for $25, one to _____ for $30, and two to _____ (half-reels) for $20.'[41]

As another who was constantly occupied with answering practical enquiries from the readers of his column, Wright reports, 'Came several letters the past few days asking if

---

38 See Ball, *The Art of the Photoplay* (1913; repr., London: Forgotten Books, 2012), 28–30 and Wright, *Photoplay Writing* (1922: repr., New York: Nabu, 2012), 197.

39 Sargent, 'The Photoplaywright', *MPW*, January 24, 1914, 406–407.

40 Wright, 'For Photoplay Authors, Real and Near', *NYDM*, 1914 May–Jun 1915, 2013.pdf: *Fulton History*: http://fultonhistory.com/Fulton.html

41 Sargent, 'The Photoplaywright', *MPW*, January 17, 1914, 282–283.

we supported the synopsis-only theory.'[42] From another letter he quotes a regular question he was asked:

> If I sell a photoplay to a company and they produce that play, giving it another title [...] have I the right [...] to claim authorship under their title?[43]

Even a cursory examination of these columns indicates that they were being accessed by a wide range of people, from professional writers through to their most amateur counterparts.

The first recorded instruction on screenwriting began to appear in the fan and trade press in early 1911. These initial column writers did not necessarily gain the renown of those who followed them. A. W. Thomas, for example, who with scenarist Marc Edmund Jones wrote a column for *Photoplay* in 1911, was also editor for *Photoplay* but would not produce a manual based on his columns until 1914, by which time his influence had waned. Summing up Thomas's achievements, Sargent states, 'He has done a few plays but nothing to attract marked attention. He holds pretty closely to the editorial end' (see Figure 30).[44]

In 1917 Sargent records that in 1912, Thadée Letendre of Universal had established the first trade journal that was totally dedicated to photoplay writing, *The Scenario Writer* (later *Photoplay Author*). He also claims that Letendre wrote the first book of instruction, which 'was presently followed by one from Wright'.[45] However, Sargent appears to contradict himself, as on at least two other occasions in 1914 he claimed that Wright had produced the first manual.[46] Liepa takes the view that 'Sargent erroneously credited Wright in 1914 as "the author of the first book on photoplay writing"' and later corrected this in his 1917 article. But this argument would mean Sargent had made the same error twice in 1914, which seems unlikely.[47] As the publication date of Letendre's manual remains unknown, there is no way of resolving this issue.

---

42 Wright, 'For Photoplay Authors, Real and Near', *NYDM*, 1914 May–Jun 1915, 2133.pdf: *Fulton History*: http://fultonhistory.com/Fulton.html

43 Wright, 'For Photoplay Authors, Real and Near', *NYDM,* 1914 May–Jun 1915, 1539.pdf: *Fulton History*: http://fultonhistory.com/Fulton.html

44 Arthur W. Thomas, *How to Write a Photoplay* (Chicago: Photoplaywrights' Association of America, 1914). The surviving six chapters of this manual are relatively well developed and their content reflects the level of advancement by 1914, http://www.oocities.org/emruf1/photoplay.html. See also Sargent, 'The Literary Side of Pictures', *MPW*, July 11, 1914, 199–202.

45 Sargent, 'Photoplay Writing, Then and Now', *MPW*, March 10, 1917, 1491.

46 See Sargent, 'Wright's Second' in the 'The Photodrama', *MPW*, July 18, 1914, 425 where Wright is credited as 'the author of the first book on photoplay writing to come from the press [...] about four and a half years ago' and 'The Literary Side of Pictures', *MPW*, July 11, 1914, 199–202, where he states, 'William Lord Wright was the first in the field with a book.'

47 Liepa, 'Figures of Silent Speech', 233.

The Literary Side of Pictures

BY EPES WINTHROP SARGENT

SUPPOSE, before we get too deep into the subject, that you take a look at the forgotten side of what this title implies. Now and then one of our cherished goats wanders from its own fireside at the call of someone who says that pictures are not literature, but we call it back, because we're careful of our goats and don't let them associate with such persons.

Stop a minute and think. Literature is old, centuries old. It started 'way back; possibly before the flood. It ought to be good by this time if, like wine and cheese, it gets savor from age. Photoplay writing is no bearded veteran. Photoplay writing was born some time or another in 1909. Can you ask the six-year-old to have the erudition of the ages?

Now to beat out the possible (and probable) objector, we'll revise that statement, but with mental reservations. The photoplay writing game started somewhere between 1894 and 1896. Don't ask just precisely when. If we could tell we would not be writing this stuff. We would be over in the Treasury Department or some place in Washington, making out next year's corn crop reports. We never said we were *that* good.

But it was about 1898 that the first editor was employed. Then there were three companies over here that lasted overnight. One of them was the Biograph. They had been doing the Jefferson family until we were sick of them. The Jeffersons were big in the Biograph in those days and if you saw a fisherman who hooked himself in the seat of his panties it was C. B. Jefferson; or Joe, Jr., or someone of the Jefferson family who were more numerous in those days than Eddie Foy's family is at present. Every time we asked Austin Fynes who a new Biograph player was he found out and added a new Jefferson to the already numerous family.

title and about one-third holding out for more money, because he was making good. This was one of his off moments and he was "writing pictures" for the then Standard. They were not moving pictures in the sense now employed, though they were indeed moving. McCardell used to write about ten captions telling a more or less complete story. Then he and the boss would hire a lot of models—mostly girls—and go out and make pictures for the captions. Somebody on the Biograph must have read the Standard, for presently McCardell was hired to go down to Thirteenth street and Broadway and write pictures for the Biograph. To be exact it was for the Mutascope, then a nickel in the slot machine. They didn't think much of the projection machine in those days. It was all mutascope.

Anyhow, Roy wrote the stuff and he was the first man on either side of the water to be hired for no other purpose than to write pictures. He did the work very successfully until he got the idea for Mr. and Mrs. Nagg, first cousins to the present Jarr family, and he went the rest of the way down to the place with the gilded dome, but he has kept on writing pictures to this day and he is still one of the most successful farcical writers. In passing, the New York World later gave two other writers to the business. With the formation of the Thanhouser Company, Lloyd Lonergan, a brother-in-law of the founder of the company, was induced to leave the paper and write stories for the films. Until the growth of the Thanhouser concern made it necessary for him to concentrate on the big stuff like "The Million Dollar Mystery," he did most of the stories for Thanhouser and later for the Princess, as well. Considering the number of stories produced in proportion to the percentage of hits, we incline to the

This is a quote about A. W. Thomas that occurs further on in this article:

Another is A. W. Thomas, of the Photoplay Magazine and the Scenario Writer. He has done a few plays, but nothing to attract marked attention. He holds pretty closely to the editorial end.

Figure 30: Sargent's article on 'The Literary Side of Pictures'
Source: *MPW*, July 11, 1914, 199-202.

Wright's short (30-page) *The Art of Writing Scenarios*, probably published in late 1910, could well have been the first.[48] Sadly, like Letendre's manual, it appears Wright's did not survive. However, Wright would go on to author two further manuals, which are still available and will be examined in this book, and he also exerted considerable influence as a column writer for *Motion Picture News* and the *New York Dramatic Mirror*.

Early in 1911, a short series of articles appeared in *Moving Picture World,* called 'Technique of the Picture Play' by George Rockhill Craw; they dealt with basic scenario structure and writer concerns, but no manual would result.[49] Thereafter Louis Reeves Harrison, an editor and staff writer for *Moving Picture World*, produced a series of articles on photoplay writing, covering subjects such as plots, characterisation, settings, scenario construction and rejected manuscripts.[50] These would later form the basis for his 1916 manual, *Screencraft*.

Within a relatively short period, regular columns and photoplay departments were created in all the major fan and trade press publications in an effort to educate the public and, in all probability, to keep industry insiders informed about the current thinking on how to write scenarios. This intense interest in writing for the screen coincided with a 'boom in trade and fan magazines that appeared throughout the teens, reaching a combined circulation of several million copies'.[51] Those who wrote regularly for these publications therefore had the potential to influence the debate about screenwriting.

Others to write manuals that are among the earliest to survive are Ralph Perkins Stoddard (1911) and James Slevin (1912). The basic nature of these manuals illustrates the infancy of the craft at this point. Stoddard's book restricts itself to rudimentary advice on the story idea, plotting and formatting, and focuses on simplicity of approach. Although his manual is more developed, Slevin views film in theatrical terms, as indicated by the title, *On Picture-play Writing: A Handbook of Workmanship*, and makes extensive references

---

48   Advertisements in mid-1914 about Wright's upcoming book, *The Motion Picture Story*, mention the earlier book, *The Art of Scenario Writing*, which has now presumably been lost. This is probably the book Sargent is referring to. See advertisement in *Movie Pictorial*, June 13, 1914, 4 for *The Motion Picture Story* (1914), which credits Wright as 'author of *Art of Scenario Writing*' too. The same credit appears in the prefaces to his manuals, *The Motion Picture Story* (Chicago: Cloud Publishing, 1914) and *Photoplay Writing* (1922). It was also given a favourable review, 'The Art of Writing Scenarios', in *MPW*, February 25, 1911, 419. This review means a likely publication date in the autumn of 1910.

49   Craw, 'Technique of the Picture Play', *MPW*, January 21, 1911, 126–127; January 28, 1911, 178–180 and February 4, 1911, 229. Although this series halted, Craw did continue to write regular features on various topics.

50   Harrison, 'The Rejected Manuscript', *MPW*, April 1, 1911, 695; 'Characterization', April 29, 1911, 937; 'Superior Plays: The Important elements of their Construction', June 3, 1911, 1233–1234; 'Settings', June 17, 1911, 1360 and 'Plots', July 1, 1911, 1493–1494.

51   Azlant, 'Theory, History and Practice of Screenwriting', 133.

to Aristotle.[52] Herbert Case Hoagland, editor for Pathé Frères, wrote a slightly more sophisticated manual, *How to Write a Photoplay*, in 1912. However, it was not only short but also simplistic in its approach to structure, as these comments indicate:

> To write a photoplay requires no skill as a writer, but it does require a 'constructionalist.' It requires the ability to grasp an idea and graft (please use in the botanical sense) a series of causes on the front end of it and a series of consequences on the other end.[53]

By far the most outstanding early publication, for reasons that I will address later, was the first edition of Sargent's *The Technique of the Photoplay*, published in 1912, which was based on his columns in *Moving Picture World*. The popularity of Sargent's manual would spawn two further editions in 1913 and 1916, both of which were substantial revisions of the previous work. In Azlant's opinion, 'it represents a distillation and on-going revision of public instruction which appeared in a respected trade journal written by an eminently qualified scenarist'.[54]

If we compare Hoagland's approach above, which appears to belittle proper story-writing skills and the role of the writer, with the following opening statements in Sargent's column, 'Technique of the Photoplay', about the nature of the photoplay and the role of the photoplaywright, it is clear that Sargent has a more developed understanding of the skills required of the writer and their role in the production process:

> The photoplay [… is] a story told in action instead of words, and therefore is written in action instead of dialogue or polished phrase. The author supplies the groundwork of action and idea, but he is dependent on the director and the actor for proper interpretation and expression.[55]

The writers of other screenwriting columns in the fan and trade press would also produce manuals as a result of their popular success. Many other scenario writers, directors and actors would also soon follow suit and, within a relatively short period, a steady supply of manuals was published:

> Over ninety books in English on the silent scenario, many by accomplished scenarists or scenario editors, were published between 1910 through 1920, perhaps the largest body of instruction in an aspect of film production within the materials of film history.[56]

---

52   See Ralph Perkins Stoddard, *The Photoplay: A Book of Valuable Information for Those Who Would Enter A Field of Unlimited Endeavor* (1911: repr., Whitefish, MA: Kessinger Legacy, 2013), 5–6; and James Slevin, *On Picture-play Writing: A Handbook of Workmanship* (1912: repr., BiblioBazaar, 2013), 57–64.

53   Herbert Case Hoagland, *How to Write a Photoplay* (1912: repr., New York: Nabu, 2012), 6.

54   Azlant, 'Theory, History and Practice of Screenwriting', 211.

55   Sargent, 'Technique of the Photoplay', *MPW*, July 22, 1911, 108–109.

56   Azlant, 'Theory, History and Practice of Screenwriting', 134.

These manuals provided instruction in film-writing technique, format, and generic and moral constraints, as well as helping to promote the interest of the general public. In mediating a space between freelance writers and the film studios, ultimately they helped the industry as a whole to define what it meant to write professionally for the screen. Liepa elaborates:

> manuals helped regulate the body of material being produced. From simple instructions on format and presentation, to specific industry requirements, these manuals collectively promoted and orchestrated a massive cultural movement of independent writing. Such instruction helped ease the industry's incorporation of writing as a fundamental element of film production. Increasingly complex, the industry needed to develop a degree of rationalization in order for writing to maintain a significant position within the process.[57]

In summary, the evidence suggests screenwriting teachers had a more industry-inclusive and broader involvement in the American film industry in this early period than at any other point in screenwriting history.

As it is not possible to survey all the material that these people produced, it is important to justify why this book will not examine a number of apparently important texts. Some of these include manuals by well-known scenario writers, trade and fan press columnists, critics, filmmakers and film stars. However, by excluding these, it is possible to focus on the most important texts so as to test the contention that certain key screenwriting teachers made a significant contribution to the development of the American film industry during this early period.

A set of criteria will next be established in order to both eliminate the work of certain individuals from the study and validate why the contribution of only five screenwriting teachers should be examined in detail.

Five Important Criteria

It is not practical to scrutinise closely all of the manuals published from 1910 to 1922, because there are so many, but it is important to select those of most significance. This is why it is necessary to establish criteria that can help decide which of these manual writers are worthy of closer examination. It establishes the basis for Chapter 6, which considers the advice and guidance that these key screenwriting teachers offered and its potential relevance to the industry and those individuals, both amateur and professional, who sought to pursue or further their career in screenwriting. Applying such criteria will also help to assess the significance of the contribution of those selected for further consideration, including how central and integral their role was in the early film industry and their influence on early screenwriting development, which is the focus of Chapter 7.

---

57   Liepa, 'Figures of Silent Speech', 232–233.

In summary, the five criteria selected are that the screenwriting teacher must have:

1. Achieved significant writing credits

2. Worked as a scenario editor

3. Written extensively for the fan or trade press

4. Written more than one manual or written a manual that was published in more than one edition

5. Had considerable industry connections.

Criterion 1. Writing Credits: The influence and authority of those who claimed to be screenwriting teachers would be considerably enhanced if they had already demonstrated they could write. Although it is not essential to be able to do something in order to teach it, screenwriting teachers were more credible if they had succeeded at what they were asking others to master. Therefore, the first requirement is that the screenwriting teachers should be scenario writers with a significant number of script credits and evidence of critical success. In addition, they may have been accomplished writers in other fields, such as journalism and writing plays or short stories.

Criterion 2. Scenario Editor: As those considered to be more central to the industry are likely to have worked as scenario editors for a major studio or film company, this will be another requirement. Azlant notes the importance of this role:

> The evolving studio system advanced not only the craft of screenwriting, but also the separate role of the scenario or story editor, who managed the various aspects of the studio's use of story materials and writing skills.[58]

Those who were appointed as gatekeepers to make judgments about scripts and to verify which of them were suitable to purchase performed a vital function. Most companies advertised widely for scripts, and the scenario editor on the staff read these submissions before selecting and adapting those they accepted. Bowser confirms the importance of these individuals and describes how they were selected:

> Out of the hundreds of journalists, magazine story writers, actors and amateurs who submitted scripts, a handful developed into professional scriptwriters and were hired as scenario editors of production companies.[59]

Legitimacy in such a context came from an individual's ability to show they had the relevant experience to instruct others, beyond an understanding of theory alone. Louella Oettinger Parsons legitimises her own work as a screenwriting teacher and manual writer by alluding to her professional experience as a scenario editor with Essanay:

---

58 Azlant, 'Theory, History and Practice of Screenwriting', 85–86.

59 Bowser, *Transformation of Cinema*, 256.

> I have studied the subject of the photoplay from every angle, and it is from my actual experience with the scenario writer that I have evolved this series of lessons for the help of those who have photoplay ambitions.[60]

Wright agrees that scenario editors are at the heart of the industry:

> The scenario editor is a very important functionary because he not only must be a writer with a keen sense of dramatics, but he must understand the policy of the producing company for which he works, and he should also have had experience in the sales end of the business.[61]

Those selected for closer scrutiny in this study were among the most highly regarded scenario editors with the greatest expertise and were recognised as such by their peers and other industry professionals.

Criterion 3. Fan or Trade Press: Potential candidates for closer study should have written for key fan or trade press publications about screenwriting. Writing for the regular columns or special departments dedicated to this purpose, which most of these publications had established, indicates that the teacher had a demonstrable audience and could have had considerable influence over the amateur writing public and/or the professional writing fraternity. It is important to consider both teachers who featured in the fan press and those who wrote for the trade press as they addressed different, but in their own way equally significant, audiences.

Criterion 4. Multiple Manuals: The candidates should have written more than one manual, or a substantial manual that was published in more than one edition, which would indicate they have a wide readership and popularity. Those who wrote regular columns and features in the fan or trade press were more likely to have also gained a wider readership of their manuals, due to the press coverage they received and the advertising potential of their copy.

Many wrote manuals based on their experience as scenario writers or directors, or they were high-profile actors with expertise that was demonstrated in their texts. In considering various manual writers, it is important to examine the context from which they arose: for example, it may be necessary to distinguish between individuals who made educating screenwriters their main priority and those who merely wrote manuals to further their own reputation or celebrity status. Although intention is not a test of quality, if the work was not born out of dedication, and was not continuous and sustained, this might signal a lack of depth or worth.

---

60   Louella Oettinger Parsons, *How to Write for the 'Movies* (1916: repr., New York: Nabu, 2012), 3.

61   Wright, *Photoplay Writing*, 55.

Criterion 5. Industry Connections: The candidates should have had some other significant industry connections, as further evidence of their centrality. They might have been producers, studio executives, directors or actors, or have actually formed, owned or run film companies. They might have established, run or participated in writing clubs or organisations, federations, leagues or courses, or adjudicated in scenario competitions. Such work might have earned them plaudits or citations from others in the industry who recognised their contribution.

The above criteria are intended to be a robust way of assessing the level of influence of significant screenwriting teachers. However, I recognise that in this kind of historical research it is always difficult to measure, or arrive at accurate judgments about, who is more or less influential, because the surviving historical documentation is rarely neutral. To mitigate this problem, I have drawn on multiple sources with the aim of making my judgments more secure and gaining a consensus view to the degree that is possible. As a starting point in establishing the reputation of each screenwriting teacher, I consulted the Internet Movie Database for Professionals (*IMDbPro*). This source has been checked and greatly expanded upon through extensive reference to the fan and trade press and any other online resources that can be located. Respected contemporary commentators such as Grau, along with earlier and modern film historians, have also been consulted where appropriate.

Peripheral Screenwriting Teachers

Many people contributed to the screenwriting discourse during the early years of the American film industry. After sifting through their materials, I have excluded many of them from this study because they do not even come close to meeting my criteria.[62] Applying the criteria did identify a number of potentially significant candidates, on which basis it was then possible to separate those of lesser importance from the most significant of these contributors. First, we consider those screenwriting teachers who only partially fulfilled the criteria, and were therefore judged to be of marginal significance.

---

62   Among others surveyed but not included are: Ardon Van Buren-Powell, *The Photoplay Synopsis* (1919: repr., Memphis: General Books, 2013); Clarence J. Caine, *How to Write Photo-Plays* (Philadelphia: McKay, 1915); Carl Charlton, *How to Write* Photoplays; Charles Donald Fox, *The Fox Plan of Photoplay Writing* (1922: repr., Whitefish. MA: Kessinger Legacy, 2013); William Lewis Gordon, *How to Write Moving Picture Plays* (1914: repr., New York: Nabu, 2013); James Irving, *The Irving System: A New Easy Method of Story and Photoplay Writing* (1919: repr., Memphis: General Books, 2012); Grace Lytton, *Scenario Writing Today* (1921: repr., Miami: Hard Press, 2013); Elbert Moore, *Elbert Moore's Textbook on Writing the Photoplay* (1915: repr., Memphis: General Books, 2012); Ernest N. Ross, *Scenario Writing* (Philadelphia: Penn Association, 1912); James A. Taylor, *The Photoplay* (Washington: Washington DC Printing, 1914); and C. G. Winkopp, *How to Write a Photoplay* (1915: repr., Whitefish, MA: Kessinger Legacy, 2013).

Joseph Berg Esenwein (1867–1946) co-wrote a manual with Arthur Leeds, entitled *Writing the Photoplay* (1913). Esenwein was a published author, novelist and academic, and became the editor of 'The Writer's Library' for the Home Correspondence School in 1914.[63] This organisation published material on many writing-related subjects, such as 'Writing for Vaudeville', 'The Art of Short Story Writing' and 'The Art of Public Speaking'. Screenwriting was just one interest among Esenwein's wide-ranging literary pursuits.

Esenwein's co-writer Leeds had written photoplays for Selig and Essanay and became scenario editor for Edison in 1915. Leeds was also an editor of and a regular contributor to *The Photoplay Author* along with Esenwein.[64] In other roles, he was the head of the photoplay section of the Home Correspondence School and, like Sargent, a member of the Ed-Au (Editors and Authors) Club.[65] The Ed-Au Club was exclusive, as membership was granted only to writers who had at least six scripts produced. Leeds later became president of the Ed-Au Club and was made vice president when the club's name changed to the Photodramatists Inc.[66]

Both Leeds and Esenwein were, no doubt, figures of some importance and worthy of attention. In general, Sargent was highly critical of correspondence schools, but he seems to have been prepared to make an exception for them:

> Arthur Leeds and Dr. J. Berg Esenwein are working on a book for a course of lessons by Mr. Leeds. We are inclined to think that this will be decently administered [...] but it is very plain that most of the correspondence schools first lie to their would-be pupils and then swindle them.[67]

In terms of screenwriting, Esenwein's reach was more limited because his activities were so diffuse and he was first and foremost an academic. Although Leeds had distinguished himself with a number of writing credits, by being a scenario editor and an occasional contributor to the trade press, Sargent's opinion of his diminishing importance by 1914 is clear:

---

63   J. Berg Esenwein was editor of *Lippincott's Magazine* from 1905–1914. First published in 1868, the magazine, according to Mott, 'must be given a high rank among American Magazines' and had published the likes of Arthur Conan Doyle, Oscar Wilde and Rudyard Kipling. See Frank L. Mott, *A History of American Magazines, 1865–1885 Vol. 3* (London, OUP, 1938), 399–401.

64   See 'Arthur Leeds', *MPW*, March 20, 1915, 1777. Leeds (whose additional roles included actor, director and short story writer) was editor of *The Photoplay Author* (journal of the Home Correspondence School and known as *The Writer's Monthly* from 1916 onwards) and 'Edison's New Editor', *NYDM*, 1914 May–June 1915, 1821.pdf. *Fulton History*: http://fultonhistory.com/Fulton.html

65   Sargent, 'The Photoplaywright', *MPW*, January 24, 1914, 406–407.

66   'Sifted from the Studios', *Motography*, May 27, 1916, 1232.

67   Sargent, 'The Photoplaywright', *MPW*, June 21, 1913, 1246–1247.

> Another book author is Arthur Leeds, who used to be a star Selig and Essanay
> writer. He was once an actor and a lecturer. [...] He is doing very little original work
> at present.[68]

Esenwein and Leeds' manual is detailed and thorough, but only one was written and,
because it was a collaborative effort, it lessens the individual achievements of its
authors.[69] It often appears on recommended reading lists by screenwriting teachers,
which lends it some credibility. However, those who made these recommendations had
far more exposure in trade and fan publications.[70] While Esenwein and Leeds must be
acknowledged as respected contributors to the discourse, others had the potential for far
greater influence.

John Arthur Nelson (1874–1960) had an impressive track record in acting, writing,
producing and directing for Universal and Warner Features.[71] He also ran his own film
company, was editor of *The Photoplay Dramatist*[72] and eventually published his manual,
The Photoplay: How to Write, How to Sell (1913). Nelson's own character was perhaps
questionable, as criminal charges for embezzlement and gun-running were brought
against him and, although these charges were later dropped, suspicions remained that
were never resolved. With socialist leanings, he was also driven by the desire for political
change and a wish to put 'radical ideas across on the screen'.[73] His one feature film, *The
New Disciple* (1921), was a commercial failure because it focused narrowly on particular
interest groups, lessening its influence and reach.[74] Nelson's manual is detailed and well
apportioned, covering 'form, structure and technique' and ran to a second edition, but he

---

68   Sargent, 'The Literary Side of Pictures', *MPW*, July 11, 1914, 199–202.

69   Esenwein and Leeds wrote articles on 'photoplay construction' up to April 1915 in *The Photoplay
Author*. This work formed the basis for their book, *Writing the Photoplay*. Esenwein also wrote a column,
'Letters to Young Authors', from January 1915 and Leeds took over a column from Sargent called 'Thinks
and Things' in March 1915.

70   Phillips, 'Photodrama in the Making', *MPM*, March 1918, 108 and 110; and Sargent, 'The
Photoplaywright', *MPW*, October 10, 1914, 181.

71   Nelson has 20 credits, of which 19 are shorts from 1913–1914. See 'Nelson', *IMDbPro*: https://pro-labs.
imdb.com/name/nm0625422/

72   Nelson's editorial role is noted in the press, but copies of *The Photoplay Dramatist* do not appear to have
survived, as no records can be located. See 'What Duluth is Reading', *Duluth MN Evening Herald*, January
28 1916, 7, 6752 pdf. *Fulton History*: http://fultonhistory.com/Fulton.html

73   Steven J. Ross, *Working-class Hollywood* (New Jersey: Princeton University, 1999), 152–153.

74   Nelson's feature film, *The New Disciple*, for the Federation Film Corporation, was shot in 1921. It
'shows how worker cooperatives could restore the harmony between employer and employee that was
shattered by wartime capitalist profiteering'. See Ross, *Working-class Hollywood*, 158. *Variety's* critic Jolo
slated it as having 'little entertainment value and even less value as propaganda [...] and the story by John
Arthur Nelson isn't convincing'. See 'The New Disciple', *Variety*, December 23, 1921, 1072 pdf. *Fulton
History*: http://fultonhistory.com/Fulton.html

wrote no more.[75] A further limit to his influence was that Nelson made no contributions to the fan or trade press. Possibly his alleged misdemeanours and propagandist tendencies contributed to his waning influence too, as his behaviour did not follow the established patterns of the industry.

Howard T. Dimick (1897–1976) wrote two manuals[76] on screenwriting, but appears to have had no film credits and little or no fan or trade press coverage, although Wright does mention in one of his articles that 'he is a successful photoplay author'.[77] Not a great deal is recorded about Dimick, apart from that he seems to have been some kind of theatrical agent and a vaudeville comedy sketch writer,[78] was interested in religion and was a historian of sorts, with a particular interest in the Civil War period. All of his books, apart from the screenwriting manuals, are out of print or unavailable.[79] One reviewer of his manual *Photoplay Making* (1915) claims Dimick was 'a disciple of W. T. Price, and his present work an attempt to adapt that stage authority's rules of play making to the newer art of the screen'.[80] This background perhaps explains his plagiarising of some of Price's statements (see Chapter 1). The foreword of Dimick's main manual, *Modern Photoplay Writing: Its Craftsmanship*, which appeared in two volumes in 1922 (with his first manual comprising the first volume), indicated that it was 'intended for the intelligent aspirant with latent ability' and also for use in 'educational establishments'. He hoped that leading universities might set up photoplay writing departments with the use of his material:

> It has been the aim of the author to adapt this book to college use by a graded series
> of exercises, beginning with analysis and proceeding to creative writing.[81]

The manual is thorough and the aim laudable in itself but, as the freelance market in screenwriting had virtually collapsed by 1922, such departments may have been his only viable audience.

---

75   Nelson, *The Photoplay*, 19.

76   See Dimick, *Photoplay Making* (New Jersey: Editor Company, 1915) and *Modern Photoplay Writing*.

77   Wright, 'For Photoplay Authors, Real and Near', *NYDM*, 1913 Mar–Apr 1914, 2440 pdf. *Fulton History*: http://fultonhistory.com/Fulton.html

78   See 'The Vaudeville Spotlight', *NYDM,* December 4, 1915. 1915 Jul–Aug 1916 - 0825 pdf, which records that he was the writer of 'The Green Woman', and advertisement in *The Billboard*, December 18, 1915; 1916, 0144.pdf. *Fulton History*: http://fultonhistory.com/Fulton.html

79   Dimick and Others ed. Halderman-Julius, *The Truth about American Evangelists* (A Little Blue Book no. 1273, 1928); Dimick, *Peace overtures of July, 1864* (1946); *Visits of Josiah Gregg to Louisiana, 1841– 1847* (1946); *Reconsideration of the Death of Josiah Gregg* (1947); *Ancestry and Some Descendants of William Gregg* (1948).

80   'Book Review', *NYDM*, July 21, 1915 See 1915 Jul–Aug 1916, 0110.pdf: *Fulton History*: http://fultonhistory.com/Fulton.html

81   Dimick, *Modern Photoplay Writing,* 8.

Louis Reeves Harrison (1857–1921) was an important voice in the industry. As well as being a relatively successful scenario writer,[82] he was an editor and staff writer for *Moving Picture World*, regularly contributing on all aspects of film production, including screenwriting. His manual *Screencraft* comprises 18 short essays drawn from articles he wrote for *Moving Picture World* between 1915 and 1916.[83] Not a manual in the conventional sense, it was, according to Brower and Glick:

> a difficult book to define [. .and] firm classification even evaded Chalmers Publishing, the parent company, and publisher of both Harrison's book and the *MPW*, which touted *Screencraft* as both an instructional tract and as a quasi-scholarly meditation in advertisements in its trade paper.[84]

Indeed, Harrison backs up this view in his own prefatory note:

> This book is intended to help in formulating a new art, not that the art may appeal to the delicate sensibilities of the super-cultivated, but that it may adequately respond to the needs of plain people the world over through addressing their sympathetic intelligence.[85]

Because Harrison's intention was to educate his readers more broadly than through instructing them on writing photoplays, *Screencraft* could be termed a quasi-manual. As Brower and Glick observe, Harrison was:

> interest[ed] in exploring the composite form of film and defining its place among the arts [...by] analyzing the artistic qualities of contemporary films and how they emerged out of, but were also separate from, literature, theatre, and painting.[86]

Harrison's broader agenda related to his roles as a well-known photoplay critic[87] and film theorist who wrote on all aspects of film production. This discounts him as a key contributor to the screenwriting discourse for the purposes of this study, as his interests were so wide-ranging, rather than focused on the craft of screenwriting alone.

82　Harrison had seven writing credits and one directing credit. See 'Harrison', *IMDbPro*, https://pro-labs.imdb.com/name/nm0365723

83　Brower and Glick, 'The Art and Craft of the Screen' in *Historical Journal of Film, Radio and Television*, 33:4 (2013), 540, accessed January 15, 2014, http://dx.doi.org/10.1080/01439685.2013.847652

84　Ibid., 540–541.

85　Louis Reeves Harrison, *Screencraft* (1916: repr., Memphis: General Books, 2012), 4.

86　Brower and Glick, 'The Art and Craft of the Screen' in *Historical Journal of Film, Radio and Television*, 33:4 (2013), 542, accessed January 15, 2014, http://dx.doi.org/10.1080/01439685.2013.847652

87　Harrison was dubbed the 'foremost photoplay critic in the country'. See 'Motion World', *The Auburn Citizen*, March 7, 1913, 13, 0071.pdf: *Fulton History*: http://fultonhistory.com/Fulton.html

Frederick Palmer (1881–?), a relatively successful early scenario writer,[88] formed the Palmer Photoplay Corporation, which functioned as a correspondence school for aspiring writers. Morey has indicated that this organisation had an agenda beyond helping its subscribers succeed as scenario writers, in that it was concerned with self-improvement as well:

> [Although] such schools promised to prepare men and women for jobs in the film industry, especially as screenwriters [...t]he thriving nature of Palmer Photoplay's business as late as the mid-1920s [...] began to shift its attention to instruction in short story writing and general self expression.[89]

Palmer's organisation could be seen as part of the handbook culture that became popular in the early twentieth century and covered many subjects (see also Chapter 3). Palmer himself published a number of manuals on screenwriting.[90] Very few of his subscribers, however, succeeded in screenwriting and Palmer's own attempts to form a production company in 1922, in order to produce selected scenarios, met with limited success.[91] In fact, by the time Palmer had formed his correspondence school in 1918, the phenomenon of 'scenario fever' was largely over 'since the freelance market for manuscripts collapsed in the late 1910s, and the likelihood of private individuals placing a screenplay with a studio was small'.[92] His organisation commissioned prominent industry professionals to write booklets and short manuals, although their effectiveness in influencing the industry is debatable, as they were all published in and around 1920.[93]

---

88   Palmer claims that he authored some 52 scenarios in just nine months during the period of 1910–11. However, as Morey points out, such scenarios were shorter and less complex in the early period. See Morey, 'Have You the Power?' *Film History* 9 (1997), 310. Palmer's unsubstantiated claims about himself were far wilder when discussing the whole of his screenwriting career: 'I have written and sold and seen exhibited upon the screen hundreds of my own film stories.' See Palmer, *Palmer Plan Handbook* (1921, repr., BiblioBazaar, 2013), 20 and 'Palmer', *IMDbPro*, which only records a modest 39 writing credits from 1917–1930 and does not account for the earlier period. See https://pro-labs.imdb.com/name/nm0658233

89   Morey, *Hollywood Outsiders,* 70–71.

90   *The Essentials of Photoplay Writing* (1921); *Palmer Handbook of Scenario Construction* (1922); *Photoplay Plot Encyclopedia* (1922); *Author's Photoplay Manual* (1924); *Technique of the Photoplay* (1924); *The Business of Writing* (1925), (Los Angeles: Palmer Photoplay Corporation).

91   According to *IMDbPro*, Palmer Photoplay Corporation had only three production credits for 1924. 'Palmer Photoplay Corporation', *IMDbPro*: https://pro-labs.imdb.com/company/co0035001/?ref_=sch_int

92   Morey, 'Have You the Power?' *Film History 9*, (1997): 300.

93   Palmer Photoplay Corporation published the following booklets: Adeline M. Alvord, *Practical Research in Photoplay Writing*; Badger, *The Point of Attack*; George Beban, *Photoplay Characterization*; Jasper Ewing Brady, *The Necessity of Original Photoplay Material*; Al E. Christie, *The Elements of Situation Comedy*; Kate Corbaley, *Selling Manuscripts in the Photoplay Market*; Denison Clift, *Dramatic Suspense in the Photoplay*; Eric Howard, *Photoplay Plots and Plot Sources*; Frank Lloyd, *The Dramatic and Undramatic in the Photoplay*; Jeanie Macpherson, *The Necessity and Value of Theme in the Photoplay*; Hugh C. McClung, *Camera Knowledge for the Photoplaywright*; Rob Wagner, *Picture Values from an Artist's Viewpoint* (Los Angeles: Palmer Photoplay Corporation, 1920).

It is also important to consider a number of women writers who rose to prominence in early Hollywood. These women were gradually 'marginalized as the film industry became a Wall Street-defined, vertically integrated big business' before 1920.[94] The *Women Film Pioneers Project*, conducted by Columbia University, has provided substantial research on their activities during the early period and has sought to highlight their significance before its decline.[95] According to Lizzie Francke, 'half of those 25,000 scripts stored away in the Library of Congress Copyright Office were written by women'.[96] Further, Karen Maher makes the point: 'Female scenario department heads were common. Indeed, many women writers in the 1910s literally defined the craft.'[97]

Several of these women also wrote manuals as a result of their success as writers and scenario editors, or their popularity as actresses and celebrities. For example, Leona Radnor wrote *The Photoplay Writer* (1913),[98] Florence Radinoff *The Photoplaywright's Handy Text-Book* (1913)[99] and Elizabeth Frye Barker *The Art of Photoplay Writing* (1917).[100] These particular works are basic, short and less scholarly than others that followed. Some guidance is offered on constructing a story and what subjects to write about, along with formatting advice and the necessary technical knowledge to prepare a manuscript and synopsis. As in many handbooks, they each give a 'model' scenario by way of an example.

More serious offerings came from Marguerite Bertsch (1889–1967), in the form of her manual, *How to Write for Moving Pictures* (1917). Hired as a staff writer by Vitagraph in 1913, she eventually became a scenario editor and also directed for Vitagraph. Her career was perhaps cut short, as she left the business when Vitagraph lost its competitiveness in 1918. It was eventually sold to Warner Brothers in 1925.[101]

---

94   Karen Ward Maher, *Women Filmmakers in Early Hollywood* (Baltimore: Johns Hopkins University, 2006), 8.

95   *Women Film Pioneers Project at Columbia University*: https://wfpp.cdrs.columbia.edu

96   Lizzie Francke, *Script Girls: Women Screenwriters in Hollywood* (London: BFI, 1994), 6.

97   Maher, *Women Filmmakers in Early Hollywood*, 182.

98   Radnor is credited with writing only two shorts. See 'Radnor', *IMDbPro*: https://pro-labs.imdb.com/name/nm1311093/

99   Radinoff has 21 acting credits but none for writing. See 'Radinoff', *IMDbPro*: https://pro-labs.imdb.com/name/nm0705627/

100   No writing credits are recorded for Barker. She appears to have founded the 'Barker Society of America' in 1928, although no details are known of its function. See *Brooklyn NY Daily Eagle*, June 30, 1938, 10; 1938, 5415 pdf: *Fulton History*: http://fultonhistory.com/Fulton.html

101   Bertsch is credited with 51 screenwriting and four directing credits. See Jennifer Parchesky, 'Profile: Marguerite Bertsch', *Women Film Pioneers Project*: https://wfpp.cdrs.columbia.edu/pioneer/ccp-marguerite-bertsch/ and 'Bertsch', *IMDbPro*: https://pro-labs.imdb.com/name/nm0078442/

Another successful scenario writer, Catherine Carr (1880–1941), was employed by The North American Film Co. (which became the Kinetophote Co. in New York) as scenario editor.[102] She had a high enough profile to be the subject of a feature in *The Photoplay Author* in 1914 after being in the business for only three years.[103] She wrote a fairly substantial manual, *The Art of Photoplay Writing* (1914), on the back of this success.

Former *Chicago Tribune* journalist Louella Parsons (1881–1972) worked as a scenario writer and editor at Essanay and later became a premier gossip columnist.[104] Her manual, *How to Write for the Movies* (1915), drew a complimentary reaction from Sargent: she 'has written little, but many promising writers owe much to her helpful advice'.[105] Her handbook was also popular enough to run to another edition in 1917, which contains a chapter written by Maibelle Heikes Justice (a successful scenarist) on 'The Photodrama'. Parsons, Justice states, is 'probably the best-known freelance scenario writer in America'. She also praises her handbook for its excellent handling of 'the technique of writing for the screen'.[106]

A sign of the prominence of Carr, Parsons and Bertsch is that they belonged to the Ed-Au Club in 1914.[107] However, while these women were successful writers, none of them wrote for the fan or trade press, which would have limited the exposure of their work on the teaching of screenwriting.

Of greater significance is the work of Anita Loos (1888–1981), a highly successful scenario writer, producer and actress. According to JoAnne Ruvoli, 'she wrote over one hundred and fifty scripts in her thirty years as a Hollywood screenwriter and elevated intertitles to an art'.[108] Around 1915–16 the studios finally lifted their initial policy of maintaining the anonymity of writers. According to Ian Hamilton, Loos 'became one of

---

102   Carr is credited with 58 screenwriting titles. See 'Carr', *IMDbPro*: https://pro-labs.imdb.com/name/nm0139636/

103   E.M. Wickes, 'So You'll Know Them Better – Catherine Carr, Editor of Kinetophote Company', *The Photoplay Author*, November 1914, 134–138.

104   Parsons has nine credits in all, but only four writing credits. See 'Parsons', *IMDbPro*: https://pro-labs.imdb.com/name/nm0663860/

105   Sargent, 'The Literary Side of Pictures', *MPW*, July 11, 1914, 202.

106   Parsons, *How to Write for the 'Movies'*, 2nd ed. (Chicago: A. C. McClung, 1917), 237 and 251; cited in Maras, *Screenwriting*, 143.

107   All three were 'admitted as new members' of the Ed-Au Club in New York. See 'New Ed-Au Officers', *New York Dramatic Mirror*, April 15, 1914; 1913 Mar–Apr 1914. 2385.pdf. *Fulton History*: http://fultonhistory.com/Fulton.html

108   JoAnne Ruvoli, *Profile: Anita Loos, Women Film Pioneers Project*: https://wfpp.cdrs.columbia.edu/pioneer/ccp-anita-loos/. However, *IMDbPro* only credits Loos with 148 screenwriting titles, eight producing titles and one acting title. A possible reason for this apparent discrepancy from Ruvoli's record could be that some of Loos' work involved collaborations with John Emerson. See *IMDbPro*: https://pro-labs.imdb.com/name/nm0002616/

the first "name" writers to have any sort of presence in the public consciousness' and she was, in his opinion, 'the first literate screenwriter'.[109]

When Loos began her writing career with the Biograph Company, Griffith directed one of her first scenarios, *The New York Hat* (1912). Actors she wrote for included Mary Pickford, Lillian and Dorothy Gish and Lionel Barrymore. Loos is credited with possessing a very specific gift with dialogue, pioneering the use of witty and humorous comment in titles, which enhanced the appeal of stars and helped some, such as Douglas Fairbanks Junior, to major stardom. Her success as a writer continued into the 1950s, when she wrote the acclaimed *Gentlemen Prefer Blondes* (1953), which starred Marilyn Monroe.[110]

Loos worked closely with her husband, John Emerson (1874–1956), on many writing projects. Among their collaborations were a series of six articles on screenwriting for *Photoplay* in 1918, which more than likely was a replacement for the successful run of articles by Peacocke that ended in 1917.[111] They followed this with another series of eight varied articles in *Motion Picture Magazine* in 1921.[112] The coverage of these articles is impressive and their substance was published as a manual, *How to Write Photoplays* (1920). A second book, *Breaking into the Movies* (1921), deals mainly with acting and other opportunities in the business, but it contains a very short section on writing scenarios.[113] It is also indicative of the eclectic and broad interests Emerson and Loos had in the film industry in all its guises.

The popularity of Loos as a celebrity, actor, director and writer meant that she could use the fan press to promote her ideas about how to write. However, brilliant though she was as a writer, the locus of her work was not the education of the screenwriter. The co-written nature of her material on screenwriting further diminishes her individual achievements in this realm. It is also worth noting that the freelance market in scenario writing was largely extinguished by the time both these sets of articles and the manuals were published.

---

109 Ian Hamilton, *Writers in Hollywood: 1915–16* (New York: Harper-Collins, 1990), 8.

110 Camille Scaysbrook, 'Anita Loos – Biography'. See 'Loos', *IMDbPro*: https://pro-labs.imdb.com/name/nm0002616/

111 Loos and Emerson, 'Photoplay Writing', February 1918, 51–52; March 1918, 53–54; April 1918, 81–82; 'About the Development of Theme', May 1918, 81–82; 'On the Study of Continuity', June 1918, 78–79; 'On the Subtitle and the Speech', July 1918, 88–89 and 121 in *Photoplay*.

112 Loos and Emerson, 'What's What in Scenarios', February 1921, 38–39, 114 and 116; 'What Makes a Photodrama?' March 1921, 60–61 and 121; 'Building the Scenario', April 1921, 40, 96 and 98; 'The Plot Thickens – Construction Information on Scenarios', May 1921, 60–61 and 105; 'Checks and Checkmates – Instruction on Scenario Writing', June 1921, 40–41, 98; 'Title Technique', July 1921, 30, 82 and 86; 'Plot Mechanics', August 1921, 65 and 111; 'The Full Close', September 1921, 45 and 94 in *MPM*.

113 Emerson and Loos, 'Scenarios' in *Breaking into the Movies* (Philadelphia: George W. Jacobs & Co., 1921), 41–43.

One further woman writer in this period, Frances Taylor Patterson, ran screenwriting courses at Columbia University, but her links with the industry were tenuous and she was hardly ever credited as a writer.[114] Patterson helped set up, with Freeburg, one of the first courses in photoplay composition; she also wrote home study courses. She soon made the university course her own, her pedagogy focusing on 'plot construction and character [...] and she clearly saw her role as instructing writing students to craft effective narrative'.[115] Her two books, *Cinema Craftsmanship* (1920) and *Scenario and Screen* (1928), were 'practical guides rather than broad philosophical manifestos [... although] we can find in her writings the rudiments of a general aesthetics of film'.[116] Polan observes that:

> Throughout her career [... Patterson] was [...] concerned with encouraging higher quality in photoplay scenarios [... and through] her occasional writings, Patterson gained some influence beyond the classroom.[117]

Cinema Craftsmanship did extend to two editions and Paramount Studios produced a pedagogical film about cinema techniques for her to use in her teaching programmes.[118] However, Patterson's own views about the students for whom her Courses in Photoplay Composition were intended reveal a broader educative agenda:

> Some of those interested in it are interested purely from the point of view of a spectator, but there are many who are interested from the point of view of the writer.[119]

Although an educator with a practical bent, Patterson was not really a practitioner herself and the inclusion of some elements of critical analysis in her courses was perhaps 'an early intimation of the division of film studies into the sorts of tracks that would remain with the discipline throughout its history: there would be those who write creative works and those who write criticism'.[120] Polan concludes:

> It is hard to know the extent to which Patterson's pedagogy or writing had any direct impact on the motion picture industry and its films, but she did receive some

---

114   Patterson had one produced screenplay, *Broken Hearts* (1926). See 'Patterson', *IMDbPro*: https://pro-labs.imdb.com/name/nm0666207

115   Polan, *Scenes of Instruction*, 58.

116   Ibid., 64.

117   Ibid., 62.

118   Polan, 'Profile: Frances Taylor Patterson', *Women Film Pioneers Project*: https://wfpp.cdrs.columbia.edu/pioneer/ccp-frances-taylor-patterson

119   Patterson, 'University Training at Home', *Photoplay*, December 1920, 126.

120   Polan, *Scenes of Instruction*, 73.

support from the studios (she was a vocal and active member of the National Board of Review) [and that] brought her a certain regular attention in the trade press.[121]

In some ways Patterson resembles some modern screenwriting gurus, in demonstrating that she could run courses in screenwriting without being a practitioner – an achievement that sets her apart from the key screenwriting teachers of the early period. The quasi-academic nature of her course is also a forerunner of the type of modern screenwriting education offered in much of the university sector today.

When discussing women writers, Lizzie Francke points out that 'the publication of books by *big names* advising on how to craft scenarios became an industry in itself [emphasis added]'.[122] This observation must be borne in mind when considering any of these lesser screenwriting teachers, male or female: they were generally capitalising on their own popularity as writers, celebrities or actors and the potential financial gain in producing a manual, although some wrote for social or educational reasons. In other words, teaching screenwriting for these individuals was a sideline rather than their principal activity. This is perhaps one explanation for the sheer number of manuals published in this period. This is not to claim that they did not make a contribution to the discourse: many of them developed a genuine interest in the craft of screenwriting and some achieved a level of recognition, which means they probably influenced the discourse through their writings to a degree.

Again I refer to the comments of Thompson, who, when discussing screenwriting manuals right back to the 1910s, admits she had 'not attempted to survey such handbooks systematically, since they often repeat the same information with minor variations'.[123] With this observation I concur, as within the remit of this study it is not possible to fully analyse the content of all extant materials. However, the cursory inspection of manuals above indicates that Thompson's assumptions are broadly correct. It appears that many of these manuals contain pertinent but similar advice. However, what is at issue here is not their content in the main, but the extent of their impact.

Although it is important to acknowledge the role of these lesser figures, it is unlikely that they were key players in the debate over screenwriting development. Of the writers mentioned so far, most had no sustained presence in the fan or trade press; a number of them had limited experience as writers; others only produced a single manual without further editions, or their later manuals simply replicated the content of the earlier ones; some did not become scenario editors; and others had limited connections with the industry itself. Their failure to fulfil important aspects of the five criteria means that, in

---

121 Polan, 'Profile: Frances Taylor Patterson', *Women Film Pioneers Project*: https://wfpp.cdrs.columbia.edu/pioneer/ccp-frances-taylor-patterson

122 Francke, *Script Girls,* 18.

123 Thompson, *Storytelling in the New Hollywood*, 11.

terms of scope, reach and influence, these screenwriting teachers should be regarded, for the purpose of this study, as of secondary importance.

It is with this understanding that I now turn to the screenwriting teachers selected for closer scrutiny. They were individuals whose main focus was to improve the craft of screenwriting. In terms of quality or relevance of content, they embrace all the elements contained in the other works, but with one key difference: all five teachers either fulfil the five criteria or make an outstanding contribution in four. Thus, the impact of their advice both on the industry as a whole and on the screenwriting discourse is likely to have been greater and longer lasting. While the difference between the peripheral and the key screenwriting teachers is relative rather than absolute, I also contend that, because the latter worked as screenwriting teachers to a greater depth and breadth, it is likely that they were more instrumental in significantly shaping the discourse and helping to develop the craft of screenwriting within the industry.

The Five Key Screenwriting Teachers

I contend that five screenwriting teachers in the early film period merit special consideration. Moreover, two of these individuals – Epes Winthrop Sargent and William Lord Wright – appear to have wielded the greatest influence, although Leslie Tufnell Peacocke, Eustace Hale Ball and Henry Albert Phillips also held considerable sway. To support this argument, here I piece together the biographical record of each from existing primary sources and examine important endorsements that the various authorities and commentators of the period gave to them, along with the commendations the key screenwriting teachers themselves gave to each other's work. This evidence will indicate that these particular screenwriting teachers fulfil the criteria almost completely and are likely to have made the greatest contribution to the screenwriting discourse during this period.

Epes Winthrop Sargent (1872–1938)

Epes Winthrop Sargent meets all five criteria. He was a successful writer and a scenario editor, wrote extensively for the trade and fan press, produced a seminal manual that ran to three editions and had significant industry connections.

Soon after beginning his career in amusement trade journalism, Sargent gravitated to become vaudeville editor at the *Dramatic News*, a theatrical journal, which was eventually taken over by the *Daily Mercury*. His caustic and critical reviews of vaudeville acts appeared under the pseudonym 'Chicot'. By the mid-1890s the *Mercury* had been acquired by the *New York Morning Telegraph*, but 'Chicot' was still writing his reviews about lacklustre performances and dishonest business practices. In 1903 Sargent moved to the *New York Evening World* for a brief stint, but by 1905 had left to help Sime Silverman found *Variety*, becoming its associate editor. Within six months he left *Variety* to start up his own theatrical publication, *Chicot's Weekly*, although this was short-lived.

In 1906 Sargent spent a brief period as a press representative and agent and then settled down to short story writing and screenwriting.[124] As vaudeville and early cinema were closely related, it seems logical that Sargent would end up in the movies. However, another influence on his decision may have been that, by around 1910, vaudeville was in decline. As Allen observes, 'By the mid-teens, big-time vaudeville had lost its position as premiere American popular entertainment form – that place taken by the motion picture.'[125] Sargent eventually returned to reviewing entertainment, albeit on a broader basis, in 1930, when he wrote a column for *Variety* and continued to do so until his death in 1938.[126]

---

124 See 'Authors' in John Francis Barry and Sargent, *Building Theatre Patronage: Management and Merchandising* (New York: Chalmers, 1927).

125 Allen, 'Vaudeville and Film', 298.

126 For a cogent summary of Sargent's career, see Azlant, 'The Theory, History and Practice of Screenwriting', 105–111.

Sargent was a prolific short story and novelette writer.[127] An indication of his meticulousness and work rate is contained in Wright's recollection that he possessed 'one of the most complete card index systems known in the business'.[128] Contrary to Norman's modern and somewhat unscholarly assumptions that Sargent was 'the first in the tradition of noted film teachers with no writing credits',[129] Sargent wrote many scenarios. According to a post-script in one of Sargent's articles in *Moving Picture World*, he had authored:

> several hundred stories for Lubin, two for IMP, two for Vitagraph and seven for Edison. Also about half a mile of photoplay advice and several miles of short stories and novelettes.[130]

Other sources are more conservative, but writers did not always receive credits before 1916, making it impossible to be sure of his actual output. His scenarios, mostly split-reel comedy shorts containing elements of slapstick and classic comic misunderstandings, probably exceeded 200 in number.[131] Most of Sargent's scenarios had been produced at Lubin and in 1909 he was appointed their scenario editor; a job he held for about a year and a half.[132] In 1914, with little doubt as to Sargent's versatility and talent as a writer, Grau writes that:

> Mr Sargent's activities are truly prodigious. [...] Scarcely a week ever passes that one of Sargent's photoplays is not released. The Lubin Company has released the greatest number, but at the time of this writing the Edison Company is producing some of the best work this author has ever done. In addition, Sargent contributes

---

127   The *FictionMags Index* lists 33 published short stories by Sargent, http://www.philsp.com/homeville/FMI/s/s4596.htm. Of particular note is a novelette, *Beyond the Banyans* (1909), which tells the story of an explorer encountering evil in the mountains of Africa. Georges Dodds argues that this story is among a number of texts that prepared the advent of Edgar Rice Burroughs's story, *Tarzan of the Apes* (1912), http://www.erbzine.com/mag18/banyans.htm. Sargent also wrote under a number of pseudonyms and contributed several hundred stories to newspapers and magazines. See Azlant, 'Screenwriting for the Early Silent Film', *Film History* 9, (1997): 248.

128   Wright, 'For Photoplay Authors, Real and Near', *NYDM*, 1914 May–Jun 1915, 0709 pdf: *Fulton History*: http://fultonhistory.com/Fulton.html

129   Norman, *What Happens Next,* 65.

130   Sargent, 'The Literary Side of Pictures', *MPW*, July 11, 1914, 202.

131   Sargent has 144 writing credits and one acting credit recorded between 1912 and 1918. See 'Sargent', *IMDbPro*: https://pro-labs.imdb.com/name/nm0765104

132   See 'The Authors' in Barry and Sargent, *Building Theatre Patronage.*

fiction stories galore to the magazines and special articles to magazines and newspapers alike.[133]

Sargent's focus on writing comedy shorts does temper Liepa's evaluation of his scenario-writing ability:

> Despite his elevated self-esteem, [… he] seems to have penned quite pedestrian stories himself […and] the simplicity of Sargent's work contrasts with the lofty stylistic goals he prescribed for the medium.[134]

However, such a focus should not be surprising, given that he came from a vaudeville tradition and had written for this particular market. His writings as a journalist and screenwriting teacher gradually took over as the feature market was developing, which possibly explains why he never wrote features. Oliver Hardy had forged his early career as 'Babe Hardy' by acting in scenarios Sargent had written. At least three of these films are still available: *The Smuggler's Daughter* (1914), *The Servant Girl's Legacy* (1914) and *They Looked Alike* (1915).[135] Despite Liepa's criticism of Sargent, he accepts, when commenting on *The Servant Girl's Legacy*, that the 'story accords perfectly with his show business sensibility towards filmmaking'.[136]

As a vaudevillian journalist, Sargent had learnt his trade well:

> Sargent provides a coherent point of view on […] the development of the comic sketch from the one-act play, the changes in comedy from slapstick to sophistication, and the range of the permissible in language and nudity.[137]

As soon as Sargent began to write scenarios and work as an editor, it was likely he would begin to cast his critical eye over the movie output and write about it. He was, Azlant claims, about to do what he 'had already done for vaudeville, helping to refine the art through intelligent, uncompromising criticism'.[138] This new direction began in

---

133 Robert Grau, *The Theatre of Science: The Volume of Progress and Achievement in the Motion Picture Industry* (New York, Broadway, 1914), 308. Grau was a theatrical agent and renowned critic of the period and his book, published in a limited edition of 3,000, has become a standard reference source for the early cinema period. It details the history and development of motion pictures in America to 1914 and champions the names of pioneers of the industry who would otherwise be forgotten. See Urbanora, 'The Theatre of Science', August 29, 2007 in *The Bioscope*, http://thebioscope.net/2007/03/29/the-theatre-of-science/

134 Liepa, 'Figures of Silent Speech', 15.

135 Oliver Hardy starred in at least 29 scenarios written by Sargent. See *IMDbPro*: https://pro-labs.imdb.com/name/nm0765104

136 Liepa, 'Figures of Silent Speech', 125.

137 Judith Stevens Pratt, 'The Vaudeville Criticism of Epes Winthrop Sargent 1896–1910 (abstract)' (PhD diss., Nebraska University, 1985 *Proquest* UMI 303387823), http://search.proquest.com//docview/303387823

138 Azlant, 'Screenwriting for the Early Silent Film', 248.

earnest in 1909 when he started writing film criticism as 'Chicot' for the *Film Index*, the *Kinematograph and Lantern Weekly* and the *Moving Picture World*, when it absorbed the *Index* in 1911.

Moving Picture World soon established a regular feature on scenario writing, headed by Sargent, to instruct his readers in the craft. While his first articles appeared in October 1910, his column, 'Technique of the Photoplay', was not launched until July 1911. As mentioned earlier in this chapter, even from the opening statements in the first article, Sargent was characteristically clear about the nature of the photoplay: it is 'a distinct dramatic form, […] a story told in action instead of in words' (see Figure 31).[139] This initial series of articles ran until September 1911;[140] Sargent then decided to publish his articles in book form. The column commenced again in mid-December 1911, under the new name, 'The Scenario Writer,' until mid-April 1912 (see Figure 32)[141] when it became 'The Photoplaywright', which continued periodically until 1919 (see Figure 33).[142] In addition, Sargent was managing editor of *Moving Picture World* for a time.

Technique of the Photoplay
By EPES WINTHROP SARGENT

Copyright 1911 by E. W. Sargent. All rights reserved.

Chapter I. The Photoplay and Its Making.

Contrary to the general belief, the photoplay is not pantomime, but a distinct dramatic form, the product of cinematography. It has its own rules of technique and an individuality distinct from pantomime, with its stilted language and rigid construction.

A story is the narration of events in words. Done into dialogue and action, it becomes a drama; substitute the conventional language of pantomime, the arbitrary gestures denoting certain thoughts and emotions, and the drama becomes pantomime. The photoplay is—or should be—related in purely natural action with such small aid as may be had from written or printed explanatory matter thrown upon the screen. The ideal photoplay is told entirely in self-explanatory action, without recourse to letters or other inserts.

The photoplay, then, becomes a story told in action instead of in words, and therefore is written in action instead of dialogue or polished phrase. The author supplies the groundwork of action and idea, but he is dependent upon the director and the actor for proper interpretation and expression.

Most photo-playwrights are familiar only with the filmed presentation of the photoplay. Only a few of the elect have the entree to the studio and editorial office where a knowledge of the possibilities and limitations of the camera may be obtained. The rest write blindly in the hope of achieving result. For the better understanding of the photo-playwright the processes are here described in brief.

scenes occurring in that set are made, the exterior scenes being made before or after the interiors or in the intervals as may be most convenient. No effort is made to follow the proper order of scenes. If the setting for the last scene is the first made ready the last scene is played first and possibly one or two others in the same setting.

These scenes are made at a speed of fifteen or sixteen pictures to the second; the film being passed through the camera by a mechanism which brings the film to a stop at the moment that a revolving shutter moves its opening in front of the lense. The camera contains up to four hundred feet of film at one loading, but any amount of film may be exposed without return to the dark room.

Rehearsal of Scenes.

In rehearsing the scenes the director explains to the players the action of a single scene and this is gone through with until the actors understand their business, then the camera is set going and the scene is taken. Then the next scene is similarly rehearsed. The number of times a scene is rehearsed varies with the director and with the intricacy of the action, five to ten times being an average, though a troublesome scene may be gone over five or ten times as often.

In the field there is often little time to rehearse, but the players run through their parts to get their bearings. Usually the exteriors are made within a few miles of the studio, the players being carried in auto busses, but it not infrequently happens that a small company may be sent hun-

Figure 31: Sargent's first article in his column, 'The Technique of the Photoplay'
Source: *MPW*, July 22, 1911, 108.

---

139   Sargent's column 'Technique of the Photoplay' made its first appearance in *MPW*, July 22, 1911, 108–109.

140   The last edition of this eight-week run of articles appeared in *MPW*, September 9, 1911, 696–697.

141   'The Scenario Writer' first appeared in *MPW*, December 16, 1911, 895–896 and it ran until April 13, 1912, 134–135.

142   'The Photoplaywright' first appeared in *MPW*, April 20, 1912, 226–227 and last appeared in September 13, 1919, 1674.

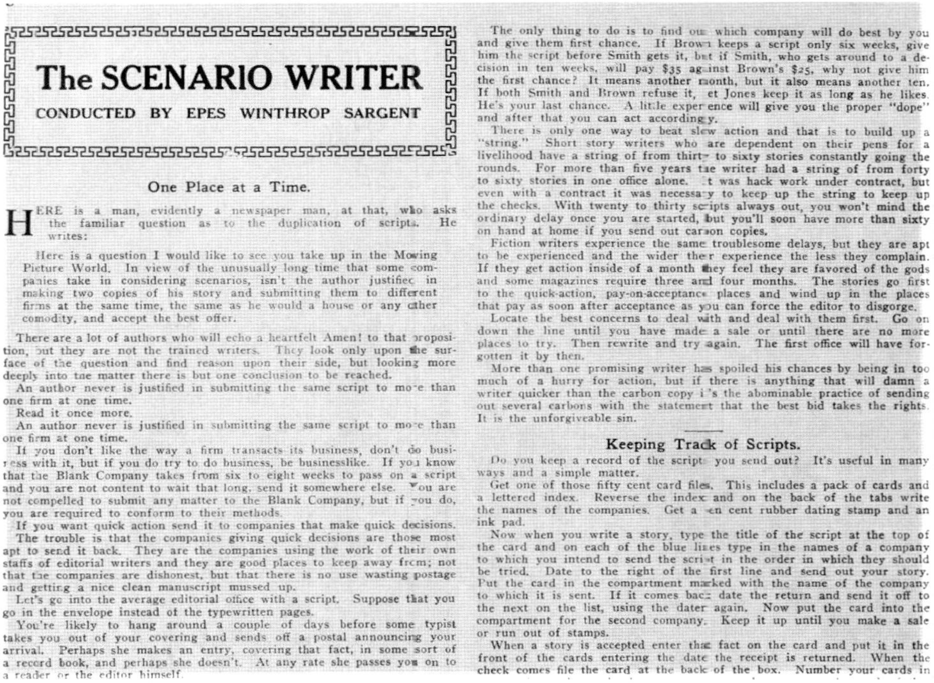

The SCENARIO WRITER
CONDUCTED BY EPES WINTHROP SARGENT

One Place at a Time.

HERE is a man, evidently a newspaper man, at that, who asks the familiar question as to the duplication of scripts. He writes:

Here is a question I would like to see you take up in the Moving Picture World. In view of the unusually long time that some companies take in considering scenarios, isn't the author justified in making two copies of his story and submitting them to different firms at the same time, the same as he would a house or any other comodity, and accept the best offer.

There are a lot of authors who will echo a heartfelt Amen! to that proposition, but they are not the trained writers. They look only upon the surface of the question and find reason upon their side, but looking more deeply into the matter there is but one conclusion to be reached.

An author never is justified in submitting the same script to more than one firm at one time.

Read it once more.

An author never is justified in submitting the same script to more than one firm at one time.

If you don't like the way a firm transacts its business, don't do business with it, but if you do try to do business, be businesslike. If you know that the Blank Company takes from six to eight weeks to pass on a script and you are not content to wait that long, send it somewhere else. You are not compelled to submit any matter to the Blank Company, but if you do, you are required to conform to their methods.

If you want quick action send it to companies that make quick decisions. The trouble is that the companies giving quick decisions are those most apt to send it back. They are the companies using the work of their own staffs of editorial writers and they are good places to keep away from; not that the companies are dishonest, but that there is no use wasting postage and getting a nice clean manuscript mussed up.

Let's go into the average editorial office with a script. Suppose that you go in the envelope instead of the typewritten pages.

You're likely to hang around a couple of days before some typist takes you out of your covering and sends off a postal announcing your arrival. Perhaps she makes an entry, covering that fact, in some sort of a record book, and perhaps she doesn't. At any rate she passes you on to a reader or the editor himself.

The only thing to do is to find out which company will do best by you and give them first chance. If Brown keeps a script only six weeks, give him the script before Smith gets it, but if Smith, who gets around to a decision in ten weeks, will pay $35 against Brown's $25, why not give him the first chance? It means another month, but it also means another ten. If both Smith and Brown refuse it, et Jones keep it as long as he likes. He's your last chance. A little experience will give you the proper "dope" and after that you can act accordingly.

There is only one way to beat slow action and that is to build up a "string." Short story writers who are dependent on their pens for a livelihood have a string of from thirty to sixty stories constantly going the rounds. For more than five years the writer had a string of from forty to sixty stories in one office alone. It was hack work under contract, but even with a contract it was necessary to keep up the string to keep up the checks. With twenty to thirty scripts always out, you won't mind the ordinary delay once you are started, but you'll soon have more than sixty on hand at home if you send out carbon copies.

Fiction writers experience the same troublesome delays, but they are apt to be experienced and the wider their experience the less they complain. If they get action inside of a month they feel they are favored of the gods and some magazines require three and four months. The stories go first to the quick-action, pay-on-acceptance places and wind up in the places that pay as soon after acceptance as you can force the editor to disgorge.

Locate the best concerns to deal with and deal with them first. Go on down the line until you have made a sale or until there are no more places to try. Then rewrite and try again. The first office will have forgotten it by then.

More than one promising writer has spoiled his chances by being in too much of a hurry for action, but if there is anything that will damn a writer quicker than the carbon copy it's the abominable practice of sending out several carbons with the statement that the best bid takes the rights. It is the unforgiveable sin.

Keeping Track of Scripts.

Do you keep a record of the scripts you send out? It's useful in many ways and a simple matter.

Get one of those fifty cent card files. This includes a pack of cards and a lettered index. Reverse the index and on the back of the tabs write the names of the companies. Get a ten cent rubber dating stamp and an ink pad.

Now when you write a story, type the title of the script at the top of the card and on each of the blue lines type in the names of a company to which you intend to send the script in the order in which they should be tried. Date to the right of the first line and send out your story. Put the card in the compartment marked with the name of the company to which it is sent. If it comes back date the return and send it off to the next on the list, using the date again. Now put the card into the compartment for the second company. Keep it up until you make a sale or run out of stamps.

When a story is accepted enter that fact on the card and put it in the front of the cards entering the date the receipt is returned. When the check comes file the card at the back of the box. Number your cards in

Figure 32: An example of Sargent's column, 'The Scenario Writer'
Source: *MPW*, January 6, 1912, 32.

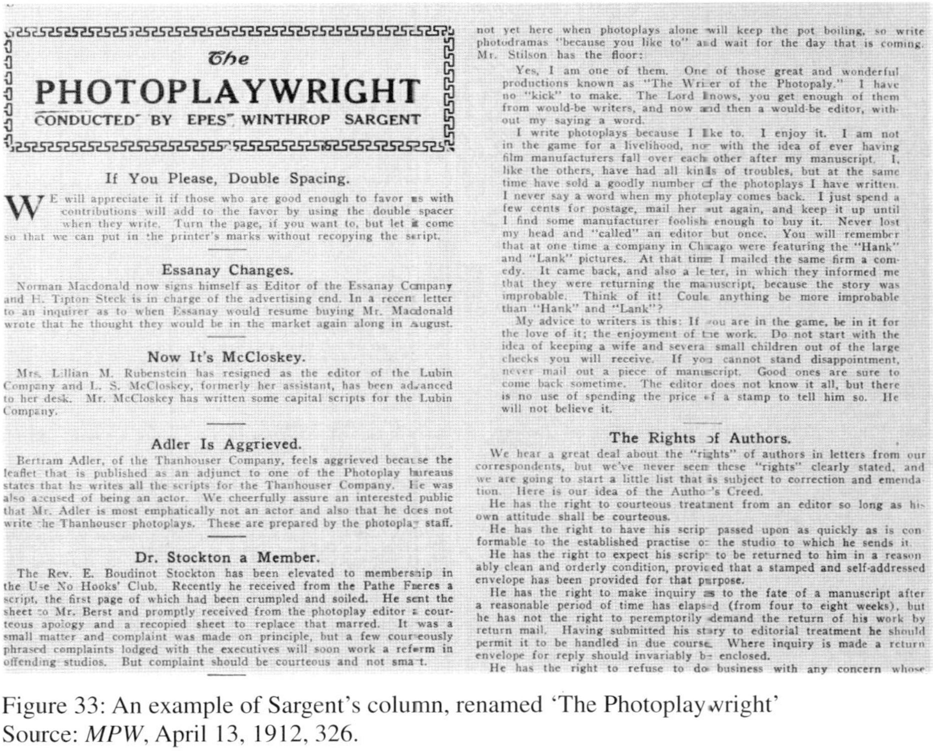

The PHOTOPLAYWRIGHT
CONDUCTED BY EPES WINTHROP SARGENT

If You Please, Double Spacing.

WE will appreciate it if those who are good enough to favor us with contributions will add to the favor by using the double spacer when they write. Turn the page, if you want to, but let it come so that we can put in the printer's marks without recopying the script.

Essanay Changes.

Norman Macdonald now signs himself as Editor of the Essanay Company and H. Tipton Steck in charge of the advertising end. In a recent letter to an inquirer as to when Essanay would resume buying Mr. Macdonald wrote that he thought they would be in the market again along in August.

Now It's McCloskey.

Mrs. Lillian M. Rubenstein has resigned as the editor of the Lubin Company and L. S. McCloskey, formerly her assistant, has been advanced to her desk. Mr. McCloskey has written some capital scripts for the Lubin Company.

Adler Is Aggrieved.

Bertram Adler, of the Thanhouser Company, feels aggrieved because the leaflet that is published as an adjunct to one of the Photoplay bureaus states that he writes all the scripts for the Thanhouser Company. He was also accused of being an actor. We cheerfully assure an interested public that Mr. Adler is most emphatically not an actor and also that he does not write the Thanhouser photoplays. These are prepared by the photoplay staff.

Dr. Stockton a Member.

The Rev. E. Boudinot Stockton has been elevated to membership in the Use No Hooks' Club. Recently he received from the Pathe Freres a script, the first page of which had been crumpled and soiled. He sent the sheet to Mr. Berst and promptly received from the photoplay editor a courteous apology and a recopied sheet to replace that marred. It was a small matter and complaint was made on principle, but a few courteously phrased complaints lodged with the executives will soon work a reform in offending studios. But complaint should be courteous and not smart.

not yet here when photoplays alone will keep the pot boiling, so write photodramas "because you like to" and wait for the day that is coming. Mr. Stilson has the floor:

Yes, I am one of them. One of those great and wonderful productions known as "The Writer of the Photoplay." I have no "kick" to make. The Lord knows, you get enough of them from would-be writers, and now and then a word of defence either, without my saying a word.

I write photoplays because I like to. I enjoy it. I am not in the game for a livelihood, nor with the idea of ever having film manufacturers fall over each other after my manuscript. I, like the others, have had all kinds of troubles, but at the same time have sold a goodly number of the photoplays I have written. I never say a word when my photoplay comes back. I just spend a few cents for postage, mail her out again, and keep it up until I find some manufacturer foolish enough to buy it. Never lost my head and "called" an editor but once. You will remember that at one time a company in Chicago were featuring the "Hank" and "Lank" pictures. At that time I mailed the same firm a comedy. It came back, and also a letter, in which they informed me that they were returning the manuscript, because the story was improbable. Think of it! Could anything be more improbable than "Hank" and "Lank"?

My advice to writers is this: If you are in the game, be in it for the love of it; the enjoyment of the work. Do not start with the idea of keeping a wife and several small children out of the large checks you will receive. If you cannot stand disappointment, never mail out a piece of manuscript. Good ones are sure to come back sometime. The editor does not know it all, but there is no use of spending the price of a stamp to tell him so. He will not believe it.

The Rights of Authors.

We hear a great deal about the "rights" of authors in letters from our correspondents, but we've never seen these "rights" clearly stated, and we are going to start a little list that is subject to correction and emendation. Here is our idea of the Author's Creed.

He has the right to courteous treatment from an editor so long as his own attitude shall be courteous.

He has the right to have his script passed upon as quickly as is conformable to the established practise of the studio to which he sends it.

He has the right to expect his script to be returned to him in a reasonably clean and orderly condition, provided that a stamped and self-addressed envelope has been provided for that purpose.

He has the right to make inquiry as to the fate of a manuscript after a reasonable period of time has elapsed (from four to eight weeks), but he has not the right to peremptorily demand the return of his work by return mail. Having submitted his story to editorial treatment he should permit it to be handled in due course. Where inquiry is made a return envelope for reply should invariably be enclosed.

He has the right to refuse to do business with any concern whose

Figure 33: An example of Sargent's column, renamed 'The Photoplaywright'
Source: *MPW*, April 13, 1912, 326.

On top of all this was a regular column, 'Thinks and Things', that Sargent wrote for *The Photoplay Author* (later called *The Writers' Monthly*) under the pseudonym of 'Gorenflot'. This humorous and chatty, but informative column covered daily concerns, requirements and any relevant industry news for writers. The style indicated his versatility, and the content his knowledge about what was current in the business.[143]

Sargent's contributions to the trade press were sustained, exhaustive and unrivalled in content and became important in the discourse on screenwriting. As Kiel observes, 'Sargent examined the principles of crafting a successful scenario in painstaking detail.'[144] This was another crucial difference between Sargent and those considered to be peripheral to this study.

In his columns, Sargent would also give news about the screenplay trade – about new writing recruits and established writers, rates of pay and the whims and fancies of story editors. These details were of direct relevance to actual and aspiring writers. Wright, a significant trade press contributor himself, makes constant mention of Sargent in his own column, 'For Photoplay Authors, Real and Near', naming him as 'one of Those Who Help You' and tagging him as a 'pioneer of the scriptwriting game'.[145]

Considerable evidence points to Sargent's influence on film companies and his standing within the industry. For example, Kalem's release of the 1912 Pathé film, *Passion Play*, was particularly sensitive due to the religious nature of the subject matter. As one of the *Moving Picture World* columnists who suggested how to handle it, Sargent 'outlined a "dignified and simple" promotional campaign for the film, and […] the film's presentation'.[146] He also suggested that a musical 'quartette […] be used […], though it should be seriously impressed upon the singers that they are accompanying the film and are not rendering a number'.[147] Marks records that this advice was heeded and: 'As envisaged by Sargent and carried out by Kalem, the presentation featured an unusual performing ensemble.'[148]

---

143   Sargent's last contribution to 'Thinks and Things' was in February 1915. Leeds then took over the column in March 1915, approaching it with a more formal style.

144   Kiel, *Early American Cinema in Transition,* 36.

145   Wright, 'For Photoplay Authors, Real and Near', *NYDM*, 1914 May–Jun 1915, 0709 pdf: *Fulton History*: http://fultonhistory.com/Fulton.html

146   Martin Miller Marks, *Music and the Silent Film: Context and Case Studies, 1895–1924* (Oxford: OUP, 1997), 90.

147   Sargent, 'Handling the Kalem Release', *MPW*, October 19, 1912, 233.

148   Marks, *Music and the Silent Film,* 91.

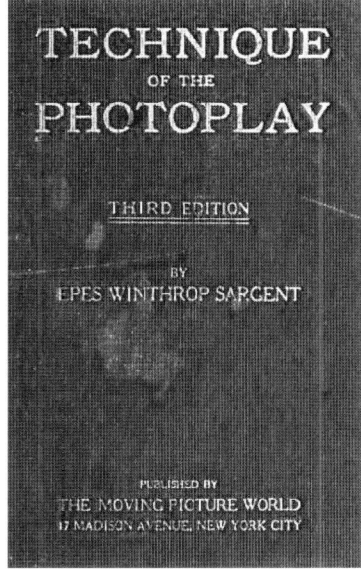
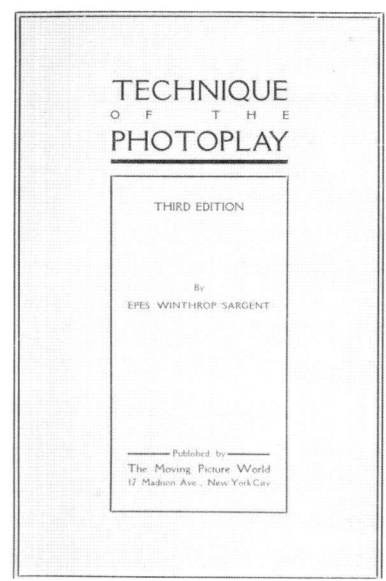

Figure 34: Sargent's *Technique of the Photoplay*, 3rd edition,
book cover and title page
Source: *mediahistoryproject.org.*

According to Grau, the first edition of Sargent's manual, published in 1912, drew considerable readership and there was 'an overwhelming receipt of advance orders' for the 1913 second edition.[149] When the third edition was published in 1916 (see Figure 34), Wright described it as a 'bully good volume' while noting the first and second editions had been 'two mighty excellent works that have aided many a photoplay author near and far.'[150] Grau confirms that:

> As scenario editor and a photoplaywright, Sargent's experience has been of that character to wholly justify his being accepted as an authority on photoplay construction from almost any angle; hence, his first volume on 'The Technique' was widely distributed and favorably reviewed all over the world.[151]

Among the many others to hold Sargent in high esteem were other well-known authors who had written about screenwriting. Freeburg suggests that his own readers should have to hand 'Mr. Epes Winthrop Sargent's *Technique of the Photoplay*, which discusses the practical side of plot building, scenario writing and photoplay filming'.[152] Manual writers

---

149   Grau, *Theatre of Science,* 308.

150   Wright, 'For Photoplay Authors, Near and Far', *NYDM*, 1915 Jul–Aug 1916, 1906.pdf. *Fulton History*: http://fultonhistory.com/Fulton.html

151   Grau, *Theatre of Science,* 308.

152   Freeburg, *Art of Photoplay Making*, The Foreword.

such as Dimick were likewise keen to recommend Sargent's book along with their own,[153] while Thomas, editor of *Photoplay*, states, 'Sargent's *Technique of the Photoplay* (the first edition) is the best book, but the edition is sold out just at the present', indicating its popularity.[154]

Sargent was so widely established in his position that contemporary figures, as well as more recent academic commentators, acknowledge him. Even early film historians such as Jacobs, not known for their coverage of screenwriting, give Sargent's work some credence:

> These magazine articles explaining the principles and technique of movie construction were, although rudimentary, subsequently incorporated in the book *Technique of the Photoplay*, which was one of the first of its kind and which crystallized a method and bred many subsequent scenarists.[155]

Jacobs also recognises that Sargent was one of those trade-paper critics who continually agitated for higher standards and can take credit for the improvement of movie art.[156] Considering the first edition of Sargent's 1912 manual and the extensively revised edition of 1913, Bordwell comments, 'Although other handbooks of film practice preceded his, Sargent's work became a classic in a field that from that point rapidly expanded.'[157] A similar view from Azlant is that the third edition of Sargent's manual is 'exemplary' and worthy of close examination because:

> In the contemporary literature on screenwriting Sargent is consistently regarded as a respected authority, and his manuals are viewed as the best available.[158]

Of all the screenwriting teachers considered in this study, Sargent has received the most attention and recognition from film academics. However, the extent and breadth of his contribution and influence across the industry and the writing community have not been adequately explored or investigated.

One demonstration of the extent of his influence and expertise is that, as well as his regular column for *Moving Picture World*, Sargent wrote 'Advertising for the Exhibitor', which carried useful trade information and advice on how advertising worked best in

---

153 Dimick, *Modern Photoplay Writing,* 392.

154 Arthur W. Thomas, 'The Photoplaywright and His Art', *Photoplay*, August 1914, 85.

155 Jacobs, *Rise of the American Film*, 131.

156 Ibid., 134.

157 Bordwell, Staiger and Thompson, *Classical Hollywood Cinema,* 106–107.

158 Azlant, 'Theory, History and Practice of Screenwriting', 211.

theatres. Much of the information in these articles was published in a book entitled *Picture Theatre Advertising* in 1915 (see Figure 35).[159]

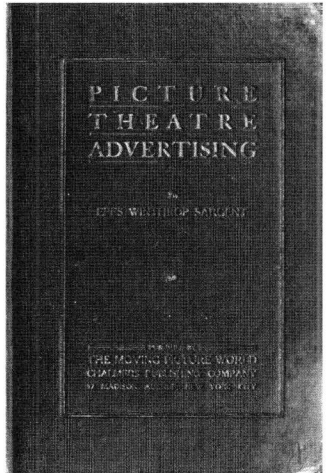

Figure 35: Sargent's *Picture Theatre Advertising*, which included much information from his 'Advertising for the Exhibitor' column
Source: *archive.org*

Activities of Photodramatists Club

The Photodramatists Club, formerly known as the Ed-Au, is making rapid strides toward perfecting an organization which promises to become a power in the photoplay field.

Composed of members, all of whom are recognized screen dramatists, the club boasts an array of talent. The president, Howard Irving Young, formerly responsible for some of Kalem's biggest hits, now a member of the Metro organization, has big plans for the coming year. He is ably assisted by Vice-President Arthur Leeds, co-author with Dr. Esenwein of the text book on photoplay writing, and until recently scenario editor for the Edison company.

At a meeting held Thursday, June 8, plans were formulated for enlarging the club by inviting recognized writers, many of whom are now lending their names to the screen, to join the club which has heretofore confined its membership to established photodramatists and directors only.

An entertainment committee was appointed to have charge of the social side of the club's activities for the coming year. Mrs. L. Case Russell is chairman of this committee, the other members being Edward J. Montagne of the Vitagraph company and C. Doty Hobart, of Famous Players. The club has arranged a trip to the Bayshore studio of the Vitagraph company on the invitation of Mr. Montagne.

After a short address by Mrs. Russell from the point of view of the free-lance writer, the club was treated to a showing of the latest Vitagraph Blue Ribbon feature, "The Destroyers," an adaptation by Mr. Montagne from a story by James Oliver Curwood, directed by Ralph Ince.

Figure 36: 'Activities of Photodramatists Club' article
Source: *Motography*, July 1, 1916, 10.

---

159 Sargent, *Picture Theatre Advertising* (New York: Chalmers, 1915); and Barry and Sargent, *Building Theatre Patronage*. See *OCLC WorldCat* for a full history of Sargent's books and editions, http://www.worldcat.org/search?q=kw%3AEpes+Winthrop+Sargent&fq=yr%3A1900..1938+%3E&qt=advanced&dblist=638

Moreover, Sargent helped to run various film-writing groups in New York, which met on a monthly basis from late 1912 until 1914 and more sporadically up to 1916. Two of the most prominent were the Inquest Club, which Sargent helped to form and was open to all, and the Ed-Au Club. Other branches of the Inquest Club were soon founded in Chicago, Ohio, Boston and Pittsburgh. By 1916 this organisation had been replaced by Photodramatists Inc. (the renamed Ed-Au Club) and, according to the trade press, was '[c]omposed of members, all of whom are recognized screen dramatists' (see Figure 36).[160] In a more detailed history of these clubs, Liepa notes that Sargent's columns provided a focus for announcements about club meetings and writing forums. Some of the best-known scenario writers and industry insiders also attended the clubs, making them important forums for discussion and debate about film form.[161] Wright recalls Sargent's role in starting the Inquest Club:

> We remember in 1913 the formation of the 'Inquest Club', originated by E. Winthrop Sargent, then a staff writer for the old Lubin Film Mfg. Company, now staff writer for the [Moving] Picture World. [...] So far as we know, the Inquest Club was the first regular gathering of the writers of film plays, real and near, ever held.[162]

According to Liepa, Sargent 'often transferred these discussions to his columns, bringing the discourse both to the industry and the wider public'.[163] Another initiative from Sargent was to form the Photoplay Authors' League, which he announced in February 1914; he also became one of its founder members (see Figure 37).[164] Formed to protect the interests of writers, the League exposed false correspondence schools, fought for a copyright bill to include photoplays and demanded payment for authors whose magazine stories were turned into films. Eminent screenwriter and reviewer Frank E. Woods was its first president and its main publication became *The Script*.[165]

---

160 'Activities of Photodramatists Club', *Motography*, July 1, 1916, 10.

161 See Liepa, 'Figures of Silent Speech', 193–200.

162 Wright, *Photoplay Writing*, 217.

163 Liepa, 'Entertaining the Public Option' in *Analyzing the Screenplay*, ed. Nelmes, 15.

164 Sargent, 'The Photoplaywright', *MPW*, March 28, 1914, 1674.

165 Anthony Slide, 'Photoplay Authors' League', in *The New Dictionary of the American Film Industry*, (Maryland: Scarecrow, 1998), 158.

THE PHOTOPLAYWRIGHT
Conducted by EPES WINTHROP SARGENT

A Photoplay League.

FROM Los Angeles comes a letter announcing the formation of The Photoplay Authors' League with the typewritten signatures of those mentioned as the incorporators. To these are added "per E. P." though there is no E. P. in the list of incorporators, however, we shall take it for granted that the signatures are used with authority. The letter follows:

On Friday evening, February 27th, 1914, there was formed an organization known as the Photoplay Authors' League, with Hettie Gray Baker, Wallace C. Clifton, James Dayton, Marc Edmund Jones, W. M. Ritchey, Russell E. Smith, Lois Weber, Rickard Willis, W. E. Wing, and Frank E. Woods as charter members.

It is the purpose of this organization of photoplaywrights to affiliate for the purpose of mutual protection and for the general uplift and advancement of the heretofore only partially recognized art of motion picture play construction, and

To bring together, in an effective and powerful organization of national and international scope, recognized photoplay writers for their mutual benefit and exchange of ideas and experiences, and

To incorporate under the state laws of California, and

To publish as often as possible a bulletin announcing new members, reporting new laws that may be enacted for the benefit of its members, and all photoplay authors, and containing a complete forum for the exchange and dissemination of the experiences and ideas of its members, and

To undertake matters of legal procedure, or any other matters that may arise, for the benefit of its members or as a majority of its members may desire, and to assist in securing whatever legislation may be needed at any time to help photoplay authors secure such rights and privileges as may be denied them

It is not intended that this organization may be of any service whatever in a social way, or to regulate prices, or to influence the sale of scripts, or to take in any way any arbitrary or aggressive stand with manufacturers.

The membership is not a resident one. Non-residents may become members by applying to the secretary, enclosing the dues, and thus signifying their intention. This is a national organization, and is for all recognized photoplay authors wherever their place of residence.

At the Ed-Au.

There was a brisk meeting of the Ed-Au club March 7th, and the interest felt in the organization was shown by the vote to have a meeting April 4th, instead of calling off on account of the dinner March 21st.

C. B. Hoadley read an interesting paper on the visualization of the copyright plays and books. This will be printed later when Pop gets time to prepare copy. In the discussion that ensued it was the sense of the meeting that presently the supply of copyrighted material would be exhausted and the original writers would again get their innings, but those who have given the matter the most careful thought seemed to believe that there will always be a chance for good copyright material as well as original matter, though the present craze for filming anything that ever used to be popular must soon abate. Captain Leslie T. Peacocke spoke for credit on the film and Mrs. Brandon went him one better by declaring that the Ed-Au club should issue a seal which, when affixed to a script would give it preference over the inferior writers. It was clear that she did not represent the opinion of a majority of the members. This writer pointed out that while he was given credit on the film for having written "The Sultan and the Roller Skates," an Edison comedy, the story as filmed was really written by C. J. Williams, the director, who built a sketchy farce into a comedy drama with a marked farcical trend, and expressed his belief that the credit more properly should have gone to Mr. Williams who had taken advantage of opportunity to make a much better story. The majority were strongly in favor of screen credit, arguing that the players were wholly dependent on their popularity, and overlooking the fact that the player presents his personality, while the writer does not.

At the business session Capt. Peacocke was elected to membership, as were John William Kellette, a writer, Carl Gregory, of Princess, Lu Senarens, of Motion Picture Stories and Richard Carroll, who won first prize in the old Universal-Powers contest and who writes scripts when he is not editing the Sewing Machine Times.

For a time it looked as though there would be thirteen members present for the third consecutive time, but the alleged hoodoo was avoided. Those present were President Phil Lang, Treasurer Pop Hoadley, Vice President Mrs. Brandon, Van Buren Powell, Dr. Stockton, Henry Albert Phillips, Edwin M. LaRoche, Monte Katterjohn, Mark Reardon, III., E. M. Wickes, of the Writers' Magazine, Arthur Leeds, of The Photoplay Author, James Cogan, B. P. Schulberg, and E. W. Sargent.

Figure 37: Sargent announces the formation of the Photoplay Authors' League in his column 'The Photoplaywright'
Source: *MPW*, March 28, 1914, 1674.

Writing about such clubs in 1913, Wright suggests that their purpose was to foster closer relationships between authors, to help get writers credited. to influence legislation, to protect photoplays against infringement and plagiarism and to raise the standard of the photoplay or 'the craft'. However, we can see a clear move towards the professionalisation of writing for the screen, as the Photoplay Authors' League required applicants to show that they had 10 produced scripts before they qualified for membership, rather than the six requested by the Ed-Au Club. Nevertheless, Wright claims that '[a]ll these organisations tend to accomplish good, not only to the members, but to the industry in its entirety.'[166]

Perhaps the respect that Sargent engendered in his contemporaries is best encapsulated in the accolade he received from Thomas, the editor of *Photoplay*: 'Sargent has had more experience in photoplay work, editorial writing and criticizing, than any other man of our acquaintance.'[167] In a similar vein, Wright comments:

---

166   Wright, 'For Photoplay Authors, Real and Near', *NYDM*, 1913 Mar–Apr 1914, 2235.pdf. *Fulton History*: http://fultonhistory.com/Fulton.html

167   Thomas, 'The Photoplaywright and His Art', *Photoplay*, August 1912, 88.

> [Sargent] has every branch of the industry at his finger ends and he has possibly accomplished more for the struggling picture playwright [...] through practical instruction than any other writer in the same line of work, for he has been in the business since its inception.[168]

When replying to a letter that asked, 'How would you go about it to become an author of photoplays?', Sargent finishes his long explanation of the process of film education with a recommended reading list: 'The books by William Lord Wright and Eustace Hale Ball, [... and] Phillips', *The Plot of the Short Story.*' In one statement, therefore, he endorses three out of the four others to whom I have devoted this study.[169] Given the apparent reputation and high regard in which Sargent was held across the industry, his backing of other screenwriting teachers is another indicator of their potentially major contribution to the screenwriting discourse.

William Lord Wright (1879–1947)

William Lord Wright also meets all five criteria. He was a prolific writer, headed a scenario department, wrote for both the trade and fan press, published three manuals and was employed by a studio as a writer and producer, from the silent era until well into the sound era.

A journalist by background, Wright initially worked in a number of US cities writing many magazine features.[170] By 1915 he was writing scenarios for the Selig Polyscope Company, which became the start of a long and illustrious career in the film business. Wright was truly prolific, writing many of Selig's early successful shorts; he moved on to join Pathé Exchange as chief story editor. He then worked for Universal Studios, becoming one of its top writers and heading the scenario department for serials and

---

168 Wright, 'William Lord Wright's Page', *MPN*, May 25, 1912, 12–13.

169 Sargent, 'The Photoplaywright', *MPW*, February 7, 1914, 670–671.

170 'Wright' in *Motion Picture Studio Directory and Trade Annual* (New York: Motion Picture News, 1916), 158.

Westerns.[171] This contract was renewed in 1926 and Wright continued to work for Universal until the early 1930s.[172]

Wright's first column for the trade press, possibly inspired by Sargent's, was in *Moving Picture News* (which became *Motion Picture News* in 1913), where he eventually became an editor. Beginning in November 1911 as 'Wm. Lord Wright's Page', it dealt with general movie topics, reviews and comment, with an occasional emphasis on writing scenarios.[173] The column soon grew to more than a page in length, as an adjunct appeared in February 1912 under the heading, 'For Those Who Worry O'er Plots and Plays', which dealt more specifically with writing issues. These columns were eventually integrated into one extended column that ran until March 1914 (see Figure 38).[174]

Among his other contributions, Wright wrote for *The Motion Picture Story Magazine* (renamed *Motion Picture Magazine* in 1914) from 1912 to 1919, on most things filmic, and some of these articles were on writing scenarios.[175] He also wrote periodically for *The Photo Playwright* (see Figure 39) [176] and *The Photoplay Author,* where in one article he comments on the use of the synopsis and other topical writing issues.[177] In 1914, Grau bestows upon him the highest of praise:

> there is no better qualified writer on the subject in this country today. […] [A]s editor of Moving Picture News, Mr. Wright conducted two distinct departments which represented the best subject matter contained in that publication, while his contributions to the Motion Picture Story Magazine have been, and still are, a feature of that amazingly successful publication.[178]

---

171 According to *IMDbPro*, Wright had 24 credits for writing, producing and script supervision. Of note are *The Indians are Coming* (1930), a sound film based on the life of Buffalo Bill (William F. Cody), which is alleged to have saved Universal's serial format into the sound era; and *Perils of the Wild* (1925), a serial directed by Francis Ford. See *IMDbPro*: https://pro-labs.imdb.com/name/nm0942936/

172 'Wright Signs New Universal Contract', *Exhibitors Trade Review,* February 27, 1926, 8.

173 See 'Wm. Lord Wright's Page', *MPN*, November 18, 1911 for the column's first appearance.

174 Wright, 'For Those Who Worry O'er Plots and Plays', *MPN*, February 17, 1912, 12–13 and *MPN*, March 14, 1914, 31–32 for its first and last appearance.

175 Wright, 'The Spark of Genius', September 1912, 135–36 and 'The Tremolo Touch', December 1912, 130 in *MPSM*.

176 Wright, 'The Idea is the Thing', September/October 1912, 11–13 and 'The Successful Plot', October/November 1912, 9 in *Photo Playwright*.

177 Wright, 'Looking Over the Field', *Photoplay Author*, October 1914, 117–119.

178 Grau, *Theatre of Science,* 311.

WILLIAM LORD WRIGHT'S PAGE

THE CAMERA MAN

The Camera Man! The Camera Man!
  What kind of a man is he?
He carries a box and dodges rocks
  And combats adversity!
Scenes of sorrow, stories of pain,
In hail and snow and sleet and rain
Looking for latest pictures to "can"
    Is the Camera Man!

The Camera Man! The Camera Man!
  He is a man of nerve!
Right in front he performs his "stunt,"
  Faithfully to serve.
On battlefield, in palace grand,
This individual takes his stand.
He's never in the "also ran"—
    The Camera Man!

The Camera Man! The Camera Man!
  He is a man of might.
Jolly and frank, he turns the crank
  When there's a thing in sight!
Deeds unwritten on history's page.
He is the product of later age.
None more worthy among us than
    The Camera Man!

       *   *   *

The people of Cleveland, Ohio, co-operated with the moving picture exhibitors on Tuesday, January 23d, and as a result the Associated Charities of the "Sixth City" received a handsome addition to their fund upon which there are urgent and numerous demands this season. One cent out of every paid admission on the Benefit Day in every moving picture theatre in Cleveland was turned over to the Charitable Organization. Cleveland Local of the League of Motion Picture Exhibitors of America decided upon the charitable enterprise, and a new record of daily attendance was set on that day. There were special programs of picture plays and extra features everywhere. Many were not satisfied with paying the usual admission to the theatres and the extra sums handed over were turned into the Associated Charities coffers by the picture exhibitors. There are 120 moving picture theatres in Cleveland and suburbs and the average seating capacity is figured at 425. If every theatre filled its seats twice on January 23d it meant a total attendance of 102,000 people. The "Forest City" boasts of a set of enterprising and public-spirited picture exhibitors, and that their efforts to assist worthy causes in Cleveland are appreciated goes without saying. More power to them, is the wish of the Moving Picture News.

       *   *   *

The motion picture shows of Youngstown, Ohio, have come under the ban of the "reform" city administration. The Mayor has ordered that the Sunday entertainments must be only between 12:30 p. m. and 9:30 p. m. The rest of the time, the boys and girls can roam the streets to their hearts' content.
Zero weather cut little figure in a majority of the picture shows in the smaller cities of Ohio, Indiana and Illinois, according to reports we have compiled. The fact that so many people did attend is evidence of the hold cinematography has upon the public. The houses, as a rule, were as comfortable, and the shows just as good, as on a night in June.

       *   *   *

Newspaper paragraphers' sayings on the pictures during the past week:
"The public faces a new terror. One man laughed himself to death in a moving picture show."
"Not one of the twenty greatest men of the world got his inspiration at a moving picture show. This is strange."

"Many of the foreign moving picture films represent drinking scenes, and the bottles are usually a quart and a half size."
"Chicago school boys ran away from home proposing to pose in 'Wild West films.' Probably they could do as well as some of the near-cowboys and Indians inflicted upon us."

       *   *   *

Man wants little here below,
  But he wants that little long.
This may be one reason for
  The Illustrated Song.

Little drops of perspiration,
  Little grains of sand
Are both essential qualities
  In Moving Picture Land.

It's easy enough to be pleasant
  When things go the way that's glad;
But the man worth while is the one who
    can smile
  When the picture show is bad.

       *   *   *

The Isthmus of Panama is picture crazy. This is the latest information received, not only from Government sources but in the letters home from the thousands of Yankees who are now engaged in digging Uncle Samuel's big ditch. It is stated that the principal medium of entertainment along the Isthmus is cinematography. It should be encouraging to those manufacturers who are working for the uplift of the picture to know, too, that the classic script is greatly favored. Word from the Isthmus is to the effect that such films as "David Copperfield," "Enoch Arden," et al., are packing the picture play houses.

       *   *   *

The assertions that the public press was antagonistic to the moving picture, once so often repeated, is happily checked. In reality, the newspapers of the United States have accomplished a great deal for cinematography. Quick to criticise, the better class of journalism has also been ready to commend. Following the leadership of the Moving Picture News, the newspapers attacked the suggestive and the exaggerated in picturedom and then took up the crusade for the educational film. Such newspapers as the Chicago Tribune, Cleveland Leader, Cincinnati Times-Star, New York World and Journal and others are giving wide prominence to the moving picture industry, and several of these newspapers conduct Sunday departments devoted to news of the cinematograph industry. The newspapers, those worthy of being called newspapers, are helping along the good cause by every means in their power.

FOR THOSE WHO WORRY O'ER PLOTS AND PLAYS

Hoadley Successful

C. B. Hoadley, who won a prize of $50 in the Imp Films Company Scenario Contest, is a former editor and professional script writer. He lives in Weehawken, N. J. Hoadley has many friends among authors, and they will rejoice over his success.

Roughly Handled

An author forwarded us a comedy script the other day that had just been returned from a certain editorial office. On the back, written in lead pencil, were comments of readers as follows: "Very good comedy," then another wrote "Fair," and then the final reader wrote on the back in indelible pencil, 'Decline.' The writer in question has a logical protest coming. He had prepared the manuscript carefully, paid $1 for having the story typewritten, and had enclosed return

Figure 38: Wright's article on 'The Camera Man' in his first column is followed by a section called 'For Those Who Worry O'er Plots and Plays'
Source: *MPN*, February 17, 1912, 12–13.

The Idea is The Thing

By William Lord Wright, Author of "Twixt Loyalty and Love,"
"For The Sunday Edition," and Many Others

HE play's the thing—but so is the idea. One must have a striking idea or situation before the picture-play can be successfully written. The present consensus of opinion among the pictureplay editors is that many have eyes and see not, and have ears that hear not. The elusive idea is here, there and everywhere. The plot-germ for a good picture-play may be at the dooryard, and all the while the ambitious author is pursuing a frantic serach elsewhere for his or her inspiration.

"I've got an idea," exclaims the author, and he chortles with glee. Then dismay shadows his countenance for the inspiration has fled.

The elusive idea—the hope that remains in Pandora's Box! The idea is always with us and always fleeting; it is the Tantalus of the pictureplaywright, the actor, and the director.

The simplest idea for a story is the narrative of some queer thing that has happened in the town or neighborhood; a thought germ quickened into life through reading something that appeals; but there is also the world under our feet and above our heads. Uncanny things, extraordinary things, queer things are stirring all around us if we have the eyes to see them or the ears to hear them as unusual or interesting events or complications.

Figure 39: Wright's article on 'The Idea is The Thing'
Source: *The Photo Playwright*, September/October 1912, 11.

In the spring of 1914, Wright left *Motion Picture News* to become editor of the Photoplaywrights' Department of the *New York Dramatic Mirror* and write a new weekly column, 'For Photoplay Authors, Real and Near'. The editorial announcement of this new departure was marketed as a positive coup:

> TO PHOTOPLAYWRIGHTS! - We have discovered since announcing our new Department that the friends and admirers of Mr. William Lord Wright number thousands and that they can be found in every section of this country.[179]

Readers were reminded in every issue that 'Mr. William Lord Wright will be pleased to answer all personal inquiries by mail', as long as they included a self-addressed envelope. This is perhaps indicative of Wright's phenomenal work rate and his intention to engage with the public on all matters of writing.[180]

---

179 Editorial announcement, 'To Photoplaywrights' in Wright, 'For Photoplay Authors, Real and Near', *NYDM*, 1913 Mar-Apr 1914, 2476 pdf: *Fulton History*: http://fultonhistory.com/Fulton.html

180 Wright, 'For Photoplaywrights, Real and Near', *NYDM*, 1915 Jul-Aug 1916, 0148.pdf: *Fulton History*: http://fultonhistory.com/Fulton.html

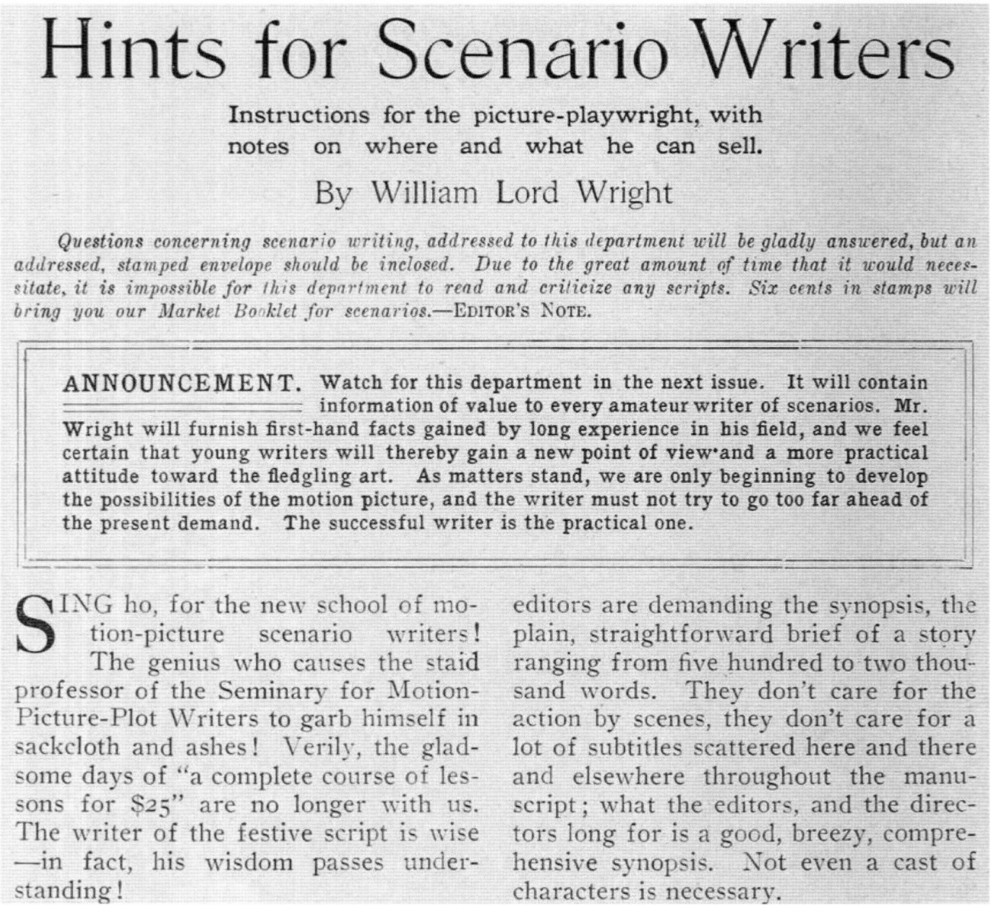

Hints for Scenario Writers

Instructions for the picture-playwright, with notes on where and what he can sell.

By William Lord Wright

Questions concerning scenario writing, addressed to this department will be gladly answered, but an addressed, stamped envelope should be inclosed. Due to the great amount of time that it would necessitate, it is impossible for this department to read and criticize any scripts. Six cents in stamps will bring you our Market Booklet for scenarios.—EDITOR'S NOTE.

ANNOUNCEMENT. Watch for this department in the next issue. It will contain information of value to every amateur writer of scenarios. Mr. Wright will furnish first-hand facts gained by long experience in his field, and we feel certain that young writers will thereby gain a new point of view and a more practical attitude toward the fledgling art. As matters stand, we are only beginning to develop the possibilities of the motion picture, and the writer must not try to go too far ahead of the present demand. The successful writer is the practical one.

SING ho, for the new school of motion-picture scenario writers! The genius who causes the staid professor of the Seminary for Motion-Picture-Plot Writers to garb himself in sackcloth and ashes! Verily, the gladsome days of "a complete course of lessons for $25" are no longer with us. The writer of the festive script is wise—in fact, his wisdom passes understanding!

editors are demanding the synopsis, the plain, straightforward brief of a story ranging from five hundred to two thousand words. They don't care for the action by scenes, they don't care for a lot of subtitles scattered here and there and elsewhere throughout the manuscript; what the editors, and the directors long for is a good, breezy, comprehensive synopsis. Not even a cast of characters is necessary.

Figure 40: Wright's column, 'Hints for Scenario Writers'
Source: *Picture-Play Magazine*, December 1917, 246.

Commenting on Wright's joining *The New York Dramatic Mirror* and his new column, Grau extends his positive view:

> in 1914 the editorial staff in this department was materially augmented by William Lord Wright, long contributing to various trade issues and magazines and a recognized authority on all scenario questions.[181]

It seems that Sargent and Wright knew each other well and were friends. Sargent refers to Wright as 'Bill' and the nickname 'Willord' on updating readers about his work in Chicago. Apparently holding Wright in high regard, he comments, 'Bill not only knows how to tell you how to do it, but if he has to he can jump in as overflow man and do it himself.'[182] When Wright's work with the *New York Dramatic Mirror* ended in

---

181   Grau, *Theatre of Science,* 253.

182   Sargent, 'The Photoplaywright', *MPW*, February 6, 1915, 821–822.

1917, Sargent laments in his own column, 'Wright quits Mirror', believing this would terminate his work as a screenwriting teacher.[183] However, by December of that year Wright had joined *Picture-Play Magazine* to write another column, 'Hints for Scenario Writers' (see Figure 40).[184] From May to November 1919 he also assumed responsibility for another department, 'The Picture Oracle', in the same publication, which focused on questions and answers about the screen.[185] In 1921, after 10 years of writing columns on screenwriting, he finally stopped writing for the fan and trade press in order to focus on his work with Selig and Universal.

Wright wrote three manuals. The first, *The Art of Writing Scenarios,* was initially advertised in February 1911, although the book itself has now been lost.[186] After it sold out quickly, the second edition was published in-house by *Moving Picture News* and offered for $2 or $1, with a yearly subscription. Full-page advertisements in *Moving Picture News* with endorsements from major film companies such as Essanay and IMP lauded its merits (see Figure 41).[187] Although only 30 pages in length, the book's contents seem to have been highly respected. In the words of one reviewer, 'We invite all our readers in this department of dramatic work, to get a copy of his book and study the formula he gives.' He does add a note of caution, however, to the effect that talent is required and no amount of study will replace it:

> The poet is born not made. So we believe is the scenario writer. Still, for the benefit of those who are not born and who think they can be made, Mr. Wright's book should be of great value.[188]

The Motion Picture Story was published in 1914. Sargent pays 'Wright's Second' manual high compliments:

> Mr. Wright not only offers sound advice, but he avoids the erroneous information that mars some otherwise helpful publications. He writes fluently and understandingly and with comprehensive knowledge of his subject.[189]

---

183 Sargent, 'The Photodrama', *MPW*, March 10, 1917, 1562.

184 Wright took over a column from Clarence J. Caine, 'Hints for Scenario Writers' in *Picture-Play Magazine,* December 1917, 246–253 and continued until July 1921, 8, 10–11.

185 See Wright, 'The Picture Oracle', *Picture-Play Magazine*, May 1919, 142 and November 1919, 86 and 88.

186 Advertisements in February 1911 are proof of its publication in late 1910. See advertisement in *MPW*, February 18, 1911, 385.

187 Wright, *The Art of Writing Scenarios* (Chicago: Cloud, 1st ed., 1911 and Cinematograph, 2nd ed., 1911). There is some confusion over the title as it is also called *The Art of Scenario Writing*. See advertisement in *MPN*, January 6, 1912, 39.

188 'The Art of Writing Scenarios', *MPW*, February 25, 1911, 419.

189 Sargent, 'The Photodrama', *MPW*, July 18, 1914, 425.

THE ART OF Scenario Writing
Second Edition   By WILLIAM LORD WRIGHT

The MOVING PICTURE NEWS has secured the sole right to republish this standard work on Scenario writing, and offers it as a premium to all new subscribers of $2.00 for one year.

ART OF SCENARIO WRITING, separately, $1.00, post free.

Read what the *Moving Picture World* of February 25th, 1911, says of this excellent aid:—

The Art of Writing Scenarios

By William Lord Wright. Author of "Twixt Loyalty and Love," "Simon Kenton," etc., etc. Published by the Scenario Instruction Publishing Co., Bellefontaine, Ohio. Price $1.00.

In a very interesting series of articles published in our pages last month, Mr. G. R. Craw told the aspiring scenario author how to write scenarios. Those articles have been favorably commented upon as being of great practical value. Now comes Mr. W. Lord Wright with a little book of about 30 pages which still further adds to our knowledge of a subject that has perplexed many would-be moving picture authors, namely: How to set about work; how to acquire its technique; how, in fact, to prepare goods suitable for the market.

Mr. Wright, who is a successful scenario writer, first of all points out what is in demand by moving picture makers. Then he indicates what is not wanted. After reviewing the function of the scenario editor, he gives some of his own experiences, his failure and his successes. Then we come to some practical advice. He tells the author how to get ideas; where to market the completed scenario; how it should be written and presented, winding up by printing a sample scenario as a guide. Finally, he points out the value of action in this branch of dramatic work, and takes the view that though unhonored, the moving picture scenario writer may some day come into his own in the way of publicity, fame and fortune. We hope he will, though we think this agreeable state of things a long way off.

Meanwhile, we welcome Mr. Wright's little book just as we welcomed Mr. Craw's articles. These things relieve us of some responsibility. We are often asked how a scenario should be written; where it should be marketed and how much money there is in it! Mr. Wright answers all these questions for us. We invite all our readers who are interested in this department of dramatic work, to get a copy of this book and study the formula that he gives. Of course, it is one thing to give a formula for a moving picture scenario, or plays, or a novel. These things may be delivered to managers technically correct in every detail; and yet lacking the one essential which no book on earth can teach: The selection of a theme which will get over; this is the divine afflatus referred to long ago by the author of the phrase: Poeta mascitur non fit: The poet is born, not made. So we believe is the scenario writer. Still, for the benefit of those who are not born and who think they can be made, Mr. Wright's book should be of great value. It will sell well on account of that. It may have a negative value, too, in that it may possibly act as a deterrent to many people who think they can write scenarios and cannot realize their unfitness for the work. There are two or three books extant, and they have run through numerous editions on how to write plays. It is not on record that any playwright who has succeeded during the last quarter of a century, traces any of his success to these manuals, which, perhaps, have been instrumental in diminishing the output of unsuitable plays. It is no easy thing to write a good play; it is no easy thing to write a good scenario. So we hope Mr. Wright's book will encourage the aspirant who aspires to some reasonable hope of success, will discourage those who have no fitness for this form of work. There are too many of the latter kind in the moving picture field to-day.

Ask these authorities what they think of the book. GILES R. WARREN, Author, Playwright, Editor, Lubin Mfg. Co.; C. B. HOADLEY, Editor Scenarios, Imp Company; HORACE VINTON, Author, Editor, Shamrock Company. We have endorsements on file from THE ESSANAY FILM COMPANY, THE POWERS COMPANY, CHAMPION COMPANY, THE IMP COMPANY and THE AMERICAN COMPANY. Also dozens of unsolicited testimonials from writers who have been helped by this work.

THE ART OF SCENARIO WRITING contains a sample scenario recommended as the best form, by GILES R. WARREN, who is acknowledged as one of the most successful and original scenario editors of the present day.

"THE WHOLE SECRET IN A NUTSHELL"

SECOND EDITION IS LIMITED! Get it promptly! REMEMBER THIS IS AN ORIGINAL, not one adapted, a copied, or a plagiarized work. FROM JUST ONE PURCHASER. This booklet cost me a Dollar: The investment netted me over $100.00 in marketable manuscripts. (Name furnished on application.)

CINEMATOGRAPH PUBLISHING CO., 30 West 13th St., N.Y.

Figure 41: Advertisement for the second edition of Wright's first manual, *The Art of Scenario Writing* Source: *MPN*, January 6, 1912, 39.

Wright's final offering, *Photoplay Writing*, published in 1922, was a summation of all he had learnt. It was used as a supplementary text in the New York Institute of Photography, which was founded in 1910 and still exists today.[190] Three of the other key screenwriting teachers, Sargent, Peacocke and Ball (misprinted as Hall), endorsed this 240-page book in an advertisement (see Figure 68 in Chapter 6).[191] The fact that they gave such recommendations and lavished praise on each other's work might suggest that they engaged in mutual back-scratching in order to boost their own reputations, and this is certainly possible. However, as demonstrated in this study, the same screenwriting teachers also received accolades from a broad base of admirers and numerous sources, lending weight to the notion that these views of their work were widely held.

As well as being a prominent member of the Ed-Au Club, along with Sargent, Wright was elected as one of the two vice presidents of the Photoplay Authors' League at its first annual meeting in 1915. He would work under its president Frank E. Woods and alongside board of control member, D. W. Griffith (see Figure 42).[192] Adding to his many

Figure 42: Officers of the Photoplay Authors' League
Source: *MPW*, July 10, 1915, 258.

190   The cover of Wright's 1922 manual, *Photoplay Writing*, states it was 'used as a supplementary text in the New York Institute of Photography'.

191   'The Motion Picture Story' (advertisement), *MPW*, August 14, 1915, 1184.

192   'Photoplay Authors' League', *MPW*, July 10, 1915, 268.

respected roles, he was asked, along with Sargent, to judge writing contests.[193] Wright also toiled to achieve copyright protection for photoplay authors by working with Congress on a new law and campaigning tirelessly against state censorship of the film industry.[194]

Captain Leslie Tufnell Peacocke (1891–1941)

Leslie Tufnell Peacocke is another who meets all five criteria. He was an accomplished writer and scenario editor. He wrote exclusively for the fan press and his manual was published in more than one edition. Peacocke was also an actor, director and producer.

Born in India and educated at Eton, Peacocke trained as an army officer at Sandhurst; he saw action in a number of military campaigns.[195] These exploits no doubt furnished him with inspiration for his many scenarios. While in India, Peacocke began writing for the *Irish Times* as a military correspondent, as well as writing plays for his regimental theatre company, even performing them before the Viceroy.[196] He travelled to the USA in 1899, where he initially worked in vaudeville and wrote articles for the *Los Angeles*

---

193   Wright and Sargent sat on a panel of judges for the Vitagraph Contest, in which the challenge was to write a suitable ending for *The Diamond Mystery* (1913); over 3,000 manuscripts were submitted. See 'The Great Diamond Mystery', *MPSM*, April 1913, 78.

194   'Scenario Copyright Law in View', *MPN*, April 4, 1914, 22; and Wright, 'Censors a Costly Luxury for Ohio', *MPN*, May 30, 1914, 25–26.

195   Peacocke served as a British Army captain in India, Burma, Africa and China and he also spent time with the French Foreign Legion fighting the Turks in Greece. He was a colourful character with a thirst for adventure and even escaped after falling into enemy hands. He had a sabre scar on his face to prove it.

196   Biographical details compiled from the following articles: Frederick James Smith, 'The Evolution of the Motion Picture, An Interview with Captain Leslie T. Peacocke, special Scenario Writer with the Universal Company', *NYDM*, 1913 Mar–Apr 1914, 0771.pdf: *Fulton History*: http://fultonhistory.com/ Fulton.html,_'This is the Man', *Photoplay*, April 1915, 117 and 'Captain Leslie T. Peacocke', *MPW*, July 11, 1914, 238.

Times. An eccentric, engaging and exceptionally literate individual,[197] Peacocke became a fecund writer with many novels, poems, plays and short stories to his name.

His rise to prominence was recorded in the *New York Dramatic Mirror* in 1913, which names him as 'special scenario writer with the Universal Company'.[198] Peacocke became very productive within a relatively short period between 1911 and 1923, becoming a highly successful scenario writer with allegedly more than 350 produced scenarios to his name.[199] He wrote for a number of the new stars of the screen, notably the 'Biograph Girl', Florence Lawrence (Chapter 2).[200]

Although Peacocke's 1914 scenario *Neptune's Daughter* was costly to produce, Laemmle was confident enough in Peacocke's skills to give it the green light. Herbert Brenon, who, according to Koszarski, would go on to be one of the most successful silent movie directors in the 1920s, directed it.[201] The film was a smash hit and Katterjohn, a former Universal scenario editor, considered that 'by writing an original motion picture play [...] and then by doing it into fiction, Peacocke had achieved 'greater success than ninety per cent of all the so-called best sellers' (see Figure 43).[202] Up until that point, scenario writers were not regarded as being in the same class as established writers of novels and plays because film did not have the status of an art form. Katterjohn comments that *Neptune's Daughter*:

---

197   Monte M. Katterjohn describes a convivial meeting with the chain-smoking Peacocke after a performance of *Neptune's Daughter* at the Globe Theatre in New York. Peacocke, whom Katterjohn respectfully dubs the 'master playwright', had viewed his own film 'many times' so he could 'remedy any faults' with 'technique'. See Katterjohn, 'Captain Leslie T. Peacocke: And What He Thinks is in Store for the Picture Play', *Movie Pictorial*, August 15, 1914, 16–17 and 32. He jokingly explained that his reason for returning to acting in the film *Betty Be Good* (1917) was that he had 'amassed a total of 42 waistcoats of which he was eager to give the public the benefit'. See *Photoplay*, August 1917, 109.

198   Smith, 'The Evolution of the Motion Picture', *NYDM*, 1913 Mar–Apr 1914, 0771.pdf: *Fulton History*: http://fultonhistory.com/Fulton.html

199   Figures on just how prolific Peacocke was as a scenario writer vary greatly. According to *IMDbPro*, he only had 65 credits (58 writing, 19 directing and 10 acting), of which over 20 are features. See https://pro-labs.imdb.com/name/nm0668813/. However, a biographical extract in 1914 records 338 scenarios. See *MPW*, July 11, 1914, 238. By 1915, *Photoplay* records it as 400 works. See *Photoplay*, April 1915, 117. A year later, in 1916, it is still recorded as over 400, but rises to a staggering 600 scenarios by 1917 and is recorded as the same for 1918. See the *Motion Picture Studio Directory and Trade Annual*, 1916, 134; April 12, 1917, 144 and 1918, 188.

200   Florence Lawrence appeared in *The Closed Door* (1913), *The Girl and Her Money* (1913), *The False Bride* (1914) and *Face on the Screen* (1917) written by Peacocke. See *IMDbPro*: https://pro-labs.imdb.com/name/nm0668813/

201   Herbert Brenon tried to top his success on *Neptune's Daughter* by working with William Fox on an epic sequel, *A Daughter of the Gods* (1915–1916), which was not entirely successful. He went on to work for Paramount and was named best director of 1927–28 in a *Film Daily* critics' poll. See Koszarski, *Evening's Entertainment*, 220–222.

202   Monte M. Katterjohn, 'Captain Leslie T. Peacocke', *Movie Pictoria*', August 15, 1914, 16–17 and 32.

16   THE MOVIE PICTORIAL   *August 15, 1914*

Captain Leslie T. Peacocke

And What He Thinks is in Store for the Picture Play

By Monte M. Katterjohn

ILLUSTRATED WITH PHOTOGRAPHS

ENTIRELY too much has been written and published about the invasion of famous authors and well-known playwrights in the field of the photoplay, and entirely too little about the men and women who have been steady contributors to the art of the photo drama since the inception of motion pictures.

That Jack London, Rex Beach, Eleanor Gates, Charles Klein, Cyrus Townsend Brady, Booth Tarkington, Louis Joseph Vance, and a hundred other as equally noted authors, novelists and playwrights have been converted to the movies has been cause for much comment and speculation by both press and public.

Picture makers are now indulging in a wild scramble for stories by big authors. What they seek is a big name and a previously advertised title. They are willing to spend enormous sums of money for literary masterpieces which have seen their heyday.

The producers have pushed aside, or seem to have forgotten, the photo playwrights who turn out never less than one successful picture plot each week for the alleged established writers with reputations. And these reputable writers —they were in a decline until the motion picture play came along and opened up a new channel of revenue. They are building summer homes and buying bungalows in California with the royalty money paid them by seemingly mad manufacturers of films for their

than one hundred dollars a week, no matter how much material he produces, nor how good, though he is expected to think up four new stories every month. The old play or old novel brings a sum equivalent to twice the staff scenario writer's salary, be it of one, two, or three-reel length.

Picture manufacturers maintained up to a few months ago that the scenario "plugger" couldn't strike the stride with the famous author. Along came Captain Leslie T. Peacocke and set their notions about plays and plots topsy-turvy. He reversed things by writing an original motion picture play, "Neptune's Daughter," and then doing it into fiction, and with both, achieving greater success than ninety per cent of all the so-called best sellers. To a degree, Marguerite Bertsch and Elaine Sterne, women, have accomplished this same supposedly impossible thing, though there is still a doubt as to the success of their offerings. Miss Bertsch is editor of scenarios for the Vitagraph Company of America and has written an original six-reel comedy entitled "Uncle John." Miss Sterne, a free lance photo playwright, recently won the thousand dollar prize in the Vitagraph Scenario Contest with an original story entitled "The Sins of the Mothers." And it is to be noted that more than a hundred famous authors, novelists and playwrights were competing. The scenarios of both Miss Bertsch and Miss Sterne are now under production.

But of Captain Leslie T. Peacocke and "Neptune's Daughter." At the Globe Theatre, New York City, this photoplay masterpiece in seven reels bids well to outlast the summer months, notwithstanding the fact that it has already been exhibited for twenty weeks to capacity business, afternoon and night—the longest run ever known on Broadway for a photoplay. In cities like Chicago, Philadelphia, Denver and San Francisco "Neptune's Daughter" is going just as big, and in the words of a well-known

is a staff writer for the Universal Film Manufacturing Company. Though he has achieved slight success as a writer, he is not considered of Rex Beach or Jack London caliber. However, the photoplay world knows him to be the foremost photo playwright in America. He has almost four hundred produced photoplays to his credit. But it must be remembered he has, as a salaried writer, outstripped all the established authors, novelists and playwrights. He has written something that gets the money.

Born in Bangalore, India, educated at Eton and the Royal Military College at Sandhurst, and for eleven years an officer in the English Army, Captain Peacocke, as his friends know him, has had a picturesque career. His life has been as full of exciting incidents and thrilling adventures as the stirring tales he scenarizes for the picture screen.

He has served in many campaigns in India, one of which was the second Chitral expedition through that part of Burmah of which Rudyard Kipling became so obsessed and wrote "On the Road to Mandalay." As a member of the Foreign Legion fighting with Greece in her war with Turkey, he was captured and held prisoner at Stamboul for weeks. A scar on his chin indicates where he was sabered by a Turk at the time of his capture. Also, he participated in the Boxer rebellion in China. He has traveled all over the civilized world, north, south, east and west.

While quartered at Bangalore as an officer in the Eighty-eighth Regiment—the Connaught Rangers—he began his writing career as military correspondent for "The Irish Times." Prior to this he had sent army happenings to his home paper, and had written numerous verses for various weekly publications, receiving a free subscription therefor.

The officers and their wives of the regiment organized a theatrical company for their own entertainment. Captain Peacocke became interested and wrote several of the plays produced which resulted in his being made stage director and manager of all productions.

Since coming to the United States fifteen years ago he has experienced all the ups and downs of theatrical life. He is the author of numerous vaudeville sketches, notably, "The Syndicate," "Married by Telephone," "The Honeymoon Suite," "Mr. Plato," and "The Happy Family." He has served as actor on stage and in studio. Also, he has directed motion picture plays as well as playing the leads in several.

Recently, when Mrs. Langtry was preparing to enter picture work in a photoplay production of "His Neighbor's Wife," she instructed Daniel Frohman to find Captain Peacocke, who, as she said, "will make an admirable villain." There was nothing else for Mr. Frohman to do but institute a search for Captain Peacocke, since Mrs. Langtry was set on having him play the leading male role. Though there is little

Captain Leslie T. Peacocke, America's Foremost Photoplaywright

With His Wife and Their Child and the Governess

Figure 43: Katterjohn's article on Peacocke
Source: *The Movie Pictorial*, August 15, 1914, 16.

has already been exhibited for twenty weeks to capacity business, afternoon and night – the longest run ever known on Broadway for a photoplay. In cities like Chicago, Philadelphia, Denver and San Francisco "Neptune's Daughter" is going just as big [… and] the photoplay world knows [Peacocke] to be the foremost photo playwright in America.[203]

It continued its run at the Globe Theatre in New York for a total of 26 weeks, a record not matched until the showing of *Birth of a Nation* in 1915.[204]

Neptune's Daughter owed its success not only to the skill of Peacocke as a writer and Brenon's direction, but also to the engagement of a major swimming and diving star, Annette Kellerman, to play the lead. Sex appeal played a part, as Kellerman appears in a swimming suit that portrays her as all but naked, which titillated but did not flout the common mores of the period. Nevertheless, *Moving Picture World* credits Peacocke for 'telling a story independent of her and doubly strong by reason of that fact'.[205] Describing it as a 'remarkable production', Grau also acknowledges 'the achievement was a triple triumph for the director, the author and the star'.[206]

A significant impact of *Neptune's Daughter* was that it drew Münsterberg's attention to the artistic possibilities of film:

> Until a year ago I had never seen a real photoplay. Although I was always a passionate lover of the theatre, [… I] risked seeing *Neptune's Daughter*, and my conversion was rapid. I recognized at once that here marvelous possibilities were open, and I began to explore with eagerness the world which was new to me.[207]

The 'epic qualities' of this 'fantasy' film, Allan Langdale contends, led Münsterberg to launch 'himself into the study, and later even the modest production, of films'.[208] Although Münsterberg does not mention the writing of this photoplay, focusing only on the effect the film had on him, it is evident that the work of Peacocke, even if by proxy, played a part in turning his attention to film theory.

Even though Peacocke was never officially credited, it appears he was one of the writers of the highly acclaimed and controversial film, *Traffic in Souls*, released by Universal in

---

203 Ibid.

204 'Great Directors and their Productions', *NYDM*, July 1916, 26; cited in Koszarski, *Evening's Entertainment*, 222.

205 George Blaisdell, 'Neptune's Daughter', *MPW*, May 9, 1914, 796–797.

206 Grau, *Theatre of Science,* xviii and 278.

207 Cited in Allan Langdale, ed., 'The Stimulation of the Mind: The Film Theory of Hugo Münsterberg', in *Hugo Münsterberg on Film – The Photoplay: A Psychological Study and Other Writings* (New York: Routledge, 2002), 7–8.

208 Ibid., 7.

1913.[209] As he was also chief scenario editor at Universal at the time, his involvement seems likely and it is also confirmed in a number of biographical features on him.[210] Peacocke does appear to have been a writer with a social conscience, as he also worked with the 'all negro' Democracy Film Company on a film about the role of Black Americans in the First World War. Its purpose was to work toward 'eliminating race prejudice', although there is no record the film was ever made.[211]

Peacocke was the writer and director for *O, It's Great to Be Crazy*, a 1918 short that starred a young Stan Laurel before he teamed up with Hardy.[212] He also worked for the Metro, Titan and Venus Film Companies during his career.[213] Peacocke wrote *The Wonderful Eye* (1911), a short directed by Sennett.[214] He also worked with the well-known playwright Edward Brewster Sheldon (1886–1946)[215] and co-wrote with Catherine Carr, another highly successful scenario writer who wrote her own screenwriting manual, as noted in the previous section.[216]

Peacocke's skills extended to acting in many successful shorts under the direction of Porter[217] and in a number of prominent features. Of particular note was the 1921 Vitagraph production of *Black Beauty*, which still survives in the Library of Congress.

---

209   The film highlighted the social evils of prostitution. The sensational subject matter led to moral panic, which resulted in the inclusion of the 'white slave trade' in the topics explicitly barred under the Hays Office's Production Code in 1921. See Ben Brewster, '"Traffic in Souls": An Experiment in Feature-length Narrative Construction', *Cinema Journal* 31, No.1, 1991, 37–56.

210   *Traffic in Souls* (1913) is listed as one of Peacocke's writing credits. See *MPW*, July 11, 1914, 238 and *Photoplay*, April 1915, 117.

211   A. H. Giebler, 'News of Los Angeles and Vicinity', *MPW*, June 7, 1919, 1491.

212   Peacocke is listed as writer and director for *O, It's Great to Be Crazy*. See *IMDbPro*: https://pro-labs.imdb.com/name/nm0668813/

213   See 'Peacocke' in *Motion Picture Studio Directory and Trade Annual*, 1917, 144.

214   Peacocke is listed as writer for *The Wonderful Eye*. See *IMDbPro*: https://pro-labs.imdb.com/name/nm0668813/

215   Peacocke wrote the scenario for Sheldon's play, *Salvation Nell* (1915). This play was filmed again in 1921 and 1931. Other films based on Sheldon's plays were *Romance* (1930), starring Greta Garbo, and *The Song of Songs* (1933) starring Marlene Dietrich. See *IMDbPro*: https://pro-labs.imdb.com/name/nm0791017/

216   Carr wrote the scenario for Peacocke's story, *The Limousine Mystery* (1916) and *The Untamed* (1917) and was author of *The Art of Photoplay Writing* (1914). See *IMDbPro*: https://pro-labs.imdb.com/name/nm0139636/

217   Peacocke worked under the direction of Porter in *His Neighbour's Wife* (1913). See *IMDbPro*: https://pro-labs.imdb.com/name/nm0668813/

In this he plays with great aplomb the dashing villain, Lord Wynwaring.[218] Peacocke also wrote for, directed and acted with a host of other early silent film stars, such as Mary Fuller of Universal, Ethel Grandin, Maurice Costello and Harold Lockwood.[219] He directed many shorts and features, including an expensive sequel to *Neptune's Daughter* entitled *Neptune's Bride*, which was another critical success.[220] Towards the end of his active period, he also worked as a producer.[221]

The first studio Peacocke worked for was Universal, under Laemmle. When he began in early 1913, he was on its editorial team but eventually became chief scenario editor. In late 1914 he moved to The World Film Corporation under Lewis J. Selznick; then in 1916 he worked briefly for the California Film Corporation, only to re-join Universal in 1917. By 1923, Peacocke had formed his own production company, Peacocke Productions, and in 1924 he founded the New Orleans Feature Film Corporation, but by then he had faded from public view (see Figure 44).[222]

NED HOLMES has returned to New York from Washington, where with Allen Glenn and Nelson R. Bell of the Crandall staff he started on its course 'Abraham Lincoln,' which was shown at Harry Crandall's Metropolitan Theatre. The formal opening was preceded by a showing at the New Willard Hotel. Prior to the screening of the picture there was a dinner given at the Washington Hotel to a number of well known residents and to representatives of the New York motion picture business publications. The picture opened well and Mr. Holmes reports that the houses have been steadily increasing in size from the initial showing.

MR. CRANDALL said that the Metropolitan

CAPTAIN LESLIE PEACOCKE, director of productions of the New Orleans Feature Film Corporation, is in New York. The Captain has finished "Prohibition?" which recently has completed a successful two weeks run in New Orleans. He reports his organization is rapidly assuming definite shape and that he expects during his stay in New York to gather about him the elements now lacking in his organization. Among these will be two directors. The company has offices at 347 Carbondale street, in New Orleans, and intends erecting a studio later in the summer. The concern is backed by half a dozen prominent residents of the southern city who have every belief in the availability of their community for a motion picture production center.

Figure 44: 'Old Lady Astor Says' article on Peacocke
Source: *Exhibitors Trade Review*, June 14, 1924, 17.

---

218 For a full synopsis, see entry for *Black Beauty* (Vitagraph, 1921) at http://www.movies.msn.com. The seven-reel original survives in fragments of two-and-half reels from a 1929 re-release and can be accessed at http://www.harpodeon.com

219 See directing and writing entries for Peacocke, where these stars are listed in the credits of his films at *IMDbPro*: https://pro-labs.imdb.com/name/nm0668813/

220 Peacocke was the writer and director of *Neptune's Bride* (1920): http://www.tcm.com. With a cast of over 700, the film premiered in Los Angeles with a full Philharmonic orchestra and, according to the 25 July issue of the *Los Angeles Times*, was held over for a second week. It was still playing to limited audiences in 1922. See John T. Soister, *American Silent Horror, Science Fiction and Fantasy Feature Films* (North Carolina: McFarland, 2012), 427–428.

221 *The Wheel of Fortune* (1923) was produced by Peacocke Productions. See 'The Wheel of Fortune', *MPN Booking Guide* (Los Angeles, MPN, April 1923), 106.

222 'Captain Leslie T. Peacocke', October 31, 1914, 648 in *MPW*; 'Beyfuss signs Capt. Peacocke', March 11, 1916, 594 and 'Three Authors Added to Universal Forces', October 20, 1917, 812 in *Motography*; and 'Old Lady Astor Says', *Exhibitors Trade Review*, June 14, 1924, 17.

Throughout his active period, Peacocke was regularly featured and written about in the fan and trade press, including in *Moving Picture World*, *Motion Picture News*, *Motography*, *The Movie Pictorial*, *Motion Picture Magazine*, *The Film Daily* and *Photoplay*.[223] Peacocke's public statements opposing correspondence schools led *Photoplay* to employ him in 1915, following its pledge to rid itself of advertising from unscrupulous correspondence schools and dodgy clearing houses (see Figure 45).[224] He was in full approval of 'the successful campaign *Photoplay Magazine* has waged against dishonest "schools" purporting to teach the art of scenario writing for a price'.[225]

This Is the Man

Whom PHOTOPLAY MAGAZINE has engaged to conduct its new department, "Hints on Photoplay Writing," which will be helpful to those interested in this work.

Captain Peacocke was for two years associated with the Universal Film Company, and prior to that was writing photoplays for various film producing companies in this country and abroad. He has had more than 400 photoplays produced, some of which were adaptations, but, for the most part, were his own original stories.

Among his most successful originals are the famous Kellerman feature, "Neptune's Daughter," "Married by Telephone," "The Closed Door," "The Nautch-Girl and the Tiger," "You, I and It," "Traffic in Souls," "A Mexico Mix," "The Polo Champions," and "A Girl and Her Money."

His adaptations number several of the country's greatest dramatic successes, including "What Happened to Jones," "As Ye Sow," "The Coward," "Salvation Nell," and "Old Dutch"—Lew Fields' first feature film, just released.

Captain Peacocke was educated at Eton, England, and before beginning his literary career was an officer in the British Army, seeing service both in India and Africa.

He is the author of more than 200 short stories and several successful novels.

If *You* are interested in scenario-writing, as a fact or as a possibility, don't fail to get PHOTOPLAY MAGAZINE for *May*. *Hints on Photoplaywriting* is going to be the best, biggest and most authoritative department of its kind published anywhere in the English language.

CAPTAIN LESLIE TUFNELL PEACOCKE is not only one of the most experienced, but one of the most successful scenario writers and scenario editors in the world. A cosmopolitan, free-lance journalist as well as a fiction writer of recognized ability, he was early attracted to the field of moving pictures, and began to study the game of the camera, from all sides, at a time when it was given little serious consideration by serious-minded people. As a matter of course, when the importance of moving pictures was recognized, Captain Peacocke had already enjoyed several years of vigorous tuition in the fundamentals of the great art-industry.

Figure 45: Article on Peacocke's 'Hints on Photoplaywriting' series
Source: *Photoplay*, April, 1915, 117.

---

223 A small survey of advertisements indicates his profile as a writer. See 'The Woman Who Dared' in *MPN*, May 20, 1916, 2975; 'Checkmate' in *MPW*, May 26, 1917, 1229; 'The Heart of Juanita', *The Film Daily*, December 14, 1919, 25; 'Neptune's Bride', *Exhibitors' Herald*, December 25, 1920, 39.

224 Peacocke is featured at the end of an article called 'Scenario "School" Advertising'. His position as chief scenario editor for Universal and the respect he held within industry circles made him the ideal candidate to clean up *Photoplay's* image when it came under new management. See *Photoplay*, April 1915, 114–117.

225 Peacocke, *Hints on Photoplay Writing*, 4.

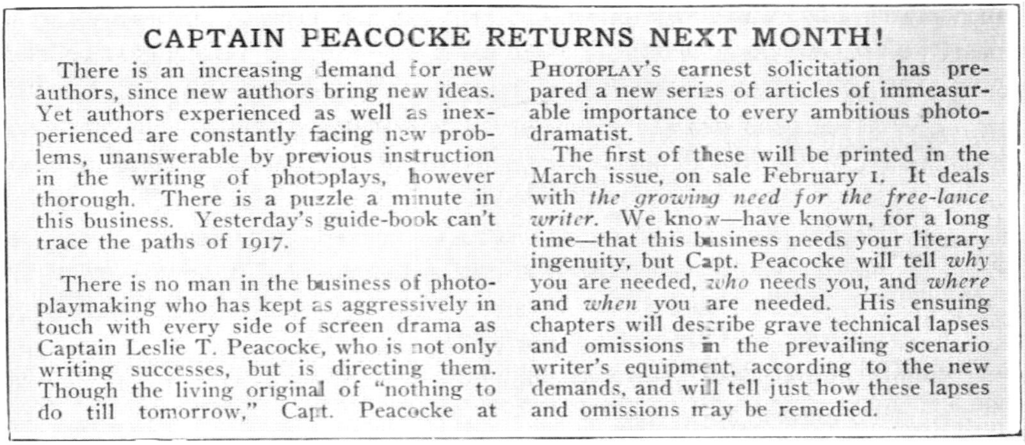

CAPTAIN PEACOCKE RETURNS NEXT MONTH!

There is an increasing demand for new authors, since new authors bring new ideas. Yet authors experienced as well as inexperienced are constantly facing new problems, unanswerable by previous instruction in the writing of photoplays, however thorough. There is a puzzle a minute in this business. Yesterday's guide-book can't trace the paths of 1917.

There is no man in the business of photoplaymaking who has kept as aggressively in touch with every side of screen drama as Captain Leslie T. Peacocke, who is not only writing successes, but is directing them. Though the living original of "nothing to do till tomorrow," Capt. Peacocke at

PHOTOPLAY'S earnest solicitation has prepared a new series of articles of immeasurable importance to every ambitious photodramatist.

The first of these will be printed in the March issue, on sale February 1. It deals with *the growing need for the free-lance writer*. We know—have known, for a long time—that this business needs your literary ingenuity, but Capt. Peacocke will tell *why* you are needed, *who* needs you, and *where* and *when* you are needed. His ensuing chapters will describe grave technical lapses and omissions in the prevailing scenario writer's equipment, according to the new demands, and will tell just how these lapses and omissions may be remedied.

Figure 46: Article announcing Captain Peacocke's second *Photoplay* series
Source: *Photoplay*, February, 1917, 114.

Over his first year with the magazine (1915–16), Peacocke wrote a series of articles, 'Hints on Photoplay Writing', that was so popular he was invited to write another series in 1917 (see Figure 46).[226] The initial article in 1915 included an offer to answer questions if letter writers enclosed a self-addressed envelope but he was so inundated with requests to read screenplays that after this he just directed readers to submit their scenarios to film companies.[227]

The success of Peacocke's articles led to their publication in manual form in 1916, under the same title, *Hints on Photoplay Writing*. This manual was widely publicised in *Photoplay* and the rest of the fan press subsequent to its publication.[228] Although at first glance advertisements seem to suggest a further manual, *Scenario Writing*, was published in 1918, closer examination reveals this is likely to have been another edition of the same work, advertised in a different way in order to boost sales.[229]

---

226 Peacocke was asked to write again at 'Photoplay's earnest solicitation', due to the popularity of his articles. See 'Captain Peacocke Returns Next Month', *Photoplay*, February 1917, 114.

227 Compare Peacocke's closing comments in his articles on 'Hints on Photoplay Writing', May 1915, 129–132 and July 1915, 129–132 in *Photoplay*.

228 Peacocke's *Hints on Photoplay Writing* was advertised over a four-year period. See *Photoplay*, August 1916, 176 and August 1919, 15.

229 Separate advertisements for *Hints on Photoplay Writing* and *Scenario Writing* appear in the same edition of *Photoplay*. The second advertisement has 'Scenario Writing' as a header. However, on closer examination, the advertisement for *Scenario Writing* reads 'Peacocke's remarkably popular book on Scenario Writing', which includes the header. The text of the advertisement of *Scenario Writing* is almost identical to the text of the advertisement for *Hints on Photoplay Writing*. The drive for this advertising appears to be that it was re-published by the Photoplay Publishing Co, *Photoplay*'s own publishing arm, which indicates the high esteem the magazine editors had for Peacocke. Compare advertisements in *Photoplay*, April 1918, 10 and 122.

Others who wrote for the trade press, such as Sargent and Wright, do not reference Peacocke as regularly as they do each other. Nevertheless, Peacocke should be counted among their number, as his easy and accessible style appealed to amateur writers and he was widely respected. In one of his articles, Wright does endorse Peacocke by including his advice on writing features and stating, 'there is no script writer better qualified than Captain Peacocke to discourse on the subject of the multiple reel'.[230] A further indication of his acceptance into the fold is that Sargent recorded Peacocke's election to membership of the Ed-Au Club in 1914.[231] The phenomenal success achieved by the likes of Peacocke and Wright led those of lesser fame to seek endorsements to give their own work more validity. Hence, for example, Thomas's *How to Write a Photoplay*[232] offers thanks 'for courtesies extended in the preparation of the work' to both Peacocke and Wright on its title page.[233]

Peacocke directed his last films in 1923 and returned to the stage in 1924.[234] Having gradually disappeared from the public arena after this period, he has since been largely forgotten, along with others who were likely to have been important contributors to the early discourse on screenwriting.

---

230 Wright, 'For Those Who Worry O'er Plots and Plays', *MPN*, September 27, 1913, 22–24.

231 Sargent, 'The Photoplaywright', *MPW*, March 28, 1914, 1674.

232 See footnote 44 in this chapter. An examination of the surviving six chapters of Thomas's *How to Write a Photoplay* shows that the advice he offered is not essentially different from that of the key screenwriting teachers.

233 'New Photoplay Textbook', *Motography*, December 19, 1914, 851.

234 Peacocke is listed for a vaudevillian playlet based on *Neptune's Daughter* in New York and a production of his play *The Bride* in London, based on *The Gay Young Bride*, which he had written 11 years previously. See *Variety*, September 1924, 'Maddock's Playlets', 7 and 'Inside Stuff', 14.

Eustace Hale Ball (1881–1931)

Eustace Hale Ball fulfils all but one of this study's five criteria. He was an outstanding writer, worked as a scenario editor, made some important contributions to the fan and trade press, wrote two manuals and worked closely with the industry as a director and producer. As will become clear, although Ball never authored a regular column for the fan or trade press, he fulfils the other four criteria in such an exemplary way that his inclusion is justified.

Ball was educated at Harvard, was an accomplished musician and became a sophisticated, multi-faceted writer, journalist, critic, satirist, scenarist, short story writer and novelist of considerable prowess. For several years in New York he held the record for marathon fiction writing, penning 60,000 words on a weekly basis for various publishers (see Figure 47).[235] His novelised version of the popular *Traffic in Souls* (1914) was based on the controversial film of the same title (1913), in which Peacocke also had some involvement (see above). The frontispiece of the book indicated its 'sensational subject matter' on prostitution among the white community,[236] displaying a provocative image from the film.[237] For a second novelisation – of the famous 1916 silent horror serial *The Mysteries of Myra* – Ball collaborated with Charles W. Goddard.[238] Among his many

---

235   'Eustace Hale Ball', *MPN*, March 29, 1913, 13.

236   Brewster, 'Traffic in Souls: An Experiment in Feature-length Narrative Construction' in *Cinema Journal* 31, no.1 (1991): 37–56. *Traffic in Souls* (1913) was written by Walter MacNamara and produced by Universal. See also *IMDbPro*: https://pro-labs.imdb.com/title/tt0003471/

237   Shelley Stamp, *Movie Struck Girls: Women and Motion Picture Culture After the Nickelodeon* (New Jersey: Princeton University, 2000), 74.

238   Charles W. Goddard and Eustace Hale Ball, *The Mysteries of Myra* (Stedman, 2010). The book is illustrated with shots from the 1916 film serial, which has been almost fully restored. See *The Mysteries of Myra: The Astonishing 1916 Cinema Serial*, http://www.mysteriesofmyra.com and *IMDbPro*: https://pro-labs.imdb.com/title/tt0007107/

EUSTACE HALE BALL

Eustace Hale Ball, general manager and part owner of the new Historical Film Company, of 1 Madison Avenue, and 4 Gerard Street, London, has had unique experience in moving picture work. He is a graduate of Harvard University and also of Cincinnati University, and for several years in New York after his graduation held the record for Marathon fiction writing, doing 60,000 words weekly under contract with Frank Tousey, the publisher, and other syndicates. Then he wrote the Nick Carter thrillers for Street & Smith not neglecting an occasional story in the current magazines along more serious lines. Mr. Ball founded and edited the little magazine "Broadway Buzz," and became successful as a dramatic critic. From this he entered the field of Cinematography, starting with the Eclair Company, as scenario editor and special writer. He has directed for Solax, Majestic, Reliance and other film companies, specializing in the production of his own plays. He attained much public attention by his productions of mid-air thrillers with Rodman Law, the sky-trouper, and is the first cinematographic director to have managed and produced an entire film-play in the breezy, "Saved by Airship," in which Mr. Ball and his aviator, Harry Bingham Brown, did some aerial duets in a biplane which caused three camera men to lose their jobs from stage fright. He is Librarian of the Screen Club, and a member of the Harvard Friars, Southern, and other well-known clubs. The Historical Film Company will soon begin releasing for the "open market" special productions along educational and historical lines, under the auspices of the great universities and the Federal government, in new lines which it is believed will surprise the "old guarders." American historical plays, with all-star casts, will be specialized upon. English scenery and history will be utilized by the London branch of the company, for American sale. A number of Wall street capitalists are backing the new organization, as well as two men high up in filmdom finances.

Figure 47: A review of Ball's credentials
Source: *MPN*, March 29, 1913, 13.

Big Booking Records

The Entire Circuit of Marcus Loew Theatres Books "The Voice on the Wire" Serial

IMPRESSED by the initial showing of the Universal's latest and greatest serial, "THE VOICE ON THE WIRE," the bookers of the big Marcus Loew Theatre Circuit booked it for every house on the list. This magnificent serial opened in the big Broadway and Brooklyn Houses of the circuit to tremendous crowds. The deep, mysterious plot captured the first episode audiences, and the following episodes showed record attendances.

Featuring Ben Wilson & Neva Gerber

The leads are played by Ben Wilson and Neva Gerber, two of the most popular Universal Stars. There is great scope for their pleasing personalities of which they make the most. The plot has to do with a series of mysterious events each of which is preceded by a ghostly warning given by a weird "voice on the wire." A strange muffled figure and a dismembered hand serve to intensify the mystery, and in the character of John Shirley, professional investigator Ben Wilson attempts to locate the owner of the "voice."

Written by Eustace Hale Ball

The fascinating story is from the celebrated novel of the same name written by Eustace

A Tense Situation from "The Voice on the Wire."

Figure 48: A review of the film serialisation of Ball's novel,
The Voice on the Wire
Source: *MPN*, May 12, 1917, 3000.

other novels, he authored the popular Jack Race series[239] and he also wrote a number of long-running syndicated newspaper serials.[240]

When Ball turned his attention to the movies, he soon became a prolific and highly successful scenarist. He wrote for major stars such as Clara Bow and Douglas Fairbanks and, when the films were produced, he would author popular novels based on them.[241] According to *Motion Picture News*, the film serialisation of his own novel *The Voice on the Wire* (1917) released by Universal:

> opened in all the big Broadway and Brooklyn Houses in the circuit to tremendous crowds. The deep, mysterious plot captured the first episode audiences, and the following episodes showed record attendances.[242] (see Figure 48)

In a favourable review, critic Robert L. McElravy described it as a 'clever combination of mystery and thrills'.[243] As Sargent confirms, Ball had an ability to turn his hand to most types of writing:

> Eustace Hale Ball is an old hand at the writing game. He is one of the few who can write a good dime novel (and few can) or he can write pretentious stuff. But he writes action when he writes photoplay, because whatever the tendency toward literature in the script he may have had that beaten out of him when he was editor for Éclair and others.[244]

The skilled and prolific nature of his scenario writing in particular attracted widespread praise. Producer W. F. Haddock, for example, stated: 'In my opinion [...] Mr. Eustace Hale Ball is the most capable scenario writer in the business today.'[245] One New York paper recorded in 1913 that Ball had 'sold 80 of his scenarios to the different moving

---

239   'Ball' in *Motion Picture Studio Directory and Trade Annual,* 1918, 210.

240   Ball wrote the long-running serialised novels, *Marigold* for the *Buffalo New York Courier* (1926), *Tiger Love* for *Brooklyn NY Standard Union* (1929) and *The Scarlet Fox* for *Binghamton NY Press* (1930). See *Fulton History*: http://fultonhistory.com/Fulton.html

241   According to *IMDbPro*, Ball only had ten writing and five directing credits, but this record is seriously deficient. His adaptation *Beyond the Rainbow* (1922) featured Clara Bow, a major star in the 1920s, and his popular novel, *The Voice on the Wire* (1917), became a long running serial. See 'Ball' in *IMDbPro*: https://pro-labs.imdb.com/name/nm0050369. Ball collaborated with Fairbanks in the writing of *The Gaucho* (1927) starring Douglas Fairbanks, which was also novelised (New York: Grosset & Dunlop, 1927). See Ball, *The Art of the Photoplay*, inside cover for more details.

242   'Universal Bulletin – Big Booking Records', *MPN*, May 12, 1917, 3000.

243   Robert L. McElravy, 'The Voice on the Wire', *MPW*, March 24, 1917, 1948.

244   Sargent, 'The Photoplaywright', *MPW*, September 11, 1915, 1825–26.

245   Haddock was a producing director with Edison, Éclair and All Star, as well as president of Mirror Film Corporation. His comments were released by the publishers. See G. W. Haddock, 'The Art of the Photoplay' (New York: G. W. Dillingham, 1913), http://tera-3.ul.cs.cmu.edu/NASD/4dcb85c3-9fee-4c83-9e6d-fe6ce5522b59/China/disk2/20050318-062/31004109/HTML/00000C04.htm

picture companies in less than 11 months'.[246] He was also the first director to manage and produce his own mid-air thriller with aerial stunts, *Saved by Airship* (1913).[247] As a writer, Jacobs recognises, Ball is deserving of 'special mention' for 'being among the first to convert stories into an effective screen idiom'.[248] Grau records in 1914 that Ball had 'prepared the scenarios for a dozen big features [… and] produced about 250 comedies, dramas, and is now busier than ever'.[249]

Ball worked for the Éclair Company as an advertising agent in 1912, where he later became scenario editor, and in same year he helped to form the All-Star Feature Film Corporation, which took many of the plays of the successful theatrical producer Charles Frohman and brought them to the screen.[250] Ball distinguished himself as a staff writer, scenario editor and director at a number of other companies, including Reliance, Solax, Majestic and Excelsior.[251] He became the manager and part owner of the Historical Film Company in 1913, with the intention of producing films about the history of the United States; a venture that appears not to have succeeded (Figure 49).[252] Ball also worked as successful producer for Universal Studios.[253]

Ball's writing talent, more than his contributions in the fan and trade press arena, seems to have pushed him to the forefront of the general public's mind and gained him industry respect. However, he was an occasional contributor to the press on issues that he considered important. One of his trade press offerings was a pithy checklist for budding scenarists, 'Ten Things I Would Tell a Beginner' (see Figure 50).[254] Another article focused specifically on how to negotiate the thorny and tricky issue of censorship and provided some guidelines for writing scenarios. The prompt for this article came when parties connected with the industry set up a voluntary body in New York, the National

---

246 'Personalities of Writers and Players', *Syracuse NY Daily Journal*, 0802.pdf: *Fulton History*: http://fultonhistory.com/Fulton.html

247 'Eustace Hale Ball', *MPN*, March 29, 1913, 13.

248 Jacobs, *Rise of the American Film*, 132.

249 Grau, *Theatre of Science,* 310–311.

250 Ibid.

251 'Ball' in *Motion Picture Studio Directory and Trade Annual*, 1918, 210.

252 The Historical Film Company had offices in New York and London and was formed to make three- to four-reel features on American and English historical themes. Ball consulted with historian Edward S. Ellis about this. See 'The Historical Film Company' in *MPW*, April 12, 1913, 177 and *Exhibitors' Times*, August 16, 1913, 7.

253 Ball was producer of 'the wonder drama, "20,00 Leagues Under the Sea"'. See 'Universal Bulletin' *MPW*, May 26, 1917, 1204.

254 Ball, 'Ten Things I Would Tell a Beginner', *Photo Playwright*, July 1912, 5. His basic advice covers formatting, censorship and being economical with casts, scenes and locations.

Board of Censorship, in an attempt to avoid legislation (see Figure 51).[255] Novelised forms of his scenarios regularly appeared in the fan press. For example, 'The Ocean Waif' was published in *The Photoplay Journal*, as well as in the *Washington Times* (see Figure 52).[256] His status as a highly competent journalist was confirmed when in 1919 he became feature editor of the *New York Sun*.[257]

As an indication of their reach, both of Ball's two screenwriting manuals ran to a number of editions. The first, *The Art of the Photoplay* (1913) was published in three editions by two publishing houses (see Figure 53 for the second edition).[258] Grau comments on its publication:

> Eustace Hale Ball, like Mr. Sargent, has had a long career as writer and photoplaywright to justify the publication of his new volume, *The Art of the Photoplay* (at least three other books have the same title).[259]

Sargent himself gives his own endorsement to the volume by identifying it as part of his essential library that every scenario writer should have.[260]

The second manual, *Photoplay Scenarios: How to Write and Sell Them*, was published in 1915 and again in 1917 in America (see Figure 54). The British version of the same book, *Cinema Plays: How to Write Them, How to Sell Them*, was published in 1917 and 1920 in Britain.[261] The mere two-year gap between the publications of Ball's two manuals is indicative of the speed of change in the industry and Ball's desire to keep up with developments – an issue that will be considered in Chapter 7.

Finally, Ball was a member and librarian of the Screen Club of New York.[262] This organisation attracted major stars and figures of note in the film industry to its events.

---

255 Ball, 'The Scenario Writer, the Director and the Censor', *MPN*, December 26, 1914, 36.

256 Ball, 'The Ocean Waif' in *The Photoplay Journal*, December 1916, 26–31 and *Washington Times*, November 19, 1916, 13. *Newspapers.com*, http://www.newspapers.com/newspage/79979449/

257 As feature editor in 1919, Ball wrote articles on high-profile people such as the millionaire railway magnate and antiquarian Henry Edwards Huntington. His imaginative descriptions of the maverick tycoon who, Ball claims, possessed 'the greatest private library in the world', won him praise and were published in many newspapers. See James Ernest Thorpe, *Henry Edwards Huntington: A Biography* (Los Angeles: University of California, 1994), 353–354.

258 Ball, *Art of the Photoplay*, published by New York publishing houses Veritas and W. Dillingam Company in two editions in 1913.

259 Grau, *Theatre of Science,* 310.

260 Sargent, 'The Photoplaywright', *MPW*, February 7, 1914, 670.

261 Ball, *Photoplay Scenarios: How to Write and Sell Them* (New York: Hearst's, 1915 and 1917) and *Cinema Plays: How to Write Them, How to Sell, Them* (London: Stanley Paul, 1917 and 1920). See *OCLC WorldCat:* http://www.worldcat.org/search?q=au%3ABall%2C+Eustace+Hale%2C&fq=&dblist=638&start=1&qt=page_number_link

262 See Ball, *Art of the Photoplay*, 3.

Big stars such as Mary Pickford attended the annual ball in 1914, for instance, along with the heads of virtually all the studios. Ball would also have been in attendance, which indicates that he was counted among their number and regarded as an important industry insider.[263]

THE HISTORICAL FILM COMPANY.

A newcomer into the film world is the Historical Film Company, with offices at 1 Madison Avenue, New York, and 4 Gerrard Street, Shaftesbury Avenue, London, W. The policy of the organization is releasing features of three and four reels based on American and English historical themes, for sale on the open markets and by state rights.

In addition, however, some unusual educational cinematography is under way, in conjunction with the great Eastern universities, to be used in college courses and for university extension work. The company is already at work on some anthropological work in recording the dances and customs of the old and the new generations of the Indians for the government records.

Eustace Hale Ball, General Manager Historical Film Co.

The company is under the general management of Eustace Hale Ball, well known in the film world as a prolific playwright and director for many companies, among which were Reliance, Solax, Majestic and Eclair. Mr. Ball is a Harvard graduate and is the author of a number of published novels and satires. He is the librarian of the Screen Club and a member of the Harvard, Friars, Southern and other well-known clubs.

The first of the feature releases will be announced in the near future in this magazine. The first educational record feature was made this week at the Carlisle Indian School, covering all branches of the Federal Government's system, under the personal direction of the superintendent, Professor M. Friedman. Trades study, military evolutions, native customs and dances, Indian plays and other unique features of the student life were recorded for the department.

Figure 49: An announcement of the arrival of the Historical Film Company under Ball's management
Source: *MPW*, April 12, 1913, 177.

Ten Things I Would Tell a Beginner

By EUSTACE HALE BALL, Scenario Editor, The Eclair Company

YPEWRITE your scenario on good paper, 8½ by 11 inches. Use a fresh typewriter ribbon so the printing will be plain. When submitting your script, enclose a stamped and addressed envelope. Never send loose stamps. It is hard work to address and stamp envelopes for a bunch of manuscripts.

2. Send complete scenarios—not single page sketches. If you expect to get money in return, give the film company something worth while. Write out the scene plot, give the captions or inserts, indicate the settings and mention the costumes and the various characters. Seven or eight lines should be sufficient to tell the scene action.

3. Too many scenes spoil the pie. Never use more than twenty-five or thirty, and this number will be trimmed at the studio. Remember—if your story calls for an elaborate scene, it should be used in the story several times to justify the expenditure and time for arranging the scene.

4. For general "speculation writing," small castes are desirable. Simple settings are needed. When great spectacles are needed the film company will hire the experts to arrange the scenes.

5. To transcribe the masterpieces and the classics is a waste of time. The studios producing this sort of stuff order such adaptions from their own staff of special writers.

6. You will save the director many heart aches by leaving knife play, shooting in the back, arson, abduction of children, etc., entirely out of the story. Such stories won't pass.

7. Eliminate drinking, dissolute women, religious subjects, and other trite ideas from your scenarios.

8. Avoid writing letters to the film companies offering to sell the "true" story of your life, or somebody else's life. Write out a complete scenario from your idea and then submit the scenario. The big film companies are too busy to establish correspondence schools.

9. Eliminate hot air. Never write an editor telling him how wonderful his company's work is, besides wishing him success and riches. (Who ever heard of a rich scenario editor?) The number of contributors who do this sort of thing is amazing—and amusing!

10. Above all, study postal weights. Don't make the editors pay "postage due" on your contribution. You get in bad right at the jump. Don't send odd pennies or one cent stamps. They are of no avail with letter postage. It is either two cents or nothing when mailing a sealed letter.

Figure 50: Ball's 'Ten Things I Would Tell a Beginner' article
Source: *Photo Playwright* July, 1912, 5.

---

263   'The Third Screen Club Ball', *Motography*, December 12, 1914, 799–800.

MOTION PICTURE NEWS   Vol. 10. No. 25.

The Scenario Writer, the Director and the Censor

BY EUSTACE HALE BALL
(Late Director and Staff Writer for Reliance, Majestic, Eclair, etc.)

Some Expert Advice by a Veteran Composer of Scripts on the Wisdom and Profit of Working with the National Board of Censorship, Realizing that Their Rules Are, at Bottom, for the Greatest Good of All Concerned, in the Business as Well as Out of It

IN view of the fact that the life blood of the industry is the continual supply of fresh, virile scenarios, the great majority of which are written by "free lances," it is essential that the photo playwrights throughout the country, as well as the staff writers should get a true perspective of the activities of The National Board of Censorship.

Producing directors have learned by hard bumps against the adamant that this and that may be, and that and this may not be; yet still they continue, in an unfortunately large number of picture plays, to insert scenes and "business," contrary to these permissions and prohibitions.

Inasmuch as the Censorship Board is maintained almost entirely by the manufacturers, as a real insurance against the printing and distribution of expensive copies which might be thrown back upon their hands by the black-listing of smaller local bodies and the ever critical public who scrutinize the screen in 17,000 photoplay theatres, it behooves the scenario writer and the director to insure his own certainty of financial return and increasing artistic reputation, by thoroughly understanding the attitude of that critical Board.

To get down to "brass tacks," it is simply a case then in which the scenario writer and the director can increase the value of their own work by keeping the rules continually in mind, and, "beating the censor to it."

Censorable Details Unnecessary

To declare that risque situations, grewsome details, exposition of the methods of offensive to good taste, in matters of race, religion and politics.

"Behind the Times" Scenario Writers

So, the scenario writer who lingers in the realms of cheap melodrama, sex thrillers, vice mongering is trying to reap a harvest from a field already trimmed to the stubble. His themes *must* keep pace with the fashions and the demand of the universal board ot censorship— the patrons who pay the nickels, the dimes and the quarters.

Never before in the history of the business has there been such opportunity for true artistry in the development of theme and action. The production of classic plays, poems and stories, as well as the staging before the camera of famous modern theatrical successes has educated the photoplay patrons to a demand for higher grade stories, interpretation and even photography.

Every scenario writer, every director, despite the vaunted value of loyalty to the "firm," is working primarily for himself. As a business proposition, every cent saved by avoiding enforced alteration in a costly production lends added value to the scenario and to the picture into which it was developed.

From a purely mercenary standpoint, every director and playwright should have in his possession the pamphlet of rules and standards, which will be sent upon the receipt of a written request by the secretary of the National Board of Censorship, 70 Fifth avenue, New York City.

friendly, personal co-operation with the directors and the playwrights, for their work is essentially altruistic in the finest sense; it is a defense of the moralities and sensibilities of the millions of theatre patrons, and its power has been so thoroughly developed that it affords an invaluable protection to the film producers.

What the Board Has Done

When it is considered that the National Board of Censorship has been the protecting bulwark of the film manufacturer against the dangers of a legal censorship, and the almost certain growth of grafting among political appointees in the case of state or federal control, the director and playwright may consider himself not harassed by the sensible standards and sympathetic latitude shown by the executive officers and the members of the General Committee, made up of cultured men and women, who have been qualified to represent the finest and broadest ideals of the American people.

The development of the programs, features and serials based on lavish outlays of money, a highly organized, creative and interpretative technique and a commercial system of distribution and sales which ranks with the biggest factors of so-called "Big Business," with the continual stimulus of keen competition between the large number of producing companies, means survival of the fittest.

OWEN MOORE GOES TO BOSWORTH

Figure 51: Ball's 'The Scenario Writer, the Director and the Censor' article
Source: *MPN*, December 26, 1914, 36.

The
OCEAN
WAIF

By

EUSTACE
HALE BALL

CARLYLE BLACKWELL
Co-star

DORIS KENYON
Co-star

CHAPTER I

The Rediscovery of Eden

CAPTAIN FARWELL, the place is ideal! Send her ahead and I'll go adventuring into the past. It looks like an old painting or a stage set, instead of a simple Yankee fishing village."

His voice thrilled with boyish delight, as he lowered the binoculars, turning with sparkling eyes toward the skipper of the steam yacht "Sea Gull."

"Ay, ay, sir. But I calculate you'll find it a bit weather-beaten," was the officer's response. "Port Sunray is the sleepiest town on the coast—there ain't none of them swell hotels or cottages which a gentleman like you is used to, sir. That place is like a country graveyard, sir, and . . ."

"Exactly what I want!" and the tall young man leaned over the taff-rail to gaze devouringly at the purple rocks which sheered so precipitously

"There ben't no hotel, friend," volunteered the most patriarchal of the reception committee. "But old Si Squiggins still runs the Holly Branch Tavern up on the Mill Brook road."

"Where is his place?" asked Roberts.

"Up this yere road," volunteered another. "It's a long walk; mebbe old Cap'n Ben 'll take ye up in his hack."

A few minutes of leisurely negotiation were necessary before the luggage could be safely stowed away on the after-deck of Cap'n Ben's craft. Hawkins was puffing and perspiring from the unwonted exercise.

"Now, point out the historical spots on the way," Roberts insisted. "And why aren't you trimming sails outside the harbor there, instead of doing this land-lubber's work, here?"

"Wall, it's a long story," observed the ancient mariner. "I was brung up when ships was ships, and not steam engines! I was master of a clipper in the days when whalin' was a perfession. And here I am now with nothin' to steer

Roberts drew his guide's attention to a white columned dwelling of Colonial architecture on the highland, back of the harbor.

"What's that place? It's the prettiest thing in the town."

"Taint with botherin' about, that place. It's been deserted for six years. Used to be a purty nice place when old man Simmons was alive, and before his gal died. But since he hung hisself, and after the gal died of fits, there ain't been no luck with the place. They rented it two or three times, all furnished up and everything. But people won't stay there."

"Why not?" Roberts already sensed some "copy" for his story.

"Oh, they does say as how the place has sperrits. Anyway, there's funny noises and sich at night, and old Mis' Sparrergrass who lived there last she said that the Simmon's gal came around at midnight every night."

"But she was dead, wasn't she?" inquired Hawkins, with true British obtuseness. "How could

Figure 52: 'The Ocean Waif', Ball's scenario in novelised form
Source: *The Photoplay Journal*, December, 1916, 26.

THE ART OF THE PHOTOPLAY

BY

EUSTACE HALE BALL

LATE SCENARIO EDITOR, STAFF PLAYRIGHT AND DIRECTOR
FOR RELIANCE, ECLAIR, SOLAX, MAJESTIC, EXCELSIOR
AND OTHER COMPANIES; NOW PRESIDENT OF
THE HISTORICAL FILM COMPANY

To

*That splendid band of good fellows: the Playwrights,
the Directors, the Actors, the Critics, the Editors,
the Publicity Men and the Owners who have
built up the motion picture industry to
its present success, ever fighting
for higher standards—*

*MY FELLOW-MEMBERS OF THE
SCREEN CLUB OF NEW YORK*

this book is fraternally dedicated by the author.

SECOND EDITION

G. W. DILLINGHAM COMPANY
PUBLISHERS   NEW YORK

Figure 53: Ball's *The Art of the Photoplay* book cover and title page
Source: *archive.org/details/artphotoplay00ballgoog.*

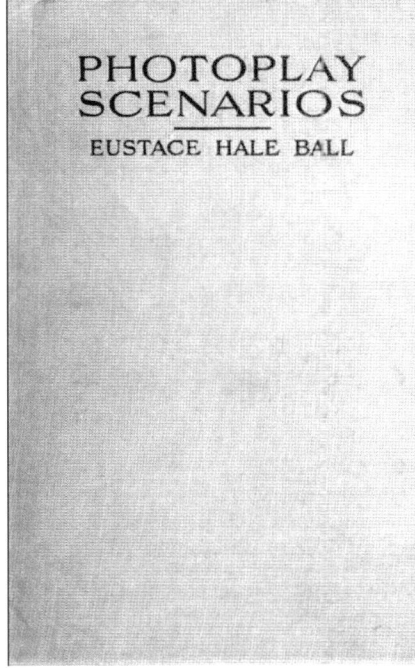

**PHOTOPLAY
SCENARIOS**

EUSTACE HALE BALL

PHOTOPLAY SCENARIOS

How to Write and Sell Them

By

EUSTACE HALE BALL

Author of " *The Art of the Photoplay,*" " *Traffic in Souls,*" " *The Voice on the Wire*"; Late
Scenario Editor, Staff Playwright and Director
for Reliance, Eclair, Solax, Majestic, Excelsior, Historical and other Film Companies

**HEARST'S INTERNATIONAL
LIBRARY COMPANY**
NEW YORK   MDCCCCXVII

Figure 54: Ball's *Photoplay Scenarios* book cover and title page
Source: *archive.org/details/photoplayscenari00ballrich.*

Henry Albert Phillips (1880–1951)

Like Ball, Henry Albert Phillips meets all but one of the five criteria. He was a versatile and highly successful writer, contributed mainly but not exclusively to the fan press, produced four manuals and lectured on one of the first photoplay courses. Even though he never worked as a scenario editor, he is too important an industry figure to omit. He was the only one of those examined in this study to teach a public course of instruction in screenwriting. Phillips also wrote more manuals than any of the others and, although less known than Ball, was more recognised and celebrated as a novelist and screenwriter than Sargent, Wright or Peacocke.

Phillips was a talented short story writer, playwright, biographer, novelist, travel writer and lecturer.[264] He was also a highly successful journalist, taking on a number of significant editorial roles, and was founder of the Playwrights' Club. Running his own photoplay correspondence school, he offered one-to-one tuition and regularly advertised the opportunity in the fan press (see Figure 55).[265] He also gave lectures on photoplay writing at the Brooklyn Institute of Arts and Sciences and the YMCA in New York. According to Eugene Brewster, editor of *Motion Picture Magazine*, Phillips authored three produced stage plays, 100 published stories, 100 special articles, five books of constructive literature and 50 produced photoplays. While the larger numbers seem rounded, indicating they are not exact, and were possibly exaggerated, they do indicate

---

264 Phillips was a novelist, travel writer, political commentator and biographer. He is recorded as writing: eight travelogues covering Germany, Spain, South America, Japan, the Caribbean and South Africa; a comedy play, *Twelve Men in a Box* (New York); a biographical work, *Other People's Lives* (New York: Boni and Liveright, 1924); and a novel *Garden of Contemplation* (Boston: The House Beautiful Pub. Corp., 1932). See *OCLC WorldCat*, http://www.worldcat.org/search?q=Henry+Albert+Phillips&fq=ap%3A%22p hillips%2C+henry+albert%22&dblist=638&start=1&qt=page_number_link

265 Advertisement for the Phillips Studio, *MPSM*, February 1914, 163.

THE PHILLIPS SCHOOL
TWO DEPARTMENTS OF INTEREST TO YOU
PHOTOPLAY Writers, send for the OPEN DOOR—
FREE. Describes Personally Conducted Course in
Scenario Writing.—**Photoplay Market 10c.** Attention,
SHORT STORY Writers, send for SHORT ROAD—
FREE. Personal Instruction with Corrected Lessons.
Story Market 10c. CRITICISM BUREAU—PHOTO-
PLAYS AND SHORT STORIES Criticized by Experts.
All under Supervision of HENRY ALBERT PHILLIPS.
PHILLIPS STUDIO, Box 12PA, 156 Fifth Ave., New York

Figure 55: Advertisement for the Phillips Studio
Source: *MPSM*, February 1914, 163.

that Phillips was probably extremely productive.[266] He wrote for important film companies such as Edison, where he was a staff contributor, and also Kalem, Vitagraph, Majestic, American and Pathé Frères. Griffith and Billy Bitzer were among the filmmakers he worked with, while he wrote for stars such as Lillian Gish and William Farnum.[267] Like the other screenwriting teachers in this study, Phillips was a member of the Ed-Au Club[268] and, like Wright and Ball, he belonged to the Photoplay Authors' League.[269]

Appointed as associate editor to *Motion Picture Magazine*, a popular fan press publication,[270] at first Phillips wrote only occasional contributions, writing on selective photoplay issues (see Figure 56).[271] Among his articles, which were generally forward-looking, was one in which he expresses his belief that one day '[p]hotoplaywriting is

266 Brewster also notes that Phillips had held editorial roles at *The Metropolitan Magazine*, *People's Magazine*, *The Scenario* and *Motion Picture Mail*. See Eugene V. Brewster, 'A Few Words from the Editor' in Phillips, 'The Photodrama', *MPM*, January 1917, 119–120.

267 According to *IMDbPro*, Phillips only has 13 writing credits between 1913 and 1920. Of particular note is his film, *The Battle of Elderbush Gulch* (1913), which was directed by Griffith, filmed by Billy Bitzer and starred Lionel Barrymore and Lillian Gish. William Farnum starred in *Heart Strings* (1920). See *IMDbPro*: https://pro-labs.imdb.com/name/nm0680450/. A further 13 credits not recorded in *IMDbPro* appear in 'Phillips', in *Motion Picture Studio Directory and Trade Annual*, 1918, 224 & 226 and 1921, 292. A full survey of the available fan and trade press literature reveals a further eight credits, making a total of 34 attested credits.

268 Mr and Mrs Phillips were recorded as 'present' at the monthly New York meeting on 3 October 1914. See 'The Ed-Au Club Meeting', *Photoplay Author*, November 1914, 138.

269 'Phillips', in *Motion Picture Studio Directory and Trade Annual,* 1918, 134.

270 *The Motion Picture Story Magazine* was founded in 1911 by Vitagraph studio head J. Stuart Blackton and his business partner, journalist Eugene V. Brewster. Renamed *Motion Picture Magazine* in 1914, its circulation reached 400,000 by 1919. See Koszarski, *Evening's Entertainment*, 193.

271 Phillips, 'Where to Get Photoplay Plots', *MPM*, February 1915, 101–105. This article was a forerunner to the plot system contained in his *Universal Plot Catalogue* (1920).

bound to become a dignified profession', a sentiment that certainly came true (see Figure 57 for the start of this article).[272] Phillips also published the full stories of many of his films in fan press publications (see Figure 58).[273]

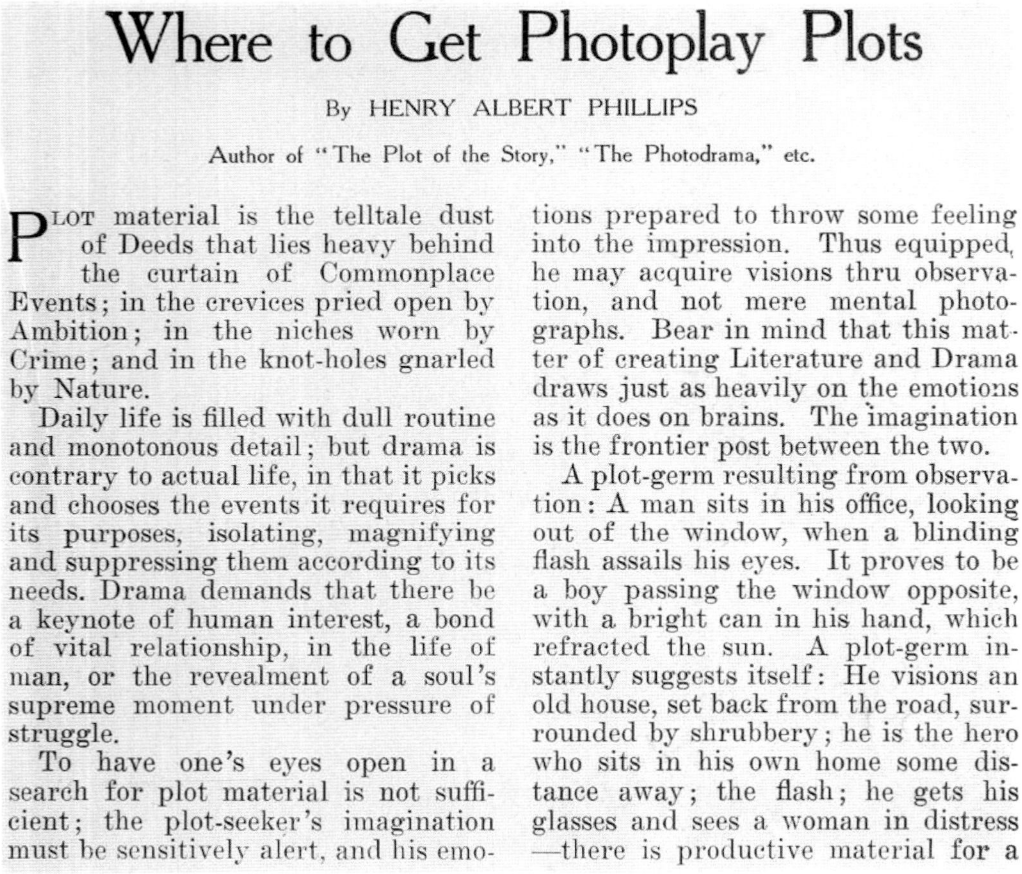

Where to Get Photoplay Plots

By HENRY ALBERT PHILLIPS

Author of "The Plot of the Story," "The Photodrama," etc.

PLOT material is the telltale dust of Deeds that lies heavy behind the curtain of Commonplace Events; in the crevices pried open by Ambition; in the niches worn by Crime; and in the knot-holes gnarled by Nature.

Daily life is filled with dull routine and monotonous detail; but drama is contrary to actual life, in that it picks and chooses the events it requires for its purposes, isolating, magnifying and suppressing them according to its needs. Drama demands that there be a keynote of human interest, a bond of vital relationship, in the life of man, or the revealment of a soul's supreme moment under pressure of struggle.

To have one's eyes open in a search for plot material is not sufficient; the plot-seeker's imagination must be sensitively alert, and his emo-tions prepared to throw some feeling into the impression. Thus equipped, he may acquire visions thru observation, and not mere mental photographs. Bear in mind that this matter of creating Literature and Drama draws just as heavily on the emotions as it does on brains. The imagination is the frontier post between the two.

A plot-germ resulting from observation: A man sits in his office, looking out of the window, when a blinding flash assails his eyes. It proves to be a boy passing the window opposite, with a bright can in his hand, which refracted the sun. A plot-germ instantly suggests itself: He visions an old house, set back from the road, surrounded by shrubbery; he is the hero who sits in his own home some distance away; the flash; he gets his glasses and sees a woman in distress —there is productive material for a

Figure 56: Phillips's 'Where to Get Photoplay Plots' article
Source: *MPM*, February 1915, 101.

---

272   Phillips, 'The New Literary Profession', *MPM*, October 1914, 81–82.

273   For example, Phillips's stories included: *A Spartan Mother* (Kalem, 1912), March 1912, 81–89 in *MPSM* and *Ashes of Inspiration* (Biograph, 1915) October 1915, 73–80 in *MPM*.

The New Literary Profession

By HENRY ALBERT PHILLIPS

Author of "The Plot of the Story," "The Photo-drama," "Art in Story Narration," etc.

A WONDERFUL event has come to pass in the annals of dramatic literature. So wonderful indeed is this new addition to the art of effective dramatic expression, that after a decade of existence, cinematography had scarcely a dozen successful writers of literature who realized its potentiality and had allied themselves with the new drama.

youngster, and the five-cent theater began to take its rightful place as "the poor man's playhouse."

Thus we have arrived at the beginnings of a need for a literature to provide for the screen portrayals. What had been the device of a moment, or the conception of an hour on the part of some ingenious—or ingenuous—director, together with the

Figure 57: Phillips's 'The New Literary Profession' article
Source: *MPM*, October 1914, 31.

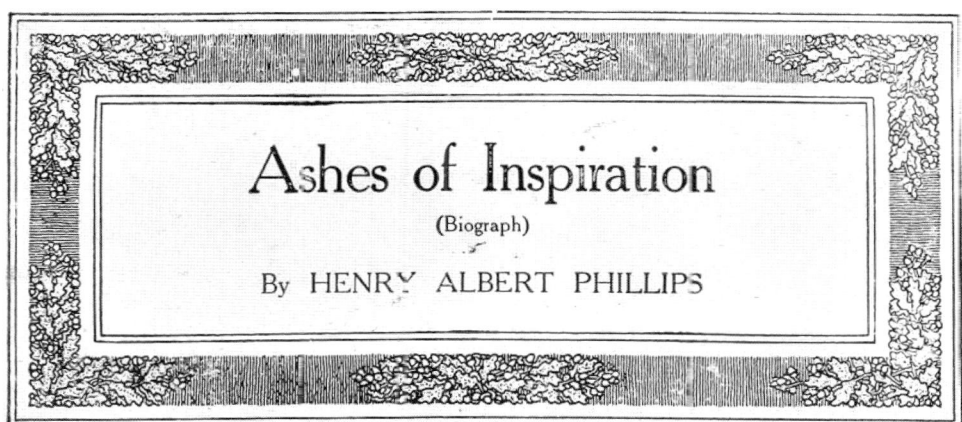

Ashes of Inspiration

(Biograph)

By HENRY ALBERT PHILLIPS

WEST'S life would undoubtedly have been one filled with commonplace, respectable insipidity, if his character had been invigorated with that energetic acumen known as tact. There was something in his nature that made him shrink from a moment's ridicule. As

straight at his unmistakable conduct. And all the while the girl stood waiting for him, her face poised, shrinking in love, yet slightly tinged with shame.

As he made his way home in the darkness, on that memorable night of discovery, he felt that the whole world was against him. His cowardice was

Figure 58: The full story of Phillips's film, *Ashes of Inspiration*
Source: *MPM*, October 1915, 73.

Photodrama in the Making

A Department of General Interest to All Readers, Showing How Photoplays Are Plotted, Written, Submitted and Sold

Conducted by HENRY ALBERT PHILLIPS

Staff Contributor; Lecturer and Instructor in Photoplay Writing in the Brooklyn Institute of Arts and Sciences; also in the Y. M. C. A. of New York; Author of "The Photodrama" and "The Feature Photoplay," and many Current Plays on the Screen, etc.

A COMPLETE PHOTOPLAY SYNOPSIS

NOTE—More than half the inquiries received by this Department ask HOW and in WHAT FORM Photoplays are submitted and sold NOW, in this year, 1918. The following Photoplay SYNOPSIS ONLY is a facsimile of a Photoplay which was sold. Furthermore, the style and form are identical with all the Photoplays I am writing and selling TODAY. This Photoplay was bought and produced by The World Film Company, Miss Alice Brady taking the lead as the *widow*. Hence this is the SALABLE FORM. This is the eighth instalment of the serial publication of this Synopsis.

A SELF-MADE WIDOW
By HENRY ALBERT PHILLIPS

SYNOPSIS—*(Continued)*

PART III.—TO THE ENDS OF THE EARTH—*(Continued)*

Butts has been a trifle suspicious from the first of his new mistress, especially when she had professed ignorance of the identity of a painted portrait of his late master. A new era begins from this date, as the romantic Sylvia proceeds to conceive a sad affection for the image in the painting and daily spends an hour worshiping before it like a shrine.

It is while Sylvia is engaged in the sad duty of worshiping the husband she has never seen that Lydia is ushered in. Strangely enough the two women conceive a deep attachment for each other on learning their mutual history. The girls are absolutely opposites in type. Lydia is masculine in tastes, appearance and preferments. Sylvia is ethereal and spirituelle.

We catch a glimpse of Bobs and Fitzhugh in the South American port. Bobs is intent on appearing like a gentleman, and Fitzhugh takes delight in appearing like a savage, cultivating, besides other rough habits, a pair of fierce whiskers. He is as brown as a berry, where formerly his skin was like a child's.

Thus, after the lapse of six months and absolutely changed, Fitzhugh now tires of the rough life, claiming that he has not found the thing that gives spice to life. So he returns to America, in sailor togs, dead broke. Arm in arm with Bobs, he comes back home, defeated and ready to assume his old life in the lap of luxury.

a rude spirit. Then he says: "AND YOU DONT KNOW WHO THE LADY IS, MASTER FITZHUGH? WHY, SHE'S YOUR WIFE!"

(*To be continued in our next*)

BOUQUETS AND BRICKBATS

I made a protest recently.

Who ever heard of an Author making a protest—and being taken seriously?

I said something to the effect that my name had *scarcely* appeared on the screen in the case of a recent release for which I had been responsible.

The fact was that my name had been Siamese-twinned with that of the person who rearranged my play in continuity or working form. In fact, both the Continuity Writer and myself were equally unhonored. Our appearance was too brief for even a quick-eyed audience to read the names. Quick eyes were outwitted in that the names were printed so *small* as to be almost invisible.

The next name to appear was that of the Director. Was his name in small letters too? No, they were so large that they crowded the space.

But it is not the Director whom I wish to want-to-know-why in this number. His turn will come later.

I merely, mildly and meekly questioned the rights, reasons and ramifications that led to another appearing as co-author of a play for which he has merely written the continuity.

It was but natural that the representative of the Producing Company should rise and tread upon such an objection, like the annoying insect he considered it.

"As to your question regarding Authors' rights in regard to writer's name and scenario writer's being given equal prominence on the screen, this is of course outside of my jurisdiction, but I believe it is the policy of the Company to so consider them."

Then the Editor gave the matter a little defensive thought and came to this polemical conclusion in a postscript to the same letter:

"What do you think Jeanie Macpherson, scenarioist of 'The Whispering Chorus' and 'Joan the Woman,' would say to your question? It all depends, it seems to me, upon *how much* the scenarioist puts into the play. Even our old friend Shakespeare assumed considerable

---

The Photodrama

A Department for the Earnest and Popular Consideration of the Photoplay in All of Its Phases—Hints and Instruction; Plotting and Construction; Selling and Production

NOTE: All readers of this magazine are invited to follow this department. For, altho it may appeal particularly to those who are already writing photoplays, yet it will be written in a popular and interesting manner that will reveal new beauties in the plays you see and read about thru knowing what they come from and how they are made. It may be that you have an underdeveloped talent that this department can turn into dollars and cents! The series will also be continued in the MOTION PICTURE CLASSIC.

A FEW WORDS FROM THE EDITOR

For some time past we have sensed the need and felt the desirability of a department that would cater to the wants of that large and growing class of Motion Picture readers, audiences and students who are interested in the construction, writing and selling of the photoplay.

We have hesitated, for two reasons, until the present time before launching such a department. The first is, that the field of photoplay writing itself has been in a state of primal uncertainty. Few there were indeed who have come anywhere near mastering its technical requirements.

In the second place, where were we to find the man?

Now, we are happy to state, the Motion Picture has truly found itself. There are lapses, to be sure, but you who attend the Motion Picture theaters regularly are rewarded by some of the finest spectacles and deep dramas that can stand without fear of reproach shoulder to shoulder with the best that our stage can offer—more than that, the stage now depends upon the screen for many plots and situations.

What we need, then, are masters of the art of photoplay making, and in Henry Albert Phillips we are going to place the selection of our judgment at your service.

We are not the first to select Henry Albert Phillips as a great inspirational force in the writing of photoplays. The Brooklyn Institute of Arts and Sciences, one of America's greatest and most conservative educational institutions, has chosen Mr. Phillips to inaugurate a course in photoplay writing in their venerable halls. The Y. M. C. A. of New York is retaining Mr. Phillips in a similar capacity for the second year.

We feel, then, in introducing a Department of Photoplay Writing that we have fully rounded out the functions of our magazine so that they now meet the requirements, desires and interests of the entire Motion Picture universe, whom we have been serving to the best of our ability for the past five years.

Welcoming either assenting or dissenting voices in the matter, we remain,

Perpetually at your service,

THE MOTION PICTURE
MAGAZINE AND CLASSIC,
EUGENE V. BREWSTER, *Editor*.

HENRY ALBERT PHILLIPS

JUST WHO HENRY ALBERT PHILLIPS IS:

(*Formerly*)—
Associate Editor of *The Metropolitan Magazine*.
Assistant Editor of *People's Magazine*.
Associate Editor of *The Scenario*.
Associate Editor of the MOTION PICTURE MAGAZINE.
Scenario Editor of *The Motion Picture Mail*.

(*Likewise*)—
Founder of The Playwrights Club.
Contributor of 100 Special Articles.
Author of 3 Produced Stage Plays.
Author of 100 Published Stories.
Author of 50 Produced Photoplays.
Author of 3 Books of Constructive Literature.
Lecturer and Instructor of Photoplay Writing in The Brooklyn Institute of Arts and in The Y. M. C. A. of New York.

Figure 59: Articles in Phillips's column 'The Photodrama' (renamed 'The Photodrama in the Making' in 1918) Source: *MPM*, January 1917, 119 and August 1918, 104.

His regular column for *Motion Picture Magazine*, 'The Photodrama', first appeared in January 1917 and ran under this title until March 1918. In April 1918 it appeared under the new name of 'Photodrama in the Making' and continued in this guise until its close in August 1918 (see Figure 59).[274] Commenting on Phillips as a department head, Brewster claims that he was one of the 'masters of the art of photoplay writing'.[275] Phillips also made contributions to the Home Correspondence School publication *The Photoplay Author* on a variety of screenwriting issues.[276] Always trying to be predictive, Phillips wrote another series of articles entitled 'The New Motion Picture' for *Motion Picture Magazine* from mid-1923 until early 1924 (see Figure 60), charting possible future developments in technology within the industry such as 3D effects, sound, colour and new camera and screen developments.[277] However, it seems that by 1924 Phillips was intent on becoming a full-time novelist; according to Brewster, he had left the *Motion Picture Magazine* staff to focus on this.[278]

Phillips's first manual, *The Photodrama*, was published in 1914 (see Figure 61). Complimenting the work, Wright dubs it 'Another "Worth While" Book' and is particularly impressed with its practical usefulness to the working author:

> It covers very thoroughly, the philosophy of its (the photodrama's) principles, the nature of its plot, its dramatic construction and technique, illumined by copious examples, together with a complete photoplay and glossary of terms.[279]

---

274   'The Photodrama' ran from January 1917, 119–120 to March 1918, 108 and 110. 'Photodrama in the Making' ran from April 1918, 60 and 122 to August 1918, 104 and 113 in *MPM*.

275   Brewster, 'A Few Words from the Editor' in Phillips, 'The Photodrama', *MPM*, January 1917, 119–120.

276   See Phillips, 'Visualisation', August 1914, 35–38 and 'Literary Construction – Its Art and Technique', March 1915, 67–69 in *Photoplay Author*.

277   Phillips wrote a series of five articles for *MPM* in 1923 and 1924 called 'The New Motion Picture': '1. The Teleview', August 1923, 35–36; '2. The Phonofilm', September 1923, 39–40 and 93; '3. Pictures in Natural Colors', November 1923, 57 and 95; '4. The Unknown World Revealed', December 1923, 61–62 and 110–111; '5. Daylight Movies', January 1924, 68 and 104–106.

278   Brewster, 'A Word About Henry Albert Phillips', *MPM*, July 1924, 47.

279   Wright, 'Looking Over the Field', *Photoplay Author*, October 1914, 117–119.

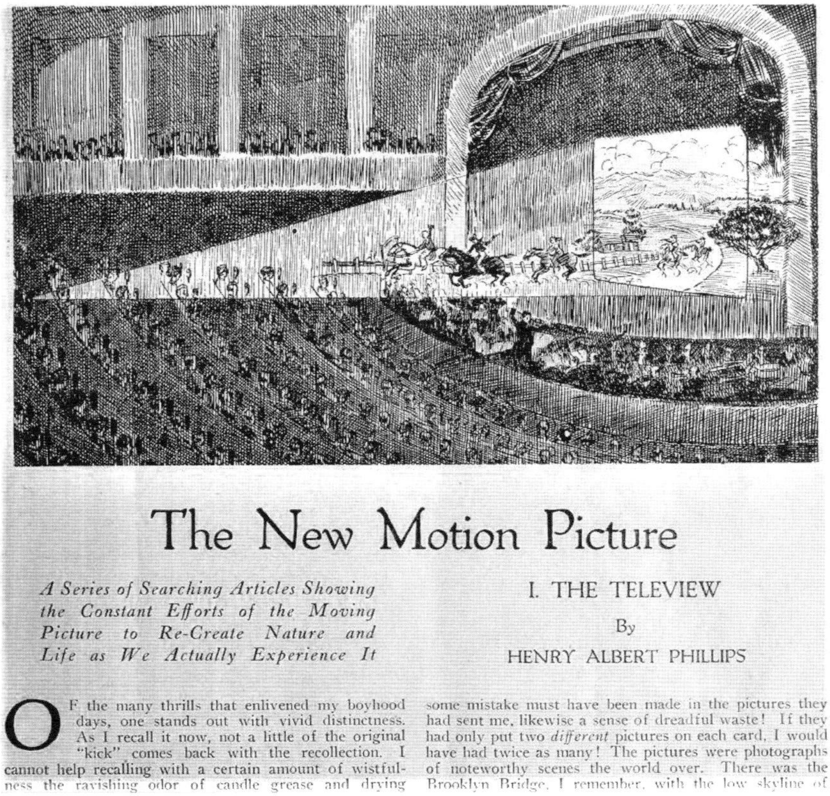

The New Motion Picture

A Series of Searching Articles Showing the Constant Efforts of the Moving Picture to Re-Create Nature and Life as We Actually Experience It

I. THE TELEVIEW

By

HENRY ALBERT PHILLIPS

OF the many thrills that enlivened my boyhood days, one stands out with vivid distinctness. As I recall it now, not a little of the original "kick" comes back with the recollection. I cannot help recalling with a certain amount of wistfulness the ravishing odor of candle grease and drying

some mistake must have been made in the pictures they had sent me, likewise a sense of dreadful waste! If they had only put two *different* pictures on each card, I would have had twice as many! The pictures were photographs of noteworthy scenes the world over. There was the Brooklyn Bridge, I remember, with the low skyline of

Figure 60: An article in Phillips's series 'The New Motion Picture'
Source: *MPM*, August 1923, 35.

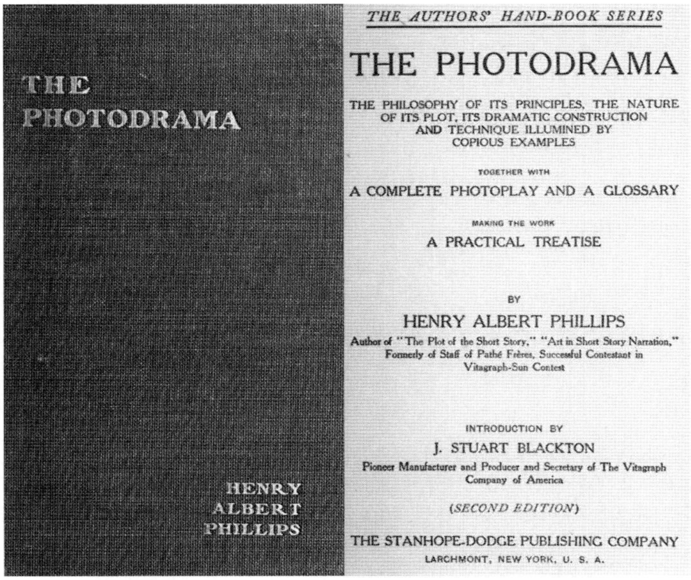

THE PHOTODRAMA

HENRY ALBERT PHILLIPS

THE AUTHORS' HAND-BOOK SERIES

THE PHOTODRAMA

THE PHILOSOPHY OF ITS PRINCIPLES, THE NATURE OF ITS PLOT, ITS DRAMATIC CONSTRUCTION AND TECHNIQUE ILLUMINED BY COPIOUS EXAMPLES

TOGETHER WITH

A COMPLETE PHOTOPLAY AND A GLOSSARY

MAKING THE WORK

A PRACTICAL TREATISE

BY

HENRY ALBERT PHILLIPS

Author of "The Plot of the Short Story," "Art in Short Story Narration," Formerly of Staff of Pathé Frères, Successful Contestant in Vitagraph-Sun Contest

INTRODUCTION BY

J. STUART BLACKTON

Pioneer Manufacturer and Producer and Secretary of The Vitagraph Company of America

(SECOND EDITION)

THE STANHOPE-DODGE PUBLISHING COMPANY

LARCHMONT, NEW YORK, U. S. A.

Figure 61: Phillips's *The Photodrama* book cover and title page
Source: *archive.org/details/photodramaphilos01phil.*

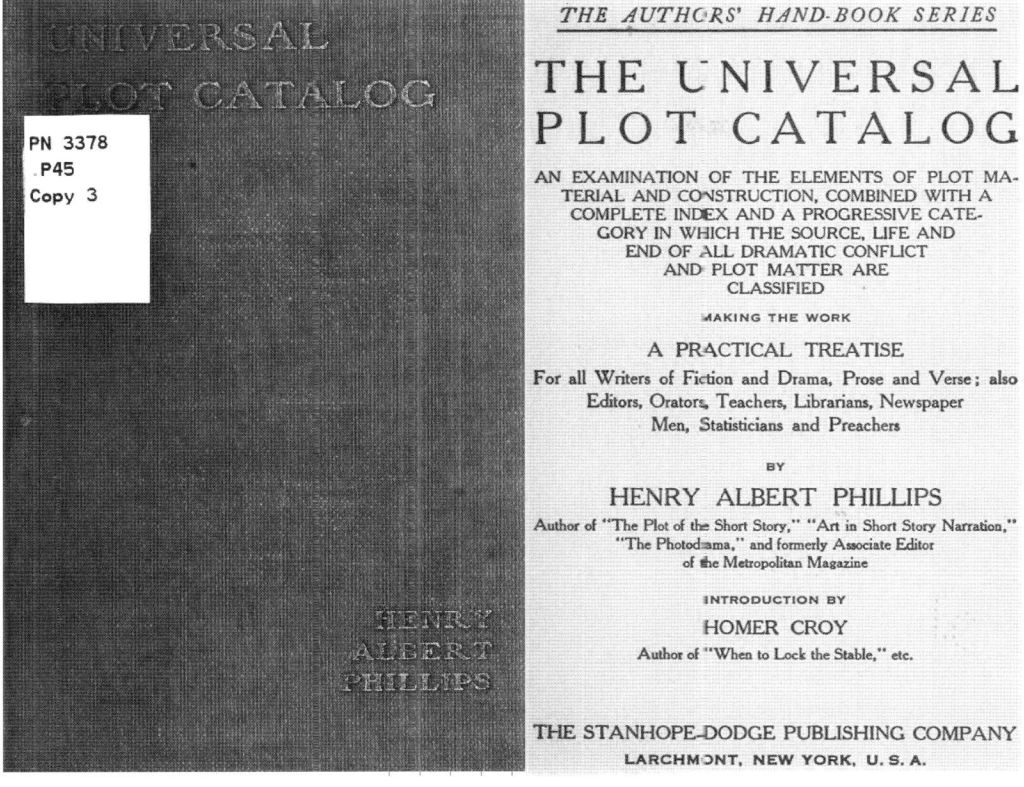

Figure 62: Phillips's *The Universal Plot Catalogue* book cover and title page
Source: *archive.org/details/universalplotcat00phi*.

Sargent claims that it was deserving of 'a thousand other words of praise'.[280] As Phillips worked closely with, and wrote for, the Home Correspondence School, it was through the school that he would publish his second manual *The Universal Plot Catalogue* in 1920 (see Figure 62), referred to in Chapter 1. This was often sold alongside *The Phillips Automatic Plot Collector, File and Index,* which was some kind of storage system for referencing and categorising potential plot material.[281] *The Universal Plot Catalogue* was not a manual in the strictest sense, but a method of organising plot material that could in turn stimulate the imagination and bring about inspiration.[282] Sargent considers, if '[u]sed intelligently [it… would guide the student', which by implication meant that it was not to be employed slavishly, but for generating ideas.[283] Phillips's third manual, *The Feature Photoplay* (see Figure 63), was published in 1921.

---

280   'Successful Photoplay Writing' advertisement in *MPM*, February 1915, 5.

281   For reference to the *Plot Collector*, see Phillips, *The Universal Plot Catalogue* (1920: repr., Nabu, 2013), 64, 75 and 158.

282   Phillips, 'Where to Get Photoplay Plots', *MPM*, February 1915, 101–105.

283   Sargent, 'The Photodrama', *MPW*, March 24, 1917, 1914.

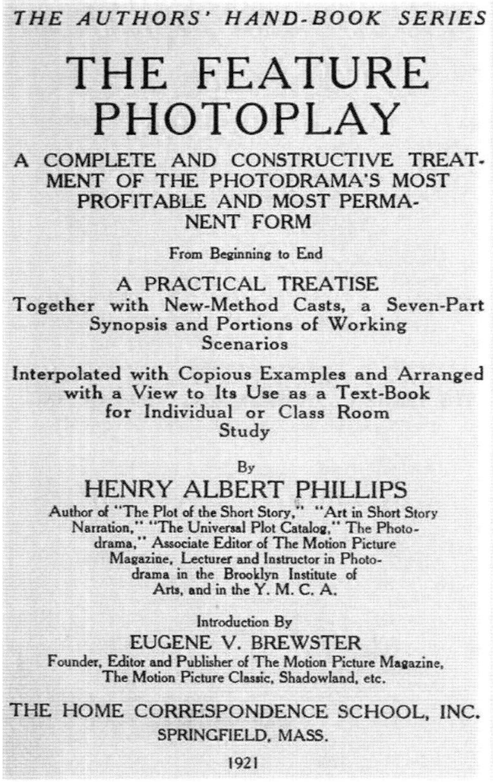
THE AUTHORS' HAND-BOOK SERIES

THE FEATURE PHOTOPLAY

A COMPLETE AND CONSTRUCTIVE TREATMENT OF THE PHOTODRAMA'S MOST PROFITABLE AND MOST PERMANENT FORM

From Beginning to End

A PRACTICAL TREATISE
Together with New-Method Casts, a Seven-Part Synopsis and Portions of Working Scenarios

Interpolated with Copious Examples and Arranged with a View to Its Use as a Text-Book for Individual or Class Room Study

By

HENRY ALBERT PHILLIPS

Author of "The Plot of the Short Story," "Art in Short Story Narration," "The Universal Plot Catalog," The Photodrama," Associate Editor of The Motion Picture Magazine, Lecturer and Instructor in Photodrama in the Brooklyn Institute of Arts, and in the Y. M. C. A.

Introduction By

EUGENE V. BREWSTER

Founder, Editor and Publisher of The Motion Picture Magazine, The Motion Picture Classic, Shadowland, etc.

THE HOME CORRESPONDENCE SCHOOL, INC.
SPRINGFIELD, MASS.
1921

Figure 63: Phillips's *The Feature Photoplay* title page
Source: *archive.org/details/featurephotoplay00phil/page/n5.*

This was followed by a fourth and final manual, *The Art of Writing Photoplays*, in 1922. Three out of four of Phillips's manuals were still being advertised in 1926, which is perhaps indicative of their enduring popularity and relevance.[284]

Two other books by Phillips are worthy of note: *The Plot of the Short Story* (1912) and *Art in Short Story Narration* (1913) (see Figure 64). Other manual writers, in particular, frequently recommended *The Plot of the Short Story* as essential reading. In a special feature article about Phillips, Leeds clearly celebrates the success of this publication:

> As for the little book, over two thousand copies were sold during the first nine or ten months, and today seventy-one states and countries possess copies of it. It goes without saying, the author of the textbook has long since taken his place as a writer of helpful books for the literary aspirant.[285]

284 Advertisement in *Screenland*, July 1926, 92.

285 Arthur Leeds, 'So You'll Know Them Better – XVI. Henry Albert Phillips – An Idealist with a Punch', *Photoplay Author*, September 1914, 69–74.

THE AUTHORS' HAND-BOOK SERIES

THE PLOT OF THE SHORT STORY

AN EXHAUSTIVE STUDY, BOTH SYNTHETICAL AND
ANALYTICAL, WITH COPIOUS EXAMPLES,
MAKING THE WORK

A PRACTICAL TREATISE
(Revised to include a Syllabus for Teachers)

BY

HENRY ALBERT PHILLIPS
FORMERLY ASSOCIATE EDITOR OF THE
METROPOLITAN MAGAZINE

Author of "Art in Short Story Narration," "The Photo Drama,"
"The Universal Plot Catalog," "The Feature Photo Play," etc.

INTRODUCTION BY

MATTHEW WHITE, JR.
EDITOR OF THE ARGOSY

Third Edition

THE HOME CORRESPONDENCE SCHOOL
SPRINGFIELD, MASS.

THE AUTHORS' HAND-BOOK SERIES

Art In Short Story Narration

A Searching Analysis of the Qualifications of Fiction
in General, and of the Short Story in Particular,
with Copious Examples, Making the Work

A PRACTICAL TREATISE

BY

HENRY ALBERT PHILLIPS
Author of "The Plot of the Short Story," and formerly Associate
Editor of the Metropolitan Magazine

INTRODUCTION BY
REX BEACH
Author of "The Barrier," "The Silver Horde," "The
Ne'er Do Well," etc.

THE STANHOPE-DODGE PUBLISHING CO.
LARCHMONT, NEW YORK

Figure 64: Title pages of two other books by Phillips,
The Plot of the Short Story and *Art in Short Story Narration*
Source: *archive.org/details/plotshortstorya01philgoog/page/n4*
and *archive.org/details/artinshortstory00philgoog/page/n4.*

EXPERT and PERSONAL
Instruction in Short Story Writing

By a Successful Author and Former Magazine Editor

Every point in the Preparation for Authorship, also in
the Conception, Plot, Construction, Narration and Dis-
posal of the Short Story treated exhaustively. You
might save a year's wasted or misdirected effort!
Any form of Literary, Editorial, Critical and Instructive
help given
Thru CORRESPONDENCE, to any part of the United
States or Canada;
Thru PRIVATE LESSONS, arranged for within the
city limits;
Thru Monday Evening COURSE OF LECTURES, in
the Metropolitan Bldg.
For further particulars, address

HENRY ALBERT PHILLIPS
507 West 111th Street, New York City

Figure 65: Advertisement for Phillips's
lectures on short story writing
Source: *MPSM*, May 1912, 171.

The popularity of these works among photoplay writers was yet another indication of the close relationship between this mode of fiction and the photoplay. Phillips gave lectures on the subject of short story writing, as he did for photoplay writing (see Figure 65).[286] This particular work again brings forth praise from Sargent:

> We think the photoplaywright will find many helpful hints in *The Plot of the Short Story*. [...] Mr. Phillips proves himself a teacher as well as an author. The renowned novelist and master of short story writing, Jack London also says of it, 'It is an excellent thing excellently done'.[287]

Meeting the Criteria

Although the status of Sargent is recognised in academic study – even if not to the extent that his contribution to the screenwriting discourse in particular deserves – the other four key screenwriting teachers have never received such recognition. Wright's achievements do not fall far short of Sargent's and yet he has received scant attention from past and present film historians for his contribution to the screenwriting discourse. Similarly, while Peacocke, Ball and Phillips are often quoted in film histories, their contributions have never been the subject of any detailed and extensive assessment.

As discussed in the Introduction, Azlant does recognise Sargent's work as significant in relation to the development of the screenplay, but this study will go further and demonstrate that the instructive work of Sargent and the other key screenwriting teachers could well have played a stronger role in the education of the screenwriter in the early 1910s than has previously been thought. Where these screenwriting teachers have been mentioned, it tends to be in relation to one or more of their other roles. For example, Azlant acknowledges that 'Ball was a fascinating figure' and discusses his literary achievements as an illustration of those who went on to become professional writers. However, he makes no reference to Ball's endeavours as a screenwriting teacher.[288]

Although guarded in his assessment of the overall impact of Sargent's work, Liepa does recognise his role in providing a forum of discussion about screenwriting: 'Though the degree of Sargent's influence can be debated, it is clear that his column functioned as a crucial discursive locus for the field.'[289] Liepa, who refers to Sargent as only a 'relative insider',[290] views him more as an interlocutor than an instigator of the debates about screenwriting:

---

286   'Expert and Personal Instruction: Instruction in Short Story Writing', advertisement in *MPSM*, May 1912, 171.

287   'The Plot of the Short Story', advertisement in Phillips, *Photodrama*, 222. See Sargent's extended comment in Sargent, 'The Photodrama', *MPW*, September 28, 1912, 1274.

288   Azlant, 'Theory, History and Practice of Screenwriting', 144–146.

289   Liepa, 'Figures of Silent Speech', 126.

290   Ibid., 202.

> Much of this discourse found its way into the press specifically through Epes
> Winthrop Sargent's columns. Sargent, in fact, in many ways served as a barometer
> for changes occurring within scriptwriting in the early 1910s.[291]

Despite Liepa's reservations, as this study has already indicated, the industry viewed
Sargent as a definite 'insider'. What Liepa's research has identified that is of interest to
this book, however, is the significant contribution that Sargent and, to some extent, the
other key screenwriting teachers made to the codification and development of the use of
intertitles; his views will be considered in Chapter 6.

Another to underplay the roles of the key screenwriters is Stempel. He makes only a
brief factual comment about Sargent and refers to one of Ball's manuals, alongside those
of less important manual writers. He writes nothing about Wright, Peacocke or Phillips.
As indicated in Chapter 3, Stempel also wrongly attributes the main origins of scenario
fever to the 'rush of books on writing screenplays' when companies opened themselves
up to outside submissions.[292] This is a case where the role of screenwriting teachers has
been overplayed: it is clear that this phenomenon was caused by a far more complex set
of circumstances (see Chapter 3).

Where the five most important candidates in this study, along with others whom I have
denoted as more peripheral, do appear frequently is in Thompson's work. However,
she draws on them merely in relation to her own contribution to the discourse on the
development of classical narrative style. She makes no attempt to evaluate or pass
judgement on the extent of their influence or to make any distinction between those of
lesser or greater significance.[293] In another essay celebrating the centenary of cinema,
Thompson compares views on film structure in early manuals with those of the modern
era. Although she again refers to four out of five of the key screenwriting teachers –
Sargent, Wright, Ball and Phillips – she appears to give them equal weight alongside
Palmer, Nelson, Bertsch, Patterson and Loos who, as indicated earlier in this chapter,
were of less importance to the screenwriting discourse.[294]

As discussed in the Introduction, in his contextual analysis of the history of screenwriting,
Maras also makes frequent reference to all the five key screenwriting teachers and
some others of lesser note He draws on their manuals as historical sources in order to
contextualise a broader argument about the development of screenwriting practice and

---

291   Ibid., 123.

292   Stempel, *Framework*, 14–15.

293   Bordwell and Staiger also make mention of screenwriting teachers but only as part of a wider film
discourse. See extended essays in Bordwell, Staiger and Thompson, *The Classical Hollywood Cinema*, 3–49
and 87–153.

294   Thompson, 'Narrative Structure in Early Classical Cinema' in *Celebrating 1895: The Centenary of
Cinema*, ed., Fullerton, 225–238

the nature of screenwriting today and in the future. The aim of this work is to 'challenge [our] understanding of screenwriting […] and ways of thinking about film in general, the production process, the functions performed by the film script'.[295] Again, as Maras's focus concerns viewpoints on the 'scripting' process, he makes little attempt to distinguish between these teachers or to evaluate their level of influence, except in the case of Sargent, whose work he describes as providing 'an interesting archive for developments in photoplay writing'.[296] Maras acknowledges that this archive is 'significant' and reiterates Azlant's endorsement that it represents a 'distillation and on-going revision of public instruction'.[297] Patterson is another whose work Maras refers to extensively for the part it played in institutionalising writing for the screen and setting up formal educational processes for teaching screenwriting.[298] While this chapter has already acknowledged Patterson's contribution in this area, her role in the early development of screenwriting practice is more questionable; it would be better expressed as codifying existing practice and formalising rather than initiating it, as her first manual did not appear until 1920.

In contrast to the position held by other scholars, I contend that the key screenwriting teachers probably played a far more significant role in the development of screenwriting practice than has previously been recognised, because they all either meet or substantially meet the five criteria. They were all writers of high regard with a significant number of produced scenarios. All but one, Phillips, worked as scenario editors. In terms of trade and fan press publications, only Ball did not write a regular column. Sargent wrote almost entirely for the trade press, Wright for both the trade and fan press, Phillips mostly for the fan press and Peacocke only for the fan press. Three produced more than one manual, while Sargent's one manual was substantially revised in each of its three editions and Peacocke's was published in more than one edition. They all had significant connections with the industry and were all viewed as industry insiders.

Undoubtedly the most celebrated of these five screenwriting teachers is Sargent, and his commendation of the other four is important. He directly endorses the manuals of three of them: 'As to the library, here are some suggestions', which include books by Wright, Ball and Phillips, among others.[299] In addition, Peacocke is one of the few influential writers who he reserves for mention in a special feature article 'The Literary Side of Pictures' in 1914.[300]

---

295   Maras, *Screenwriting*, 1.

296   Ibid., 145.

297   Ibid., 148.

298   Ibid., 149–152.

299   Sargent, 'The Photoplaywright', *MPW*, February 7, 1914, 670–671.

300   Sargent only mentions the most significant writers: 'The Universal staff is headed by Captain T. Peacocke who is also a dramatist and novelist.' See Sargent, 'The Literary Side of Pictures', *MPW*, July 11, 1914, 202.

The five key screenwriting teachers operated in the most fertile period for the amateur scenario market (1910–1917) and while the industry was in a state of flux. By the late teens, when the Hollywood industry had become virtually a closed shop for outsiders, the industry was dealing with questions about how to write scenarios as an internal matter. Those who wrote later, such as Loos (1920), Patterson (1920) and Palmer (1921), were only codifying and confirming practices that had already been established, rather than initiating or engaging in a seminal discourse with the general public and the industry. Although Loos and Emerson wrote columns for the fan press publications *Photoplay* in 1918 and *The Motion Picture Magazine* in 1921, this activity was possibly linked more to the advancement of their own celebrity status than to a desire to help the struggling writer of scenarios. Certainly the manual by Leeds and Esenwein, published in 1915, had some credibility but the authors' broader influence was limited: Esenwein had eclectic interests and Leeds's star had already begun to wane. Among the other manual writers whom I have considered, either they lacked a sufficient profile to exert a major influence or their manuals were too simplistic.

It should be noted that the four key screenwriting teachers who had columns wrote them between 1911 and 1921: Peacocke, 1915–1917; Phillips, 1917–1918; Sargent, 1911–1919; and Wright, 1911–1921. The first manual of each of the five teachers was published before 1917: Wright, 1911; Sargent, 1912; Ball, 1913; Phillips, 1914; and Peacocke, 1916. These dates are a further indication that all these individuals were involved in screenwriting instruction during the most crucial period of 1911–1917, when they could exert most influence.

6. The Discourse – What the Key Screenwriting Teachers Advised

Having established that certain screenwriting teachers were more influential than others on the developing discourse about how to write for the screen, it is now possible to turn to the discourse itself.

This chapter begins by identifying that the advice taken from the most relevant editions of the manuals of the five key screenwriting teachers focused on three areas – how to train for, write for and sell to the industry. The following sections then examine each of these areas in more detail: the learning, filmic and storytelling processes that had to be mastered in order to train for the industry; the protocols of visual writing, photoplay form and screen technique that had to be followed in order to write for the industry; and the manuscript requirements and marketing strategies that had to be employed in order to sell to the industry.

This discussion sets the foundations for the comprehensive assessment of the main contribution that the key screenwriting teachers made to the discourse in Chapter 7.

The Nature of the Advice

In establishing what advice the five key screenwriting teachers offered, I have based my study on their manuals. One reason for this choice is that the contents were mainly drawn from their columns in the trade or fan press and/or from their personal experience of writing and editing the work of others; another is that the manuals clearly represent the views of these individuals. In addition, all but one of these teachers wrote more than one manual or made significant changes to their original manual in a new edition, which also provides some insight into how they adapted their approaches during periods of transition in the film industry. Where necessary, however, this discussion is supplemented by primary and secondary material from other sources, and from the fan and trade press.

Sargent's one manual, *The Technique of the Photoplay*, appeared in three editions, 1912, 1913 and 1916. As this is a large body of material to examine, the issue of which edition(s) to use as the main reference presents itself. As noted in Chapter 5, Maras argues that Sargent's work offers an interesting archive for developments in photoplay form. By way of illustration, Maras compares Sargent's own comments in the first and second editions of his manual to indicate how Sargent believed the craft of screenwriting had developed over a very short period:

> [In] the first edition of his Technique of the Photoplay [...] 'the writing of photoplays is at once the most simple and the most difficult form of dramatic construction.'

By the second edition, 'the art of writing photoplays has become possessed of a technique that is applicable only to the writing of picture plays and to no other form.' A distinct and separate domain of technique opens up, beyond the normal sphere of dramatic construction.[1]

According to Maras, Sargent's second edition viewed screenwriting as a highly specialised craft, which was a clear development from the first. On this basis, the second edition should take precedence over the first for the purposes of this study. However, Azlant selects the third edition as the basis for his study, because he claims it is a major revision of the second edition (1913) and represents a 'distillation and on-going revision of public instruction' of the period.[2] Maras quotes this comment from Azlant, but incorrectly attributes it as applying to all the editions by claiming that 'the three editions [...] form a significant archive'.[3] From Azlant's original work, however, it is clear he means only the third edition.

A cursory examination of the second edition and comparison with the third edition confirm that the third contains significant reorganisations of material, substantial additions and also some extensive revisions of the original content, which comprise Sargent's detailed description of the craft. Given that Azlant appears to provide the clearest endorsement of the value of the third edition, and he is the only scholar to have investigated Sargent's work extensively, his opinion carries weight. Moreover, as this study is not specifically focusing on the development of the screenplay, there is little need to analyse the similarities and differences of these two editions in detail, so I have decided to focus on the third edition as the basis for study, while referring to the second where necessary. In support of this decision, I also note that Sargent chose to keep the original title, presumably because he believed it to be fundamentally the same manual, but a much-improved version.

With regard to the other key screenwriting teachers, no such problems are encountered. Of Wright's three manuals two survive: *The Motion Picture Story* (1914) and *Photoplay Writing* (1922). These are fundamentally different books, written years apart, and present contrasting views of screenwriting practice and the role of the screenwriting teacher in relation to the film industry. Among the five teachers, Peacocke is the only one with just one surviving and unchanged manual, *Hints on Photoplay Writing* (1916), although it appeared in more than one edition. The material for this manual was drawn directly from his 1915–16 articles in *Photoplay* and, as a body of work, it is of particular interest with regard to the freelance market for amateurs. Ball's two manuals, *The Art of the Photoplay* (1913) and *Photoplay Scenarios, How to Write and Sell Them* (1915),

---

1   Maras quotes from Sargent, *The Technique of the Photoplay*, 1st ed. (New York: MPW, 1912), 3 and *The Technique of the Photoplay*, 2nd ed. (1913: repr., BiblioBazaar, 2012) 7. See Maras, *Screenwriting*, 145.

2   Azlant, 'Theory, History and Practice of Screenwriting', 211.

3   Maras, *Screenwriting*, 148.

were written only two years apart yet they are very different books. It is clear from the substantially different content that Ball wrote the second book from scratch rather than by revising the first. His two manuals offer some significant insights into the changes that occurred in the industry, from a writing and instructional perspective, during this short period (1913–15).

The differences between Sargent's second edition of *The Technique of the Photoplay* (1912) and the third (1916) are also considerable but, for reasons already suggested, unravelling all the intricate differences would be beyond the realm of this study. Suffice to say, a cursory examination of these differences does confirm the increasing sophistication of the writing process and, as the opportunity to make these comparisons is already offered by comparing the manuals of three of the other key screenwriting teachers, repeating the process with Sargent's various editions is unnecessary.

Three of Phillips's four manuals are instructional. The first two, *The Photodrama* (1914) and *The Feature Photoplay* (1921), are completely different books, written years apart, and offer us an understanding of the many changes that had occurred in the approach of screenwriting teachers over this period. The third, *The Art of Writing Photoplays* (1922), is aimed at the professional writer and focuses on how to write a 'continuity'. It is an interesting addition to *The Feature Photoplay*, which was written for the freelance market and concentrates solely on how to write an extended synopsis.

These five key screenwriting teachers were in a position to shape, influence and guide the discourse in three broad areas: how to train for the industry; how to write for the industry; and how to sell to the industry. These three concerns are clearly exemplified in the writings of all five teachers.

Although Wright's first manual, *The Art of Writing Scenarios*, can no longer be located, an early review of its contents in *Moving Picture World* indicates that it clearly addressed the above three questions:

> [This…] little book of about 30 pages […] adds to our knowledge of a subject that has perplexed many would-be moving picture authors, namely; how to set about work; how to acquire its technique; how in fact, to prepare goods suitable for the market.[4]

The hierarchy of importance of these questions for their readers was a matter of discussion. In identifying the question that the general public most commonly asked, some playful comments by Sargent in his own column in response to comments from Wright in his column are indicative of areas of disagreement:

> Now and then William Lord Wright will step on a banana peel and slip up. He says the question most frequently asked is how to write scripts. That is not so. That is

---

4 'The Art of Writing Scenarios', *MPW*, February 25, 1911, 419.

question number two. The most frequent one – and we think he will agree with us – is 'I have written a photoplay. Where can I sell it?' This is before they even dream that what they have done is not a photoplay.[5]

First and foremost, Sargent is concerned that his readers should understand what a photoplay is, as indicated by his final comment. In other words, for him, education about the nature of photoplay writing was paramount. However, he recognised that, for many, the possibility of selling work and making money was the priority rather than first learning 'how to write scripts'. A need he perceived, perhaps more keenly than Wright, was to reorient the general public's priorities in this respect. That is, those who wrote needed first to understand the process involved in becoming a writer, second to acquire the knowledge and technique to do it, and third to concern themselves with selling their work.

In the foreword of Peacocke's book, where the publishers set out its purpose, the same issues are implicit:

> Do you want to write a moving picture scenario? Do you want to know how to write it so that it will stand a chance of acceptance? [...] This book is full of instructions – hints and helps [. . and] is published for the purpose of helping YOU [...] become a part in the development of moving pictures.[6]

For Peacocke, a person must understand what is involved in becoming a writer and 'know how to write' material that has 'a chance of acceptance'. In an interview for a feature article in *Movie Pictorial* in 1914, he also prioritises these three issues. First, he states how people can school themselves as writers: 'Beginners should study pictures and see how things are done. The motion picture theatre is the best teacher available.' Then he adds, almost as an afterthought, how important it is to gain knowledge of how to write and then to sell: 'Of course one should know plots, and know how to market his scenarios after he has written them.'[7]

Just as succinctly, Ball sums up the aims of his first book, *The Art of the Photoplay*:

> To learn how a scenario is received and produced, through the various stages of the studio and outdoor work; to learn what are its essentials; to learn the technical needs of the companies, and the drawing and selling power of various kinds of motion picture plays.[8]

---

5   Sargent, 'The Photoplaywright', *MPW*, March 13, 1915, 1601–1602.

6   Peacocke, *Hints on Photoplay Writing*, 1–4.

7   Katterjohn, 'Captain Leslie T. Peacocke', *Movie Pictorial*, August 15. 1914, 16–17 and 32.

8   Ball, *Art of the Photoplay*, 9.

For Ball, the writer must 'learn' about the writing and filmic process, 'learn […] its essentials' or how to do it and then gain knowledge about the 'selling power' of their work.

In his column, Phillips sums up his approach with four statements:

> First, learn what a photoplay is. Second, know how to write one. Third, follow the market needs. Fourth, write the photoplay that will sell on its merits.[9]

Phillips's summary repeats the same three-pronged mantra, as his third and fourth statements both address the issue of selling work.

To consider what these five key screenwriting teachers taught about screenwriting, it is helpful to probe their thinking using the three logical questions that they all aimed to address. The issues raised in answering them are not exclusive to each question, as their concerns overlapped, just as they are likely to have done in the minds of prospective freelance writers. The overlap can also be demonstrated from the writings of these screenwriting teachers, who do not always address these questions sequentially in designated sections or in an organised chapter-by-chapter manner. However, using these three questions to interrogate the large body of work that these screenwriting teachers produced, both in their handbooks and their columns, allows a more incisive and purposeful investigation and makes it easier to organise and codify their responses in a focused way. As a natural corollary, it will also permit a comparative analysis and evaluation of some of the main similarities and differences that existed between their approaches to screenwriting instruction.

How to Train for the Industry

Those who wanted to train for the industry needed instruction in how to approach it; knowledge across the population of how the industry worked was limited early in the century. Frederick Talbot was inspired to write a popular volume about all the technical aspects of the industry, because:

> A vast industry has been established of which the great majority of picture-palace patrons have no idea, and the moment appears timely to describe the many branches of the art.[10]

The opinion of W. Hanson, scenario editor for Western Vitagraph, about writers' lack of industry knowledge is typical:

---

9   Phillips, 'The Photodrama', *MPM*, January 1917, 119-120.

10   Frederick Talbot, *Moving Pictures: How They are Made and Worked* (1912: repr., Whitefish, MA: Kessinger Publishing, 2013), vii.

> The average author has no idea of the close serious study, which must be given to each script previous to production to make the salable scenario a working scenario.[11]

In answer to these concerns, the key screenwriting teachers would impart information on the distinctive skills required for film writing, basic instruction on how films were made and technical advice on submission formats and the mechanics of scenario writing. For clarity, these three broad realms of knowledge will be addressed separately as 'The Learning Process', 'The Filmic Process' and 'The Storytelling Process'.

The Learning Process

The advice that the key screenwriting teachers offered in their manuals was always optimistic and positive, as if reading the manual were the first step in a potentially lucrative and successful writing career. In reality, the claims probably held an element of exaggeration. Their readers had more than likely purchased a manual after reading a column by the author and/or coming across one of the numerous advertisements in the fan or trade press and/or seeing or reading about a photoplay the author had written (see Figures 66 and 67).[12] Advertisements about manuals written by peer authors also commonly appeared in the flyleaves of a manual they had already purchased, or the author recommended the manuals of others as further reading.[13] However, as noted in the Introduction, the advertisements of these more legitimate teachers generally contained far more muted claims than those of the correspondence schools.

As a first step, it was important to restate the assurances contained in any advertisements that had originally drawn the fledgling writer to buy the manual. Such opening gambits verged on hyperbole, but were also designed to enthuse, inspire and kindle the fire of ambition in the individual to write for the screen and to convince them that the manual they had chosen would not disappoint.

---

11   W. Hanson, 'A Few Particular Points', *The Photoplaywright*, November 1912, 4.

12   See sample advertisements and features for Sargent's 'Technique of the Photoplay', *MPW*, January 2, 1915, 69 and *Photoplay Journal*, May 1916, 31; Wright's 'The Art of Writing Scenarios', *MPW*, February 18, 1911, 385; Peacocke's 'Hints on Photoplay Writing', *Photoplay*, December 1916, 14; Ball's 'Photoplay Scenarios: How to Write and Sell Them', *MPN*, January 15, 1916, 248; and Phillips's 'The Photodrama', *MPM*, March 1915, 181.

13   Sargent, *Technique of the Photoplay* 3rd ed., 358. See also the advertisement for the 2nd edition of Sargent's 'Technique of the Photoplay' in Wright, *Motion Picture Story*, 229. Esenwein and Leeds endorse the works of Sargent and Phillips in the appendices of their manual. See Esenwein and Leeds, *Writing the Photoplay*, 293–294.

More measured is Wright's viewpoint on the potential opportunity in his manual, in keeping with its trade literature advertisement (see Figure 68):

> Writing the motion-picture story has assumed the dignity of a separate and distinct literary profession. For anyone with a fair amount of education and talent may enter it and attain some success.[14]

In stark contrast, the opening statement in Peacocke's manual is brash, but again is in line with the fan press advertisement (see Figure 69): 'This book, by a foremost authority, contains all that can be taught on the conception and preparation of motion picture scenarios.'[15]

One other ingredient that all the key screenwriting teachers stressed was that proficiency and accomplishment could only be achieved through application and perseverance. According to Sargent, being prepared to face rejection and failure was a prerequisite.[16] Similarly Wright asserted, 'You may have to write for a year or two before you really know how to do it [...]. It is likely to take time and patience – and a great deal of effort.'[17] Peacocke's upbeat tone is also laced with warnings: 'A lazy person never has time for anything; he is always behind in every endeavor.'[18] As all five key screenwriting teachers saw it, success was never assured: instead it depended on diligence and dedication as well as ability.

Once students were aware of the commitment, cost and potential rewards of this enterprise, they needed to know how to school themselves in it. In 'How to Become an Author', Sargent advises that the prospective scenario writer should 'study the screen, and the papers, and the books'.[19]

---

14   Wright, *The Motion Picture Story* (Chicago: Cloud Publishing, 1914), 8.

15   Peacocke, *Hints on Photoplay Writing*, 1.

16   Sargent, *Technique of the Photoplay*, 3rd ed., 305–306.

17   Wright, *Photoplay Writing,* 7.

18   Peacocke, 'Hints on Photoplay Writing', *Photoplay*, March 1916, 125.

19   Sargent, 'The Photoplaywright', *MPW*, February 7, 1914, 670.

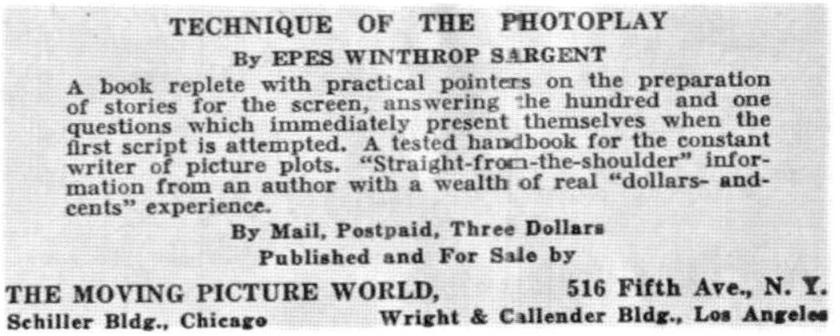

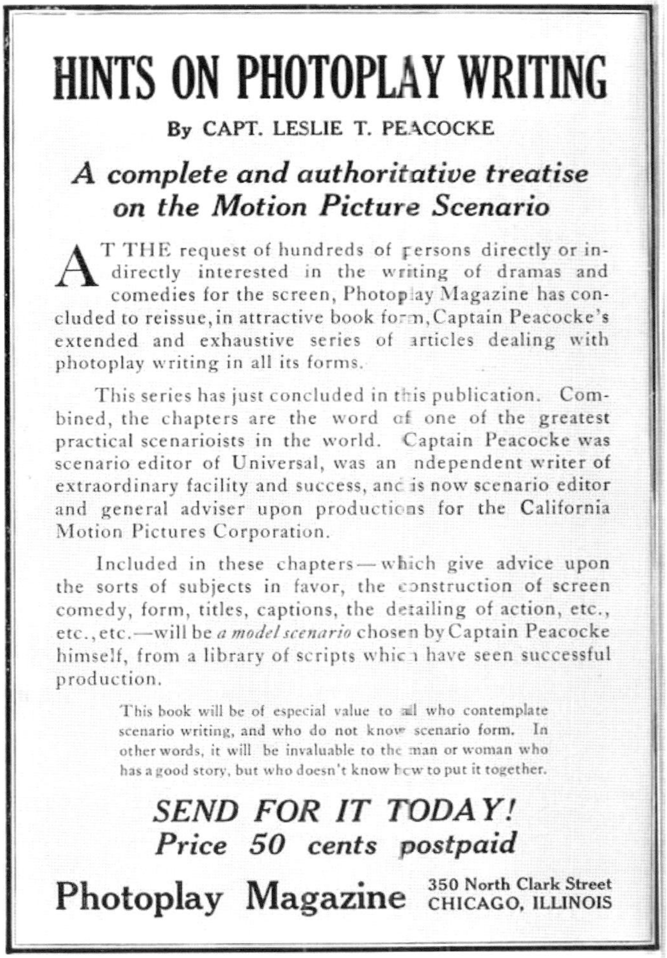

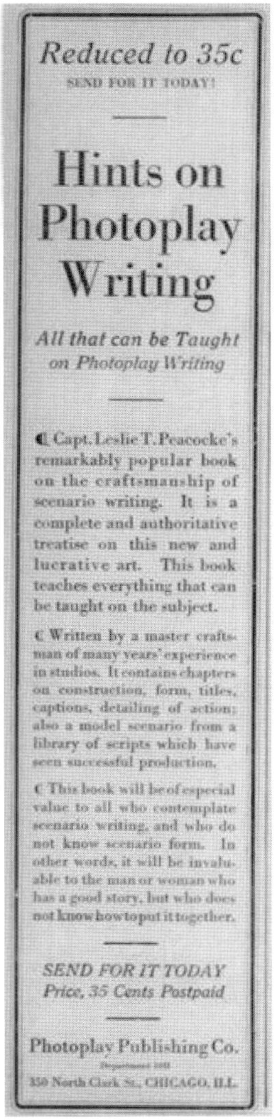

Figure 66: Advertisements for Sargent's *Technique of the Photoplay* and Peacocke's *Hints on Photoplay Writing*
Source: *MPW*, November 9, 1918, 660, *Photoplay*, December 1916, 14 and *Photoplay*, August, 1919, 15.

"The Art of Writing Scenarios"

By WILLIAM LORD WRIGHT

A TEXT BOOK FOR BEGINNERS

Price $1 Postpaid

GILES R. WARREN, well-known Scenario Editor with several prominent concerns, says: "I recommend its use to all beginners. By far the best work of its kind I have ever seen."

Another Scenario Editor says: "Shall cheerfully recommend it whenever opportunity offers."

PICTURE PLAY MANUSCRIPT CRITICIZED and available markets suggested by a successful author. A charge of $1 for manuscript up to and including 1,000 words.

Scenario Instruction Publishing Company
BELLEFONTAINE, OHIO

BALL WRITES BOOK ON PHOTOPLAY SCENARIOS

"Photoplay Scenarios, How to Write and Sell Them," by Eustace Hale Ball, a volume of 186 pages, published by Hearst's International Library Company, New York, is the most recent addition to the increasing number of manuals for aspirants to successful photoplay writing.

Mr. Ball is himself a successful scenarioist, having been connected as staff playwright scenario editor or producing director with the Reliance, Eclair, Majestic, Solax, Excelsior and Historical Film Companies.

The book is a practical treatise on subjects which the screen writer must understand thoroughly if he is to succeed—manuscript preparation, methods of sale and recording, present day script markets, with lists and addresses; dramatic principle; theme and plot construction; comedy; tragedy; romance; historical plays; characterization; costuming, scenes and sets; technical terms and their uses; editorial rules; censorship conditions; feature scenarios, and sample forms of scenarios.

The author makes it very clear that there is no royal road to photo-dramatic success. He writes from an angle of common sense that is usually absent from books of this kind. Insofar as a general discussion of any art can be valuable, Mr. Ball's volume is good.

Successful Photoplay Writing

—is nine-tenths a matter of choosing the right ideas and using them in the right way. It is Technique, yet something a thousand times more. It is a matter of knowing **Where to Get Plots** whenever you want them and after that a knowledge of **Dramatic Construction.** These two prime requisites are now set forth for the first time in the history of Photoplay Writing by the greatest authority on the subject in a manner that begets immediate Inspiration and puts a sure finger on all the material you can use in a lifetime!

THE PHOTODRAMA

By HENRY ALBERT PHILLIPS

Formerly of the Staff of Pathé Frères; Associate Editor Motion Picture Magazine; Successful Contestant in Vitagraph-Sun Contest; Author of "The Plot of the Story," "Art in Story Narration," etc.

Introduction by J. Stuart Blackton, Vitagraph Co.

224 Pages—Cloth-Bound—Stamped in Gold—Postpaid $2.10

It is the only serious work on the subject. It shows you everything:

What Plots Are—Where to Get All the Plots You Can Use—How to Build Them—How to Make Any Material Dramatic—How to Get the Punch Every Time

Also a SPECIMEN PHOTOPLAY and a REVISED GLOSSARY. Used in Schools, Colleges and Libraries thruout the United States.

ALL AUTHORITIES AGREE IT IS THE BEST!

"All of us here at the Majestic-Reliance—in Los Angeles for that matter—consider THE PHOTODRAMA the very best work that has appeared on the subject."
—RUSSELL E. SMITH, Editor.

"A book which the novice will find immensely helpful and informative, yet will be of especial value to the writer who has sold more than one script. It will assist him wonderfully in plot building, showing him how to take a mere idea and build it up into a strong, salable script!"
—ARTHUR LEEDS, in the "Photoplay Author."

"It contains just the information that fiction writers—or anyone with a good idea—who has never tackled a scenario requires."
—AUTHORS LEAGUE OF AMERICA.

"I find it one of the best works of any kind that has ever been written."—CARL H. GETZ, Professor in University of Montana.

"It is the best thing Mr. Phillips has done—and that is saying a whole lot."
EUGENE V. BREWSTER, Editor Motion Picture Magazine.

"The newness of Mr. Phillips' ideas starts with the cover. It is one of the sanest discussions that has been done. It is a book worth while. Better still, it is not a rehash of any other work, but original in treatment and thought."
—EPES W. SARGENT, in "Moving Picture World."

—and a thousand other words of praise!

By the same Author: **THE PLOT OF THE STORY** / **ART IN STORY NARRATION**

Both valuable to the Photoplaywright, $1.20 each. Either, with "Photodrama," $3.10. All three books, $4.00

THE CALDRON PUBLISHING CO.
173 DUFFIELD ST., BROOKLYN, N. Y.

Figure 67: Advertisements for Wright's *The Art of Writing Scenarios*, Ball's *Photoplay Scenarios: How to Write and Sell Them* and Phillips's *The Photodrama*
Source: *MPW*, February 1911, 385, *MPN*, January 15, 1916, 248 and *MPM*, March 1915, 181.

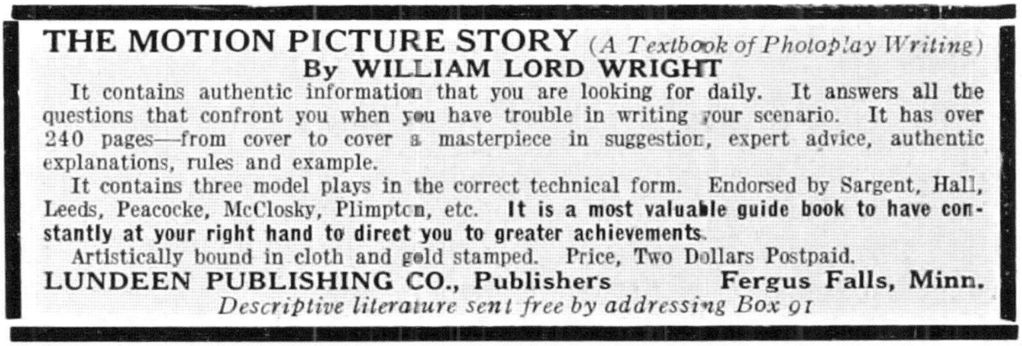

THE MOTION PICTURE STORY *(A Textbook of Photoplay Writing)*
By WILLIAM LORD WRIGHT

It contains authentic information that you are looking for daily. It answers all the questions that confront you when you have trouble in writing your scenario. It has over 240 pages—from cover to cover a masterpiece in suggestion, expert advice, authentic explanations, rules and example.

It contains three model plays in the correct technical form. Endorsed by Sargent, Hall, Leeds, Peacocke, McClosky, Plimpton, etc. **It is a most valuable guide book to have constantly at your right hand to direct you to greater achievements.**

Artistically bound in cloth and gold stamped. Price, Two Dollars Postpaid.

LUNDEEN PUBLISHING CO., Publishers   Fergus Falls, Minn.
Descriptive literature sent free by addressing Box 91

Figure 68: Trade literature advertisement for Wright's *The Motion Picture Story*
Source: *MPW*, August 14, 1915, 1184.

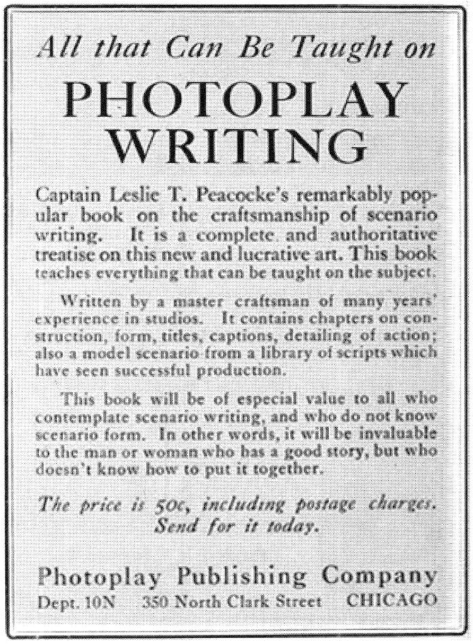

All that Can Be Taught on
PHOTOPLAY WRITING

Captain Leslie T. Peacocke's remarkably popular book on the craftsmanship of scenario writing. It is a complete and authoritative treatise on this new and lucrative art. This book teaches everything that can be taught on the subject.

Written by a master craftsman of many years' experience in studios. It contains chapters on construction, form, titles, captions, detailing of action; also a model scenario from a library of scripts which have seen successful production.

This book will be of especial value to all who contemplate scenario writing, and who do not know scenario form. In other words, it will be invaluable to the man or woman who has a good story, but who doesn't know how to put it together.

The price is 50c, including postage charges. Send for it today.

Photoplay Publishing Company
Dept. 10N   350 North Clark Street   CHICAGO

Figure 69: Fan press advertisement for Peacocke's
Hints on Photoplay Writing
Source: *Photoplay*, August 1918, 8.

The Study Regime

Without exception, the key screenwriting teachers believed that watching and analysing films was a crucial part of screenwriting education. Wright urges, 'Repeated visits to the motion-picture theater are recommended to those wishing to write the successful photoplay.'[20] More than just passively observing, students should undertake active notebook 'study' and analysis of all aspects of the film.[21] One way Peacocke believed he could improve his own writing was to go to watch his own successful photoplay, *Neptune's Daughter*, repeatedly, to find 'some discrepancy in the plot or technique'.[22] As well as dissecting the plots of films they had seen, Wright encouraged his readers to try to write them out from memory. It was also important to study character development and how the circumstances in the picture wrought character change.[23] Sargent believed, as did the others, that his students should put themselves through a rigorous training regime, and the motion picture theatre was their starting point:

> There is only one school of experience, and the classroom is the motion picture theatre, but you must regard it, for the time being, as a classroom and not as a place of amusement.[24]

Where students could not see a film, the key screenwriting teachers encouraged them to access the film press for story summaries. They could then attempt to write their own versions from reviews they had read or titles they had encountered. Ball lists most of the 'trades' as essential reading:

> In particular, the *Moving Picture World* contains many interesting articles by well-known critics on photoplay technique [presumably including Sargent and Wright] as well as showing brief synopses of the weekly releases.[25]

After emphasising the clear distinction between writing for the screen and writing for the theatre, Phillips, Ball, Wright and Sargent specifically state that it was absolutely necessary that their students should comprehend the same skills of dramatic construction as a playwright. For Peacocke, the same belief is implicit but he never openly refers to this connection – oddly, given he was a successful stage actor and playwright himself and this knowledge more than likely informed his understanding of dramatic technique in film.

---

20 Wright, *Motion Picture Story*, 52–53.

21 Ibid., 53.

22 Katterjohn, 'Captain Leslie T. Peacocke', *Movie Pictorial*, August 15, 1914, 16–17 and 32.

23 Wright, *Photoplay Writing*, 39–43.

24 Sargent, *Technique of the Photoplay*, 3rd ed., 307.

25 Ball, *Art of the Photoplay*, 30.

Keen that his students grasp the 'technical knowledge of dramatic construction', Ball refers them to a well-known work by Price, *The Analysis of Play Construction and Dramatic Principle*.[26] To succeed, the freelance writer had to:

> apply [their] vigorous and unhackneyed thoughts so as to produce artistic results along the lines laid down by centuries of necessary conventions, [which] is the simple and complex art of dramatic technique.[27]

Further, Ball makes the clear link between writing 'good scenarios' and understanding 'dramatic development, professional presentation of theme and movement, which makes a scenario worth while'.[28] He wants his readers to 'gain a broad technical knowledge of dramatic construction'.[29] In beginning his instruction about photoplay writing, he underlines the connection with the comment: 'just as with a drama for the stage or a novel'.[30] His choice of description for the film writer is 'photoplaywright', which underscores his particular view that film writing is an extension of writing for the theatre.[31]

Wright is equally clear about the connection between the principles of play construction and film narrative:

> A great deal of theatrical parlance has been handed down to the motion-picture industry for the reason that the majority of the directors of motion pictures are former directors of the spoken drama, as are a majority of the motion-picture supporting casts of today.[32]

In his columns, Sargent refers to a number of theatrical manuals quite regularly and he encourages his readers to purchase them. One article is devoted completely to considering the views of Brander Matthews, a well-known dramaturge (Chapter 1).[33] Sargent also includes Price's *The Technique of the Drama* as part of his essential reading list for aspiring photoplay writers.[34] In an attempt to announce his work as definitive, Sargent may even have gained inspiration for the title of his manual, *The Technique*

---

26 Ibid.

27 Ibid., 34.

28 Ibid., 31.

29 Ibid., 30.

30 Ibid., 33.

31 Ibid., 9.

32 Wright, *Photoplay Writing*, 176–177.

33 Sargent frequently discusses the writings of dramaturges such as Freytag, Price, Archer, Matthews and Andrews in his columns. See Sargent, 'The Photoplaywright', December 18, 1915, 2171; March 25, 1916, 2001; May 13, 1916, 1165 and September 8, 1917, 1537 in *MPW*.

34 Sargent, 'The Photoplaywright', *MPW*, February 7, 1914, 670–671.

of the Photoplay, from both Price's manual, *The Technique of the Drama*, published in 1892, and Freytag's 1863 work of the same name, although the structure and content of these earlier books are decidedly different from Sargent's.

These commendations of sources beyond the film industry were not limited to books about playwriting. As Chapter 5 has noted, Phillips's *Plot of the Short Story* was another of Sargent's recommended readings. It is pertinent to Sargent's discussion when he quotes from the dramatist Hamilton about the decisions the dramatist must make in the process of writing. When people lose interest in the play, he claims it is due to an 'error of proportion', where too much secondary material has been used. *Hamlet* and *Much Ado About Nothing*, he argues, illustrate this point. The dramatist must make a 'definite selection of events' and, furthermore, 'All this has been written of the drama of the stage, but it applies with equal force to photoplay.'[35] Similarly, Phillips plainly affirms his trust in theatrical principles: 'The man who writes photoplays should study and master the principles of dramatic construction. Before all things he is a playwright.'[36]

As well as being recommended by the key screenwriting teachers, Price's manual and manuals by other leading dramaturges, such as Archer, Matthews, Andrews and Hamilton, were regularly advertised and discussed in the fan and trade press (see Figure 70).[37] Hamilton was also a well-known drama critic, who in 1911 expressed interest in the possibilities that film presented. Both he and Andrews would go on to write successful photoplays.[38]

It is also evident that the key screenwriting teachers were aware of the views of early film theorists and their contribution to the debate about writing photoplays. These works of theory appear between 1915 and 1918, later than all the first manuals or columns of the five key screenwriting teachers. Therefore, they did not initiate or pre-date the discourse of the key screenwriting teachers, but did assist in clarifying, formulating and organising some of their ideas. The theorists were trying to get to grips with the new art form and, as such, their books were seen as useful learning tools. While the Introduction has already noted that the views of the theorists were not always helpful to the cause of the screenwriter, the key screenwriting teachers still often recognised and recommended their work.

---

35 Sargent, 'The Photoplaywright', *MPW*, March 20, 1915, 1757–1758.

36 Phillips, *Photodrama*, 151.

37 See advertisement in *MPSM*, March 1912, 170; 'The Philosopher's Advice', *Photo Playwright*, September/October 1912, 10; Harrison, 'Theatrical Plots', *MPW*, October 23, 1915, 586; and Palmer, 'Today and Tomorrow', *The Story World and the Photodramatist*, September 1923, 73–75.

38 Hamilton, 'The Art of the Moving Picture Play', 50–52. See 'Hamilton' in *IMDbPro*: https://pro-labs.imdb.com/name/nm0357793/ and 'Andrews': https://pro-labs.imdb.com/name/nm0028602/

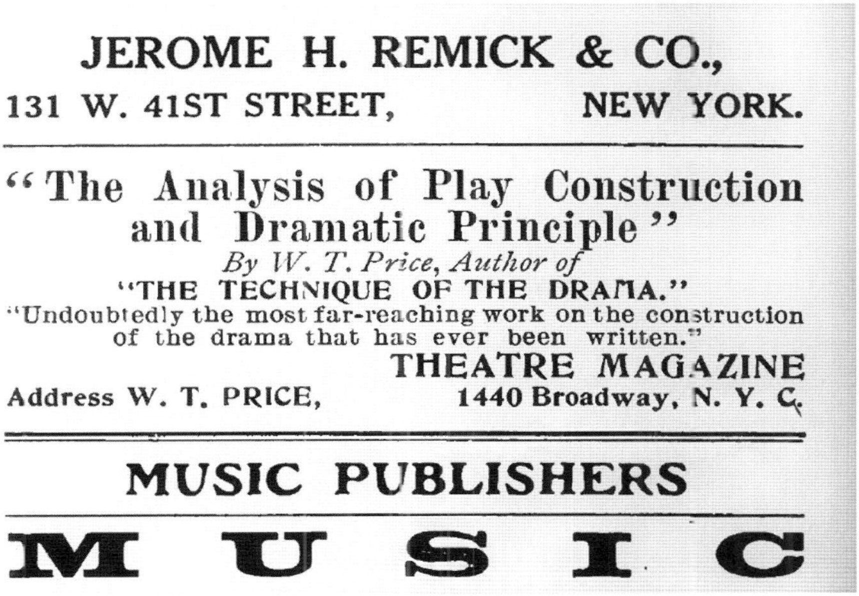

Figure 70: Advertisement for Price's playwriting manual
Source: *MPSM*, March 1912, 170.

William Morgan Hannon's short treatise on film, *The Photodrama: Its Place Among the Fine Arts* (1915), struggled to give film full definition. As a silent medium, film was largely visual (except for musical accompaniment), yet it had a semblance to many art forms, such as sculpture and painting, and obviously exhibited basic dramatic structure for 'the technique and dramaturgy of the photodrama [… were] dynamic rather than static'.[39] He also understood film to be 'allied to the art of pantomime on one side, and to drama proper on the other'.[40] Manual writers such as Sargent were aware of Hannon's work; in fact, Sargent is complimentary about Hannon's attempts to define photoplay writing as an art and to compare it to other artistic disciplines. According to Sargent, Hannon's defence of film as an art form 'assigns it its true place, defining both its advantages and limitations'.[41]

Another important early film theorist was Hugo Münsterberg (1863–1916), who was also an eminent psychologist. In his analytical work, *The Photoplay: A Psychological Study* (1916), he foresaw the possibilities of making 'the art of the film […] a medium for an original creative expression'.[42] According to Passi Nyyssonen, Münsterberg 'draws an analogy between mental processes and cinematic functions [– for example,]

---

39   Hannon, *The Photodrama*, 16.

40   Ibid., 13.

41   Sargent, 'The Photoplaywright', *MPW* October 30, 1915, 784–785.

42   Münsterberg, *The Photoplay*, 121.

memory corresponds to the "cut back" in the cinema'.[43] In other words, in Münsterberg's opinion, the medium of film resembled the human thinking process of the spectator with its cinematic elements of close-up, cut-back, and parallel cutting:

> the act which in the ordinary theater would go on in our mind alone is here in the photoplay projected into the pictures themselves [... and consequently the] objective world is molded by the interests of the mind. Events which are far distant from one another [...] are fusing in our field of vision, just as they are brought together in our own consciousness.[44]

Sargent also engages with Münsterberg's ideas about film writing and commends his work to his readers. Although disagreeing with Münsterberg's purist ideas about not using subtitles, as will be seen later, he praises him for realising the value of the cut-back 'as one of the real individualities of the photoplay'.[45] Münsterberg understood one of the most important differences between stage and screen to be 'liberty of movement from scene to scene and capacity for being in two or more places at seemingly the same time'[46] and, properly used, the cut-back meant 'an annihilation of time and space'.[47] These features distinguished the screen from the stage, where imagination and memory or 'past fact and future hope must alike be dealt with in the spoken word'.[48] Sargent realised, that, like himself, Münsterberg grasped the power of cinema to visualise people's very thoughts. To support this understanding, he quotes Münsterberg: 'Our imagination is projected on the screen' – that is, visions of the future and memories can be visualised.[49]

Scholar and poet Vachel Lindsay (1879–1931) wrote *The Art of the Moving Picture* (1915). Approaching film as high art, he saw it as a means of bringing 'motion' to visual arts such as sculpture, painting and architecture.[50] He believed 'that the printed page had counted too much' and that, as a visual medium, 'the ideal film has no words printed on it at all'.[51] For Lindsay, stories were to be told through images redolent with symbolic meanings, and there was no place for subtitles. Egyptian hieroglyphics, as a

---

43   Passi Nyyssonen, 'Film Theory at the Turning Point of Modernity', in *Film-Philosophy Electronic Salon*, October 17 (1998), 2, accessed September 1, 2014, http://www.film-philosophy.com/vol2-1998/n31nyyssonen

44   Münsterberg, *The Photoplay*, 56 and 62.

45   Sargent, 'What Is Photoplay?' *MPW*, July 21, 1917, 369–370.

46   Sargent, 'Münsterberg on the Photoplay', *MPW*, July 15, 1916, 436–437.

47   Sargent, 'What Is Photoplay?' *MPW*, July 21, 1917, 369–370.

48   Sargent, 'Münsterberg on the Photoplay', *MPW*, July 15, 1916, 436–437.

49   Ibid.

50   Lindsay writes extensively on bringing sculpture, painting and architecture to life. See Vachel Lindsay, *The Art of the Moving Picture*, 2nd ed. (1922; repr., London: Forgotten Books, 2012), 79–150.

51   Ibid., 5 and xxix.

means of picture writing that also told stories, fascinated him and he drew on them as a model rather than 'Anglo-Saxon' language with its sense of 'algebraic formulas'.[52] As he examined these images, he claimed it was '[as] though I were looking at a "movie" in a book'.[53] To the modern reader, Lindsay's views can seem rather odd and antiquated, but he does draw attention to the importance of film as a powerful visual medium.

From his contemporary perspective, Sargent recommends Lindsay along with Münsterberg as worth reading, but with some qualification: 'Between the somewhat fantastic speculation of Vachel Lindsay and the scientific exactness of Münsterberg lies the photoplay of the future.'[54] Sargent acknowledges that both Münsterberg and Lindsay had recognised:

> that the motion picture is not the bastard offspring of the dramatic stage, but the legitimate child of drama and story with an entity of its own.[55]

In fact, Lindsay had taken the trouble to list 30 differences between the photoplay and the stage to make this point. In seeing that '[t]he supreme photoplay will give us things that have been but half expressed in all other mediums allied to it', he identified the potential of film.[56]

The author of *The Art of Photoplay Making* (1918), Victor Oscar Freeburg (1882–1953), was an important early film theorist. Although his book is more of an academic treatise than a manual in the conventional sense, it recognises the potential of the photoplay. It was based on a series of lectures on photoplay composition delivered at Columbia University between 1915 and 1917. In Freeburg's view, the photoplay 'inherits something from each of the elder arts, and yet differs essentially from them all' because it 'is silent and practically wordless', which he does not regard necessarily as a limitation.[57] Freeburg suggests that:

> Any means of effective expression which will help us dispense with words is to be welcomed, because the photoplay cannot be developed into great art as long as it remains hybrid, half literary and half pictorial.[58]

In recognition of the visual requirements of photoplay writing, he suggests that the 'scenario writer must not only imagine his pictures, but he must learn to imagine them in

---

52 Ibid., 171–188.

53 Ibid., xxxv.

54 Sargent, 'The Photoplaywright', *MPW*, October 7, 1916, 70.

55 Sargent, 'Münsterberg on the Photoplay', *MPW*, July 15, 1916, 436–437.

56 Lindsay, *Art of the Moving Picture,* 169.

57 Freeburg, *Art of Photoplay Making*, 1.

58 Ibid., 119.

terms of the screen'.[59] Freeburg, uniquely, argues that the writer should rank their images according to the:

> accelerating progression of the pictorial values in the play, [meaning] the pictures should become more beautiful, more impressive as they progress towards the climax of the play.[60]

This linking of the images to the dramatic structure of the play is insightful. However, he still emphasises a tripartite scenario structure, reminiscent of Aristotle's beginning, middle and end, by suggesting that a photoplay should have a 'premise, complication and solution',[61] although he does not want it to be directly compared with the stage drama. He insists that the 'cinema play is a new art distinct from all the other arts which were invented and have been developed before it'.[62]

Freeburg's books gain Sargent's attention: he recommends *The Art of Photoplay Making* as essential reading and describes a second book, *Disguise Plots in the Elizabethan Drama* (1882), as helpful.[63] Returning the compliment, Freeburg rates Sargent's manual as 'first' in discussing 'the practical side of plot building, scenario writing, and photoplay filming', presumably in contrast to his own theorising.[64] Sargent was also supportive of Lindsay's and Freeburg's idea to designate 'Columbia University as the home of the first museum of photoplay writing and production'.[65] The idea came to fruition as the university would house the first educational centre and seek endowments to allow it to store scripts and other materials as a permanent record.[66] As part of this programme, Freeburg had already 'gathered working material for his class in photoplay construction'[67] and Sargent was also pleased to record that the third edition of his own manual, *The Technique of the Photoplay*, was to be used 'as a textbook' on the course at Columbia University alongside the books of Münsterberg and Lindsay.[68] Lindsay was occasionally invited to lecture on this course, but there is no record of Sargent ever doing so. As Freeburg's aesthetics are philosophically oriented, they belong more in the academic tutorial than the world of the practitioner. Much of the work of Patterson in

---

59   Ibid., 29.

60   Ibid., 255–256.

61   Ibid., 238.

62   Ibid., 205.

63   Sargent, 'The Photoplaywright', *MPW*, October 21, 1916, 386.

64   Freeburg, *The Art of Photoplay Making*, Foreword.

65   Sargent, 'Wanted – A Museum', *MPW*, September 9, 1916, 1704.

66   Sargent, The Photoplaywright', *MPW*, February 24, 1917, 1170.

67   Ibid., 1704.

68   Sargent, 'The Photoplaywright', *MPW*, March 24 1917, 1914.

further developing these courses at Columbia University would grow out of Freeburg's efforts and would eventually give rise to her own manual, *Cinema Craftsmanship* (1920).

The work of these early theorists had positive and negative effects on screenplay writing and on the instruction of the key screenwriting teachers. As already noted, both Münsterberg and Lindsay tended to downplay the literary merits of screenwriting, although some of their insights were of use to screenwriting teachers. Freeburg's work formed the basis for the academic study of screenwriting; Sargent's endorsement of his work, and of that of Münsterberg and Lindsay, indicates his willingness not only to engage with the works of early film theoreticians but to recommend them to his students as a source of enrichment.

Along with Sargent, the other key screenwriting teachers saw these theoretical works as potentially valuable learning tools for their readers and followers. Further, they contributed to the discourse about film theory themselves by making comment through their articles, columns and manuals. So where does this place their manuals in relation to the theoretical texts? As Macdonald suggests, 'Screenwriting manuals thus represent "metaprescriptive texts" or "low intensity theory," lying between practice and high theory.'[69] That is, they functioned as a bridge between the two and brought the attention of aspiring writers to the more theoretical material, which could act as an additional learning resource.

In the view of the key screenwriting teachers, their manuals should still be central to the learning process. His own manual, Sargent argues, ought to be a constant point of reference for the prospective writer; after reading it, they would have 'received a complete course of instruction in photoplay writing'.[70] Both Sargent and Wright were not averse to their students reading other screenwriting manuals and encouraged them to build up a library of books about writing.[71] However, merely reading a book did not in itself mean that students had absorbed its content and was not sufficient to develop the skills needed for screenwriting. Sargent encouraged his readers to apply themselves to 'study the rule and then learn, through experience, to apply it'.[72] Wright emphasises the doing part: 'The best way to learn to write is to write.'[73]

In regard to constructive criticism from others, Sargent considered it could be useful, providing it was backed by 'practical knowledge'. However, submitting to criticism from just any source was of little value and he admitted that even some editors gave poor

---

69   Macdonald, 'Forming the Craft' in *Early Popular Visual Culture*, 8.1 (2010): 79.

70   Sargent, *Technique of the Photoplay*, 3rd ed., 356.

71   Sargent, *Technique of the Photoplay*, 3rd ed., 358 and Wright, *Photoplay Writing*, 216.

72   Sargent, *Technique of the Photoplay*, 3rd ed., 305.

73   Wright, *Photoplay Writing*, 33.

feedback. Advocating a process of 'self-criticism', Sargent offered a series of 10 probing questions, originally published in *Moving Picture World*, as a test of any work.[74] Wright wholeheartedly agreed that students need to be self-critical:

> Endeavour to be your own critic. After completing your story, lay it away for a week or so and try and forget it. Later, go over it again carefully, analyze every scene, every action, every motive.[75]

To further aid students' development, Sargent's manual ends with a section called 'The Unasked Question' to address all the questions he believed the new writer might ask. In introducing them, he claims that '[t]he questions are those that have been most frequently repeated in the thousands of questions answered by the writer in the past five years'.[76] As the key screenwriting teachers had supplied a full course of instruction, they suggested that there was little point in their students joining correspondence courses, even those that appeared legitimate. As Chapter 5 mentioned, the teachers characterised most of them as bogus, along with the agencies, clearing houses and prize schemes, which generally required money for services that the teachers deemed to be improperly rendered and a waste of time.[77] Sargent advises writers to stay away from such correspondence schools, which he viewed as fake and fraudulent:

> Do not believe the misleading statements contained in the advertisements of the self-styled schools [...] that one could begin to write photoplays within three hours after receipt of instructions. It cannot be done![78]

Instead, Sargent counsels that:

> Until the real success comes the author must cut his own path, and none of these schemes will help. They may hinder progress very materially or completely spoil all chances of success. [...] No matter what the contest, the damage done through delay in progress will far outweigh the possible financial gain. You can make more money keeping out of contests and selling in the market.[79]

---

74   The 10 questions are: '1. Is the plot new or novel? 2. Is it practicable? 3. Will it pass the censorships? 4. Has it struggle? 5. Has it suspense? 6. Is it properly motivated? 7. Are the characters well chosen? 8. Are the settings correct? 9. Is the plot adhered to? 10. Is the climax correct?' See Sargent, *Technique of the Photoplay*, 3rd ed., 315.

75   Wright, *Motion Picture Story,* 223.

76   Sargent, *Technique of the Photoplay*, 3rd ed., 366.

77   Sargent, *Technique of the Photoplay*, 3rd ed., 305 and 354–356; Wright, *Photoplay Writing*, 196 and 214–216.

78   Sargent, *Technique of the Photoplay*, 3rd ed., 305.

79   Ibid., 354 and 356.

Likewise Ball saw these schools as mere money-making schemes and counselled that 'no wise writer' should believe their claim that 'no literary training nor skill is necessary'.[80] Peacocke's condemnation of correspondence schools is equally stinging and, as mentioned in Chapter 5, was the reason *Photoplay* hired him to write about scenario writing:

> I cannot tell you how bitterly I am opposed to the schools, clearing houses and other schemes of like nature. I have been fighting against them for years. […] I have never heard of anyone having benefited from having enlisted in one of these schools.[81] (see Figure 71 for more on this article)

Scenario "School" Advertising

PHOTOPLAY MAGAZINE has decided to eliminate motion picture school advertising.

This action has been taken only after careful investigation of the merits of these schools, and is the result of a determination that no advertising, to which the least suspicion is attached, shall be allowed space in this publication.

The scenario editors of the leading moving picture companies of the country seem to be unanimous in the opinion that these

> "I was a staff writer with the Universal Company for two years, and while I was there no scenario was ever accepted from a so-called school or clearing house."
> LESLIE T. PEACOCKE,
> World Film Corporation.

and authoritative publication in its field, and to permit no advertiser, whose claims the magazine cannot guarantee, to have access to its advertising columns.

One of the first acts of the new management was to investigate the merits of the so-called motion picture schools, clearing-houses, and correspondence schools of photoplay acting. As a result of this investigation it was decided to entirely eliminate this class of advertising.

The scenario editors of the motion picture

Capt. L. T. Peacocke, scenario editor World Film Corp.:

"I cannot tell you how bitterly I am opposed to the schools, clearing houses and other schemes of like nature. I have been fighting against them for years. I was a staff writer with the Universal for two years and whilst I was there, no scenario was ever accepted from a so-called school or clearing house. They were always considered a form of petty graft. I have never heard of anyone having benefited from having enlisted in one of these schools.

Barred by Photoplay Magazine

that idea and may be paid $50 or $100 for it.

"Scripts submitted by correspondence school students are generally worthless. They can be immediately detected from other submissions because they are frequently crowded with senseless designations supposed to be technical, and the idea or plot germ, provided there is any, is generally lost in a mass of mysterious terms which neither the author or the producer understands.

"Why pay $25 for a 'course' in a correspondence school when for ten cents more knowledge can be obtained? Visit the motion picture theatre, not for entertainment but for the purpose of study.

> "We wish to congratulate you on your determination to eliminate the motion picture school advertisements. The art of photoplay writing cannot be taught by correspondence, and the same rule applies to the art of acting."
> JOHN F. PRIBYL,
> Selig Polyscope Company.

by studying the pictureplays, but that talent to devise new plots, new situations, new atmosphere—in other words that talent to write original pictureplay stories cannot be acquired in any school, in any theatre, in fact, no where but in the heart and mind of the writer. Originality is a God-given talent that cannot be acquired.

"Why pay $25 tuition for a school course, sometimes conducted by incompetents, when the ambitious can acquire 250 practical lessons, at ten cents a lesson, in the motion picture theatre?

"We wish to congratulate you upon your determination to eliminate the motion picture school

Figure 71: Peacocke's article, 'Scenario "School" Advertising Barred by Photoplay Magazine'
Source: *Photoplay*, April 1915, 114 and 116.

---

80 Ball, *Art of the Photoplay*, 30–31.

81 'Scenario "School" Advertising Barred by Photoplay Magazine', *Photoplay*, April 1915, 116.

Of course, the views of the key screenwriting teachers about correspondence schools may have not been entirely objective, given they could have seen these operators as competitors. However, their altruistic attitude in recommending other screenwriting teachers, who definitely were competitors with the potential to limit their own financial gain, may legitimise their opinions about some of the more unscrupulous operators.

Writing clubs, by contrast, received a positive response from the key screenwriting teachers. A forum for discussing films and commenting on each other's work, these clubs also often had visiting speakers and provided networking opportunities. As Chapter 5 has established, the teachers were involved in setting up a number of these clubs – including the Inquest Club, the Ed-Au Club, the Photoplay Authors' League and the Screen Club – and were often in attendance.

Talent versus Tenacity

The argument over whether someone requires a high level of literary skill and story-writing talent to become a screenwriter is an enduring one. It feeds into a wider debate about the difference between 'art' and 'craft', terms that have been widely used to articulate the belief that a 'craft' or 'skill' can be learnt, but the mystified conception of artistic expression cannot. This division or dualism has a long history: according to Larry Shiner, it was institutionalised in the eighteenth century and has been a strong notion ever since. He argues that, up to that point, there had been no conceptual distinction between art, in the sense of masterpiece making, and what would later be termed artisanal craftsmanship. Shiner asserts that the old system of art had been broken apart:

> arrogating intellect, imagination, and grace to fine art and disparaging craft and popular culture as the realm of mere technique, utility, entertainment, and profit.[82]

The five original 'fine arts' of music, painting, sculpture, architecture and poetry shared a common essence and were regarded as 'art', while furniture-makers and potters – and, by extension, popular musicians and movie-makers – were relegated to the category of 'craft'. These notions of the two realms remain strong in contemporary Western culture. Because the art–craft dichotomy has only existed as a modern 'Western' cultural construct, Shiner contends, failing to recognise it will skew any debate. The continuing art–craft opposition can be traced in twentieth-century philosophers and critics, who 'reiterated their belief in a deep opposition between serious art and popular art'.[83] The same tension is evident in much of the discourse of the key screenwriting teachers.

It is inherent in one of the issues the key screenwriting teachers constantly address: how likely is an individual to succeed as a scenario writer? Their answers entail the fundamental tension or contradiction – depending on interpretation – between what

---

82 Larry Shiner, *The Invention of Art: A Cultural History* (London: University of Chicago, 2001), 307.

83 Ibid., 286.

might be deemed the realm of 'art' and what could be achieved through craft. On the one hand, all the key screenwriting teachers seem to stress that some kind of innate talent or artistic ability was necessary for success but, on the other hand, they also appear to indicate that most people could succeed with application and tenacity.

Of course, limiting the appeal of their advice to those who had proven writing skills would not have been a sensible marketing ploy for anyone who wanted to sell a lot of manuals. However, it is also possible that the manual writers themselves were not entirely sure whether the new skill of writing for film, which certainly required a different kind of writing ability from play, short story or novel writing, could be acquired through instruction or was in fact more innate. They certainly realised that it did not involve a mastery of exactly the same kind of literary skills required for previous kinds of writing, even though they often recommended play and short story writing manuals as useful study aids. They also understood that additional skills, such as the ability to visualise and to write in action, were more important than writing in fine prose; but could these skills be acquired through application or were they also to some extent innate? Throughout their writings, this tension is clearly evident, whatever view on this issue they ultimately may have settled on.

When the key screenwriting teachers slip into vagueness, it may also be a way of avoiding the apparent contradiction between notions of 'unteachable' art and teachable craft. It could be, most likely at a subconscious level, a strategy or means of avoiding really dealing with the issue head-on. On occasions they appear to want to invest somewhat in the higher notions of art, in order to appeal to loftier elements, but this does not fit easily with an often strongly pragmatic approach towards the material. Most of the advice they give appears to be of a craft/skill nature, but they convey a vague sense that writing ought to be something more grandiose. These elusive notions of art often seem quite functional and blurry: simmering below the surface of comment and remaining as unresolved conflicts. The key screenwriting teachers seem to want to see themselves as occupying that kind of artistic realm, at least in part, and not just peddling methodologies to create skilled technicians.

These tensions surface regularly in Peacocke's manual, which is not an instructional manual in the conventional sense, as it is not structured systematically, but instead is filled with pithy statements and insights about screenwriting. Peacocke's sporadic, scattergun approach is in keeping with what its title claims it to be: 'Hints' on how to write photoplays. For most of the book, Peacocke presents himself as an experienced writer dispensing wise advice, rather than a methodical and systematic teacher of photoplay writing. His book is filled with easy-to-grasp, practical statements, such as:

> Make your scenes short; do not elaborate; don't try to be technical. Be clear and
> concise in the description of your scenes and of your characters. Don't aim to be
> literary.[84]

Emphatic in his view that it is not possible to teach people how to write photoplays, he
states that he does not want his 'readers to get the impression that I am aiming to teach
the art of photoplay writing, because I do not believe that any mortal being can do that'.[85]
His constant reiteration of this theme throughout the book gives the impression that some
mysterious or artistic conception is present that cannot be put into words or described:

> Scenario writing (the sort that brings acceptance checks from producers) cannot be
> taught; hints to help are the extent of the instruction possible.[86]

Peacocke insists, 'I am merely giving to others the experience I have gained, and pointing
out pitfalls which beset the unwary writer.'[87] And yet, at some points he becomes entirely
pragmatic, implying the complete opposite – that most people can learn this skill:

> There is no mystery about writing photoplays. Anyone who makes a study of
> pictures on the screen and who can visualize a story and who can put that story into
> words, which constitute short, crisp scenes, which will bring the story to a logical
> conclusion, can write a photoplay.[88]

His statement seems at worst contradictory and at best ambiguous or confused, as the
'anyone' described here was clearly 'someone' who in fact had considerable ability or
skills. Peacocke could perhaps be accused of falsely raising his readers' hopes of entering
the industry, if he truly believed that screenwriting could not be taught and yet he had
published a book to do just that. One may well ask, what was the point of trying to help
freelance writers if they could not learn how to do it or benefit from instruction anyway?
In reality, his motives were probably more nuanced, as a mix of a genuine desire to
improve the writer's lot and a drive to gain financial reward and enhance his own status.

This fundamental tension is evident in the writings of the other key screenwriting teachers,
although subtlety of argument sometimes masks its presence. Sargent seems to imply
that a great deal of innate talent is required, when he claims that the 'fact that literary
style is not required does not also excuse the lack of inventiveness, of creative ability,
of originality of thought' when writing a scenario.[89] At another point, Sargent seems to

---

84 Peacocke, *Hints on Photoplay Writing,* 31.

85 Ibid., 32.

86 Ibid., 4.

87 Ibid., 32.

88 Ibid., 39.

89 Sargent, *Technique of the Photoplay*, 3rd ed., 306.

leave open the possibility that such creative skills might be developed in someone who is not innately talented. The 'real author', he maintains, is either born that way or has laboured very hard to acquire the elusive but key skill of being able to 'sense the story; to look past the action, past the technique, past the plot and past the punch itself and see the soul of the story'.[90] Here, Sargent appears to be appealing to a rather mysterious quality that he believes makes someone a writer but that is not necessarily an inborn talent. Perhaps his vagueness on this issue again functions as a way of avoiding confronting the contradiction head-on.

In his discussion of creativity, Wright focuses on the learning potential someone might have, but also indicates that talent resides within:

> It is a thing that can be cultivated, rather than taught. […] It does not require years of study of technical terms, but rather, study of human nature. There are a few simple things that can be taught, and that anyone can learn – after that, it's what you have in you, yourself, that counts.[91]

Every now and then, this tension over whether talent or tenacity is required to succeed as a scenario writer would surface in debates over screenwriting in the trade press. In 1916 Phillips was appointed to lecture on screenwriting at the YMCA in New York. Writing about this appointment in his column, Sargent objected to some of the publicity about the course that the press had released. According to Sargent, it claimed that Phillips had said, 'I can teach anyone how to write a good photoplay.' Sargent's response in his column was emphatic: 'He can't teach anyone to write a photoplay […] He can, because he is competent, guide those who are qualified and earnest.'[92] Exactly what Sargent meant by the word 'qualified' is unclear – another awkward issue evaded perhaps.

Although Sargent berates Phillips for his apparent claims, Phillips himself is probably the key screenwriting teacher who expresses most clearly what he thought art actually was. In *Art in Short Story Narration* (1913), Phillips states, 'Art consists in an endeavor to express thru an outward and visible symbol some great inward and invisible truth or spiritual struggle.'[93] Ironically, however, a little further on in the same text he also appears to denigrate and downgrade artistic understanding: 'artistic appreciation is simply emotional response'.[94] Art surely cannot be both 'truth' and mere 'emotional response'. However, to achieve whatever Phillips saw as 'true art' would depend, according to him,

---

90   Ibid., 309.

91   Wright, *Photoplay Writing*, 5.

92   Sargent, 'The Photoplaywright', *MPW*, March 25, 1916, 2001.

93   Phillips, *Art in Short Story Narration*, 15.

94   Ibid., 20.

'as much upon knowledge and practice as it does upon special gifts and imagination'.[95] In this statement, he still exhibits the classic dualism and, like the other screenwriting teachers, emphasises the 'craft' element of screenwriting; but at least he does try to define what he thinks art is. For example, the statements 'We may be born with the soul of the artist, but we must also cultivate the hand of the artisan skillfully'[96] and 'Every artist must master technique; or he is but an artisan whom technique masters'[97] underline his view that acquiring skills and becoming an artisan are important, irrespective of artistic notions.

In addition, the key screenwriting teachers drew a clear distinction between writing for the screen and the 'literary' skill required to write novels and short stories. Making a further division between 'literary skill' and 'literary expression', Sargent points out that '[f]lorid expression [...] is out of place',[98] but recognises that:

> Literary skill and judgment are [...] required of the author in plotting his story as well as in originating ideas, but literary expression can only be shown in the leaders.[99]

Contrast what Wright states about the literary skills required to write short stories and those of writing for the screen. Of stories, he writes, 'It requires toil, patience, education and worldly experience, not to speak of talent.'[100] However, on writing for the screen, he claims:

> [T]he fact that you have not had a great deal of education from books will not necessarily stand in your way. It is far more important that you should know people.[101]

The absence of spoken dialogue in the silent period and the relatively simple construction of the earliest of films, which often required no writer at all, perhaps perpetuated the idea that literary skill was not relevant, and gave birth to the notion that only the plot idea or story mattered. However, Phillips counters this view to some extent by emphasising that proficiency in English was essential on the grounds that only through 'clear, forceful English alone can the playwright hope to give searching expression to an exquisite

---

95   Ibid., xiii.

96   Phillips, *The Art of Writing Photoplays* (Cincinnati: Writer's Digest, 1922), 7.

97   Ibid., 23.

98   Sargent, *Technique of the Photoplay,* 3rd ed., 5.

99   Ibid.

100   Wright, *Photoplay Writing,* 150.

101   Ibid., 6.

impression!'[102] His argument does not necessarily imply higher literary skill is required; rather, a person needs enough facility with language to craft a screenplay.

For his part, Ball is quite optimistic that the freelance writer could learn this dramatic technique and write material in a manner that did not require adjustment:

> The well-executed, thoroughly practical and professional type of photoplay scenario, which can be handed to the producing director as it has been purchased, for immediate and unaltered staging, without the additional expense and delay of rewriting, is the one which is worth the most to a motion picture company.[103]

What should not be overlooked is that all the key screenwriting teachers came from a highly literate background. They had all been successful journalists or fiction writers of one kind or another and had acquired the skills to write scenarios through their experience and training. For example, Peacocke had a privileged background, having been educated at one of the best English public schools and had army training at Sandhurst; he was a highly unusual, gifted, intelligent and well-read individual. Ironically, when discussing the possibility of making the transition from freelance writer to staff writer, he largely describes his own skill set as the main qualifications: namely, success in the literary field as a result of journalistic training, experience and education.[104]

Wright also claims that a journalistic background was of great help, even if it was a more pragmatic form of writing:

> If you will look over the lists of successful fiction writers, yes, and those who have succeeded in motion picture story writing, you will notice that nine out of ten have been newspaper men or women.[105]

His advice to those who might be tempted to sign up to one of the fake correspondence schools is illuminating – follow a journalistic training instead, by taking 'an apprenticeship in the "city room"'.[106] Wright's emphasis on this form of pragmatic writing skill also implies 'applied craft' rather than art.

The belief that very little or no literary skill is required to write a screenplay would today be scorned and regarded as an anachronism. The modern screenplay writer has to be terse and to the point and must be able to think and write in a style that conveys visual imagery – all of which are literary skills. Modern screenwriters would claim that it is just as difficult to write a visually conceived screenplay with sub-textual dialogue

---

102   Phillips, *Photodrama*, 116.

103   Ball, *Art of the Photoplay*, 8.

104   Peacocke, 'Hints on Photoplay Writing', *Photoplay*, November 1915, 119–122.

105   Wright, *Photoplay Writing*, 33.

106   Wright, *Motion Picture Story*, 18.

as it is to write a novel, even if the style of language is markedly different. The ability to construct stories also requires an understanding of structure and character. Although this understanding of the literary nature of screenwriting was not fully developed in the early period, its beginnings are evident by the late teens of the twentieth century, particularly when it came to writing synopses, as will be explored in the next section of this chapter.

The Original Plot

The key screenwriting teachers constantly emphasised the need for originality and the industry's demand for 'original' scenarios, as opposed to those that had been plagiarised or breached copyright. Notions of originality appear to be associated with the realms of art, as already suggested, and in this context were often vaguely framed. However, it is clear from their writings that the key screenwriting teachers' ideas of originality were essentially rooted in very conventional, routine and formulaic tropes, which included advice on structure, genre and melodrama. What they seemed to recommend were fresh versions or unstolen reworkings of fairly standard routines, while couching their advice in what would be understood as artistic terminology.

The consensus among the key screenwriting teachers was that freelance writers did have something fresh to offer the industry, and they were writing at a time when this was most needed. As Part One has established, the film industry was desperately short of 'original' material in the early to mid-teens, when several of these manuals were published. Recognising the reach of the new medium, Ball observes that 'the photoplaywright has a greater audience with one picture than Shakespeare had in two centuries'.[107] It would require new authors who could exploit this opportunity.

Peacocke went straight to the heart of the matter with his plea for 'Original stories! Original photoplays',[108] which, he claims, 'the directors have fully demonstrated that they are not capable of producing'.[109] To support his views, he points to the output of the industry, which he saw as comprising many poor-quality films and ill-conceived adaptations of old stage plays and novels.[110] Another of Peacocke's concerns with the current state of the industry was that it did not give the freelance writer a proper hearing. At some points he almost seems to suggest the reason was conspiratorial: 'Their stories have long been wilfully kept back, through the selfish motives of others in salaried positions.'[111] However, it is hardly surprising to find Peacocke on the side of the amateur, as he was playing to this particular gallery, which included his *Photoplay* readership.

---

107   Ball, *Art of the Photoplay*, 27.

108   Peacocke, *Hints on Photoplay Writing*, 11.

109   Ibid., 128.

110   Ibid., 9.

111   Ibid., 129.

The ability to 'plot', as distinct from just writing good prose, was critical:

> the success of a photoplay depends mainly on the originality of its plot. A novel or short story, on the other hand, can be negligible in plot but sustain interest by pleasing descriptive matter and clever dialogue.[112]

Peacocke never clearly articulates exactly what he means by an original plot, other than stating that '[t]he public is clamoring for logical stories, replete with human interest and full of action and suspense'.[113] Further, they should be 'virile, human, up-to-date stories, well worked out into scenes, with logical continuity'.[114] In practice, originality seemed to amount to just variations on themes or a novel idea.

With a similar belief that the problem was industry-related, Ball claims that those who called themselves professional writers in the industry had mainly been drawn from the ranks of unsuccessful journalists and second-rate theatrical actors and managers. He argues that they were blinkered, hackneyed, out of touch and unable to adapt their writing style to the screen, whereas the freelance writer was free of past conventions and such limited vision. It may be that Ball was attempting to flatter his readership when he observed of the amateur writer that '[h]is thoughts are apt to be fresher, and while perhaps lacking the technical skill of the scenario staff writer, he views life from a less professional vantage point'.[115] Ball's solution was simple:

> the encouragement of the independent writer, who understands technique and applies it, with variation and artistry, to every scenario [… as he] can read more, see more staged plays, and mingle more with the people who are interested, as laymen, in the picture productions.[116]

While agreeing it was not a completely level playing field, Phillips considers freelance writers had a real chance of success, because they were more open-minded, lacking the preconceptions of the professional:

> The trained writer has only a slight advantage over the untrained writer, because he must reject all his well-grounded rules of fiction and dramatic technique. The novice has a better chance in photoplay writing than in any other field of expression, providing he is mentally and temperamentally equipped to take it up.[117]

---

112   Peacocke, 'Original Photoplays – versus Adaptations', *Photoplay*, July 1917, 127.

113   Peacocke, *Hints on Photoplay Writing*, 97.

114   Ibid., 12.

115   See Ball, *Art of the Photoplay*, 33.

116   Ball, *Photoplay Scenarios*, 168 and 171.

117   Phillips, *Photodrama*, xxv.

Likewise, Wright claims that freelance writers were capable of injecting fresh life into the industry by providing original material. However, originality in this context generally meant they could take a newspaper clipping of some amusing or amazing incident and weave it into a story that could happen to real people:

> anyone can write for the screen; that is, anyone who has a feeling for the thing that makes a screen story, for the right kind of plot – anyone who has inventive ability, and can devise new situations, and show us old ones from an angle that is new enough to interest us; anyone who can show us everyday people on the screen, in such a way that we like to look at them, and to see what they are going to do next.[118]

Although he seems to indicate that the field was wide open to everyone, his qualification that it was for 'anyone who has inventive ability' makes his statement rather elusive and even contradictory. Oddly, the one quality that appeared to count was the ability to come up with an innovative idea or novel approach to any extant material, rather than the use of literary skill:

> You do not have to be able to express yourself well, as you would have to if you were going to write short stories, for instance. It is the idea that counts, rather than the way in which it is told. [119]

Apparently emphasising the craft element of screenwriting, Wright indicates that even a carpenter is as well-placed to write screen stories as a novelist, as long as they can take inventive ideas and plot them into an engaging story:

> The novelist must forget his word paintings and get right down to screen terms and action along with the contributor who may be unskillful in the assembling of adjectives, but who can plot, and who can visualize.[120]

In one of Wright's articles, we are confronted with the blunt and uncompromising statement: 'A book cannot teach originality.'[121] Again, the precise definition of originality is rather unclear in this context, since it could be argued that very little sold work was truly original. Some clarification comes from his manual, where Wright admits that '"[f]reshness and originality" are generalities [and the] best we can do is to try to put something new and fresh into an old plot or an old situation'.[122] Similarly, Sargent alludes to originality by referring to the need for a plot to have a 'new twist', which means 'the viewing of an old plot from a really new angle'. In other words, 'a story [must] either

---

118 Wright, *Photoplay Writing,* 5–6.

119 Ibid., 6.

120 Ibid., 228.

121 Wright, 'For Photoplay Authors, Real and Near', *NYDM*, 1916 Sep–Nov 1917, 0261.pdf: *Fulton History*: http://fultonhistory.com/Fulton.html

122 Wright, *Photoplay Writing,* 147.

have a new plot or a new use of an old idea'.[123] Phillips also admits that originality is 'doing an old thing in a new way' and that we must 'invent new ways to reveal truth […] – that is originality'.[124]

In summary, the key screenwriting teachers presented their adherents with a clear process of study that included exposing themselves to the medium, reading playwriting manuals and works of theory and, most importantly, scrutinising the teaching manual. Their instructions about the type of learning involved were more confused.

At the time, the key screenwriting teachers were wrestling with a fundamental question: were they right to appeal to lofty artistic notions in order to justify a role as sponsors of talent, or should they simply admit that they were dispensers of practical skills that produced artisans with craft-based expertise? The tension between these constructs or definitions about the nature of creativity opens up space in between – a space in which the genus of this debate about the nature of screenwriting is located and continues to be located to this day. Interpretations of the different aspects or tasks involved in screenwriting exist on the space continuum between these two positions of 'art' and 'craft', leaning more towards one or the other.

Although the key screenwriting teachers occasionally waxed lyrical about the concept of 'art', their instruction mostly tended towards 'craft'. It was easier to impart a set of skills and pragmatically discuss screenwriting using craft-based terminology. Mobilising these kinds of skills made the debate easier to handle too, whereas mystified notions of art were much more difficult to deal with. The idea of 'originality' generally related to working within well-understood and specified dramatic conventions and applying them to plot material, rather than thinking up completely new ways of doing things or inventing novel ways of thinking about film as an art form.

The Filmic Process

In line with a pragmatic and craft-based approach, all the key screenwriting teachers attempted to educate their readers with varying levels of detail, via their columns and manuals, about the industrial process of filmmaking, the terminology that the industry used and, in particular, the role of the writer in this process. Acquiring such knowledge would allow the writer to fit into the specific, practical requirements of the business.

Learning about the technical aspects of the business was matter-of-fact, hands-on and of direct relevance. It was information that the teachers could convey more easily than the challenging issue of developing artistic ability and sensibility and the relatively vague notion of 'how to write' in an artistic way.

---

123   Sargent, *Technique of the Photoplay*, 3rd ed., 69.

124   Phillips, *Art of Writing Photoplays*, 22.

To enable his readers to be fully versed in how films were made, Sargent summarises the whole procedure in a step-by-step manner, including: the initial reception, selection and development of the script in the manuscript department; the type and operation of the studio; the selection of indoor and outdoor locations and their cost implications; the role and activity of the director; and the manufacture and distribution of the film.[125] Further, his glossary inducts his readers into industry jargon, although he discourages the overuse of these terms in a manuscript as he advises it could appear 'amateurish' to an editor: those who truly know do not need to parade their knowledge.[126] In addition, Sargent's columns in *Moving Picture World* provided up-to-date industry information.

In *The Motion Picture Story* (1914), Wright confines himself to explaining how editorial departments work, as well as providing a 'list of terms', which he calls the 'professional vernacular'.[127] Understanding the editorial process was crucial, as this was the part of the industry with which the aspiring writer would have to engage. His third manual, *Photoplay Writing* (1922), gave details on the production process in a chapter on 'How your Story is handled'.[128] Like Sargent, Wright also supplied up-to-date industry information through his articles and columns in *Motion Picture News* (1911–14), *The Motion Picture Story Magazine* (1912–14), *New York Dramatic Mirror* (1914–17) and *Picture-Play Magazine* (1917–1921).

Although Peacocke's writing style was less organised, he offered industry information sporadically throughout his manual. For example, he highlights the importance of various roles in filmmaking: 'A capable camera-man is quite as important to the success of a film production as is the director', as it was the cameraman who filmed what the writer had already visualised with their 'camera eye'.[129] In an extensive glossary, he included terms more directly relevant to the writer.[130] His first series of articles for *Photoplay* (1915–16) was largely a distillation of his manual, but his second series, published in 1917, relayed more information about the process of filmmaking and included articles on the role of the director, the workings of the studio and understanding camera work.[131]

---

125   Sargent, *Technique of the Photoplay*, 3rd ed., 6–17.

126   Ibid., 359–366.

127   Wright, *Motion Picture Story*, 218–221.

128   Wright, *Photoplay Writing*, 165–175.

129   Peacocke, *Hints on Photoplay Writing,* 13.

130   Ibid., 138–146.

131   See Peacocke, 'The Scenario Writer and the Director', May 1917, 111–114; 'Studio Conditions as I Know Them', June 1917, 127–130; and 'Knowledge of the Camera Essential to Successful Photoplay Writing', October 1917, 108 and 118 in *Photoplay*.

In his first manual, *The Art of the Photoplay* (1913), Ball wrote a whole chapter on 'The Adventures of the Scenario', which described the process of making a film from scenario right through to manufacture and distribution.[132] His second manual, *Photoplay Scenarios: How to Write and Sell Them* (1915), was limited to the vital process and requirements of submitting a scenario to a studio; however, it also contained insights on acting for the camera and how this differed from acting in stage plays. Ball emphasises that facial expression and actions were more important than dialogue as agents in storytelling, forming vital knowledge for a writer to acquire.[133]

In his first instructional manual, *The Photodrama* (1914), Phillips includes a brief chapter on the filmmaking process. Information covered the studio, the editor's role and the possibilities and limitations of the camera.[134] He also provided a glossary of terms in common use by various studios, in an attempt to encourage standardisation.[135] His second instructional manual, *The Feature Photoplay* (1921), focused entirely on the process of writing synopses, and the final manual, *The Art of Writing Photoplays* (1922), concentrated on continuity writing. It seems he assumed that those who read these subsequent manuals were already attuned to the knowledge contained in his first manual. His articles in *Motion Picture Magazine*, published in 1917–18, supplemented the manuals with important information about the workings of the industry. In another series of articles in *Motion Picture Magazine* in 1923–24, he attempted to predict possible future technical developments in the industry – predictions that have since proved to have had some degree of accuracy.[136]

The Storytelling Process

The advice the key screenwriting teachers provided about storytelling – the craft of writing – has a practical feel to it, with the application of dramatic conventions. However, it also involved what might be deemed artistic choices about character and the imaginative process of envisioning and creating the storyline. Much of the guidance is comparable across the five different teachers, which indicates its significance, as the teachers all focused on the most important issues. Where they agree, I will deal with these issues collectively, but I will also carefully examine crucial differences of opinion and any notable specific insights that individual teachers offer. (For details on the technical process of writing, see the next section, 'How to Write for the Industry'.)

---

132 Ball, *Art of the Photoplay,* 11–32.

133 Ball, *Photoplay Scenarios.* 1–26.

134 Phillips, *Photodrama*, 107–118.

135 Ibid., 212–221.

136 Phillips's series of articles for *MPM.* 1923–24, included possible developments in the use of colour, sound technology and innovative camera techniques.

The Initial Idea, Theme and Plotting

The key screenwriting teachers generally distinguished between the initial ideas for a story – which could be a thought, an experience, real or imagined, or some literary source often termed as 'original' – and the theme, which was the overall meaning or import of the photoplay. This relates closely to the distinction that Archer outlines: the 'germ of a play' relates to its story, whereas the 'theme' expresses its subject or meaning.[137]

A major preoccupation of the key screenwriting teachers was how to help their readers devise what they considered 'original' ideas for the screen, given the industry was constantly seeking new and fresh material. Oddly, although Peacocke constantly implores his readers to come up with 'original stories', he gives little or no advice in his manual or columns on how to do this and, as we have already seen, what he meant exactly by 'original' is not entirely clear. Whatever this was, when it related to the theme, he suggests that '[e]ach story should have an idea in it greater than merely an interesting series of events'.[138]

In contrast, Sargent was by far the most detailed on this subject; he spends two whole chapters in his manual on how to cultivate the power of the imagination to come up with these ideas.[139] He suggests, 'Imagination is creative only in that it can develop and embroider known facts. It cannot imagine new ones.'[140] According to Sargent, the imaginative process works through actively observing, absorbing and recollecting facts throughout daily life in the hope that they would lead to what he termed a process of 'transmutation; projecting the base material of unoriginal idea into the gold of unusual thought'.[141] Again, this notion seems rather nebulous and it is hard to know exactly what Sargent is meaning, other than that an unusual thought pattern or inkling could be the inspiration for a story. He advocates a notebook and card index for recording these 'novel and strongly suggestive ideas'.[142]

As to theme and plot, Sargent appears to treat them as virtually synonymous, never really distinguishing between them. When it comes to devising a plot, Sargent avers that: 'Plotting is the imaginative and creative part of photoplay writing. Form is merely the expression of the plot in the simplest and most direct manner.'[143] In other words, the suggestive idea for the plot is then creatively worked upon. Sargent appears to use

---

137   Archer, *Play-making*, 13–22.

138   Peacocke, *Hints on Photoplay Writing*, 102.

139   See Sargent, *Technique of the Photoplay*, 3rd ed., 18–24.

140   Ibid., 19.

141   Ibid., 21–22.

142   Ibid., 24.

143   Ibid.,18.

Archer's analogy of the skeleton, which is the 'fundamental element in the human organism',[144] to describe the structural function of the plot:

> the skeleton upon which the flesh of incident is hung and the spirit which animates that flesh, for plot comprises both the outline of incident and the idea which that incident seeks to tell. One gives form and the other soul.[145]

In *The Motion Picture Story* (1914), Wright is also rather vague about the source of inspiration, terming it the 'elusive idea' or 'plot germ', which could be as simple as a 'fleeting' thought suggested by some incident or something a person had read. Basically, it could come from anywhere, but it must be an idea redolent with 'dramatic possibilities'.[146] Fleshing out this issue in an article for *The Photo Playwright,* he claims that '[a]n idea is good in proportion as it concerns some event that determines a man or woman's happiness or unhappiness'. In other words, for it to be dramatic it must involve decisions with huge consequences and life-changing possibilities.[147] In *Photoplay Writing* (1922), Wright's description was more concrete: inspiration could come from a theme, a character, an incident or a moral teaching.[148]

However, Wright does not go into detail about plot construction, other than referring to it as 'the art of story plotting' and pointing the prospective writer to the study of the various masters of this art, such as Charles Dickens, Wilkie Collins and Edgar Allan Poe, and their skill in arousing emotion, showing clear motivation and providing suspense in their plots.[149] While not using the word 'theme', Wright identifies 'the tremolo touch' or 'soul of the story' – sometimes referred to as the 'punch' – which he regards as 'that element which makes the story significant for life, which gives it a bearing on our existing problems, which brings to us heart-felt human interest'.[150] Achieving this through plotting again requires skill and technical craft.

Similarly using 'plot germ' as the term for the inspiration for a plot, Phillips considers it might be 'an isolated incident, phrase, deed, relationship, fragment, or moment, vitally connected with and suggestive of man's emotional life'.[151] It is noteworthy that Price had

---

144   Archer, *Play-making*, 18.

145   Sargent, *Technique of the Photoplay*, 3rd ed., 25.

146   Wright, *Motion Picture Story*, 21–27.

147   'The Idea is the Thing', September/October 1912, 11–13 and 'The Successful Plot', October/November 1912, 9 in *Photo Playwright*.

148   Wright, *Photoplay Writing*, 23.

149   Wright, *Motion Picture Story*, 42–47.

150   Ibid., 28–29.

151   Phillips, *The Photodrama*, 120.

already used the term 'plot germ' in his playwriting manual[152] and Phillips's language in describing it is very similar. In an attempt to systematise the process of coming up with these ideas, Phillips produced a plot catalogue that classifies subjects, characters, emotions and experiences under broad groupings linked to humankind's concerns and circumstances.[153] In essence, with reference to constructing the 'complete plot', he states that:

> It is a combination of the stability of science and the subtlety of art. It requires the brains of structure, the imagination of artifice and the fancy of adornment.[154]

In other words, a good plot requires some blend of the imagination of the artist and the skill of the artisan and no system can replace the creative element, which, as always, is hard to quantify or describe. As Phillips sees it, the overall theme is the 'big idea' or 'master idea'. It must embrace the whole story and be of noble worth, but he admits that such themes are rarely original.[155]

Ball only briefly discusses how to obtain ideas for photoplays, suggesting similar sources to the other key screenwriting teachers. However, he does stress the importance of 'theme' in a similar way to Phillips. Specifically it must be expressed in one sentence and be regarded as 'the backbone which gives the strength, action and effectiveness to the photoplay', which means it must have a moral foundation.[156]

These ideas again draw on familiar homilies rather than any strong notion of originality. Coming up with ideas and then plotting them into a story that has an over-arching theme involves combining some kind of ill-defined artistry with, in much greater measure, artisanship. Again these ideas express the fundamental tension that runs through all these manuals.

Dramatic Construction

The classical elements of dramatic action, unity of action, probability of action, the unified three-act dramatic structure and the well-honed rules of the 'well-made' play are all present in the key screenwriting teachers' instruction. This guidance is presented alongside advice on what writers can use from the melodramatic tradition.

---

152   Price, *Technique of the Drama,* 227.

153   Phillips, *Universal Plot Catalogue,* 71–106.

154   Ibid., 22–23.

155   Phillips, *Photodrama,* 119–123; and *Feature Photoplay* (Springfield: Home Correspondence School, 1921), 91–95.

156   Ball, *Art of the Photoplay,* 33–38.

After admitting that a 'play may be partly a drama and partly a melodrama', Sargent goes on to write a whole chapter on melodrama.[157] However, he warns that 'recourse to melodrama alone will not suffice'.[58] Wright sees no reason why the 'ambitious writer' should not study melodrama and Peacocke regards 'melodramas with a strong "heart interest"' as a legitimate form. [159] Going even further, Ball claims that '[e]very good serious play [...] is a melodrama pure and simple'.[160] Less enthusiastically, Phillips states that '[m]elodrama is at best Art over-exaggerated' and rejects sensationalism, implausibility and extremely good heroes and totally evil villains whose only emotion is passion. However, he appears to consent to melodrama's milder elements, provided they are governed by dramatic rules 'we can admit it only as far as the threshold of good photodrama'.[161]

As indicated, all the key screenwriting teachers advocated a methodological approach to plotting, although writing within these parameters still involved making some creative choices. Sargent articulates this in 1913:

> The successful writer of the moment is well equipped technically as the novelist or the dramatist. He writes in strict accordance with the rules of construction and he observes with care the hundred and one details that go to make the perfect script.[162]

While likewise acknowledging writers must apply clear, unalterable rules of construction, Ball argues this understanding can be acquired:

> What can be learned can be taught! Many successful dramatists have derided the idea of a practical application of systematized technique to the writing of plays. [...It] can be seen that there are certain definite laws upon which the permanence of their excellence is based.[163]

Phillips relates it back to theatrical tradition, drawing a clear parallel:

> The presentation of a photoplay, through the medium of actors, on a screen-stage, before an audience, and in a theater. is almost identical with that of the Stage Play. Both are drama, hence both are dependent on the same larger laws for their larger effects.[164]

---

157 Sargent, *Technique of the Photoplay.* 3rd ed., 250 and 267–269 on 'melodrama'.

158 Ibid., 295.

159 Wright, *Photoplay Writing*, 127 and Peacocke, *Hints on Photoplay Writing*, 90.

160 Ball, *Photoplay Scenarios*, 58.

161 Phillips, *Feature Photoplay*, 53 and *Photodrama*, 154.

162 Sargent, *Technique of the Photoplay*, 2nd ed., 9.

163 Ball, *Photoplay Scenarios*, 28–29.

164 Phillips, *Feature Photoplay*, 19.

The key screenwriting teachers set out a process for clear storytelling. They all have an Aristotelian understanding of narrative structure. In addition, the formulaic influence of Freytag, largely evident with Price, can be detected. This perspective diverges from Archer's rather more loosely rhythmic approach to structure, despite the teachers' regular recommendation of his manual to their readers. Sargent and Phillips clearly articulate Aristotelian structure in their plotting, Wright makes brief reference to it and for Peacocke it is implicit. When discussing plot, Sargent states:

> the centuries-old definition of Aristotle declares that a play must have a beginning, a middle and an end. [...A] beginning, which is the statement of the object of the play and the obstacle to be encountered; a middle, or struggle against this object made interesting through suspense; and an end or termination of the struggle, wherein either victory is gained or defeat sustained.[165]

In elaborating, he explains that 'a plot can have but a single objective point' which is 'the objective' of 'the protagonist' who 'must carry the interest'. The 'antagonist opposes' this objective through 'obstacle', which the protagonist must 'overcome through struggle'. This struggle will produce 'suspense,' which is resolved at the climax.[166]

Although not specifically referring to Aristotle in this way, Phillips explicitly links photoplay structure to the three-act structure in the stage play:

> the Act principle will always be the same. There must be a beginning, the middle, and the end; the Introduction, the Crisis, and Dénouement. These requisites are met in the three Acts of the Stage Play.[167]

The 'complete plot', he states, is a 'perfect syllogism', which raises three questions the plot must answer: '1) What is the cause? 2) What is the effect of the cause? 3) What climax does the effect lead to?' In *The Feature Photoplay* (1921), he develops this structure by breaking it into: 1) 'Sequence', where the purposes of the protagonist and antagonist are set out; 2) 'Consequence', where the protagonist and antagonist are at war; and 3) 'Solution', where the protagonist emerges victor at the climax.[168]

With a simpler approach, Wright identifies the structure as 'motive', 'cause' and 'effect' or 'preliminaries, complications and dénouements' in *The Motion Picture Story* (1914), while in *Photoplay Writing* (1922) he describes it as 'the opening of the story, the building and the plot development, the big situations and the climax'. Neither of his manuals elaborates.[169] As Chapter 1 has noted, Phillips subscribed to an understanding

---

165   Sargent, *Technique of the Photoplay*, 3rd ed., 26–27.

166   Ibid., 29–31.

167   Phillips, *Feature Photoplay*, 20.

168   Phillips, *Photodrama,* 122 and *Feature Photoplay*, 99.

169   Wright, *Motion Picture Story*, 37 and 42 and *Photoplay Writing,* 60.

of 'situational dramaturgy' that was inherited from the more melodramatic tradition Brewster and Jacobs identified.[170] In contrast, Ball's structure is entirely reminiscent of Freytag with its five parts: 'introduction', 'rising action', 'climax', falling action' and 'dénouement'.[171]

The key screenwriting teachers all concur with, as Sargent puts it, the Greek triad of time, place and action.[172] All five agree about the importance of Aristotle's unities of 'one time', 'one place' and 'one action'.[173] Time is compressed by extracting all unnecessary scenes, such as time lapses of six months or ten years between the action, in order to avoid any break in the sequence of the observer's thought. The number of locations is reduced to the minimum. What takes place in them is appropriate to those locations and the story follows the action of a single character, while any extraneous action or characters are removed.[174] Keeping the number of locations to a minimum made sense for economic as well as dramatic reasons. As Ball suggests, 'Unity of place possesses unusual advantages in pictureplay production. The number of sets and outdoor scenes should be held down as much as possible.'[175]

In accordance with Aristotelian principles, the key screenwriting teachers agree that all actions must be 'in accordance with probability or necessity'.[176] Nothing must happen at random, and all actions, characters and settings must be plausible and logical.[177] Further refining the idea of narrative coherence, Sargent stresses that incidence on its own does not comprise plot, but 'plot is that which makes these connected incidents a story by giving those incidents some reason for being shown'.[178] In other words, the progress of the action must be completely apparent and logical with regard to the elements of character and place. This progress of action involves a protagonist who must have an 'underlying reason' or goal and the dramatic aspect of the plot should be 'the recital of the means by which a definite and predetermined object is gained or lost'.[179]

---

170   Phillips, *Photodrama*, 163–164.

171   Ball, *Art of the Photoplay*, 49–50 and *Photoplay Scenarios*, 46–47.

172   Sargent, *Technique of the Photoplay*, 3rd ed., 26.

173   Although the view is implicit in Peacocke's understanding, again he never discusses it.

174   Sargent, *Technique of the Photoplay*, 3rd ed., 34–35; Wright, *Photoplay Writing*, 18; Ball, *Art of the Photoplay*, 47–49 and *Photoplay Scenarios*, 47–50; and Phillips, *Photodrama*, 175–184.

175   Ball, *Photoplay Scenarios*, 49.

176   Aristotle, *Poetics*, 16.

177   Sargent, *Technique of the Photoplay*, 3rd ed., 37–39; Wright, *Motion Picture Story*, 68 and *Photoplay Writing*, 8; Peacocke, *Hints on Photoplay Writing*, 106; Ball, *Art of the Photoplay*, 55; and Phillips, *Photodrama*, 138–145.

178   Sargent, *Technique of the Photoplay*, 2nd ed., 66.

179   Sargent, *Technique of the Photoplay*, 3rd ed., 25–26.

Like Sargent, Phillips is characteristically clear: 'we must have a single action by knitting and welding together [...], everything must agree with our purpose and be essential to its being, or be eliminated' and nothing extraneous must be present.[180]

A key theme in most of the early manuals, as Staiger usefully points out, is 'continuity', which 'stood for the smoothly flowing narrative, with its technique constantly in the service of the causal chain'.[181] Continuity is a constant preoccupation of all the key screenwriting teachers. Two measures of its increasing importance are that Ball includes it in his second manual in 1915 after barely mentioning it in his first (1913); and that Wright only briefly mentions in his second manual in 1914, but by his third in 1922 the requirements of smooth storytelling have evolved into a script form known as the 'continuity'.[182] Audiences from a broad social range and background could not be left wondering about time or spatial relationships that did not make complete sense in films. Hence, films needed a careful arrangement of scenes, clear action and intertitle use to avoid plot interruptions and achieve a logical chain of causality. Phillips's pithy description captures its importance in the photoplay: 'Perfect continuity [e]nsures perfect illusions.'[183]

However, it seems that to some extent the teachers tolerated the non-classical narrative structural elements found in melodrama, as identified by Singer and discussed in Chapter 1. Although Wright and Peacocke do not elaborate, Sargent states his openness to the idea that '[e]xact truth may be strained' if 'the visual effect is of greater importance than strict probability'.[184] He admits to the 'dominance of the melodramatic feature'[185] but wants writers to moderate the more extreme elements when drawing from this form:

> It must be *fairly* logical, plausible and with a plot that can be followed by those incapable of depth of thought and yet sufficiently intelligent to interest those of a higher order of intelligence [emphasis added].[186]

With a similar perspective, Phillips states that these elements 'should never be employed for pictorial effects alone, and they should always be consistent in spirit with the theme'.[187]

---

180   Phillips, *Feature Photoplay*, 112.

181   Bordwell, Staiger and Thompson, *Classical Hollywood Cinema*, 194–195.

182   Sargent, *Technique of the Photoplay*, 3rd ed., 220–224; Wright, *Motion Picture Story*, 45 and *Photoplay Writing*, 49–59; Ball, *Art of the Photoplay*, 46 and *Photoplay Scenarios*, 4; Peacocke, *Hints on Photoplay Writing*, 21 and 28; and Phillips, *Photodrama*, 138–145.

183   Phillips, *Photodrama*, 144.

184   Sargent, *Technique of the Photoplay*, 3rd ed., 267.

185   Ibid., 270.

186   Ibid., 269.

187   Phillips, *Feature Photoplay*, 35.

As discussed above, his *Plot Catalogue* indicates that Phillips had a 'situational' view of plotting, which could make use of such effects. Ball also endorses the use of 'tableaux vivants' as a means of unifying the action.[188] Given how wedded they were to Aristotle's principles, it is surprising the key screenwriting teachers were willing to tolerate the use of spectacular effects and allow some degree of implausibility and improbability. However, this stance was likely to have been driven by market considerations, as Sargent points out that a 'melodrama' is one of the 'best selling' scripts, providing it is 'well-planned' and 'well-written'.[189]

On the issue of linearity of storytelling, some differences open up between Sargent's view and Phillips's as expressed in his later manual, *The Feature Photoplay* (1921). In 1916 Sargent writes that

> Theoretically the photoplay should move in chronological order, beginning with the earliest action and continuing in logical sequence to the last action recorded.[190]

Sargent's model for the scenario appears to be the short story; in 1912 he quotes from Phillips's book, *The Plot of the Short Story*, in support of his view: 'The short story plot should set out to do one thing and then complete it.'[191] Similarly, in 1913, Sargent again states the photoplay should follow the same principle: 'Not only must each scene be played in chronological order, but each scene should aid in advancing the plot.'[192] These two forms, according to Sargent, are virtually indistinguishable: 'Photoplay is merely a plot in action instead of words, and most of Mr. Phillips's statements are as applicable to the photoplay as to the fiction story.'[193] This position is understandable in the first two editions of Sargent's manual, as feature-length films were not completely dominant at this point. However, their dominance was well established by 1916, when the third edition of his manual was published, so Sargent's continued support for this position seems rather antiquated.

When Phillips's book on short story writing was published in 1912, it may have been a model for scenario writing at that time. But in *The Feature Photoplay*, Phillips opens up other storytelling possibilities and suggests two other forms. First, the 'Logical Sequence' involves 'choosing related events and applying the law of syllogism to them'.[194] This is still cause-and-effect, as one event logically follows another, but it does not have to

---

188   Ball, *Art of the Photoplay*, 24.

189   Sargent, *Technique of the Photoplay*, 3rd ed., 269.

190   Ibid., 203.

191   Sargent, 'The Photodrama', *MPW*, September 12, 1912, 1274.

192   Sargent, *Technique of the Photoplay*, 2nd ed., 38.

193   Sargent, 'The Photodrama', *MPW*, September 12, 1912, 1274.

194   Phillips, *The Feature Photoplay*, 123.

be chronological. Second, he proposes the 'Dramatic Sequence' as a combination of chronological and logical sequences, whereby the storytelling may move in and out of chronological sequence at will. By this means, a film can portray incidents occurring simultaneously or depict a character's thoughts.[195] As forms of storytelling, these sound decidedly modern and advanced and less applicable to the scenario writing of the period. This more flexible approach to storytelling also refers back to Münsterberg's ideas about creating emotion within the viewer by manipulating events, as the next section considers in relation to advice on how to write for the industry.

Establishing Characters

The key screenwriting teachers draw on the prevailing Western tradition of character-centred narrative and generally discourage characters with simplistic melodramatic traits. According to Azlant, Sargent's view of character is 'complex', as characters must be understood in order to comprehend their actions. Each character must 'possess a clear, distinct identity and maintain some degree of consistency if their actions are to be credible to the audience'.[196] For Sargent, characters are also defined by what they do and the photoplay is no place for literary character sketches. Through their actions, '[t]he characters, particularly the leading character, must be so finely drawn that the persons seem real and convincing'.[197] Characters must exhibit constancy in their behaviour and actions, although Sargent does allow for the possibility of character development:

> It is necessary to select a type of character for each person and hold to that type, unless a change in character is a basis of your play, when you must prepare your audience for the change by showing a gradual deepening in feeling.[198]

Nevertheless, indications are that even Sargent lapsed into melodrama when describing character traits by sometimes depicting characters as simple heroes and villains.[199]

Phillips's view of character is as developed as Sargent's. Characterisation, he believes, is symbolic of inner psychological truth and must be logical and consistent:

> When we seek what it is that characters express, we find that they express their characteristics, which in turn are largely symbols of the vices and virtues of humanity.[200]

---

195 Ibid., 124.

196 Azlant, 'Theory, History and Practice of Screenwriting', 222.

197 Sargent, *Technique of the Photoplay,* 3rd ed., 58.

198 Ibid., 51.

199 Ibid., 86.

200 Phillips, *Feature Photoplay*, 168.

Phillips claims that 'characters must be delineated in terms of emotion – repressed or active – or described in words of action – commonplace or dramatic'.[201] Intertitles gain his approval as a quick way to establish a character if necessary.

Although offering far less detailed comments on character, Wright advises that the writer should limit their number and 'make them "human beings"' by drawing them from life, which presumably means basing them on real people.[202] In both his manuals, Ball suggests drawing upon the 'stock company characters' of melodramatic tradition for establishing basic character traits. However, with a more developed view of character in the second manual, he also advises the writer to try to understand the psychological profile of the character by attempting to think as the character would think, in order to ensure 'logical action and realism'.[203] Peacocke's advice on character is similarly limited. Nonetheless, he is clearly aware that actions define character. For example, he explains that if a girl is reading in a park, it means she is possibly a 'girl of leisure and probably wealthy'.[204]

The key screenwriting teachers see character motivation as the main driving force behind the plot; and they appear to agree with Archer that 'action ought to exist for the sake of character', rather than the reverse.[205] Sargent claims that '[e]very action must be motived to show its connection with the plot, and so must be related to plot'.[206] Wright advises, 'never let the interest shift for a moment from the central figure'; and every action must have a reason behind it, 'for no human act can be rightly understood without the motive for that act'.[207] With equally clear views, Phillips believes that desire is 'the basic motivating force behind all Drama'[208] – a sentiment shared by Ball, who claims that '"want" […] is the steam of the dramatic engine'.[209] The only comment on this topic from Peacocke is that the writer should '[a]lways create a logical reason for each character to be in each scene depicted'.[210]

---

201 Phillips, *Photodrama*, 80.

202 Wright, *Motion Picture Story*, 167–175.

203 Ball, *Art of the Photoplay*, 46–47 and *Photoplay* Scenarios, 56–59.

204 Peacocke *Hints on Photoplay Writing*. 25.

205 Archer, *Play-making*, 19.

206 Sargent, *Technique of the Photoplay*, 3rd ed., 33.

207 Wright, *Motion Picture Story*, 40 and 43.

208 Phillips, *Feature Photoplay*. 190–191

209 Ball, *Art of the Photoplay*, 50.

210 Peacocke, *Hints on Photoplay Writing*. 41.

Azlant's assertion that Sargent has a 'complex' view of character implies that his viewpoint is special. As the above discussion indicates, however, most of the other key screenwriting teachers' views about character were just as developed.

The Beginning

The key screenwriting teachers agree that the beginning of a photoplay is very important, as it is essential to grab the audience's attention from the start. Wright states:

> Your story must begin with action – something must happen right away […] and then go back afterward and explain who the people were and why they were doing what they did.[211]

According to Sargent, Wright's position is actually more extreme than the above advice indicates in that he proposes a 'striking first scene':

> The device will serve at times, but as William Lord Wright has pointed out, the striking first scene is a promise to the spectator that must be kept. If you promise a big play, […] you must keep your promise by pitching the play in that key.[212]

Phillips agrees:

> The problem to be met by those who open up in the midst of a fire, is to explain how things became so hot and to get back to Sequence gracefully.[213]

Wright's only other instruction about the composition of an opening scene appears to be simply – and rather vaguely – to: 'Start the story where it should start.'[214] More specifically, Phillips suggests getting 'into the heart of the theme with as few scenes as possible […and the] first scene must be suggestive at least of the climax'.[215] Ball also urges that the 'opening scene should […] show […] the line upon which the theme of the subsequent action is directed'.[216] Reiterating this advice, Sargent explains, 'the statement of the question is the start of the play […] and the reply the climax or end'.[217] This is reminiscent of Archer's 'point of attack', which signifies a first scene that will capture the spectator's interest and will of necessity lead to the 'obligatory scene', or the scene that must happen at the end.

---

211   Wright, *Photoplay Writing,* 24.

212   Sargent, *Technique of the Photoplay,* 3rd ed., 217.

213   Phillips, *Feature Photoplay,* 126–127.

214   Wright, *Motion Picture Story,* 83.

215   Phillips, *Photodrama,* 135–136.

216   Ball, *Photoplay Scenarios,* 43.

217   Sargent, *Technique of the Photoplay,* 3rd ed., 29.

The Struggle

If characters have a clear motive, they will be pitched into a struggle. For Sargent, 'Struggle must be directed against a specific and not a general object [... and] the objective must be concrete.'[218] In other words, it must have a definite physical end point so that the struggle can be terminated. Wright points out that precision is important, as '[e]xactly the right amount of motive is necessary for action', meaning that the writer should think out a logical reason for every detail in the photoplay, because otherwise the struggle will not be effective.[219] Ball asserts that:

> Struggle is this foundation stone of drama. Some one or some several want something: they try to get it. Some others or something resists the efforts to obtain it. The continuation of those efforts, now succeeding temporarily, now failing, here changing in plan, there surprising the antagonist, is the action of the drama.[220]

In his advice on struggle, Phillips emphasises its internal nature, in contrast to the external:

> Actions must express and portray an internal struggle with which the audience is in sympathetic understanding. There must be an underlying emotional meaning for every prominent action [221]

Particular references to the 'struggle' are strongly suggestive of Freytag's playwriting manual: 'What the drama presents is always a struggle, which, with strong perturbations of soul, the hero wages against opposing forces.'[222] Freytag uses the idea of 'struggle' to completely frame the action in all three acts, with the claim that 'the beginning of the struggle' takes place in Act One.[223] This idea also figures heavily in the playwriting manuals of Archer and Matthews.[224] Moreover, like Archer, who advises that once 'the tension sets in' at the beginning of the struggle, it should not be relaxed until the end, Phillips reiterates that '[e]ach minor effect, tho begun in the first scene, must heighten and tighten the climax'.[225]

---

218 Ibid., 40.

219 Wright, *Motion Picture Story*, 44.

220 Ball, *Photoplay Scenarios*, 32–33.

221 Phillips, *Photodrama*, 156.

222 Freytag, *Technique of the Drama*, 104.

223 Ibid., 196.

224 Archer, *Play-making*, 23; and Brander Matthews, *The Principles of Playmaking* (New York: Charles Scribner's Sons, 1919), 40.

225 Archer, *Play-making*, 148; and Phillips *Photodrama*, 163.

The 'Punch' or 'Tremolo Touch'

All five key screenwriting teachers see the need for 'heart interest' in a story, as a quality in the actions of the characters that engenders emotions of pathos, sympathy and warmth in the audience.[226] It reaches its zenith with what these screenwriting teachers refer to as the delivery of the 'punch' or the 'tremolo touch'. Broadly, these terms seem to mean the emotional impact of the story produced at the climax, although their writings vary in their level of precision on this point. It is certainly reminiscent of some of the melodramatic elements discussed in Chapter 1, but the terms are not derived from theatrical tradition.

An important element in delivering an effective punch was suspense, or delaying the outcome for as long as possible, to heighten the climactic effect. Therefore careful planning was needed to ensure that the climax occurred at exactly the right moment to produce a punch with maximum impact, usually followed by a happy ending.[227] Ball sums it up:

> The uncertainty of outcome, the surprise of the successive incidents of the play, – these keep the audience in sympathy with the participants holding them spellbound until the final scene or dénouement.[228]

In respect to the positioning of the climax and the delivery of the punch, Sargent differs strongly from Ball and seems to take issue with Freytag's five-act structure. In Sargent's opinion, the photoplay follows more closely the structure of the one-act play:

> This differs from the teaching of the drama where the last act is supposed to be reserved for the falling action following the climax, but photoplay is not drama, and in the photoplay the climax should be so led up to that there is nothing more to follow and detract from the interest.[229]

Using language similar to Freytag, Ball describes how the '"rising action" follows the introduction, showing the development of the situation. Then the series of powerful incidents culminating in [...] the climax', which constitutes the penultimate act. Following it is the 'falling action', which signals the dénouement of the play.[230]

Characteristically light on specifics, Peacocke, although he regularly refers to the 'punch', does not discuss what it actually is. It is important, he advises, to 'create plenty

---

226   See Sargent, *Technique of the Photoplay,* 3rd ed., 56–60; Wright, *Motion Picture Story,* 125; Peacocke, *Hints on Photoplay Writing,* 6; Ball, *Art of the Photoplay,* 53 and *Photoplay Scenarios,* 39–40; and Phillips, *Photodrama,* 69 and *Feature Photoplay,* 106.

227   Sargent, *Technique of the Photoplay,* 3rd ed., 92–98; Wright, *Motion Picture Story,* 28–34; Peacocke, *Hints on Photoplay Writing,* 30; Ball, *Photoplay Scenarios,* 179; and Phillips, *Photodrama,* 173.

228   Ball, *Art of the Photoplay,* 70.

229   Sargent, *Technique of the Photoplay,* 3rd ed., 43.

230   Ball, *Art of the Photoplay,* 49–50.

of suspense and keep the interest up to fever heat until the actual "thrill" occurs [...] and you have landed the "punch".[231] Ball discusses the importance of feelings and that the:

> necessary emotion [or] heart interest [...] is satisfied by the rounding up of the action into a dénouement which exemplifies dramatic justification. [...T]he goal of the play must be worthwhile: there must be a reason for the ending, and that ending must satisfy the audience.[232]

However, although Ball mentions 'the punch' a handful of times in his second manual, he never develops or clearly defines its meaning.

In place of the term 'punch', Wright calls the same concept the 'tremolo touch'. While describing it as 'the soul of the story' and 'that element which makes the story significant for life', otherwise his definition is rather obscure and, as already mentioned, he only vaguely relates it to the theme.[233] He takes up the idea under the guise of 'emotionalism' in an article for *The Motion Picture Story Magazine*, where he claims that the 'tremolo touch' is that moment when you play the 'heart strings' of the audience and 'is an inherent emotionalism essential to success in Literature, Music, Art and the Drama'. This description is more reminiscent of an approach found in conventional melodrama.[234] Perhaps Wright's lack of clarity in his own mind on this issue is emphasised by the credence he gives to a 1913 article in *The Writer's Magazine,* in which five writers attempt to define the 'tremolo touch' or 'punch' and none of them agrees on the analysis.[235] Wright even locates it in the power of the acting as one possibility.[236] In summary, he is content with it as 'a mystery' and states, 'It means an infinite variety. It is heart-interest, gripping action, suspense, climax, and unusual idea, all rolled into one.'[237] Such descriptions underline the melodramatic tendencies of the concept.

Based on a much clearer understanding of the punch, Phillips explains it is the moment 'when the dramatic struggle that has waged uncertainly from side to side suddenly pitches forward with the victor for good'.[238] It is in these moments that the reason behind the action or, as Phillips puts it, 'the effective expression of the movement that underlies the action [... or] the force behind the Climax' is exposed.[239] According to Phillips, the

---

231　Peacocke, *Hints on Photoplay Writing,* 30.

232　Ball, *Photoplay Scenarios,* 39–40.

233　Wright, *Motion Picture Story,* 28–29.

234　Wright, 'The Tremolo Touch', *MPSM,* December 1912, 130.

235　Wright, *Motion Picture Story,* 33.

236　Ibid., 31.

237　Ibid., 34.

238　Phillips, *Photodrama,* 173–174.

239　Phillips, *Feature Photoplay.* 142.

'Climax-Punch' should have the power to move people and:

> must be sufficient to make the audience literally hold its breath, or emotionally rise
> to the occasion [… as it] is the motive-idea of the play summed up in a cumulative
> stroke [… and] the emotional truth of the author's vision come home to dwell in the
> heart of each one who sees the vision.[240]

Phillips clearly links emotional impact with the thematic intentions of the writer, as
discussed earlier. He also seems to articulate the potential emotional power of the film
experience more clearly than the other screenwriting teachers. In this, his writing sounds
distinctly modern. However, the following description displays strong elements of pathos
verging on melodrama, similar to Wright's approach, when he claims that in the 'perfect
play' it is possible to find 'sufficient emotion released to shatter the soul of the strongest
man God has created'.[241]

With similar views on the punch, Sargent presents it as the 'idea' behind the incidents of
the plot, strongly related to the theme and heightening the effect of the climax:

> Punch is the idea back of the narrative. It makes narrative interesting through idea.
> In this it differs from motivation, which makes for interest through explaining the
> reason for action.[242]

In other words, the punch 'is the effect of action heightened by our knowledge of facts',
thus providing the underlying reason for the plot.[243] It is what gives the story 'dramatic
intensity' and, as with Aristotle, it is through this that the audience experiences 'strong
and gripping effects'.[244] Sargent illustrates it in the following way:

> The sight of one man trying to kill another may be exciting, but not of real interest.
> If we know the slayer is unwittingly trying to kill his own son, then this idea gives
> interest to the physical action.[245]

According to Sargent, the punch can only be effective if we fully understand the reason
or motive behind the action. However, he does not rule out the inclusion of melodramatic
elements at this point if 'it is desired to increase or heighten the effect toward the close'.[246]

---

240 Phillips, *Photodrama*, 174.

241 Phillips, 'The Photodrama', *MPM*, January 1917, 119–120.

242 Sargent, *Technique of the Photoplay*, 3rd ed., 93.

243 Ibid., 96.

244 Ibid., 230.

245 Ibid., 93.

246 Ibid., 268.

As Azlant correctly identifies, Sargent's view of the punch is more 'subtle' than that contained in many other screenwriting manuals, because he links it with the theme or 'the "idea" behind the incidents of the plot'.[247] As an example of a less subtle manual, Azlant offers James Slevin's 1912 manual, because it fails to link emotion to theme and argues that '[t]he dramatic crisis deals in emotions, and the more emotion and greater variety you can get out of a situation, the nearer you are to the dramatic'.[248] However, Azlant incorrectly aligns Phillips[249] with Slevin's position, as well as overstating the uniqueness of Sargent's views. As outlined above, Phillips also clearly expresses the view that the punch could powerfully relay the theme or intention behind the drama in a similar way to Sargent, even if his arguments are tinged with melodramatic overtones.

In summary, the approach the key screenwriting teachers adopted to the learning, filmic and storytelling processes lent itself to a more pragmatic 'craft' type line, even though they often broached artistic notions too. Through their manuals and articles, they proposed a clear study pathway, conveyed appropriate information on the film industry and laid down a form of storytelling that was based on familiar mechanisms such as the 'well-made' play and melodramatic devices, overlaid with more sound instruction from the playwriting tradition, which advocated a product that would appeal to the mainstream. Although their material essentially contained nothing new, the key screenwriting teachers were the first industry insiders to have an opportunity to propagate it widely in a consolidated and easy-to-understand format.

How to Write for the Industry

All five key screenwriting teachers gave strongly practical advice on the specialised technical skills that the freelance writer needed to acquire in order to write for the film industry. The three particular skills of particular importance were: developing the skill of writing visually; comprehending how to write in photoplay form; and gaining an understanding of screenwriting techniques.

Visual Writing

One important skill that the prospective writer needed to acquire was the ability to think visually, a dimension specific to the medium.

To Sargent, using 'the eye of the mind' or being able to 'think in action and to visualize that action' is indispensable. In other words, the writer must see the action so clearly in their mind that they can write it as they see it. Along with the other key screenwriting teachers, Sargent regards this skill as the one that distinguishes the writing of photoplays from all other forms of writing:

---

247   Azlant, 'Theory, History and Practice of Screenwriting', 220.

248   Slevin, *On Picture-play Writing,* 24.

249   Azlant, 'Theory, History and Practice of Screenwriting', 270.

> Without the picture eye it is not possible to write convincingly of your action since you cannot see your action and do not know what it is, but a little practice will enable you to acquire the picture eye if you have the proper imagination.[250]

Strangely, Azlant only mentions the issue of visualisation briefly and then makes little of it. Instead he tends to focus on Sargent's treatment of the literary aspects of photoplay writing, even though Sargent stresses visualisation as a crucial skill in writing for film. Azlant does recognise that Sargent 'considers the province of "imagination"' important and that he would expect such a skill to be 'attached to a craft that requires the mental picturization, transformation, and embroidery of complex events'.[251] However, he writes no more on the subject apart from a comment relegated to an endnote, where he acknowledges that '[m]any of the screenwriting manuals make much of this capacity for "imagination" or "picturization", often calling it the "picture eye"'.[252] This endnote lists some of the peripheral manual writers of this study, who considered the skill of visualisation important, but it only mentions one of the other key screenwriting teachers, Phillips.[253] Nonetheless, as the following discussion will show, all five key screenwriting teachers considered this skill of specific relevance to the medium and absolutely vital in writing photoplays.

In emphasising the skill of visualisation just as strongly as Sargent, Wright asserts, 'You must be able to visualize your story as you write it – you must be able to see it.' Like Sargent, he gives absolute pre-eminence to acquiring this skill: '*Above all* learn the "Picture eye" and when you can clearly visualize, natural, unforced and logical construction will come to you almost unawares [emphasis added].'[254] The ability to 'visualize a story' is a skill that Peacocke also stresses more than once. Urging, 'Try and look at things with a "camera eye"', he even advocates taking up photography as a means of facilitating this skill.[255] The issue of visualisation is omitted from Ball's first manual, *The Art of the Photoplay* (1913). However, he makes amends just two years later in his second, *Photoplay Scenarios: How to Write and Sell Them* (1915), when he contrasts writing for the screen with writing for the theatre. He claims that the photoplay writer:

---

250   Sargent, *Technique of the Photoplay*, 3rd ed., 137.

251   Azlant, 'Theory and History of Screenwriting', 255.

252   Ibid., 273.

253   Azlant lists Esenwein and Leeds, Thomas, Barker and Bertsch and Freeburg alongside Phillips when discussing visualisation. See ibid.

254   Wright, *Motion Picture Story*, 83 and 85.

255   Peacocke, *Hints on Photoplay Writing*, 13 and 39–40.

eliminates the explanatory speeches of the stage play which must describe things seen and done out of view of the audience, by going through every phase of the action before the camera-eye.[256]

Backed by his stance that visualisation is 'both the key and keynote of all photoplay-writing',[257] Phillips devotes a whole chapter to it in his first instructional manual, *The Photodrama* (1914), and constantly refers to it in his second, *The Feature Photoplay* (1921).[258] In his first manual, he also gives visualisation a new twist by suggesting that 'perfect visualization' occurs when the 'dramatic development', represented visibly 'in terms of action', functions as 'symbols of emotion' for the audience.[259] In *The Feature Photoplay* he terms this 'Dramatic Visualization', which he claims means 'feeling while we see'.[260] Interestingly, the views of Phillips line up with Münsterberg's ideas. According to Sargent, Münsterberg actually moots the possibility of 'reproducing in the mind of the spectator the actual emotion and not merely the record of an emotion in another' by rearranging scenes and putting them in a particular order.[261] Münsterberg puts it thus:

> Every shade of feeling and emotion which fills the spectator's mind can mold
> the scenes in the photoplay until they appear the embodiment of our feelings.[262]

This is an effect Sargent thought was too difficult to achieve at the time: the photoplay could only depict emotion to the viewer and not suggest it to the viewer's own experience.[263] However, Münsterberg's belief that the pictures on the screen could in some way project or mirror the thought processes of the human mind certainly opens up new storytelling possibilities and combines with Lowe's understanding that narrative processing of the Aristotelian variety is intuitive and an innate part of the human make-up. As this was the kind of visual storytelling that screenwriting teachers like Phillips were advocating, it could be viewed as doubly powerful.

Although playwriting manuals also advocated the idea of visualisation, it was not to the same degree. For example, Archer advises that the playwright must 'at some point in the working-out of his theme, visualize the stage-picture in considerable detail' by paying 'great attention to [...] the topography of their scenes and the shifting "positions"

256   Ball, *Photoplay Scenarios,* 6–7.

257   Phillips, *Photodrama*, 65.

258   Ibid., 65–74.

259   Phillips, *Photodrama*, 67 and 69.

260   Phillips, *Feature Photoplay*, 146.

261   Sargent, 'Münsterberg on the Photoplay', *MPW*, July 15, 1916, 436–437.

262   Münsterberg, *Photoplay*, 93.

263   Sargent, 'Münsterberg on the Photoplay', *MPW*, July 15, 1916, 436–437.

of their characters'.[264] However, the key screenwriting teachers frequently voice and emphasise the need for this particular skill. Maras correctly identifies Sargent's concern: 'The plot of action demands a specific style of writing, one that demands a specific kind of visualization.' In other words, 'Literary style and the picture eye come together' for Sargent. This issue is clearly enunciated in the 1913 edition of Sargent's manual, as Maras observes:

> His overall view of 'writing photoplays' is that while 'the mastery of phrase and literary style that are demanded of the other forms is not required,' it is 'offset by the need for being able to write in action so clearly that this action is as plain and understandable as the written word.'[265]

The ability to 'write in action' was a fundamentally different skill from writing the fiction prose narrative or novel. In contrasting the visual skills of the photoplay author with the skills of the novelist, Ball claims that, in the novel, a:

> character is shown by long dialogues, letters, descriptions of scenes, manners, expressions; the entire portrayal depending primarily upon the story-telling individuality or 'style' of the author.[266]

Phillips concurs, explaining how a film must approach that dramatic conflict in an entirely different way: 'An internal struggle of one being with himself can sustain but a few scenes at most.' Extended inner monologues and introspection had no place in the photoplay. According to Phillips, ideas had to be conveyed through 'psychological action, suggestive attitude and mimetic expression'.[267]

In making a similar contrast, Sargent points out that '[t]he fiction author is free of the fetters of time':[268] it is easier to move back and forth in fiction with a few words of explanation. However, '[w]hat the fiction writer must do in words, the photoplay writer must do with business and situation'.[269] For Wright, screenwriting 'does not depend so much upon word painting, dialogue and tricks of the literary craft' as on the visualisation of action.[270] Ball sums up the main differences:

> Contrasted with the novel, then, the scenario must tell its story within a limited time, its characters must be differentiated by their type, as shown in movement,

---

264   Archer, *Play making*, 51.

265   Sargent, *Technique of the Photoplay*, 2nd ed., 144; cited in Maras, *Screenwriting*, 148.

266   Ball, *Photoplay Scenarios*, 8.

267   Phillips, *Photodrama*, 77 and 69.

268   Sargent, *Technique of the Photoplay*, 3rd ed., 247.

269   Sargent, *Technique of the Photoplay*, 2nd ed., 10.

270   Wright, *Photoplay Writing*, 223.

costume and motives. Their actions must be practically self-explanatory because long captions, or 'subtitles' of printed matter use up valuable film space to the detriment of the action in the scenes: and the photoplay is primarily action, from start to finish.[271]

The key screenwriting teachers also wanted their students to understand the clear distinction between the skills required to write plays and those for film. Again, Ball clearly articulates these differences in his 1915 manual, where he explains the stage play is dependent on:

action, interpreted by dialogue, [...] the emotional appeal is made to the ear rather than to the eye [...] while the action of the motion picture story must be self-explanatory *or shown through action*. The ideal photoplay is that one which contains the least number of explanations in the form of subtitles and screen letters [emphasis added].[272]

As Peacocke states, films needed to be 'visualized', making them 'absolutely distinct from the art of the spoken drama or from the art of pantomime', which consisted of showing emotions and feelings through gestures.[273] In sharp contrast, '[t]he really good screen play [...] written by trained screen play writers especially for [...] the motion picture camera' was more naturalistic.[274] Similarly, Phillips recognised that this new form of writing required more than just a transfer of skills: it needed 'a new type and a new school of artists' as well.[275]

However, Ball also understood that many of these skills were interchangeable. If people learnt how to write a photoplay, they were also developing the skills that would help them to write for the theatre and literature:

The development of the technique of good photoplay creation leads to a skill in dramatic composition which can be applied to original compositions for theatrical productions and literary work of the broadest nature.[276]

Although photoplay writing was a literary form, in all its guises – whether it was the synopsis, the scenario or the continuity – these teachers presented it as inseparable from a process of visualisation. This process was facilitated by brief, present-tense descriptions of actions that focused on only what the viewer of the finished film would see. The fundamental way that literary and theatrical storytelling differed from film

---

271   Ball, *Photoplay Scenarios,* 9.

272   Ibid., 2–3.

273   Peacocke, *Hints on Photoplay Writing,* 97.

274   Peacocke, 'Hints on Photoplay Writing', *Photoplay*, Sept 1915, 149.

275   Phillips, *Photodrama,* 151.

276   Ball, *Art of the Photoplay,* 9.

writing was that writing for film could only be related visually. This had to be achieved with minimal dialogue in what was a transitional document that would be discarded once it was realised in film. As Maras notes, in the writing of today, 'notions like the picture eye' have merged with more modern 'concepts such as writing for the camera and eventually writing for the screen'.[277]

This emphasis on the ability to visualise in order to write for the screen is perhaps one of the most important legacies of this early period of theorisation about writing for film. The key screenwriting teachers were among the first to fully articulate and disseminate these ideas within the industry and to a wider public.

Photoplay Form

There is a great deal of debate over the origin of the current form of the screenplay. Azlant sets out the purpose of his research as to pursue 'the problem of identifying the screenplay', which he ultimately links in his conclusion with 'Sargent's views on the nature of the screenplay'.[278] His use of the identifying words 'some format of the screenplay' when describing different kinds of 'film script' is a point Maras picks up on because no one had previously used the term 'screenplay' for this concept. This is inappropriate, Maras suggests, as relating the modern screenplay to a document that had been variously called '"plot of action," "scenario," "photoplay," "continuity," "treatment," "screen dramatization," "cinema play," to name a few terms' involves projecting a notion back into the past that was not applicable at that time.[279] Maras rightly cautions against reading back our 'present day terminology understanding' of the 'screenplay' into 'the complex and shifting terminology of screen writing in the 1910s and 1920s'.[280] However, Nannicelli rejects Maras's view that Azlant's account is teleological, arguing instead that Azlant's use of the word 'screenplay' does not necessarily imply that he regarded the 'screenplay' as the predetermined end point of the script. Instead, Azlant was simply asserting that 'the screenplay has, in fact, evolved historically out of earlier, similar script forms'.[281]

On this issue, Steven Price's research on the history of the screenplay is useful, indicating that the variance in terminology reflects the infant industry's state of flux and its attempts to define how narrative film should be written. Price identifies that 'writing for film encompasses a large number of different kinds of texts [… and] the history of these writings does not simply see one form replaced by another in a straightforward

---

277 Maras, *Screenwriting*, 148.

278 Azlant, 'Theory, History and Practice of Screenwriting', 1 and 338.

279 Maras, *Screenwriting*, 81.

280 Ibid., 81.

281 Nannicelli, *Philosophy of the Screenplay,* 56.

chronological sequence'.[282] Moreover, Sargent had reproduced a sample format from 1908 in one of his articles in *Moving Picture World* in 1911.[283] In this article, Sargent claims that the 'photoplay manuscript consists of two essential parts – the scenario and the synopsis. Cast and scene plot are optional.' [284] While he promotes that particular format here, in a 1912 article he indicates that writer and director Bannister Merwin could well have developed the 'permanent form of the photoplay', as he saw it at that time. It showed promise because Merwin's scripts had lengthy motivational descriptions and were full of detail, which, according to Sargent, made for 'absolute clearness' and standardised production.[285] In his 1916 manual, where he supplies a sample from a Merwin script in the appendix, Sargent again confirms his belief that this could become 'the standard form of script'.[286] However, he presents it alongside nine other forms of script[287] and claims that a writer 'is at liberty to adopt any one of these or combine parts of two or more into a new form, if he pleases'.[288] A glance at the range of samples in his manual indicates how different these documents were and gives some idea of how fluid the format was at this time, which reinforces Price's point.

It is beyond the scope of this study to trace this history further or to assess the level of influence that particular screenwriting teachers might have had over specific submission formats or the nomenclature of what ultimately came to be known as the 'screenplay' and its supporting documents. Suffice it to conclude that some further light may be shed on this area of interest by investigating photoplay form as it was viewed by the key screenwriting teachers selected for this study. What is confirmed is that throughout the 1910s no fully standardised form or terminology had yet emerged for the photoplay and that studio requirements varied. This variation is reflected in the writings of the key screenwriting teachers, although they agree on certain basic aspects of the submission format and terminology employed. The fact that all but one of these screenwriting teachers wrote more than one manual, sometimes years apart, is helpful in tracing some of the developments that took place in photoplay form up to the early 1920s, by which time continuity scripts were usually written in-house by staff writers and scenarios had been largely replaced by a lengthier synopsis.

---

282 Price, *History of the Screenplay,* 10–11.

283 Ibid., 81.

284 Sargent, 'Technique of the Photoplay', *MPW*, July 29, 1911, 197–198. Sargent reproduces a short synopsis, cast of characters and the beginning of the scenario of Lubin's *For His Sister's Sake* (1908).

285 Sargent, 'The Photoplaywright', *MPW*, June 8, 1912, 926–927.

286 Sargent, *Technique of the Photoplay*, 3rd ed., 374 and 397.

287 Ibid., 376–398.

288 Ibid., 99.

Examining the views of the key screenwriting teachers will at least confirm and clarify the nature of the documents that were generally referred to as photoplays in the early 1910s and the general terminology that was in use. It will also be possible to comment on how their views about these documents changed in response to the industry's requirements. Such evidence is not definitive, because it focuses on the views of only five individuals, but these individuals have already been identified as likely to be among the most significant contributors to the discourse about screenwriting during this early period, so their opinions carry weight.

The key screenwriting teachers all stress the need for the writer to present their work in a 'form' that was acceptable to the industry. However, Sargent's main concern is that the writer is not overwhelmed by form, as he sees it simply as a means to an end: 'Precise adherence to form – a placing of form before plot – is one of the pitfalls that yawn for the unwary [… and] form is merely a means of telling a plot succinctly and understandably.'[289] This view is echoed by the others. For example, in his first manual Wright claims that:

> many writers pay too much attention to technique, and not enough attention to the story. To develop an idea in the most forceful and most clear manner possible – that is the form of technique most to be desired.[290]

Here, Wright uses the word 'technique' to refer to writing in photoplay form yet sometimes he appears to use it in the sense of story-writing technique instead. His use becomes ambiguous a little further on in the same chapter: for example, 'a skilled *technique* is as highly to be desired in writing the motion-picture story as it is in writing the story of fiction [emphasis added]'.[291] The comparison he makes with fiction writing, which did not have to be presented in a highly specialised form, is confusing and seems to suggest that 'technique' refers also to story writing.

Confusion over what was precisely meant by 'technique' seems to have been more widespread. It even led to a public spat between Sargent and Peacocke, although there is no evidence the dispute went beyond this incident. One of Peacocke's articles in *Photoplay* in 1916, which was also reproduced word for word in his manual, began:

> What is the 'Technique' of a photoplay? I'm sugared if I know! All the wise-acres who are writing on the art of photoplay writing keep continually harping on that word, as if it was a mystical something that we grasp from nowhere, but which must be vitally essential to ensure success.[292]

---

289 Ibid., 373.

290 Wright, *Motion Picture Story,* 62.

291 Ibid., 63.

292 Peacocke, 'Hints on Photoplay Writing', *Photoplay*, April 1916, 123 and *Hints on Photoplay Writing,* 37.

It is unlikely to have escaped Peacocke's notice that Sargent's book, then on its third edition, was actually entitled *The Technique of the Photoplay*. His comments may therefore have been a sideswipe at Sargent. Certainly Sargent makes his own rather caustic response in his column for *Moving Picture World*:

> We quite agree with the gentleman that he does not know what technique is. But it does not follow that because he does not know what technique is that it is not necessary to those who would build a lasting success.[293]

Despite the confusion over the meaning of 'technique', these men did not really disagree. In his manual, Peacocke follows his opening comment from the article with the simple statement: 'Of course there are certain forms to be observed in the construction of a scenario' and then describes all the technical aspects of script preparation and presentation. It seems that Peacocke regarded 'technique' as referring to photoplay format, rather than the actual story.[294] He is just as concerned as the others that story should take precedence over form. The very first lines of his book are, 'If you have a strong, original plot. you already have ninety-nine per cent of a successful scenario.'[295] A careful reading of Sargent confirms that what the other screenwriting teachers sometimes refer to as 'technique', he describes as photoplay format, as his statement quoted earlier confirms: photoplay 'form is merely a means of telling a plot succinctly and understandably'.[296] Sargent divides these subject areas in his manual into sections on 'Plotting' ('technique') and 'Photoplay Form' ('form').[297] Therefore, Sargent understands 'technique' as referring to the ability or skill to write a photoplay, and 'form' as the way in which it should be presented.

Demonstrating much the same view, Ball states, 'the story is the life-blood of the play. No matter how clever the technical presentation, [...] without the backbone of a good theme, all effort is wasted.'[298] Likewise Phillips clearly sees the distinction between photoplay form and storytelling and notes that the former is only used to enhance the latter:

> we are not teaching technique. or laying down rules; rather, we are trying to interpret the laws of human conduct, the science of being natural and the art of entertaining effectively.[299]

---

293 Sargent, 'Technique of the Photoplay, *MPW*, May 13, 1165.

294 Peacocke, *Hints on Photoplay Writing*, 37.

295 Ibid., 5.

296 Sargent, *Technique of the Fhotoplay*, 3rd ed., 373.

297 Ibid., iii.

298 Ball, *Photoplay Scenarios*, 53.

299 Phillips, *Photodrama*, 106.

The surface debate over exactly what 'technique' meant could be slightly misleading and mask a deeper, more resentful undercurrent of feeling about the gradual drift towards 'literary particularism' or the professional exclusivity of a writing elite. As Maras observes, 'the study of technique becomes a key marker of the difference between the aspirant or amateur writer, and the successful scenario writer'.[300] Such views about specialist expertise would eventually begin to shut the freelance writer out of the film industry. By 1922 Wright confirms that the freelance writer was definitely relegated to providing only the story without the detailed continuity:

> there is no chance for a free lance writer, one not a member of the motion picture studio staff, or not familiar with the rules of a studio, to write and sell a motion picture continuity.[301]

Continuity or staff writers were appointed for their years of experience in the studio and their demonstrable writing skill. Opportunities for outsiders were diminishing rapidly. This trend perhaps explains the strength of Peacocke's reaction, as he sides with the freelance writer – although, as noted in the previous section, this was the audience he was writing for in *Photoplay*, an organ of the fan press. The freelance writer had value, Peacocke claims, given the urgent need of manufacturing companies is for 'original photoplays especially written for the screen by competent scenario writers'. In his opinion, the staff writers are subservient to the freelance writers in this process, as 'their chief duties should be in reconstructing good original stories that reach the scenario departments from various sources'.[302]

The debate over what the key screenwriting teachers actually meant by 'technique' again relates to the art–craft dichotomy discussed in the previous section. Their attempts to define 'technique' further indicate the level of confusion over what screenwriting actually was. When Sargent uses 'technique' in the title of his manual, he assigns it a more artistic meaning and Peacocke allots it a mystical quality, whereas the others interpret it in a more mechanistic sense. The imprecision of their language is to some extent understandable, since they were at the heart of the dispute and were not privy to the overview that today's scholars have of the historical art–craft constructs Shiner has identified. When it comes to photoplay form, however it is described, it is certainly situated more towards the craft end of the spectrum, as it involves the application of screen technique to story.

What, then, did the five key screenwriting teachers regard as photoplay form or format? Were they in agreement on the main points or did they have major differences? Their manuals and articles actually show considerable overall agreement on what was required, although some important differences arise over the synopsis in particular, as it developed

300   Maras, *Screenwriting*, 162.

301   Wright, *Photoplay Writing,* 49.

302   Peacocke, *Hints on Photoplay Writing,* 11.

into a lengthier document. Their advice is generally pragmatic on these issues because the industry was changing so fast.

The whole of Part Three of Sargent's *The Technique of the Photoplay* (1916) is devoted to photoplay form; he asserts that it:

> consists of a title, a synopsis, a cast of characters, a scene plot and the plot of action […], which is more properly termed the scenario [… and] is supplied with leaders [or subtitles] and other inserts.[303]

In *The Motion Picture Story*, Wright lists the same constituent parts as Sargent.[304] Phillips's *The Photodrama* is similar, except that he replaces the scene plot with the 'Author's Remarks'.[305] Ball, in both *The Art of the Photoplay* and *Photoplay Scenarios: How to Write and Sell Them*, calls the 'scene plot' a 'set list', but adds a document that the others leave out, which he calls a 'Director's Sheet'.[306] In *Hints on Photoplay Writing*, although Peacocke lists the same documents as Sargent and Wright, he omits the 'scene plot' altogether and instead suggests writing two synopses of the story: one short and the other a more detailed one that could form the basis for what he terms a 'working scenario', written by someone at the studio.[307]

With regard to 'Photoplay Form', Sargent claims, 'Nowhere in photoplay writing is there such a variety as in the form in which a play may be written.' He makes no attempt to present what he considers a standard form or a 'unification of style', but instead provides examples of 'ten different styles of form' from various studios by way of demonstration in his appendix, as described above.[308] Similarly, the other key screenwriting teachers do not espouse a particular form but provide samples of produced scenarios of their own and from others, which also indicate a variety of form.

While it is important to acknowledge variety and a lack of standardisation in the way submissions were made, studios had in common a number of key features that they required: a title, a cast of characters, a scene plot, a synopsis and a scenario.[309]

---

303   Sargent, *Technique of the Photoplay*, 3rd ed., 101.

304   Wright, *Motion Picture Story*, 82.

305   Phillips, *Photodrama*, 39–44.

306   Ball, *Art of the Photoplay*, 65–72 and *Photoplay Scenarios*, 16–23

307   Peacocke, *Hints on Photoplay Writing*, 37–43.

308   Sargent, *Technique of the Photoplay*, 3rd ed., 99–101 and 373–398. These examples include a synopsis with a cast of characters, a scene plot and various scenario extracts.

309   See Appendix One for a sample studio submission, *The Chap from Broadway*, a short released as *The City Fellow* (1913), written and directed by Ball.

The Title

All five of the key screenwriting teachers stress the importance of the title, but to varying degrees. In an overall sense, the title was important at two levels: to sell the screenplay and to help sell the completed film.

To Sargent, the title is the crucial first point of contact with the editor and a major selling point on billboards. In all cases it should be 'brief' and 'easily remembered', 'fluent – easily spoken', 'applicable to the story' but 'not self-explanatory'; it should 'rouse curiosity' or 'sentiment', while the 'trite' and any 'controversy' should be avoided at all times. He counsels readers to 'try to gain proficiency in title writing' by keeping a record of anything of interest from newspapers, magazines, advertisements and trade papers, 'as you never can tell where your title will come from, and you are as apt to find it in the bottom of your cocktail glass as on the top of a twenty-story building'.[310]

Like Sargent, Wright considers the title is critical but for a different reason. In *The Motion Picture Story* (1914), he presents it more as an advertising and marketing tool for the completed film than as a means of selling the original idea to the editor: 'A good photoplay with a bad title will be purchased very often and another title substituted.' Nevertheless he still advises the writer to 'submit his script in as perfect a form as possible [and if it …] is submitted under an ordinary name it is not perfect'. Therefore, the title should be 'apt, interesting, original and brief' while it should not 'give too much idea of the plot'. Thus the writer should give time and consideration to 'originating appropriate and attractive names' for photoplays.[311] By 1922, Wright seems to have adjusted his thinking on the title: in *Photoplay Writing*, he, like Sargent, now sees it as a crucial selling point for getting the work read by an editor. A 'striking, significant title for your photoplay […] will make the scenario editor want to read your story'. Perhaps his views changed because the level of competition in the photoplay market had become even higher than before. In general, he claims that most '[p]hotoplay titles are derived from the theme of the play [… except] where the theme is exemplified by the main character', meaning the title must precisely represent the product.[312]

Having a brief title is what Peacocke focuses on as a main selling point both to an editor and for the final film: '[t]he shorter the title, the better. One word will often be more potent than four or five.' He encourages every writer to carry a notebook and to jot down anything that comes to mind, as '[a] title will often suggest a theme for a story'.[313]

---

310 Sargent, *Technique of the Photoplay*, 3rd ed., 105–109.

311 Wright, *Motion Picture Story*, 161–166.

312 Wright, *Photoplay Writing*, 44–46.

313 Peacocke, *Hints on Photoplay Writing,* 42–43.

According to Ball, 'two-thirds of the scenarios have been bought because of a clever and salient title'. He also includes ideas on the topic that the other teachers do not cover: 'the best title is one which is so expressive of the theme it almost gives the entire story in a word or two or three', but does 'not tell the dénouement of the story' as this is still the 'bait which attracts the spectator to the theatre'.[314] Like Peacocke, he considers that the title is often the 'first step' to writing and 'that the most virile results are attained when a concrete idea is in the mind'.[315]

In *The Photodrama* (1914), Phillips gives a hierarchy of three reasons for a good title. The first two involve its commercial potential, namely to 'add a drawing power to the poster' for the general public at the theatre front, and its potential to attract the 'attention of the exhibitor' to include it in his programme. Oddly, the reason he relegates to last, without explaining why, is its potential 'appeal to the photoplay editor because of its promise of high-class literary or dramatic material'.[316] Later, Phillips appears to have adjusted his thinking on the title, making no mention of the above three reasons for a good title in *The Feature Photoplay* (1921). Instead he emphasises its importance for the writer by advising it is best 'conceived before the story is begun' and the writer should '[s]pend hours – days if necessary – on [their] title and then live up to every letter in it!'[317] For Phillips, the title has now become the wellspring from which the story flows.

Cast of Characters

The cast of characters served two purposes: to make the package easier to read for an editor in hope of a sale; and to serve as a practical aid when producing the film. In essence, it was none too different from what playwrights called the 'dramatis personae' or list of characters in the drama.

'The Cast of Characters', Sargent instructs, should be divided into 'leads' or those that carry the story, 'secondary personages' and 'extra parts and bits'. Writers should give distinguishing features to only key characters who are 'essential to the play' and provide characters with names that are appropriate and easy to remember.[318] Wright's advice in *The Motion Picture Story* (1914) is very similar, but he also counsels the writer to use 'few' characters because, as well as being more economical, 'the fewer the principals, the clearer the action'. Peacocke limits his advice to providing a list of the characters and

---

314   Ball, *Art of the Photoplay,* 36–37.

315   Ball, *Photoplay Scenarios* 23–24.

316   Phillips, *Photodrama*, 40.

317   Phillips, *Feature Photoplay*, 155–156.

318   Sargent, *Technique of the Photoplay*, 3rd ed., 115–119.

'a short description of their ages, sex and calling in life'. Similarly, Ball states that only a list of names with a 'three or four-word description' for each is sufficient.[319]

Of greatest interest is the fundamental change in Phillips's approach in the years between his first and second instructional manual. In *The Photodrama* (1914), the 'cast of characters' is written merely 'for the convenience of the director' and 'should mention individual characteristics […] and clearly show relationships at a glance'.[320] However, in *The Feature Photoplay* (1921), Phillips recommends a greatly enhanced 'cast of characters' that goes beyond a list of well-chosen names to also delineate the 'psychological attributes' of the leading character or characters and relevant details about supporting characters.[321] In contrast, although publishing at the same time, Wright in *Photoplay Writing* (1921) is still content that the 'cast of characters' should just comprise 'a list naming each one, and telling briefly who the person is'.[322]

Such a difference in advice indicates that, even into the early 1920s, no standard way had been established for how to convey details about characters. Further, Koszarski has pointed out how pre-1914 cinema was strongly influenced by the melodramatic tradition known for its 'instant characterization of heroes and villains'. After *Birth of a Nation* (1915), these melodramatic influences continued, but Koszarski indicates that feature-length films permitted filmmakers to give their characters 'a richness of detail', although this generally stopped short of psychological realism.[323] It appears that Phillips's writings may more accurately reflect, and show more sensitivity to, the way film was developing at this time than Wright's.

Scene Plot

The 'Scene Plot' served a highly practical purpose for the potential director of the script, giving details of locations and the order they appeared in the script plus budget implications.

For Sargent, it referred to a carefully drawn-up list of settings, with scenes marked as 'exterior' or 'interior' and given simple, short descriptions. The writer's 'choice of scenes [should] give a maximum of effect with a minimum of expense and trouble', although 'economy […at] the expense of the story' should never be countenanced. Sargent was concerned that the document should be 'exact', allowing the director to shoot all the

---

319   Wright, *Motion Picture Story,* 169–175; Peacocke, *Hints on Photoplay Writing,* 38; and Ball, *Photoplay Scenarios,* 20.

320   Phillips, *Photodrama*, 39–43.

321   Phillips, *Feature Photoplay*, 160–170.

322   Wright, *Photoplay Writing,* 17.

323   Koszarski, *Evening's Entertainment,* 181.

scenes in location order rather than chronological order.[324] Concurring on almost all points, Wright's only caveat is that a 'scene plot' is 'not necessary to complete the sale of your story' but its provision shows 'a willingness to aid the producer […] and creates a favorable impression with both editor and director'.[325]

Ball stresses the importance of correctly numbering the scenes, in what he denotes as a 'set list' instead of a 'scene plot' as they correspond with the numbers shown on a board held up during the filming of each scene on set. An additional document he mentions is a 'Director's Sheet', which he claims 'is a simple list showing scene after scene in chronological order' with numbering to act as a checklist for the director.[326] Interestingly, when asked about this document in a letter, Sargent replies he has to 'confess ignorance' but surmises it might be just the front page of the script giving the cast, synopsis and scene plot. This lack of common knowledge may indicate that it was not widely used.[327]

As mentioned above, Phillips replaces the scene plot with the 'Author's Remarks', which deal with period, locale, suggestions for 'ideal locations,' properties and 'specific actors whom you have in mind'.[328] For his part, Peacocke only discusses this document in the glossary of his manual: under 'Script', he explains that it was 'the written form of the plot and its related instructions for producing', which presumably includes the 'Scene Plot'.[329] The variety of approaches again underlines the lack of standardisation at this time.

The Synopsis

All the key screenwriting teachers agree on one point: that the synopsis functions as the main selling point for the scenario.

In the early teens, the synopsis was a short document that served as a means of introducing the scenario. However, Azlant notes:

> By the late teens this format will come to be called the 'continuity,' like the modern shooting-script […] and the 'scenario' will come to mean a highly detailed synopsis, like the modern treatment.[330]

---

324   The scene plot consists of numbered scenes that correspond to the scenario, e.g. '41. John's parlor. Typical country stuff. Portrait of Lincoln on wall essential.' See Sargent, *Technique of the Photoplay*, 3rd ed., 119–128.

325   Wright, *Motion Picture Story*, 183–186.

326   Ball, *Art of the Photoplay,* 67 and 71 and *Photoplay Scenarios,* 16–23.

327   Sargent, 'The Photoplaywright', *MPW*, April 5, 1913, 41–42.

328   Phillips, *Photodrama*, 43.

329   Peacocke, *Hints on Photoplay Writing,* 144.

330   Azlant, 'Theory, History and Practice of Screenwriting', 259.

In 1916 Sargent stresses that the synopsis, written in the present tense, is the most important document, even though it should be the last one to be written and usually consists of only around 250 words. It primarily 'exists only to interest the editor in reading that scenario' and ultimately achieving a sale:[331]

> Your title is your brand name, the synopsis the descriptive label and the preparation of the script the packing. [...] It is your business to present your story in a few words so attractively that the editor will decide to read the action. You are not telling the story, but merely telling what the story is about.[332]

In another analogy, Sargent likens effective presentation of the freelance scenario package to the eye-catching qualities of a newspaper story: '[T]he title functions as a headline, the synopsis functions as a seductive first paragraph summary, and the scenario as the story proper.'[333] In keeping with this approach, he advises the writer to put 'the punch in the opening: the editorial attention is far more apt to be held with a striking statement [... and] the rest does not matter so long as it is well written and informative'.[334] As Azlant points out, Sargent's view on the synopsis was not universally accepted among other manual writers.[335] This was because, according to Azlant, the 'synopsis, with its first sentence punch, violates the very dramatic structure of the scenario, which builds to a crescendo of conflict'.[336]

The other key screenwriting teachers instead view the synopsis as a summation of the story. For Ball, the synopsis is the document that should be written first, in preparation for the eventual writing of the scenario, and should contain 'every important phase of the story, every dramatic "kick," every essential scene'.[337] Peacocke counsels the writer: 'Tell your story as simply as you know how.' It must be as succinct as possible, even as little as 50 words, but must be the full story. Like Sargent, he also stresses the importance of its sale value as a document: '[a] good synopsis won't sell a poor scenario, but many a good scenario has lost a hearing because of a poor synopsis'.[338] Peacocke, by advising the writing of a second lengthier synopsis, was signalling one of the changes occurring

---

331   Ibid., 256.

332   Sargent, *Technique of the Photoplay*, 3rd ed., 109–110.

333   Azlant, 'Theory, History and Practice of Screenwriting', 257.

334   Sargent, *Technique of the Photoplay*, 3rd ed., 112–113.

335   Among those who disagreed, Azlant lists some peripheral manual writers such as Esenwein and Leeds, Carr, Emerson and Loos, along with two of the key screenwriting teachers, Ball and Peacocke. All viewed the synopsis as performing a genuine design function by serving as an initial outline of the scenario. See Azlant, 'Theory, History and Practice of Screenwriting', 257 and 273–274.

336   Ibid., 257.

337   Ball, *Photoplay Scenarios,* 17.

338   Peacocke, *Hints on Photoplay Writing,* 5–7.

in the industry at the time. Some studios were accepting a longer document from which the scenario editor or director would 'have to evolve the working scenario'.[339]

One point Wright holds to that is similar to Sargent's advice is that it is best to write the synopsis after the scenario has been completed, otherwise some important story detail might be left out. He also argues, 'The synopsis should be an outline of your entire plot and action, couched in as brief a form as is conducive to clarity.'[340] However, Wright was frustrated by the arbitrary word limits some studios imposed, because many writers were unused to the rigours of 'boiling down' as journalists did and so could be restricted from telling their story properly. Wright was pleased to see 'the form of the synopsis [was] undergoing alteration' and some directors were beginning to 'prefer a full synopsis', even as early as 1914.[341] As Maras comments, the development of 'a very complete synopsis including all the important points in the plot and climax', as recorded by Wright, was part of a wider trend towards a read-through that provided a visualisation or 'complete' picture of the film.[342] The synopsis became the main selling document and a staff writer would write a detailed continuity. As a consequence, the story could be told unencumbered by technical detail and the script read in a 'more artistic process [...] evoking rhythm and powerful images'.[343]

The change in the role of the synopsis in the industry, sparked by the development of the features market, is clearly seen in the change in the way Phillips treats it over the time from the publication of *The Photodrama* (1914) to the completion of his second manual, *The Feature Photoplay* (1921). In 1914 Phillips regards the synopsis as 'an abridgement' of the story. He advocates writing a synopsis 'without missing a single essential point [... in] a style of telling [...] that is terse, crisp and suggestive'. Because of the pressure of time, it is to be written 'for the convenience of the editor or reader who takes up your manuscript with a view to its acceptability'.[344] Later, in August 1917, comments in his column capture how the industry was in a state of flux over the role of the synopsis: '[T]here exists a disagreement among editors and producers as to what a synopsis is'. He then attempts to define it, indicating a significant change not only to

---

339   Ibid., 41.

340   Wright, *Motion Picture Story*, 176.

341   Ibid., 177.

342   Wright, *Motion Picture Story*, 61; cited in Maras, *Screenwriting*, 75.

343   Maras writes extensively on the development of the read-through as a means of experiencing a film through a process of mental visualisation See Maras, *Screenwriting*, 71 and 69–75.

344   Phillips, *Photodrama*, 40–42.

its length but also to its level of importance.[345] To illustrate how he believes a synopsis should be written, he publishes a lengthy one of his own over a seven-month-period.[346]

Reflecting on the state of the industry in 1917, Sargent concludes that 'in the past decade we have worked in a circle back to the starting point of synopsis'. He recognises that the industry now required a 'detailed synopsis' and entrusted the writing of the continuity to the staff writer.[347] For Bordwell, 1917 is also a watershed moment, as the point at which 'a system of formal principles that were standard in American filmmaking [now known as] *classical Hollywood cinema*'[348] was established. This is not a coincidence, as both Sargent and Bordwell are signifying the movement towards the professionalisation of writing for the screen, not only for the continuity, but for any form of screenwriting.

According to Phillips, the synopsis had become a fully rendered, highly readable story, entirely visualised with capitalised leaders and dialogue. In his 1921 manual, he provides another example of a 41-page synopsis in seven parts entitled *Pierre Le Grand*,[349] which was produced in 1920.[350] Reiterating the importance of the synopsis in his 1922 manual, *The Art of Writing Photoplays*, he emphasises the read-through in particular as a way of creating a sense of rhythm because 'each paragraph represents a complete cycle or sequence of action'.[351] Prose also had to suggest the right imagery, because 'if the author fails to use the precise word in the synopsis, he will fail to create the exact picture in the mind of the producer that his vision calls for'.[352] Most importantly, the synopsis was not only to be used as a selling point, but also for production purposes, so it must be written 'in such a manner that a group of producers – readers, editors, directors, actors – shall envision it perfectly'.[353]

While largely concurring with Phillips and the change in the basic form of the synopsis, Wright, in *Photoplay Writing* (1922), does not insist on capitalised leaders and dialogue:

---

345   Phillips, 'The Photodrama', *MPM*, August 1917, 81.

346   Phillips publishes his synopsis, *(The Romance of) The Self-made Widow* (World Film, 1917), from February to August 1918. See Phillips, 'The Photodrama', February 1918, 50–52 and 'Photodrama in the Making', March 1918, 108 and 110; April 1918, 60 and 122; May 1918, 89 and 127; June 1918, 114; July 1918, 95 and 116; August 1918, 104 and 113 in *MPM*. See 'Self-made Widow', *IMDbPro*: https://pro-labs.imdb.com/title/tt0008557/

347   Sargent, 'Photoplay Writing Then and Now', *MPW*, March 10, 1917, 1491–1492.

348   Thompson and Bordwell, *Film History,* 32.

349   Phillips, *Feature Photoplay*, 224–265. See Appendix Two for a full reproduction of this synopsis.

350   See Phillips, *Feature Photoplay*, 224–265. *Pierre Le Grand* (released as *Heart Strings* by Fox, 1920) starred William Farnum. See *Heart Strings*, *IMDbPro*: https://pro-labs.imdb.com/title/tt0011268/

351   Phillips, *Art of Writing Photoplays*, 83.

352   Ibid., 86.

353   Ibid., 82.

> The synopsis should tell the editor the plot of the story; […] the characterization of the people who carry out the plot, […] an idea of the environment or locale of the story, […] the big climaxes as the plot develops; and it should always carry a happy ending.[354]

Simplicity was the order of the day. As Wright describes it, studios required from a writer: 'manuscripts contain[ing] the bare skeleton of his idea, written in simple language, so that editors […] could see clearly just what was in the mind of the author [… and] could visualize immediately the story he had in mind'.[355] He also accepted that a feature play synopsis could now be as long as 2,000 words, which is still somewhat shorter than Phillips's recommendations.[356] He includes a sample synopsis by way of illustration.[357]

According to Phillips, the synopsis is also to be preceded by the 'motif', which is a 'paraphrase of the story' in one or two lines.[358] In his 1922 manual, Wright terms this feature simply as 'the first paragraph' that, as in a newspaper article, 'frequently contains a short and snappy résumé of the entire' story. Without going as far as Sargent to advocate telling the 'punch' up front, Wright does recognise that 'the first paragraph should be so written as to hold the attention of the editor so he will read further'.[359] Phillips also advocates an 'outline' of the synopsis, breaking it into its constituent parts. However many parts it has – which can be up to seven according to Phillips – these are always based on 'three component divisions' making up the beginning, middle and end.[360] He argues that 'as the main title must contain the essence of the entire play, so must each of the subtitles of the 'outline' contain the essence of its part'.[361] Just as in a book or play, division into parts helps focus the attention of the editor and 'greatly adds to the pleasure of reading it'.[362]

---

354 Wright, *Photoplay Writing*, 10–11.

355 Ibid., 224.

356 Ibid., 11.

357 Wright reproduces the synopsis for *The Dream Girl* written by George Morgan and directed by Cecil B. DeMille (1915). See Wright, *Photoplay Writing*, 15–17. However, IMDbPro lists Macpherson as the writer of the story and gives a release date of 1916. Wikipedia also claims it was released in 1915. See *The Dream Girl, IMDbPro*: https://pro-labs.imdb.com/title/tt0006605/ and 'List of Lost Silent Films (1915–19)' in *Wikipedia*, http://en.wikipedia.org/wiki/List_of_lost_silent_films_(1915–19)

358 Phillips, *Feature Photoplay*, 156.

359 Wright, *Photoplay Writing*, 10.

360 Phillips, *Feature Photoplay*, 149.

361 Ibid., 153.

362 Ibid., 13.

Plot of Action, or Scenario

The 'plot of action', or 'scenario', was the main script and was the most important document in the 1910s before it was mostly replaced by the synopsis. On a number of issues with regard to this document, which had its basis in theatrical tradition, the five key screenwriting teachers share common ground. Archer regards the play 'scenario' as a preliminary document – a 'skeleton' or 'scheme of scenes' that functions as the 'groundwork of a dramatic performance'.[363] However, for the key screenwriting teachers it was more than just a schema, because this document would transmit the whole story.

They are also consistent in their term for this document: Sargent refers to it as either the 'plot of action' or 'scenario', and the others refer to it consistently as the 'scenario'.[364] However, it had no definitive form in terms of layout, typeface and style of heading, as the samples referred to earlier show and both Sargent and Wright confirm.[365] They all counsel writers to keep it brief, include a variety of settings to avoid monotony, tell the story clearly by writing action in the present tense, carefully weave the scenes together, number scenes, and use good, clear English. As with an extended synopsis, the 'plot of action' or 'scenario' demanded a highly visualised form of writing, as discussed at the start of this section.[366]

With regard to segmentation, Sargent advises writers, when beginning to write a scenario, to break down the action into 'important facts and isolate those into [numbered] scenes', keeping the 'action as brief as possible' and making use of (silently mouthed but understood) dialogue only when it 'will tell more than action will'. Scene numbers were included so they could be identified in the editing process.[367] As Azlant points out, 'the basic sense of the segmentation, serial representation of the film's activity that Sargent presents in 1916 survives [...] minus the dialogue'.[368] Sargent's understanding of the 'scene' is linked to theatrical use, where an ambiguity already existed: it could refer either to a place or setting, or to the time-period over which an activity or a single experience took place. But, Azlant observes, Sargent offers a further clarification by defining 'the "scene" [... as] one continuous run of the camera'. This unit of segmentation has now

---

363 Archer, *Play-making*, 44.

364 Sargent, *Technique of the Photoplay*, 3rd ed., 213.

365 Sargent, *Technique of the Photoplay*, 3rd ed., 99; and Wright, *Motion Picture Story,* 187.

366 See Sargent, *Technique of the Photoplay*, 3rd ed., 119–145 and 213–220; Wright, *Motion Picture Story*, 186–191; Peacocke, *Hints on Photoplay Writing*, 20–43; Ball, *Art of the Photoplay*, 68-72 and *Photoplay Scenarios*, 15–26; and Phillips, *Photodrama*, 43–47.

367 Sargent, *Technique of the Photoplay*, 3rd ed., 128–136.

368 Azlant, 'Theory, History and Practice of Screenwriting', 260–261.

been redefined in the industry as the 'shot' and become part of a larger unit, usually termed a scene or sequence.[369]

> All of the action made in one set or location at one time is one scene. If the camera is stopped, then the scene stops, though the action of the scene, as it may be understood in dramatic work, may be continued.[370]

However, although Azlant comments only on Sargent's understanding of the scene as one continuous run of the camera, all the other key screenwriting teachers in this study, except Ball, show the same comprehension; so Sargent's understanding is nothing unusual, and no evidence points to who originated it.[371] Of significance is Phillips's dissatisfaction with the use of the term for this purpose; he thought it was confusing because the etymology of the word 'scene' is connected to location or setting, as Sargent also observes. Phillips prefers 'scenes' to be called 'acts' because 'they are distinct units of action and definite and complete acts in the development of the play', but would be numbered chronologically as before. His view seems to be that scene numbers should be attached to each 'act' and, when a setting is first used, it would be numbered as scene 1 and any return to it in a subsequent 'act' would have the same scene number ascribed to it.[372] Phillips's comments possibly show that ideas about the practice of segmenting were varied at this point and, as a result, aspiring writers were often offered conflicting advice.

Going into far more detail than the other key screenwriting teachers, Sargent spends no less than 43 chapters of the third edition of his book dealing with the 'technique' of how to write the scenario and the methodological skills to ensure that it was presented in a suitable 'form'.[373] To Sargent, the 'plot of action' is a crucial initial instigator and interim vehicle of the production process. Azlant clearly demonstrates that Sargent's understanding of what constituted a scenario or screenplay was 'a complex, challenging commentary on the nature of the early film scenario [which] clearly invites application'.[374] As the Introduction has described, Azlant goes on to test Sargent's views by successfully applying them in a critical analysis of the exemplary screenplay, *Selfish Yates* (1918) by Sullivan.[375] In Azlant's opinion, this use of Sargent's approach in 'the analysis of this particular screenplay indicated the high level to which the craft of screenwriting had

---

369   Ibid., 262 and 266.

370   Sargent, *Technique of the Photoplay*, 3rd ed., 135.

371   See Wright, *Motion Picture Story*, 219; Peacocke, *Hints on Photoplay Writing*, 27; and Phillips, *Photodrama*, 44.

372   Phillips, *Photodrama*, 47.

373   Sargent, *Technique of the Photoplay*, 3rd ed., 18–249.

374   Azlant, 'Theory, History and Practice of Screenwriting', 267.

375   Ibid., 276–334.

evolved by 1918'.[376] However, it is important also to credit the other key screenwriting teachers with extensive input on the scenario. Phillips spends virtually all of the first three parts of his first manual dealing with the 'principles', 'plot' and 'dramatic construction of the photoplay'. Wright and Ball are equally detailed on plotting the story and writing the scene plot and scenario in their manuals, while Peacocke analyses and annotates a sample script to indicate how it should be written. They all provide extensive advice on how to write in photoplay form.[377]

Continuity Script

It is beyond the remit of this study to attempt to discern whether what was termed the scenario simply evolved into what came to be known as the 'continuity script', or whether these were entirely separate documents. What we know is that the trade press recorded in 1911 that 'most directors prefer the well-developed scenario' and, as the 'continuity script' was not mentioned at this point, the terms may have been synonyms for the same document.[378] In the period up to 1920, the fundamental shift in the role of the freelance writer and consequently that of the staff writer had flow-on effects on how people trained for and entered the industry. It appears that submissions increasingly involved providing an extended synopsis rather than a 'scenario' and staff writers were given the job of writing the 'continuity script' from these documents.

In his 1916 manual, Sargent dubs the studio writers who rewrote submitted stories as mere 'reconstructors'.[379] Although he discusses the issue of 'continuity' in great detail, he never associates the word 'continuity' with the particular role of a staff writer. As noted in the discussion on the synopsis, Peacocke indicated in 1916 that a synopsis might form the basis for a 'working scenario' and it could be evolved by a staff writer.[380] Peacocke instructs the freelance writer, whom he believed to be an engine of creativity and originality, to focus on the idea, or the story or plot, rather than trying necessarily to write a detailed continuity. Like Sargent, Peacocke seems to relegate the studio writers to a secondary role as:

> constructionists, not hack photoplay writers [...] their chief duties should be in reconstructing good original stories that reach the scenario departments from various sources.[381]

---

376 Ibid., 338–339.

377 See Phillips, *Photodrama*, 27–184; Wright, *Motion Picture Story*, 21–65, 80–85, 114–124, 161–214; Ball, *Art of the Photoplay*, 33-79, 116–124 and *Photoplay Scenarios*, 1–93, 162-182; and Peacocke, *Hints on Photoplay Writing*, 5–43, 84–97, 115–134.

378 'Technique and the Tale', *MPW*, November 18, 1911, 541.

379 Sargent, *Technique of the Photoplay,* 3rd ed., 8.

380 Peacocke, *Hints on Photoplay Writing,* 41.

381 Ibid., 11.

Nevertheless, even in 1917 Peacocke strongly advises that, although the synopsis did not have to be necessarily accompanied by a 'continuity', it should be provided if possible. His belief that the real creativity lay with the scenarist rather than the staff writer made him surprisingly optimistic about the chances of a studio accepting the freelance writer's work in its entirety and bypassing the work of the professional writer.[382]

No matter how upbeat Peacocke was about the future of freelance writing, Phillips correctly signals in his articles that the market had changed by 1917, with studios requesting a synopsis rather than a scenario.[383] Although it is beyond the reach of the present study to carry out a detailed analysis of script nomenclature, it was clear that by this time rapid changes were happening not only to the language describing the documentation, but to the policy of the studios too. By 1921, in *The Feature Photoplay*, Phillips actively discourages the freelance writer from providing a scenario in favour of an extended synopsis. Confirming this view in his 1922 manual, *Photoplay Writing*, Wright ascribes a specialised role to the 'continuity man' who has had a 'thorough studio education', has spent 'years of study' and has gained 'much experience in the motion picture industry'.[384] Even though the fate of the freelance writer was sealed, Phillips still believed that the really creative work was located in crafting the story. In *The Art of Writing Photoplays* (1922), Phillips asserts that the creation of synopses 'is the real art' whereas continuity writers are 'interpreting' the vision of the photoplaywright, although by this time it is clear that much of the writing of photoplays was in-house.[385]

The key screenwriting teachers appear to try to cast the freelance writer as the artist or originator of ideas and the staff writer as the artisan or craftsman. This again feeds into the wider debate over notions of art and craft. The argument over synopsis/continuity was another attempt by the key screenwriting teachers to articulate elements of the debate, by positioning themselves as encouraging artistic development while on the other hand actually providing advice on very specific, practical skills.

Screen Technique

An important part of writing the 'plot of action', 'scenario' or film script was to decide how to use a range of techniques to enhance the storytelling process. These consisted of two main kinds: techniques that involved putting some kind of written material on the screen; and techniques to complement the action on screen by moving to action occurring in a parallel scene or showing some kind of close-in view of the current scene. The latter, coming to be known as parallel editing and close-ups, would become well-established elements of classical style by the mid-teens. The advice of the key

---

382   Peacocke, 'How to Sell a Photoplay Scenario', *Photoplay*, August 1917, 127–130 and 142.

383   Phillips, 'The Photodrama', *MPM*, August 1917, 81–83.

384   Wright, *Photoplay Writing* 49–59.

385   Phillips, *Art of Writing Photoplays,* 107–109.

screenwriting teachers was practical and pragmatic, and leant more towards the craft-based aspect of screenwriting in this respect.

Subtitles and Inserts

Including written material on screen posed considerable problems for the writer. Striking a balance between expositional material that was necessary for audiences to make sense of the story and overloading the viewer with too much to read involved making skilful choices. The key screenwriting teachers were probably influential in the discourse that established the protocols related to titles and inserts.

Although the key screenwriting teachers are inconsistent in the terminology they used for these devices, Sargent offers the greatest range of terms and the most detail of what they involved. Subtitles or captions that convey exposition or signify a shift in time, which he calls 'leaders', are categorised into three types. First, a 'straight leader' occurs between scenes and conveys some statement about an incident that arises between the scenes.[386] Second, a 'fact leader' is character-based and is an unspoken expository statement that clarifies the character's action to avoid any misunderstandings, or obviates the need for an extensive action sequence to convey the story. For example, presenting the words 'John tells Nellie of his intended trip to the city' would save extensively on footage.[387] Third are 'leaders' connected with time, which comprise two further kinds: a basic 'time leader' serves to mark the passage of time, such as 'the next day', whereas a 'break leader' is 'used [when it is…] not necessary to tell that time has elapsed' but it 'replaces some extended but not essential action', such as a journey or lengthy illness.[388] According to Wright, all of these techniques can be called 'sub-heads', 'sub-titles' or 'leaders', but he makes no further delineation other than to state they signify time lapses or clarify action. Peacocke refers to them simply as subtitles, Ball calls them 'captions', 'subtitles' or 'leaders' and Phillips uses only 'captions', considering the terms 'leader, subtitle' to be misnomers.[389]

Similarly, the teachers differ in their terminology for dialogue. While referring to written dialogue as 'cut-ins' or 'dialogue leaders', Sargent admits that 'spoken insert' would be a better description but one not in common use. Wright uses 'cut-in subtitle' and Phillips prefers 'spoken line', while Peacocke and Ball make no comment on this subject.[390] On the matter of filming written material to be used in the scene, however, all agree

---

386   Sargent, *Technique of the Photoplay,* 3rd ed., 163.

387   Ibid., 166.

388   Ibid., 169–170.

389   See Wright, *Motion Picture Story,* 192–199; Peacocke, *Hints on Photoplay,* 28; Ball, *Art of the Photoplay,* 24 and *Photoplay Scenarios,* 9 ;and Phillips, *Photodrama,* 48–53.

390   Sargent, *Technique of the Photoplay,* 3rd ed., 163–164; Wright, *Motion Picture Story*, 196; and Phillips, *Photodrama*, 62–64.

(except Ball, who again makes no comment) that this is 'the insert'. Inserts included letters, telegrams or any other form of printed material that could convey information within the scene.[391]

Despite the great confusion over terminology, the teachers had a clear view of when to use these techniques. In particular, if the information could be expressed effectively through action, they recommended avoiding these devices. However, like the other key screenwriting teachers, Sargent regards 'leaders' and 'inserts' as a necessary addition to action if this conveyed insufficient information. Seeing the 'cut-in' or 'spoken insert' as the least distracting type of 'leader', he recommends it, but cautions even then that 'Dialogue is used in the action only if dialogue will tell more than action will.'[392] Sargent regards the 'insert' as 'less of an interruption' to action, even though 'it does not picture action'.[393] The words of Peacocke typify the attitude: 'they are to be sparingly used and avoided when possible'.[394]

Liepa's extensive research into the use of intertitles during this period indicates that manual writers probably played an important role in the development of their effective use. He argues that:

> The language used to identify intertitles, both dialogue and expository, and describe their function, reveals something of how these authors conceptualized the function of these devices, influencing the popular perception of the role these devices should play.[395]

In illustrating this contention, Liepa draws from a wide pool of manual writers, including some of the periphery ones identified in Chapter 5. However, the views and comments of the five key screenwriting teachers also feature extensively, which to some extent further legitimises his work, and theirs. As Liepa points out, these writers 'continually returned to intertitle writing as a crucial element of the screenplay; many manuals devoted a chapter to the writing of "leaders"'.[396] Of the five key screenwriting teachers, Sargent, Wright and Phillips devote more than one chapter to the acquisition of this skill. Liepa makes a convincing case for the centrality of the manual writers in this development.

---

391   See Sargent, *Technique of the Photoplay*, 3rd ed., 153–163; Wright, *Motion Picture Story*, 200–205; Ball, *Art of the Photoplay*, 69–70; Peacocke, *Hints on Photoplay Writing*, 29; and Phillips, *Photodrama*, 54–61.

392   Sargent, *Technique of the Photoplay*, 3rd ed., 132.

393   Ibid., 153.

394   Peacocke, *Hints on Photoplay Writing*, 28.

395   Liepa, 'Figures of Silent Speech', 241.

396   Ibid., 234.

Although it is not possible to be certain of their overall impact, as it is not easily measurable, the evidence does point in this direction.

During this period, two groups at completely opposing poles were engaged in a lively debate about the role of intertitles:

> on one extreme were the 'purists' who resented the presence of orthography among their beloved pictures, and on the other were the 'integrationists' who realized a necessity of intertitles, for storytelling and otherwise, and argued for the creative integration of text into cinematic storytelling.[397]

The chief proponent of the 'purists' was the film theorist Münsterberg, who saw the photoplay as a new form of art and rejected all leaders on the grounds of visual purity.[398] Taking a less extreme view, Freeburg saw a value in the use of expository titles, although his use of them would be as a stimulus to auditory imagination, providing a running commentary on the play in the vein of a Greek chorus.[399] According to Liepa, 'those who promoted the creative integration of intertitles won the debate' by the early 1910s.[400] Among those who adopted 'integrationist' views, we find all five of the key screenwriting teachers, although they exhibit shades of opinion on the matter. Both Sargent and Wright give cogent advice on the effective use of intertitles, but they still appear to cling on to the notion that ultimately they are best avoided altogether. Sargent claims that '[t]he play without a leader is the ideal play, because here there is no interruption to the action'. When a leader is used, '[y]ou must stop thinking about the picture and read the words'.[401] An additional concern Wright suggests is that leaders 'frequently confuse the interest, and sometimes even exasperate the spectator', who did not go to the 'theater to read' but 'to be entertained'.[402] On the triumph of the 'integrationists', Phillips observes, 'Optical delusion is a negligible quantity in the face of dramatic illusion, which sweeps everything mechanical before it.'[403] As the key screenwriting teacher with the most positive view on the use of intertitles and inserts, Phillips sees them as 'an integral part of the play; units in the development of the story'.[404]

---

397   Ibid., 254.

398   Münsterberg regards the photoplay not as an imitation of theatre, but as a completely new art form 'composed of pictures'. He likens it to other forms of art such as painting that require no words except a title. See Münsterberg, *Photoplay*, 102–112.

399   Freeburg, *Art of Photoplay Making*, 174.

400   Liepa, 'Figures of Silent Speech', 256.

401   Sargent, *Technique of the Photoplay*, 3rd ed., 164.

402   Wright, *Motion Picture Story*, 193.

403   Phillips, *Photodrama*, 58; cited in Liepa, 'Figures of Silent Speech', 256–257.

404   Phillips, *Photodrama*, 49.

The key screenwriting teachers were concerned to offer pertinent and important practical advice to writers on the effective use of intertitles. In taking up this theme, Liepa claims that '[p]reserving narrative continuity and producing a more unified or integrated story was one of the primary motivations behind the development of intertitles'.[405] They were important for a range of reasons, not least because they helped to shape the action and to construct a scenario. As Sargent points out, the leader produces a shock effect, as it interrupts the action: 'Each time a leader flashes you must adjust your mind to the fact and readjust it to the story.'[406] Azlant admits that the perceptual change this requires is problematic but it also serves, in Sargent's words, to 'make definite the end of one development of action and the commencement of a second'.[407] In one sense, it was similar to the curtain drop in the theatre. Sargent even saw a legitimate use for intertitles instead of pictorial action in delivering the 'punch', as Liepa observes in quoting from Sargent's column:

> 'the real punch is not the visual action, but the idea behind the action.' For intertitles to have this forceful effect, 'the words must be used at the moment of greatest tension and the entire action must be planned to support the stated fact.'[408]

As Azlant suggests, Sargent's understanding of the 'leader' was that it 'automatically imparts a definite rhythm, which can be used in marking extensive segments of the plot's development'.[409] Phillips is willing to go even further, claiming that the use of textual inserts 'is a great factor for economy, and when properly used in this respect may contribute to heightened effects thru suggestive condensation'.[410]

Another practical problem that surfaced with leaders was determining the correct number to use within a scenario and how many feet of film to use on each one. This was a matter that all five key screenwriting teachers addressed because, in the context of a 1,000-foot film, using up valuable film footage on too many leaders could be highly detrimental. If the commonly held measure that each titled word took up one foot of film was applied, Ball observes, just 200 words would 'deprive' a one-reel film of one-fifth of its entire length.[411] Sargent suggests leaving an insert on the screen for as long as it takes 'a person

---

405 Liepa, 'Figures of Silent Speech', 242.

406 Sargent, *Technique of the Photoplay*, 3rd ed., 164.

407 Sargent, *Technique of the Photoplay*. 3rd ed., 163; cited in Azlant, 'Theory, History and Practice of Screenwriting', 227.

408 Sargent, 'Leader and Action', in 'The Photoplaywright', *MPW*, June 5, 1915, 1598; cited in Liepa, 'Figures of Silent Speech', 241.

409 Azlant, 'Theory, History and Practice of Screenwriting', 227.

410 Phillips, *Photodrama*, 55.

411 Ball, *Art of the Photoplay*, 24–25.

not used to rapid reading to decipher it'.[412] According to Liepa, Sargent's preferred measure of length for each title was to allow three feet for the first line and two feet for each succeeding line of the same leader. This would mean that a two-line leader would use up five feet of film and a three-line leader would consume seven feet. Sargent advises that no more than one-tenth of a one-reel film should be taken up with leaders.[413] Another means of controlling the amount of space that titles took up was limiting sentence length, a view favoured by Wright, who suggests that each title should be no longer than 10 to 15 words.[414]

Given that audiences in America were amorphous, as a result of large-scale immigration, and many were of lower class with limited English skills, titling was a problem. All the key screenwriting teachers addressed the issue of language in dialogue titles. According to Liepa:

> A common thread connecting the advice offered in screenplay manuals emphasized that the language of dialogue titles must reflect the everyday conditions and environment of the writer. In both choice of subject and development of character – a quality that could draw heavily from character language – the desire for the vernacular was strongly emphasized.[415]

Choice of accessible language extended to the way writers told the story and chose their subject material. Amateur writers were distanced from the rich and famous in the cosmopolitan ranks of society, and were courted for this very reason. According to Ball, the amateur writer should avoid 'oratorical and poetic profuseness of language' and tell the story in 'concise English, with description of action'. They should focus on writing 'modern American plays with simple casts, powerful action and themes of every-day life'.[416] This is a sentiment echoed by Peacocke, who encourages the writer to '[s]tick to American subjects. [...] Lay your scenes in the cities and localities with which you are familiar' and '[d]o not attempt to be "literary." Stick to simple language;- the simpler, the better.'[417] This emphasis on writing plain language, as opposed to good literary prose, again exposes the tensions in the debate over whether the key screenwriting teachers were engaged in teaching a craft or an art form.

---

412 Sargent, *Technique of the Photoplay*, 3rd ed., 160.

413 See Sargent, 'Technique of the Photoplay', *MPW*, August 12, 1911, 363–364; cited in Liepa, 'Figures of Silent Speech', 238–239.

414 Wright, *Photoplay Writing,* 186.

415 Liepa, 'Figures of Silent Speech', 272.

416 Ball, *Art of the Photoplay*, 31 and 28.

417 Peacocke, *Hints on Photoplay Writing,* 94 and 20.

For Sargent, dialogue titles should be 'everyday speech or they will sound absurd. People of today do not speak in blank verse.'[418] Wright is concerned that the language used should reflect the make-up of audiences, which he realised were 'mixed' and as 'both the educated and the uneducated throng the movie theatres […] the task of the writer is to strike a happy medium'.[419] Characteristically, Phillips's focus is on the internal emotional effects of a line of dialogue: 'The words pierce the spectator with personal sympathy, or antagonism, and fairly thunder thru the silence'.[420] This is to be achieved by imitating the mental process of the viewer – which presumably includes their form of language.

As the film theatre became mass entertainment across class and ethnic barriers, poor grammar and spelling, vulgarity and slang proliferated within intertitles. There were strong pressures to improve language in films, for the purposes of moral uplift. As Liepa points out, 'The proper writing of intertitles was a major concern for those invested in maintaining a mode of address acceptable to the middle class guardians of culture.'[421] It was easier to bring about change in the expositional title, as this did not have to reflect speech idioms. Loos had achieved this through complex, witty and clever prose and did much to improve the practice of titling. Although Sargent was not focused on moral uplift, he certainly approved of the effective use of the leader. Dealing with this issue extensively in his 1916 manual, he explains the leader is 'the sole part of the script in which the literary ability of the author may really be shown [… hence it] should be fluent and pleasing, though not grandiloquent'.[422]

Despite the efforts of Sargent and the other key screenwriting teachers, as industry requirements changed the author of the piece would seldom have the opportunity to exercise the skill of intertitling. In his 1913 manual, Ball comments that the titles provided by scenario writers were rarely acceptable to the director, who would 'prune and slice his titles to fit his own needs'.[423] By the 1920s, titles were not required at all from writers, as Wright confirms in *Photoplay Writing* (1922), where he confines the writing of titles to a specialist 'movie title writer' who has 'expressive and fine writing skills'.[424]

---

418   Sargent, *Technique of the Photoplay*, 3ᵈ ed., 171.

419   Wright, *Photoplay Writing*, 185.

420   Phillips, *Photodrama*, 63–64.

421   Liepa, 'Figures of Silent Speech', 264.

422   Sargent, *Technique of the Photoplay*, 3ᵈ ed., 171.

423   Ball, *Art of the Photoplay*, 24.

424   Wright, *Photoplay Writing*, 185.

Busts and Close-ups

'Busts' and 'close-ups' were close-in views of action or of a character's face. They were among the most important features that distinguished film from theatre. The magnification of the facial expressions and actions of characters intensified the emotional involvement of audiences, because the close-up view fostered a feeling of intimacy with the screen persona. The key screenwriting teachers saw these devices as integral to effective storytelling.

With a clear understanding of the importance of these devices, Sargent concurs with Münsterberg's belief that the close-up view was 'the most striking feature of the new art' because it would centre the viewers' attention on a particular object. In the absence of words, the importance of movement is heightened. However, Sargent argues that Münsterberg attributes an 'over-importance to its use'.[425]

The precise meaning of 'bust' as distinguished from 'close-up' is a matter of contention. Azlant claims that 'Sargent's [...] discussions of "busts" and "close-ups" are not always clear or consistent' and that 'Sargent's terms of segmentation seem to be reaching for some real difference'.[426] In support of his view, he quotes Sargent to show that the teacher also recognises the problem:

> the bust may be written as a close-up or close-up used to designate a bust, but the clearest technique makes a distinction that really is a difference.[427]

However, a careful reading shows that Sargent's thinking is clear and consistent throughout. In the quote above, Sargent is referring to the practice of some studios that confuse these terms, but he himself makes a clear distinction between the 'bust' and the 'close-up'. The 'bust' is 'a detailed exposure of some action, not so large as to take in any considerable portion of the figure. This is what makes the distinction.' In other words, it is the magnification of a significant action by a character such as a murderer whose 'hand steals into the picture and drops a pistol into the pocket' of another unsuspecting character.[428] Sargent later defines 'close-ups' as:

> scenes made with the players close to the camera [... because] the story is or should be told in facial expression. This may be seen to advantage only when the image of the player is large and distinct.[429]

---

425   Sargent, 'Münsterberg on the Photoplay', *MPW*, July 15, 1916, 436–437.

426   Azlant, 'Theory, History and Practice of Screenwriting', 263–264.

427   Sargent, *Technique of the Photoplay*, 3rd ed., 173.

428   Ibid., 148–149.

429   Ibid., 173–174.

Azlant interprets Sargent's comments about 'busts' and 'close-ups' inaccurately:

> 'Busts' are *generally* small segments of the main action, which replicate the larger activity or master shot. 'Close-ups' are *generally* close facial expressions of the players [emphasis added].[430]

The subtle use of the word 'generally' in his comment indicates that Sargent's terms are broad and ill-defined, incorrectly implying a lack of clarity in Sargent's thinking on this matter. Yet Sargent's own use of the phrase 'generally' is referring to the misconceptions of others rather than his own understanding of the differences. He is, in fact, clearer and more detailed than the other key screenwriting teachers who discuss this issue and gives a precise function for the 'bust' as close-on action by a character, distinguishable from the 'close-up', which focuses on the facial or bodily activities of a character. Wright, Ball and Phillips conflate these terms entirely. For Wright, '"the bust" is an enlarged or close up view of any object upon which emphasis is to be made' and his glossary lists them as having the same meaning; Ball appears to refer only to close-ups. Phillips prefers the words 'close-view' in place of 'close-up' but still equates it with the 'bust'.[431] Peacocke's specific suggestion of a '"close-up" of an infant's tiny foot, with the weeny toes wiggling' clearly shows that he saw what Sargent would call a 'bust' as a close-up.[432] Although Sargent's rendering of these distinctions is the most defined, all the key screenwriting teachers espoused the value of 'close-ups' or 'busts' for the purposes of clarifying action, creating a feeling of intimacy and relaying the thoughts and emotions of the characters as a form of, in Ball's words, 'psychological action'. All five also recognised these devices were unique to the medium.[433]

Cut-backs and Visions

All the key screenwriting teachers saw the value of the cut-back, or the 'flash-back' or 'flash' as some called it, as a tool for writers. It was another feature distinguishing film writing from writing for theatre because of the sheer speed with which changes of scene could be effected. Phillips renames it the 'return', claiming 'cut-back' is misleading because it 'suggest[s] going back'.[434] Sargent's views are representative of how the teachers saw its usage:

---

430 Azlant, 'Theory, History and Practice of Screenwriting', 264.

431 Sargent, *Technique of the Photoplay*, 3rd ed., 148–152 and 173–182; Wright, *Motion Picture Story*, 213–214 and 220; Peacocke, *Hints on Photoplay Writing*, 25; Ball, *Art of the Photoplay*, 18–19 and *Photoplay Scenarios*, 51; and Phillips, *Photodrama*, 60–61.

432 Peacocke, *Hints on Photoplay Writing*, 18.

433 Wright, *Motion Picture Story*, 214; Peacocke, *Hints on Photoplay Writing*, 25; Ball, *Photoplay Scenarios,* 51; and Phillips, *Photodrama,* 59–61.

434 Phillips, *Photodrama*, 140.

a device used to bridge awkward gaps in the action, to heighten the effect of a situation through contrasting action or to raise suspense through delaying the crisis or climax.[435]

In other words, cutting to another scene, or a parallel line of action or plot, can mask less interesting action that does little to advance the story. Alternatively, it can provide other information that develops the main action, before returning to the former line of action via another 'cut-back'. They all agree that, in a particularly tense scene, cutting back and forth creates more suspense, as the action is significantly slowed at the approach of a climactic moment. They also assume that audiences will not lose a sense of continuity with the use of simultaneity.[436]

In Sargent's opinion, 'visions', such as picturing the thoughts of a character in the present, recalling a past incident or dreaming of the future, are problematic because they could interrupt narrative momentum.[437] Jumping back to the past could disturb the 'continuous flow of narrative' that Sargent believed was important in a film. According to Azlant, continuity for Sargent meant 'designing the narrative film in the progressive, continuous dynamic present'.[438] But Sargent was pragmatic: if faced with a choice between a leader and a vision, he would choose the latter as the 'less intrusive of the two'. Similarly, Wright warns against trick effects, but accepts that a vision can reveal the motives of a character that have 'some bearing on the action' in a scene. Ball considers they should not be 'overworked' and Peacocke saw a use for them. Of the vision, Phillips perceptively advises that a 'play should progress even when it appears to go back', as well as that 'every scene should contribute action' and 'advance the play in the mind of the audience'.[439] As discussed in the previous section, Phillips's views on chronological order were more adventurous and opened up the possibility of using flashbacks, visions and non-linear editing if required to maintain suspense.

Other trick effects achieved through lighting, colouration of the film, under-cranking the camera to speed up action, or sending it in reverse, are denoted as 'shop stuff', and the teachers discourage the amateur or novice from loading a script with such technical terms or suggestions. The same advice applies to 'dissolves' (fading down and up) and 'stop camera' work (where something is made to disappear or appear). The consensus was that effects were best used sparingly and left to the director. Moreover, according

---

435 Sargent, *Technique of the Photoplay*, 3rd ed., 182.

436 Sargent, *Technique of the Photoplay,* 3rd ed., 182–194; Wright, *Motion Picture Story,* 206–209; Peacocke, *Hints on Photoplay Writing*, 28–30; Ball, *Art of the Photoplay,* 20 and *Photoplay Scenarios,* 7; and Phillips, *Photodrama,* 140–141.

437 Azlant, 'Theory, History and Practice of Screenwriting', 236.

438 Ibid., 238–239.

439 Sargent, *Technique of the Photoplay,* 3rd ed., 202–208; Wright, *Motion Picture Story,* 210–213; Ball, *Photoplay Scenarios,* 85; Peacocke, *Hints on Photoplay Writing,* 146; and Phillips, *Photodrama,* 142.

to Sargent, if the writer really thinks such an effect is necessary, they should simply 'tell what happens. The director will understand.'[440] Sargent presciently discusses the prospect of 'talking pictures' by setting out dialogue in a form that is none too different from modern screenwriting practice. However, he admits, 'It is not possible to foretell the precise form that talking pictures will next assume.' This was understandable because the technical difficulties of synchronising picture to sound had not yet been resolved.[441]

With regard to screen technique overall, it is important to recast Azlant's views on Sargent, which overrate his contribution in this area. Azlant represents Sargent as espousing a view that the photoplay writer could exercise a greater freedom in the 'selection of activity, compression of time and fluid sense of location' in 'designing the narrative film in the progressive, continuous, dynamic present' and that this is expressed in his detailed treatment of screen technique.[442] However, Sargent's approach was not unique. As this section has shown, the other key screenwriting teachers held similar views and provided significant instruction, albeit in less detail.

Acquiring expertise in order to write in a visual style, in correct photoplay form and using the appropriate screen techniques, was again placed firmly at the craft end of the spectrum. The key screenwriting teachers were in a position to reinforce and codify this instruction in order to ensure writers adhered to industry standards.

How to Sell to the Industry

The issue of how to sell to the industry takes up a great deal of space in the manuals of the five key screenwriting teachers. The advice covers two aspects: first, writing the manuscript; and second, marketing it. Much of it has been implicit in the previous sections. The advice is pragmatic and useful, relating to what is likely to sell based on the prevailing trends of the market at any given moment.

Writing the Manuscript

The key screenwriting teachers realised that a prospective writer was faced with a series of important decisions at the beginning of the writing process, which they should address in order to ensure they had a saleable script at the end of it.

What Photoplay to Write?

Addressing the most important issue with regard to achieving a sale involved reiterating and emphasising the arguments about the importance of so-called original material, for

---

440 Sargent, *Technique of the Photoplay*, 3rd ed., 194–212; Wright, *Motion Picture Story*, 212–214; Ball, *Photoplay Scenarios*, 85; and Phillips, *Photodrama*, xvi.

441 Sargent, *Technique of the Photoplay*, 3rd ed., 302–304.

442 Azlant, 'Theory, History and Practice of Screenwriting', 234 and 239.

which demand was relentless. In 1914 Sargent predicts that being original will give the freelance writer the best opportunity for a sale:

> it is only reasonable to suppose that, in the time to come, when the best of the book rights have been exhausted, the author who writes photoplays for photoplay production will command a better price than the man who writes books that may be adapted.[443]

Similarly, Peacocke claims in his 1916 manual: 'It is becoming an open market for the competent scenario writer, and is becoming more so every day.'[444] In response to this opportunity, he clearly articulates the need for original material:

> Originality is the Worcestershire of the screen. Don't waste your time trying to sell stale stuff. Stale stuff is as easy to get as orange culls in California. Better make out any day a crude but plotty original story than the most polished stale stuff![445]

As the first section of this chapter has shown, much of this so-called original material involved routine and familiar tropes. Nevertheless, Peacocke re-states his optimistic prediction for the role of the freelance writer in his contribution to an article for *Motography* in 1917:

> The coming year will see the stage play and fiction story adaptations in the discard, and original stories, specially written for the screen will be the only things in demand. [...] Nearly all the big moneymakers have been productions made from stories specially written for the screen.[446]

In his manual, Peacocke publishes letters from various scenario chiefs such as Woods, which support his views that 'the original story' is in short supply:[447]

> What the studio directors – the ultimate buyers of manuscripts – want is not the details, but THE STORY, and always a brief clean-cut synopsis with it. A plot will be bought if it is good; the mere technique of the idea is not saleable. The studios have their own experts to take care of the technique.[448]

While also quoting from Woods about the demand for original material, Sargent is keen to stress that 'demand increases for scripts with ideas of a higher degree of literary

443   Sargent, 'The Literary Side of Pictures', *MPW*, July 11, 1914, 202.

444   Peacocke, *Hints on Photoplay Writing,* 12.

445   Ibid., 127.

446   Peacocke, 'The Story's The Thing', *Motography*, March 31, 1917, 687.

447   Peacocke includes letters about studio requirements from Woods of the Fine Arts Studio, Harry R. Durant of the Famous Players and Jasper Ewing Brady of Vitagraph, which were published in *Photoplay* (1916).

448   Peacocke, *Hints on Photoplay Writing,* 2.

merit'. The merit here is not literary expression, but skill 'in plotting [the] story as well as in originating ideas [... as] literary expression can be shown only in the leaders'.[449]

Likewise, Wright agrees that once the writer has 'the original idea as a basis, all that is needed is skill in plot construction to develop the photoplay'.[450] Further, the story needs greater priority:

> It is the idea and not the technique that counts heavily in the end. [...] We are of the opinion that many writers pay too much attention to technique, and not enough attention to the story.[451]

Although he does not dwell on the opportunities for the freelance writer as much as Peacocke does, Wright nonetheless emphasises them even in 1922: 'The demand is now and will be in the future for original stories for the motion picture screen.'[452] The other manual writers focus on the opportunities for original scenarios in a similar way. Ball recognises the 'dearth of good stories'; Phillips claims that they could only be supplied by competent 'photoplay technicians' and not necessarily those who had populated the ranks of fiction or dramatic literature.[453]

By 1917 it was clear that the market had substantially changed. Peacocke acknowledges the staff writer was now responsible for the continuity while the contribution of the scenarist had been reduced to an extended synopsis. Yet he remains optimistic. In one of his articles for *Photoplay*, he envisions the possibility of writer–director cooperation. While clearly distinguishing between the freelance writer and the staff or continuity writer, who should work closely with the director, he sees a role for both kinds of writer and emphasises 'teamwork'. The contribution of the freelance writers, he argues, continued to be essential:

> The plots of their stories are original and well worked out in logical continuity, their photoplays will find a ready market. [...] Changes may have to be made to suit the particular requirements of the company which purchases a story from a freelance writer, but the scenario editor can easily have this done [...] because nowadays [...] good, original stories are hard to find.[454]

In reality, continuity writers often had to completely rewrite the offerings of freelance writers, which sometimes involved 'discarding a half or a third' of their work, according

---

449   Sargent, *Technique of the Photoplay*, 3rd ed., 5.

450   Wright, *Motion Picture Story*, 26.

451   Ibid., 62.

452   Wright, *Photoplay Writing* 189.

453   Ball, *Art of the Photoplay*, 15 and Phillips, *Photodrama*, xx.

454   Peacocke, 'The Scenario Writer and the Director', *Photoplay*, May. 1917, 111–114.

to successful writer and editor Jeanie Macpherson in 1922.[455] This was if the submission ever made it past the first hurdle, and most did not. As Jasper Ewing Brady, scenario editor at Vitagraph, pointed out in 1916, on some days they could 'receive as high as three and four hundred scripts, and many times not one is found acceptable'.[456]

By 1922 Wright was still claiming, in *Photoplay Writing*, 'there is an alarming scarcity of material of worth for motion pictures'.[457] However, on the whole, he is more sanguine, aiming to skill the freelance writer for the market that still exists. Although more muted, he still does on occasion give vent to the belief that:

> The market demands material [... and] more careful consideration is being given to
> the outside contributory, not so much for the literary excellence of their stories as
> for the ideas or plots contained therein.[458]

At the same time, in the search for originality the writer should beware of being inspired 'by newspaper stories, as [...] whenever anything sensational occurs in the public prints, the scenario editor is deluged with plots similar in character and based on the same foundation'.[459]

Although the market was shifting with regard to much of the material film companies required, particularly as the demand for features opened up, one constant remained: the general advice was not to attempt to write a 'continuity'. In 1922 Wright advises that 'for some years continuity has been written only by those on the inside, who were trained to write it – and the outsider can't do it'.[460] Freelance writers were only to provide a scenario or synopsis from which a continuity script would be prepared. In this they could be successful, if the work was of a high standard. As Wright points out, 'it makes no difference to them who submits a story, so long as the story meets requirements'.[461]

The advice that the key screenwriting teachers gave about subject material was fairly consistent and conventional, but continually updated through their columns. They encouraged freelance writers to focus on contemporary subjects set in America, as the cost of staging was always a consideration. Locations were to be generalised, to give the director choice, and seasonal aspects should be taken into account. For example, a story set in summer should not be submitted in winter, as it could not be filmed at that

---

455 Jeanie Macpherson, 'Functions of the Continuity Writer', *Opportunities in the Motion Picture Industry*, 26.

456 Peacocke, *Hints on Photoplay Writing*, 112.

457 Wright, *Photoplay Writing*, 188.

458 Ibid., 147.

459 Ibid., 31.

460 Ibid., 9.

461 Ibid., 190.

time. Drama, comedy and melodrama were generally considered appropriate and happy endings were advocated.[462] There was a general consensus as to what to avoid: farcical comedy or slapstick, as this was a peculiar specialism with a great deal of 'business'; adaptations; historical costume dramas; Biblical topics, which studios were flooded with; reworkings of plots the writers have seen; and plots based on the latest newspaper articles, as these were freely available. Seemingly more open to a variety of script genres in his 1913 manual, Ball has a relatively broad list of what was acceptable, noting a:

> demand for well-conceived, carefully written and strongly original photoplay scripts dealing with comic, tragic, historical, educational and moral themes.[463]

However, just two years later in 1915 he is more conservative, encouraging the freelance writer to focus on 'logical themes from the life and people about him'.[464]

All five key screenwriting teachers deal with issues regarding film length. The scenarist had to work within the various categories of film length that were in industry use: scenarios that were split (half) reel, multiple (two to three) reel, or feature (three to five) reel in length. The consensus appears to be that it was best to master the writing of one-reel scenarios before moving on to longer forms, although this form did require great skill in compression and simplification. However, film length did depend on the scale of the plot idea. According to Wright, the writer should:

> let everything be determined by the demands of your story. The location, the number and kind of people, and the things they do will all be decided by the telling of your tale.[465]

They all agree that as few characters as possible should be used, for economy in the resulting film. Sargent is cautious about advising how many scenes to have in a reel of film, as there are too many variables to take into account: some directors will work a scene quicker than others and 'leaders', 'letters' and 'inserts' also have to be included.[466] While similarly admitting that scene length can vary from director to director, Peacocke does offer some guidelines on the number of scenes in a 'scenario'; from his experience, 'dramatic or melodramatic' stories are usually around 40 scenes and comedy between 50 and 75 scenes.[467]

---

462   Ball, *Art of the Photoplay*, 28; Peacocke, *Hints on Photoplay Writing*, 91; and Wright, *Photoplay Writing*, 32.

463   Ball, *Art of the Photoplay*, 3.

464   Ball, *Photoplay Scenarios*, 62.

465   Wright, *Photoplay Writing*, 18.

466   Sargent, *Technique of the Photoplay*, 3rd ed., 145–148.

467   Peacocke, *Hints on Photoplay Writing*, 28.

It is possible to track the move from one-reelers to features through the changes in the key screenwriting teachers' manuals over that period. The earlier manuals of all five of them, published from 1912 to 1916, show that the market for one- and two-reelers was extensive. Yet by the time Wright and Phillips had written their final manuals in 1922, features were clearly by far the largest market. Wright cautions: 'A five-reel feature may call for only a small cast, but it must have a big theme and plenty of quick action.'[468] He encourages the freelance writer to focus instead on the two-reeler, where the market offered more opportunities than for lengthy five- and seven-reel features, which, by the early twenties, were more likely to be written by staff writers. In his own later manuals, although Phillips gives little market information, he does advocate writing lengthy and extended synopses, without appearing to rule out the features market.

Censorship, Copyright and Stardom

Ben Hecht wrote of the advice Herman Mankiewicz gave him in 1925 when he arrived in Hollywood: 'in a novel a hero can lay ten girls and marry a virgin for a finish. In a movie this is not allowed.'[469] All the key screenwriting teachers gave extensive advice on censorship, which was essential if the finished film was to avoid falling foul of the censor. In response to local efforts to control the content of movies, the National Board of Censorship of Motion Pictures had been formed in 1909 for the purpose of reviewing films and providing a seal of approval for those that would not give offence.[470] Films were to have no suggestiveness, sex stories, vampire stories, underworld plots or vice – nothing of a sordid nature.[471] According to Wright, 'clean stories of adventure, full of romance and devoid of crime are what are wanted'.[472] It was crucial for would-be writers to understand this kind of pressing restriction. For Sargent, the best approach was for the writer to 'avoid the necessity for being censored' in the first place, as 'the outside writer stands small chance if there is any question or doubt'.[473] The chief aim was to achieve a 'pass' from the editor and for this issue never to be raised.

Not all the key screenwriting teachers necessarily agreed with censorship. In particular, Wright used his influence to actively campaign against it, as noted in Chapter 5, and he contributed to a wider discussion about this issue. He frequently expresses his distaste for censorship, connecting it with vested interests:

---

468   Wright, *Photoplay Writing,* 82.

469   Cited in Black, *Hollywood Censored,* 4.

470   Azlant, 'Screenwriting for the Early Silent Film', 241.

471   Sargent, *Technique of the Photoplay,* 2ⁿᵈ ed., 342–345; Wright, *Motion Picture Story,* 58–60; Wright, *Photoplay Writing,* 158; Ball, *Photoplay Scenarios,* 66–79; Peacocke, *Hints on Photoplay Writing,* 93; and Phillips, *Photodrama,* 87–96.

472   Wright, *Photoplay Writing,* 109.

473   Sargent, *Technique of the Photoplay*, 3ʳᵈ ed., 344 and 315.

> So why censors would be wished on the motion picture industry is a question that has never been satisfactorily answered, except by saying that censorship provides additional political positions for political workers.[474]

Nevertheless, Wright pragmatically advises writers to keep to hand a copy of the pamphlet covering the rules and standards from the National Board of Censorship (Review). Quoting Ball, who worked with the Board, he agrees that even with censorship it is still possible to write engaging scenarios:

> To declare that risqué situations, gruesome details, exposition of the methods of criminals are necessary for dramatic punch shows a complete misunderstanding of the possibilities of the 'struggle', the fundamentals of every real play, whether on the screen or on the stage.[475]

Ball points out that writers needed a 'thorough understanding of and even sympathy with the fundamentals from which the Board's critique is carried on'.[476] According to Peacocke, 'The censors should be allowed to decide upon the script before it leaves the scenario department, or is touched by the director.' After all, it was pointless showing films in their completed state to censors when it was too late to make changes and could lead to financial ruin.[477] On this matter, they all agree: submitting scenarios that do not qualify would be a waste of time and effort.

All the key screenwriting teachers strongly condemned copyright breaches. Plagiarising was no longer an option as a result of the 1911 Kalem copyright debacle over *Ben Hur* (see Chapter 1); as Daniel Eagan confirms, the judgment on this lawsuit was a critical moment in the establishment of copyright law.[478] Sargent sums up the situation for the scenario writer: 'You may derive inspiration but not material from the work of another.'[479] Peacocke advises, 'Never, under any circumstances, take your plot from anything that has been printed', while Ball tells the writer not even to 'model [...] scenarios after the themes of the others'.[480]

---

474 Wright, *Photoplay Writing,* 154.

475 Ball, 'The Scenario Writer, the Director and the Censor', *MPN*, December 26, 1914, 36; cited in Wright, 'Photoplay Authors, Real and Near', *NYDM*, 1914 May-June 1915 – 1465.pdf: *Fulton History*: http://fultonhistory.com/Fulton.html

476 Ball, *Photoplay Scenarios,* 69.

477 Smith, 'The Evolution of the Motion Picture', *NYDM*, 1913 Mar–Apr 1914, 0771.pdf: *Fulton History*: http://fultonhistory.com/Fulton.html

478 Daniel Eagan, *America's Film Legacy: The Authoritative Guide to the Landmark Movies in the National Film Registry* (New York: Continuum International, 2010), 24.

479 Sargent, *Technique of the Photoplay* 3rd ed., 345.

480 Peacocke, *Hints on Photoplay Writing,* 6; and Ball, *Photoplay Scenarios,* 178.

Further complicating the issue was that authors of other materials, such as magazine articles, plays and novels, were protected by copyright. However, at this time the scenario could not be copyrighted unless printed in book form, so scenario writers themselves could be plagiarised. This led some to suggest that writing the story for a magazine format first would at least afford the original work some protection if the rights were reserved. This prevented hack writers from working a successful scenario back into magazine format and benefiting from it financially. Peacocke, Wright and Phillips advise this route as a precursor to writing for the screen, seeing it as an advantage not only because it was a way of improving writing skills but also because, due to the shortage of original plots, the industry saw the short story market as a possible source of material.[481]

Both Wright and Peacocke argue that a reader or staff writer was unlikely to purloin a plot, as they consider these people to be 'honorable' and to take a dim view of plagiarism. However, Peacocke is more cautious of those closer to home, advising: 'The original plot. Have you one? If you have, guard it as carefully as the pupil of your eye. Be careful to whom you submit it. Do not whisper it, even to your best friend.'[482]

Writers were also to be aware of the stars associated with particular studios and the characters they were likely to play. At the same time, it was important not to be too specific in order to ensure the scenario would appeal to a number of studios and avoid narrowing the market.[483]

Marketing the Script

Preparing the Submission

As all the key screenwriting teachers had served on the editorial staff of film companies, their roles in that capacity gave weight to their recommendations. Wright claims that he had:

> read and analyzed thousands of manuscripts submitted for motion pictures, and [...] the principal objection to most of the stories comes from the author's misconception of the requirements for the screen.[484]

As discussed in detail in the previous section, the submission consisted of the following elements: a 'cast of characters', a 'scene plot', a 'synopsis', and a 'plot of action' or 'scenario'; importantly, it also included a covering letter. By the end of the decade,

---

481   Peacocke, *Hints on Photoplay Writing*, 125 and 132; Wright, *Photoplay Writing*, 145–147; and Phillips, *Photodrama*, 117.

482   Peacocke, *Hints on Photoplay Writing*, 13–14; and Wright, *Motion Picture Story*, 114–117.

483   Sargent, *Technique of the Photoplay*, 3rd ed., 54; Ball, *Photoplay Scenarios*, 59–60; Wright, *Photoplay Writing*, 37–38; and Peacocke, *Hints on Photoplay Writing*, 101–102.

484   Wright, *Photoplay Writing*, 224.

the 'plot of action' or 'scenario' was often replaced by an extended synopsis. These teachers were most concerned that the first contact with the editor was impactful. For Sargent, 'first impressions' are important, as an editor 'cannot help being influenced, if only unconsciously, by the feel of the paper, the neat appearance of the writing, the arrangement of the page, the general air of knowingness' in an 'attractively prepared' manuscript.[485] The other key screenwriting teachers offer similar advice about creating the right impression with the editor by submitting well-thought-out documents.[486] As an experienced editor, Wright admits that:

> faced with a pile of scenarios that heap themselves up on an editor's desk [...] it's the neat, clean, business-like looking manuscripts towards which he has the most kindly feeling.[487]

Peacocke indicates that, if it is well presented, the scenario should 'speak for itself'.[488] Again, the key screenwriting teachers advocate a pragmatic and hands-on approach to this issue.

The most detailed advice comes from Sargent on the basic parameters of how to set out a manuscript, the paper to be used, the copies to be made, appropriate bindings, the importance of a good-quality typewriter along with the skill to use it, and keeping a plot book and manuscript record. Writers should always keep carbon copies of the original script and never mail it to more than one editor at a time to avoid competing offers.[489] The other teachers also devote space to this important topic, as they are all concerned with presentation.[490] Ball's pithy article, 'Ten Things I Would Tell a Beginner', summarises this technical advice on how to make a manuscript presentable to a scenario editor.[491]

Genre Classification

All the advice the key screenwriting teachers gave was time-limited, transient and closely linked to the contemporary state of the industry. Their columns give an on-going account of an industry in a state of change, whereas their manuals give a snapshot of the industry at their moment of publication and the popularity of certain genres at that particular time.

---

485   Sargent, *Technique of the Photoplay*. 3rd ed., 104.

486   See Peacocke, *Hints on Photoplay Writing*, 84–88; Ball, *Art of the Photoplay*, 11–14 and *Photoplay Scenarios*, 15–16; and Phillips, *Photodrama*, 39–40.

487   Wright, *Photoplay Writing*, 160.

488   Peacocke, *Hints on Photoplay Writing*, 86.

489   Sargent, *Technique of the Photoplay*. 3rd ed., 99–104 and 319–342.

490   See Wright, *Motion Picture Story*, 215–218 and *Photoplay Writing*, 160–164; Peacocke, *Hints on Photoplay Writing*, 84–88; Ball, *Art of the Photoplay*, 64–69 and *Photoplay Scenarios*, 80–83; and Phillips, *Photodrama*, 115–118 and 192–193.

491   Ball, 'Ten Things I would Tell a Beginner', *Photoplaywright*, July 1912, 5.

In his manual, Sargent devotes a great deal of space to the 'Classification of Photoplays', while acknowledging that 'the various forms of drama blend into one another'.[492] His purpose in classifying films into various genres, as they were understood at the time, was to ensure writers are able to categorise their work correctly on the title page and know what is popular and with which particular film company. The genres he lists are: drama (general); historical and costume; problem (presenting a life dilemma); purpose (drawing attention to a social injustice); propaganda; melodrama; comedy drama; comedy farce; and slapstick. Sargent, Wright and the other key screenwriting teachers concern themselves with the contemporary understanding of these divisions and supply plenty of scenario samples to illustrate them.[493]

Market Awareness

The key screenwriting teachers encourage their freelance adherents to study the market closely so that they are aware of the kind of material the various companies are producing. Sargent and Wright, in particular, give meticulous and up-to-date advice on a weekly basis through their columns, which was a vital facet of their value to aspiring writers.[494] It was usually direct insider information; for example, Sargent writes in *Moving Picture World* in 1914: 'The American Company announces that it is particularly interested in scripts adapted for comedies or light dramas for the use of the Beauty Company.'[495] A tip from Wright is to read the trade journals such as the *Exhibitors Herald of Chicago*, *Moving Picture World*, *Motion Picture News*, *Exhibitors Trade Review* and the *Exhibitors Herald of New York City*.[496] The information Peacocke provides in his manual on the addresses of various companies would soon have been out-dated, but his columns regularly contain the latest on what the industry wanted.[497] For example, he writes:

> Mr. Russell E. Smith, scenario editor of the Famous Players Film Company [...] will be pleased to consider detailed synopses of good strong stories that would make four or five reel photoplays.[498]

---

492   Sargent, *Technique of the Photoplay*, 3ʳᵈ ed.,250.

493   See Sargent, *Technique of the Photoplay*, 3ʳᵈ ed., 250–304; Wright, *Motion Picture Story*, 66–79 and 125–160 and *Photoplay Writing*, 60–150; Ball, *Photoplay Scenarios*, 94–161; Peacocke, *Hints on Photoplay Writing*, 89–97; and Phillips, *Photodrama*, 185–191 and *Feature Photoplay*, 43–54 and 60–73.

494   Sargent focuses on 'What Kalem Wants' and Wright details 'The Needs of Éclair' by publishing direct requests on freelance submissions from editors. See Sargent, 'The Photoplaywright', *MPW*, April 5, 1913, 41–42; and Wright, 'For Those Who Worry O'er Plots and Plays', *MPN*, November 8, 1913, 21–23.

495   Sargent, 'The Photoplaywright', *MPW*, April 4, 1914, 55.

496   Wright, *Photoplay Writing,* 197.

497   Peacocke, *Hints on Photoplay Writing,* 135–137.

498   Peacocke, 'Hints on Photoplay Writing', *Photoplay*, September 1915, 150.

Like Wright, Ball encourages freelance writers to study the trade press so as to be aware of the requirements of various companies and of the market.[499] As part of the regular industry information Phillips gives in his column for *Motion Picture Magazine,* he provides a 'List of Photoplay Markets' with company details and their requirements.[500] As to the market value of scripts, writers could stay abreast of the trends again through the fan and trade press as well as the various columns of the screenwriting teachers. Sargent's advice was to either 'offer a script at usual rates or to state a price'. Ball reminds the writer that price is always related to the 'value of the work and the fame of the writer'.[501] Membership of various clubs and associations, which have already been discussed in this chapter and in Chapter 5, was also a source of useful information and contact with industry insiders. With particular attention to this matter in his chapter, 'The Value of Organizations', Wright argues for 'cooperation' with other writers through discussion and exchange of ideas as a source of inspiration and a means of career development.[502]

The key screenwriting teachers gave expert practical advice to would-be writers on what was marketable at any given time and how to sell effectively to that market. In so doing, they demonstrate their considerable knowledge and awareness as 'industry insiders' and also give us a detailed understanding of the practices of the period.

---

499 Ball refers his readers to *Motography*, *MPW* and the *NYDM* among other publications. See Ball, *Art of the Photoplay*, 28–30.

500 Phillips, 'The Photodrama', *MPM*, November 1917, 91–92.

501 Sargent, *Technique of the Photoplay,* 3rd ed., 336–337, Wright, *Motion Picture Story,* 20; Ball, *Art of the Photoplay,* 56; and Peacocke, *Hints on Photoplay Writing,* 109.

502 Wright, *Photoplay Writing*, 217–220.

7. The Discourse – Impact of the Advice

Following on from the detailed description of the advice from the key screenwriting teachers in Chapter 6, this chapter offers a comprehensive assessment of their main contribution to the discourse. It ends with a brief summary of the reasons why the era of the early screenwriting teacher – and their influence with it – came to a sudden end.

The Contribution of the Key Screenwriting Teachers

In this book, my main contention is that the key screenwriting teachers played a crucial role in helping to translate, adapt and develop stage and literary conventions for the screen. In other words, they acted as a conduit for transforming theatrical understanding into screen practice. The five key screenwriting teachers identified: the skills that the prospective writer would need to acquire and how they could put this learning process into train; what the writer needed to know about their role in the process of making films; and how they could draw upon the rich storytelling conventions in literary and theatrical traditions in order to write for film. They dealt with what the writer specifically needed to do to write for the film industry; namely to tell their story in action and visually in photoplay form by presenting the correct documentation and by employing techniques such intertitles, busts, close-ups and cut-backs that were peculiar to the medium of cinema. They also coached the writer about the process of selling their work to the industry by: knowing what kind of material to write; submitting the correct documents in an acceptable format; being aware of how to negotiate the issues of censorship, copyright and writing for stars; and understanding where to market their work and what strategies were more likely to lead to a sale.

Although the key screenwriting teachers were not the only voices in this discourse, nor were they inventors of it, I argue that they made an important contribution to articulating the debate and codifying screen and writing practice. To some extent, more recent literature has recognised their impact, but not in any systematic or sustained manner. For example, Nannicelli states that:

> scenario writing manuals […] like the trade press, simultaneously reflected, shaped and normalized standards of screenwriting practice based on the narrative principles of the legitimate theatre.[503]

Yet, while ascribing them some limited role here, Nannicelli gives little supporting evidence or detail as to why he takes this view. However, I contend that the evidence I have put forward in this study suggests that the key screenwriting teachers were leading and active participants rather than passive and reactive agents in this process. This is a possibility that has been barely considered or acknowledged up until now.

---

503 Nannicelli, *Philosophy of the Screenplay*, 95.

These screenwriting teachers wrote for different interest groups. Sargent and Wright initially wrote for the trade press and industry insiders, although the general public increasingly accessed their columns once the market for freelance material had developed. Their broadening readership is evidenced by the proliferation of columns in different publications and some recorded effects. In his column for *Moving Picture News*, Wright claims, 'The number of readers have grown rapidly over the last year. This department is read by script writers in almost every known country.'[1] When Wright was engaged to write a column for the *New York Dramatic Mirror* in 1914, Grau notes that 'the *Mirror*'s already large circulation immeasurably increased'.[2] Sargent's weekly articles also draw Grau's attention as a reason for much of the 'amazing success' of *Moving Picture World*.[3]

Logical, organised and comprehensive in covering writing technique and providing industry information, Sargent and Wright tended to write in a relatively formal style. By contrast, in his equally prolific writing for the fan and trade press, both as a manual writer and columnist, Phillips adopted a style that is a little less formal. His writings are detailed and long-winded in places, but always remain accessible. In particular, he emphasises that technique should only be employed for one purpose – emotionally engaging the audience, for reasons discussed in Chapter 6. Ball's popularity was based on his profile as a short story columnist and successful scenarist. His manuals are also highly accessible and easily understood, readily drawing upon an understanding of theatre as a source of technique. In a terse and practical style, Peacocke wrote exclusively for the fan press. He offers a more down-to-earth, plain-speaking approach. His writings are informal and conversational in style, if a little repetitive in places.

The last two chapters have demonstrated that all five of the key screenwriting teachers were well-known, highly regarded and in a position to wield influence with a great number and wide spectrum of people both inside and outside the film industry. As experienced professional writers and editors, they probably contributed to a complex and developing industrial discourse and, in collaboration with many other film professionals, helped to establish patterns of working, requirements for submissions to film companies and the dissemination of expertise to the growing number of industry professionals and the freelancers hoping to join them.

All the key screenwriting teachers responded to market conditions through what they wrote in their columns and in publishing either revised editions of their manuals or new manuals altogether. The development of Sargent's thinking over the span of three editions of his manual and almost a decade of column writing is indicative of this openness to change. The third edition of his manual, in particular, is exhaustive in its treatment of

---

1 Wright, 'For Those Who Worry O'er Plots and Plays', *MPN*, September 27, 1913, 22.

2 Grau, *Theatre of Science,* 311.

3 Ibid., 308.

every conceivable aspect of screenwriting. In fact, its comprehensive coverage gives an excellent insight into how developed the craft of screenwriting had become by 1916. Wright's three manuals, published with considerable gaps of time in between, and his columns are likely to have made a sustained contribution to the discourse over a 10-year period. His two surviving manuals show the contrast in market conditions between 1914 and 1922. His extensive knowledge, gained from his practical experience as a writer, editor and producer throughout this period, put him in a position to give cogent and coherent advice.

Likewise demonstrating the breadth of his understanding of the craft, Phillips took varying approaches to it in his four manuals, which again signalled the seismic shift in the industry's requirements between 1914 and 1922. His columns in 1917–18 and 1923–24 also indicate his continual engagement with the industry. As Ball explains it, he wrote his two manuals only two years apart because he wanted his comment to be 'up-to-the-minute in its presentation of the new conditions, and the author believes that his own knowledge has been considerably broadened by his producing and scenario creations'.[4] Ball's second manual is more organised, much longer and more thorough than his first. Peacocke shows an in-depth knowledge of the market conditions in his 1916 manual and his columns around that time, 1915–16. His continual engagement is indicated through the second set of articles he wrote in 1917 dealing with pertinent industry issues.

Collectively, the five key screenwriting teachers appear to have made a sustained, detailed contribution of material of direct relevance to the prevailing conditions in the film industry throughout this early period. The study of a group of screenwriting teachers, rather than of one individual, adds an important wider perspective on what it meant to write for the broader system of the industry.

The key screenwriting teachers offered a complete how-to guide – from script inception right through to sale. It is impossible to determine whether they were the originators of specific aspects of the scripting process, but in all probability they contributed to its development through confirming and clarifying technique. As already suggested, perhaps one of the reasons why these screenwriting teachers have not received the recognition they deserved was the low status of the writer in the industry. As Phillips points out, 'All authority in too many instances has been given to the director.'[5] In addition, in the beginning photoplay writers received no credit. If writers were not highly regarded, this would also affect the status of those who gave instruction and possibly explain why they have also been largely marginalised and in some cases virtually forgotten.

These key screenwriting teachers owed much of their understanding of dramatic construction to theatre and other literary forms. All of them were journalists, but four also

---

4   Ball, *Photoplay Scenarios*, xv.

5   Phillips, *Photodrama*, xxiii.

had strong theatrical connections. Sargent wrote for theatrical journals as a vaudeville critic, both Peacocke and Phillips were playwrights, and Ball's versatility meant that he could turn his hand to almost any kind of writing. The key screenwriting teachers were thus in a unique position, in the early teens of the twentieth century, to be able to influence and impart knowledge about the new skill of writing for film. As Tibbetts observes, 'the movies had no tradition, no academy, no system of instruction and training, no centralized industrial plant or business headquarters and no critical record'.[6] However, what the new industry did have was the narrative tradition of the well-made play with its melodramatic overtones and pictorial realism, which would be a rich source of material to mine, adapt and reformulate.

The lack of recognition of the likely role that the key screenwriting teachers played in this process is perhaps typified by Nannicelli's negative assertion about the claims manual writers made about the importance of their work:

> that the manuals' promulgation of an understanding of photoplay writing as a new kind of dramatic literary art was nothing more than a ploy to sell more manuals [… as] the ideas they expressed were echoed in the legitimate theatrical press.[7]

Of course, the key screenwriting teachers did want to market their product, but to argue that they did nothing more than repeat information that was already available in a different guise – namely theatrical – is, I believe, incorrect. Nannicelli's comment is not supported by evidence and does not appear to acknowledge the significant differences between theatrical and cinematic storytelling, as highlighted in Chapter 6. These differences were even more marked in the silent era, when storytellers did not have the option of dialogue other than by using subtitles.

The key screenwriting teachers functioned as more than just intermediaries between the world of the playwright and the new film medium. As this study has indicated, these teachers were not simply involved in reiterating dramatic principles: I contend that they helped to adapt, reformulate and construct a highly visualised form of storytelling called cinema. I concur with Blackton, one of the founders of Vitagraph, who wrote in the foreword to Phillips's manual that a new approach was needed, because '[p]hotoplay writing is a new profession, for the simple reason that the photodrama is a new form of dramatic expression'.[8] Sargent recognised that the roots of his work were in playwriting and classical dramatic principles, but he also knew it was distinct from them:

---

6   Tibbetts, *American Theatrical Film*, 4.

7   Nannicelli, *Philosophy of the Screenplay*, 102.

8   Phillips, *Photodrama*, xxi. Blackton was one of the founders of Vitagraph in 1897. By 1912–13 it grossed an income of between $5 million and $6 million a year; his recognition of Phillips's writing approach is indicative of the need for writing expertise in the industry. See Hampton, *History of the American Film Industry from Its Beginnings to 1931*, 22–24 and 96.

> Photoplay [...] is not an adaptation of another branch of literary work, but is possessed of a technique all of its own. There are [...] the broad basic rules of literary construction and dramatic development, applicable to all forms of literature [... but] the art of writing photoplays has become possessed of a technique that is applicable only to the writing of picture plays and to no other form.[9]

Presenting a story visually through the eye of the camera was the main difference between film and theatre. Because the camera could be moved for point of view and location, and the material, once filmed, could be edited, the use of space was more fluid and time could be compressed. According to Hamilton, the medium of film gave the scenario writer a new 'freedom in handling the categories of place and time'.[10] This presented not only new opportunities but also fresh challenges for the writer. If there is a distinction between theatre and cinema, Susan Sontag observes, it is that:

> Theatre is confined to a logical or continuous use of space. Cinema (through editing, that is through the change of shot – which is the basic unit of film construction) has access to an alogical or discontinuous use of space.[11]

No longer were the positions of the spectator and the performer fixed at a set distance and the action and storytelling possibilities restricted by the limitations of the stage space, as in the theatre. Gone were many of the restrictions in showing how time passed. As Hamilton observes:

> [A character] can walk, run, ride, sail, or fly for any distance, and yet be accompanied through his entire transit by the actual eye of the observer [... and the writer has] the ability to alter in a fraction of a second, the point of view from which the story shall be looked upon.[12]

It was also possible for the writer to use, subject to cost, whatever number and type of settings they felt appropriate to tell their particular story and arrange their tale 'in fifty scenes instead of four' if that was advantageous.[13] Ball compares this flexibility with the restrictions of the theatre:

> The stage play is presented upon a broad platform, from which the audience may be observed from all parts of the house [whereas] motion picture production presents to the [...] director an unlimited scenic wealth [which] eliminates the explanatory speeches of the stage play [...] by going through every phase of the action before the camera-eye.[14]

---

9   Sargent, *Technique of the Photoplay,* 2ⁿᵈ ed., 7.

10   Hamilton, 'The Art of the Moving Picture', 51.

11   Susan Sontag, 'Film and Theatre' in *Film Theory and Criticism*, eds. Mast, Cohen and Braudy, 367.

12   Hamilton, 'The Art of the Moving Picture', 51.

13   Ibid., 51.

14   Ball, *Photoplay Scenarios,* 4, 6–7.

Another advantage of film is that screen images can be arranged in any way that would assist in the storytelling process, as Sontag observes:

> The theatre's capacities for manipulating space and time are, simply, much cruder and more labored than film's. Theatre cannot equal the cinema's facilities for the strictly-controlled repetition of images [...] and for the juxtaposition and overlapping of images.[15]

In terms of devices, this capacity was particularly evident in the use of the various forms of the close-up and the cut-back, which gave the storyteller a new power to control the perspective of the viewer and to avoid monotony by breaking up scenes. No longer were spectators free to choose what they focused on within specified theatrical sightlines, because the camera directed their eye. Ball was keen to stress the power of the close-up in this respect, because 'facial expression and the subtlety of gesture [...were] so necessary to take the place of dialogue'.[16] Peacocke's advice is to '[m]ake your characters human. Bring them close to the camera, so that we can see their facial expressions and know what they are thinking about.'[17] As Phillips observes, the 'cut-back' or 'return' makes it possible to 'cut' to another scene 'that has a contributive effect on the thematic scene'.[18] Every close-up and cut-back had to be effectively used in a seamless continuous narrative that cumulatively developed and drove the plot towards its eventual climax.

Telling a story visually posed problems with continuity that were particular to film. Ball explains that in a stage play:

> [t]he development of the action can be carried along clearly with [...] verbal assistance [...] in the words of the characters. But with motion pictures, the prime essential is continuity. There must be smoothness, logical progression, synchronism, and each step of the action must be clear.[19]

Focusing on Sargent's work specifically, Azlant sums up the importance of continuity as 'the fruition of all the techniques of screenwriting properly exercised' and it had to be maintained to ensure a filmgoer's 'constant participation in the "happening" of the story'.[20] However, the other four key screenwriting teachers espoused the importance of continuity in a similar way.

---

15 Sontag, 'Film and Theatre' in *Film Theory and Criticism*, eds. Mast, Cohen and Braudy, 368.

16 Ball, *Art of the Photoplay*, 19.

17 Peacocke, *Hints on Photoplay Writing*, 45.

18 Phillips, *Photodrama*, 141.

19 Ball, *Photoplay Scenarios*, 4.

20 Azlant, 'Theory, History and Practice of Screenwriting', 253.

Managing the experience of the viewer or guaranteeing 'continuity' required careful use of point of view. According to Azlant, Sargent expresses in his manual the understanding implicit in most early motion pictures that point of view was 'ubiquitously omniscient, all-knowing and capable of viewing the action from any possible vantage'.[21] Point of view had become an incredibly powerful tool in the hands of the writer, permitting a diegetic form of storytelling from the interior perspective of the character in a way hitherto unknown. However, the experience of the filmgoer needed to be carefully handled through skilful storytelling in an unbroken and seamless way, because verisimilitude or the illusion of real life could be easily lost, as Azlant observes:

> this omniscience is not [...] automatic. It is deeply dependent on the sustenance of [...] the uninterrupted, continuous flow of narrative [...] and fragmentation, works against the audience's active participation in the plot, instead promoting a distanced deciphering of the film's form.[22]

This method of storytelling was unique to the motion picture and required an adroit and accomplished use of novel narrative devices previously unavailable to the playwright. Instruction in this new form of storytelling was essential if it were to thrive and develop, and the key screenwriting teachers were instrumental in supplying this, through their manuals and columns.

Sargent understood that the photoplay plot mediated the relationship between the fiction film and its actual sources: a 'photoplay reproduces life and should be animated by life'.[23] Phillips agrees that 'we find something in this newest of the Arts that none other of the Fine Arts has; that is, the animated deed – the verisimilitude of life itself!'[24] Such rhetorical statements echo Aristotle's treatment of the imitation of art in the *Poetics*:

> When constructing plots and working them out complete with their linguistic expression, one should so far as possible visualize what is happening. By envisaging things very vividly in this way, as if one were actually present at the events themselves, one can find out what is appropriate, and inconsistencies are least likely to be overlooked.[25]

As Barnaby Dallas perceptively suggests, 'Aristotle could not have possibly meant his words for the cinema, yet his statement could have been made by a photoplay theorist.'[26]

---

21   Ibid., 237.

22   Ibid., 237–239.

23   Sargent, *Technique of the Photoplay,* 3rd ed., 25.

24   Phillips, *Feature Photoplay,* xii.

25   Aristotle, *Poetics,* 27.

26   Colonel Barnaby Dallas, 'Play, Photoplay, and Screenplay Structure: Dramatic Principles from Theater to Cinema' (MA Diss., Jan Hose State University, 2000), 39. ProQuest (UMI 1399789).

The imaginings of the scenarist could be fully realised in visual terms in a way that no theatrical production could match. These possibilities were also appreciated by theorists like Freeburg:

> what distinguishes the photoplay from all other narrative and dramatic arts is the possibility of representing an action in its natural setting. For the first time in the history of the arts which mimic human happenings it has become possible for the spectator to go to the very spot where the action takes place.[27]

Leaving aside Freeburg's indulgence in a certain amount of hyperbole, his treatise *The Art of Photoplay Making* was advertised in the trade and fan press. However, while theorists were not without influence, what differentiated the key screenwriting teachers from them was not necessarily their inventiveness but their potential reach and sphere of influence and the timing of their work. They were able to articulate this new understanding to a huge number of people both inside and outside the industry due to their prominence in the trade and fan press, their roles as editors, directors and writers, and the extensive and sustained comment they made through columns and manuals. All this was achieved before the theorists had even published their ideas.

Further, because visual storytelling had to be done without the dialogue that the theatre so liberally afforded, the writer had to learn to use expository and dialogue subtitles skilfully. The key screenwriting teachers, in all probability, played an important role in helping to clarify and codify this practice; and were responsible for imparting valuable instruction in the concise, effective use of intertitles as unique literary devices that both aided segmentation and enhanced the storytelling possibilities. As Liepa's research has identified:

> Screenwriting manuals both adopted and developed a specific lexicon for discussing filmmaking devices and practice. The language used to identify intertitles, both dialogue and expository, and describe their function, reveals something of how these authors conceptualized the function of these devices, influencing the popular perception of the role these devices should play.[28]

Despite drawing heavily on the key screenwriting teachers as sources, Liepa does not pinpoint them as the most influential in this process. Yet, for the reasons identified in Chapter 5, we can surmise from the evidence that they probably were among the most influential, although this cannot be conclusively proved.

According to Maras, such early handbooks played a significant part in the development of writing for the screen, their contents largely reflecting industry practices that were becoming increasingly established. Sargent's handbook, in particular, is presented as

---

27 Freeburg, *Art of Photoplay Making*, 137.

28 Liepa, 'Figures of Silent Speech', 241.

a guide for successful writing and the selling of photoplay scenarios, grounded in the point of view of the scenario editor. He sets out the 'rules for the guidance of the author ... with the full knowledge of the needs of the studio gained through service as an editor of scenarios'.[29] With his regular references to industry practices and figures, Sargent gives the impression he belonged to an extended 'club'.[30] Of course, the possibility that he exaggerated his influence for the purpose of self-promotion cannot be excluded. But even if this is true to some extent, it must be balanced against the wealth of evidence that he was highly regarded by 'industry insiders'. Azlant describes his view of Sargent's achievements in this way:

> The sum of Sargent's descriptions of the many techniques by which the scenarist works his materials into a finished scenario is extremely full, and he recognizes the almost incomprehensible complexity of combining all these considerations [... and] the working of a staggering number of variables and contingencies [...] into one craft, one exercise of creativity.[31]

In some respects, I believe it is possible to go further than Azlant and Maras in recognising Sargent as perhaps an even more highly significant and influential voice in the development of early screenwriting practice than previously acknowledged. In addition, the other four key screenwriting teachers identified in this study need to be recognised for their role in this process, which again is likely to have been extremely important.

Summary

In summary, storytelling in the new medium of the screen presented considerable challenges for the writer of the early twentieth century, and the skills required to do it were acquired within a span of just 20 years. In the early days of cinema, writing for film was not even a recognised activity; but by 1920 the craft was well established. Contrast this with literary and theatrical storytelling, which had developed over more than 2,000 years. It is impossible to prove definitively what actual, specific impact the key screenwriting teachers had, but the evidence suggests they may well have significantly facilitated and aided the speedy development of the skill of writing for the screen and its professionalisation.

The tension over whether the key screenwriting teachers considered that they were providing artistic or artisanal instruction, or a blend of both, permeates their writings. As Chapter 6 has mentioned, Shiner regards this as a false dichotomy; for him, the answer to this perception of art divided is to unite 'freedom, imagination, and creativity

---

29   Sargent, *Technique of the Photoplay* (New York: MPW, 1912), 3; cited in Maras, *Screenwriting*, 160.

30   Maras, *Screenwriting*, 160.

31   Azlant, 'Theory, History and Practice of Screenwriting', 254-255.

[…] with facility, service and function'.[32] The discourse of the key screenwriting teachers is of special interest, because it locates and reflects the genesis of this debate in early film writing.

I contend that the role of the screenwriting teacher was inextricably linked to the development of the screenwriting process in early cinema. Not only did that process affect the kind of advice that was offered by screenwriting teachers, but their input also fed into, spurred and shaped the development of that process. The advice that they gave was specific, detailed and closely attuned to the specific circumstances and developments in the industry. They were part of the melting-pot process in which writing for the screen was negotiated over this decade – from the ill-defined practice before 1910 until film companies had developed a self-sufficient means of producing their own story material and no longer welcomed the submissions of amateur writers.

The End of an Era

After an intense period of screenwriting teaching and advice for freelance writers, the five key screenwriting teachers saw a decline in demand for their instruction as the market for freelance writers shrank and the role of the professional writer grew.

Decline in Freelance Submissions

The public promotion of scenario fever gradually abated, for two major reasons. First, out of the many thousands of scripts that the industry received, most were of poor quality. By 1911, *Moving Picture World* reported that the operations of the average scenario department were highly organised and that the typical scenario editor was passing judgment on 60 scenarios a day, the vast majority of which were rejected: 'the scenarios that are accepted, according to the authority of the various editors, does not exceed one per cent'.[33] The article continues:

> scenario editors [had] to consider the reams of manuscripts that began to pour into their offices from unsuccessful playwrights and short story writers, who, in many instances, sent not scenarios, but complete plays, novels and short stories, most of them no more adapted to moving picture production than five wheels would be on a wagon.[34]

It is not possible to determine how many complete scripts by amateurs were ever turned into saleable films. Information from studios suggests that they only accepted a very low percentage of these submissions. For example, when discussing Vitagraph, *Moving Picture World* noted that, during a four-month period, 'only about two per cent were

---

32   Shiner, *Invention of Art*, 307.

33   R.V.S., 'Scenario Construction', *MPW*, February 11, 1911, 294.

34   Ibid., 294.

accepted and only four of these were practical working scenarios'.[35] According to Harrison, writing original material was easier said than done:

> Original stories of high merit [...] are few and far between [... and] the best paying productions have been wrought by those who have something new to say.[36]

In 1916 Sargent appears to be slightly more optimistic: 'Probably eighty per cent of the scripts do not pass the first reader. The remainder are sent along to the editor.'[37] On this basis, 20 per cent were at least considered. It is also probable that amateur submissions provided the industry with inspiration, albeit indirectly.

A gloomier view comes from William De Mille, head of the story department of the Jesse Lasky Feature Play Company. His estimate is that within one year he received as many as 10,000 submissions from unknown writers. His company 'bought two, made one of them into a picture – and it flopped'. It then gave up reading outside material as it was too time-consuming and gave a poor return on investment.[38]

Peacocke admits to a similar problem, in quoting Woods of the Fine Arts Studio about the disappointing quality of material he is receiving:

> If we buy so little, it is because out of the mass of material that is being constantly offered we find so little that is adaptable to our peculiar wants. Everything we receive is carefully read, in the hope of finding somewhere a diamond in the rough; occasionally we find one, but not often.[39]

Even bleaker is Durant of Famous Players, who Peacocke also quotes: 'Out of the mass of material, which is submitted to us we purchase only half of one percent!'[40]

The most detailed record of a story department of this period is in the *Biograph Logbook* from 1910–1915. In 1910 Biograph bought 162 stories, of which 114 were made into films. By 1915 it was buying 238 stories, of which 158 became films.[41] Clearly then, even out of the small percentage of bought materials, much was never filmed. By 1920 Patterson directly attributes the decline to the poor quality of scenarios received, because:

---

35   'Scenario Writing for Moving Pictures', *MPW*, March 5, 1910, 335.

36   Harrison, 'Five Reels', *MPW*, February 7, 1914, 652.

37   Sargent, *Technique of the Photoplay*, 3rd ed., 7.

38   William de Mille, *Hollywood Saga* (New York: E. P. Dutton, 1939), 126; cited in Stempel, *Framework*, 13.

39   Woods, 'What Producers Want', *Photoplay*, July 1916; cited in Peacocke, *Hints on Photoplay Writing*, 100.

40   Ibid., 110.

41   *Biograph Story Department Logbook* (New York, MOMA, 1910–15); cited in Stempel, *Framework*, 11.

everyone was attempting it [… and] scenario writing was becoming the most popular form of 'indoor sport' […but people] had absolutely no idea of the technique, of the form, of the camera, or of the procedure in the business of making a photoplay.[42]

The second major reason for the decline in the freelance market was that producers began to suffer accusations of plagiarism. Such scares were fanned by the celebrated, spurious lawsuit Mrs Mattie Thomas Thornton, an Atlanta housewife, brought against Cecil B. DeMille, claiming she had written the original screen story for *The Ten Commandments*.[43] Although such practice was not widespread, the editorial problems and legal jeopardy that accompanied amateur screenwriting drove the studios away from the public towards professional exclusivity. By the mid-teens, studios were no longer seeking freelance work and were wary of accepting work from unknown sources because of these issues.

Professionalisation of Writing for the Screen

The demand for freelance submissions gradually lessened. In 1913–1914, 'feature fever' had taken hold and it was 'the beginning of a limited number of major production companies that would end up with greater control of distribution and exhibition'.[44] The First World War had largely eliminated European competition, placing America in a completely dominant position. Given this enormous business opportunity to fill the vacuum, Hollywood become a major exporter of films. The general public was gradually cut out of writing and it was far more difficult to get a story past the gatekeepers. The process of writing for the film industry had also become immensely more complex and the professional screenwriter was in the ascendancy. By the end of the decade, writing for film had largely been institutionalised and was done in-house by professionals.

Wright signals this shift even in 1912, when he records how few freelance writers actually make it: 'Ten thousand writers in the Moving Picture scenario field, and one in a hundred fairly successful.'[45] In his own column, Peacocke laments the shifting practices of the studios, which had begun to employ their own staff writers to rework freelance scenario submissions. Appearing to share this concern, Sargent allies himself with Wright and Peacocke in his column:

> I think that you [Peacocke], William Lord Wright and myself have taken up the cudgels on behalf of the free lance writer more than others and endeavored to get

42 Patterson, *Cinema Craftsmanship,* 126

43 Mrs Thornton claimed she submitted the script to the Players-Lasky Film Company but it had never been returned. It was later discovered that she had copied her version of the scenario from a pre-release account of the plot printed in the *Los Angeles Times*. See Charles Higham *Cecil B. DeMille* (New York: Da Capo, 1973), 137–138.

44 Bowser, *Transformation of Cinema,* 224.

45 Wright, 'The Spark of Genius', *MPSM*, September 1912, 136.

manufacturers to see that the author and not the director or staff writer is the logical person to make the continuity.[46]

The next year, in assessing 10 years of the industry in 1917, Sargent considers that photoplay writers had ended up where they began. The continuity writers had taken over the main task of writing the scenario and ideas were sometimes supplied by outsiders. As he puts it, 'There are inside writers and tipsters.' In effect, he was stating that the current phase was over for the freelance writer:

> In the past decade we have worked in a full circle back to the starting point of synopsis. […] Today the detailed synopsis or scenario is sent instead of a letter of fifty or one hundred words, but the idea is the same.[47]

However, *Motography* refers to the bleakness of the situation for the amateur writer more directly in 1917, as the separation of classes of writers became more defined:

> There are only two classes of motion picture scenario writers – a few whose work is in real demand, who collaborate with the producers and get good prices; and a great many whose work is of little or no value and most of whom will never succeed.[48]

Only three years later, in 1920, Patterson openly refers to the pathway that any prospective writer must take if they were to succeed in the profession. The only opening for an amateur was the submission of a synopsis, but the real professionals were the staff writers who had a proven track record:

> Continuity writing […] has become a profession in itself, and the writer […] needs long and careful training before he can handle a script successfully. […] Writers must submit their ideas in synopsis form, and if they were purchased the company would farm out the continuity to scenarioists whose skill had been tried and proved.[49]

This view is the reverse of Peacocke's ideas that staff writers were simply 'constructionists' who were employed to rewrite the original ideas of freelance writers into workable scripts. The freelance writer had, in fact, been relegated to the sidelines. Registering this shift in 1922, Wright begins his chapter on 'What scenario editors want from you' with the directive: 'You must write your story in synopsis form.'[50] As Chapter 6 has noted, this position is confirmed in Phillips's last two manuals, which are written with the synopsis particularly in mind.

---

46   Sargent, 'Necessity of Encouraging the Author', *MPW*, July 22, 1916, 623.

47   Sargent, 'Photoplay Writing Then and Now', *MPW*, March 10, 1917, 1491–92.

48   'Better Treatment for the Story Writer', *Motography*, September 29, 1917, 651.

49   Patterson, *Cinema Craftsmanship,* 126.

50   Wright, *Photoplay Writing,* 9.

Within three years, therefore, the film industry had completely turned away from the general public as a major source of story material and toward the professional screenwriter:

> By the mid-twenties, the work of the amateur photoplay writer was no longer destined for the screen but for the wastepaper basket. The motion-picture business was now the exclusive domain of the professionals. The days of experiment were over.[51]

According to Maras, the trade press advice reflected what he calls 'particularism', or the drift towards an exclusive professional writing elite that fashioned screenwriting technique as a specialised field of knowledge. The possibility of amateur writers continuing to flood the market with their material affected the prospects of the more professional writers, who were attempting to improve their status. Initially, this put the industry management in a powerful position in relation to writers. However, in the long run the only writers to survive in screenwriting were those who could easily participate in this arena, which demanded specialised knowledge determined by the gatekeepers and authorities in the field.[52]

This knowledge of the proper technique, Maras believes, begins to serve as 'a key marker of the difference between the aspirant or amateur writer and the successful scenario writer'.[53] Ironically, Sargent himself marks the demise of the freelance writer in 1918, with the declaration that 'photoplay writing is no longer the toy of the multitude. It is a profession.' He then states categorically, 'There is no opening for the untrained man at present.'[54] His original intention, and that of the other key screenwriting teachers, may have been to broaden the base of writers and to help skill these people. Ultimately, though, they had helped to narrow the field of writers to those few amateurs who managed to succeed and the talent culled from the journalistic and literary establishment, thereby encouraging further specialisation, which would strengthen the position of the insiders. Even though the earlier 'eminent authors' programme had failed, Sargent admits in 1917 that a 'gradual absorption of real writers by the studios' had occurred.[55] Screenwriting had been professionalised.

---

51 Brownlow, *Parade's Gone By,* 278.

52 Maras, *Screenwriting*, 24–25

53 Ibid., 162.

54 Sargent, 'The Photoplaywright', *MPW*, May 25, 1918, 1136.

55 Sargent, 'Photoplay Writing Then and Now', *MPW*, March 10, 1917, 1491–1492.

Demise of the Early Screenwriting Teacher

With writing largely in-house, film companies were no longer openly seeking submissions from freelance writers. Writing schools, such as the Palmer Photoplay Corporation, continued to advertise their wares sporadically in the trade and fan press throughout the early 1920s, but such advertisements gradually tailed off. Wright's manual, *Photoplay Writing* continued to be advertised into the early 1920s.[56] The publication of new manuals gradually ceased and screenwriting columns dried up. Of the key screenwriting teachers, Peacocke ceased writing a regular column in 1917, Phillips in 1918, Sargent in 1919 and Wright in 1921. The final manuals published among the five were Wright's in 1921 (see Figure 72) and Phillips's in 1922. The role of the screenwriting teacher was over for this phase of screenwriting history.

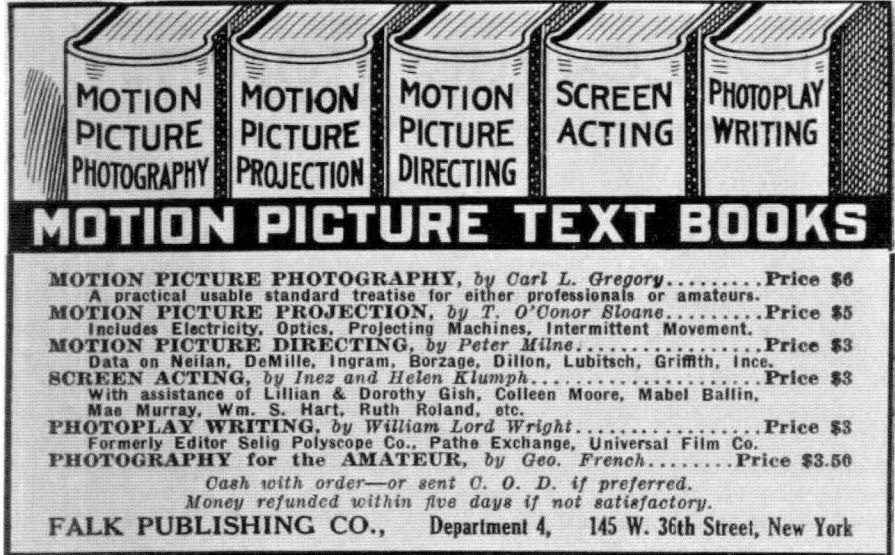

Figure 72: Advertisements for Palmer Photoplay Corporation and Wright's *Photoplay Writing*
Source: *Photoplay*, March, 1923, 144 and *MPN*, March 10, 1923, 1205.

---

56   See advertisements for Wright's manual in 'Photoplay Writing', *MPN*, March 10, 1923, 1205 and 'The Palmer Photoplay Institute', *Photoplay*, March 1925, 127.

PART THREE

LEGACY

PART THREE: LEGACY

8. Similarities to Modern Screenwriting Gurus

So far, this book has located early screenwriting teachers within their historical context and demonstrated their importance and contribution to the industry during that period. This part moves on to consider their legacy, while recognising it is not possible to measure precisely what might have flowed down from early screenwriting teachers to their modern-day counterparts, because so much film history has happened in between. However, by making associations, tracing connections and drawing out some possible similarities between then and now, this brief analysis will speculate on some possible contributions that early screenwriting teachers may have made to modern screenwriting gurus and the current screenwriting community. This chapter focuses on similarities between early screenwriting teachers and modern screenwriting gurus; the following two chapters assess their involvement in the evolution of the screenplay, and their impact on the education of screenwriters.

As indicated in the Introduction, the work of screenwriting teachers can be situated within three broad phases of screenwriting history, classified by how the Hollywood industry was structured. At the end of each of these periods, a major shift in organisation occurred, which directly affected the level and type of activity in which screenwriting teachers were engaged. The first of these periods (1895–1920s) has formed the main basis of this study, although screenwriting teachers were only fully active from around 1911 onwards. Subsequent periods were the studio era (1920s–1950/60s) and the era of the package unit system and resultant independent production (1950/60s to the present day).

During the studio era, the studios controlled everything, from the conception of an idea through to its execution. Story departments largely took over the script development role of the early screenwriting teachers and instruction went in-house. It was, therefore, a particularly lean period for widely shared instruction about screenwriting. However, in Liepa's opinion, the earlier involvement of the wider public had been beneficial:

> The participatory reputation of film writing would help the industry retain a connection to its popular base even as production became closed to the general public, and moreover granted early film writing considerable cultural influence beyond its impact on studio production.[1]

Because of the industry's dalliance with the amateur freelance writer, shared knowledge about technique and process entered the public domain and the consciousness of the general populace. A wide-ranging and open discourse about screenwriting had taken place in the fan and trade press columns and through the many manuals that had been

---

1   Liepa, 'Entertaining the Public Option' in *Analyzing the Screenplay*, ed. Nelmes, 8.

published over a 12-year period. No such open discourse had ever taken place on the subject of playwriting. According to Liepa, the public engagement on screenwriting would mean that:

> [although] industry concerns would certainly dominate the later developments of film writing, they would always be tempered and in many ways underwritten by popular influence.[2]

Moreover, despite the general exclusion of outsiders from the industry, a few notable works on screenwriting were still written during the studio era. Six manuals stand out among them: Tamar Lane's *The New Technique of Cinema Writing* (1936), Frances Marion's *How to Write and Sell Film Stories* (1937), Eugene Vale's *The New Technique of Screen Writing* (1944), John Howard Lawson's *Theory and Technique of Playwriting and Screenwriting* (1949), Clara Beranger's *Writing for the Screen* (1950) and Lewis Herman's *Practical Manual of Screen Playwriting* (1952).

Figure 73: Frances Marion (1888–1973) and Clara Beranger (1886–1956)
Source: *upload.wikimedia.org/wikipedia/commons/6/65/Frances-Marion.jpg* and *wikidata.org/wiki/Q2975468#/media/File:Clara_Berenger01.JPG.*

These manuals were integral to, and representative of, the development of screenwriting practice during this period.[3] They were more than likely written for the insider, although some seem to leave open the possibility that the freelance writer could still succeed. In 1936 Lane still addresses both freelance and professional writers, although the bar is set high. Professionalism was required from both 'those in the elementary stages of screen writing [and] experienced authors and playwrights' who must 'give much time

---

2   Ibid., 20.

3   The writers of all six manuals have extensive writing credits. Lane wrote *The Isle of Destiny* (1920) and *A Self Made Failure* (1924); Marion has 188 writing credits and won Oscars for *The House* (1930) and *The Champ* (1931); Vale's credits include *The Bridge of San Luis Rey* (1944) and *A Global Affair* (1964) and he was Oscar-nominated for his documentary, *The Dark Wave* (1956); Lawson was Oscar-nominated for *The Blockade* (1938), but his career was hampered by accusations from the House Un-American Activities Committee on his Communist sympathies; Beranger was prolific, with 96 credits, and is known for *Dr Jekyll and Mr Hyde* (1920); and Herman is known for the film noir *Strange Impersonation* (1946). See *IMDbPro:* https://pro-labs.imdb.com

and thought to a thorough study of the new studio demands'.[4] Marion (see Figure 73) claims in 1937 that the studios were 'welcoming stories by talented free-lance writers'.[5] A similar contention from Beranger (see Figure 73) is that, because of 'the dearth of good stories [, …] the author with visual and dramatic imagination has a good chance of selling an original screen story' through an agent.[6] However, she also admits that opportunities to be engaged as a staff writer are few and far between.[7] It is hard to know whether these appeals were a ploy to sell more manuals or came from a genuine conviction that a complete amateur could break through. Both Vale and Beranger also taught screenwriting on university courses, so these particular students of their work may have had a greater chance of success.[8] Precisely how this particular discourse and the dissemination of the content of their manuals interacted with the studio system and outsiders is a question that is beyond the reach of this study.

What can be affirmed is that the understanding developed in the early period was largely internalised and refined by the industry over a 40-year period; and the 'classical Hollywood cinema', as Bordwell and Thompson have identified it, was established.[9] A cursory examination of the content and organisation of these manuals confirms that they broadly reflect this continued refinement and codification. Principally concerned with the conversion from silent films to sound, Lane is less detailed in his description of story construction.[10] Marion's aim is to dispense all necessary information in order to help orientate the prospective writer 'toward giving the motion-picture studios what they want', so the manual is detailed and comprehensive.[11] Herman clearly delineates the three-act structure as the model for screenwriting and Vale, Lawson and Beranger all unmistakably link the skills required for screenwriting to playwriting tradition.[12] Oddly, none of these screenwriting teachers acknowledges their indebtedness to any teachers of the silent era for laying the groundwork.

---

4   Lane, *The New Technique of Screen Writing*, vi.

5   Frances Marion, *How to Write and Sell Film Stories* (New York: Covic. Friede, 1937), 13.

6   Clara Beranger, *Writing for the Screen* (Iowa: Brown, 1950), 162.

7   Ibid., 167.

8   Both Beranger and Vale lectured on screenwriting at the University of Southern California. See 'Clara Beranger', *Women Film Pioneers Project*, https://wfpp.cdrs.columbia.edu/pioneer/ccp-clara-beranger/ and 'Eugene Vale', *IMDbPro*: https://pro-labs.imdb.com/name/nm0883884/?ref_=sch_int

9   Thompson and Bordwell, *Film History,* 32.

10   Lane, *New Technique of Screen Writing*, 3-35.

11   Marion, *How to Write and Sell Film Stories*, vii.

12   Lewis Herman, *Practical Manual of Screen Playwriting for Theatre and Television Films*, (1952: repr., New York: Meridian, 1974) 21–22; Vale, *Technique of Screenplay Writing*, 95–99; John Howard Lawson, *Theory and Technique of Playwriting and Screenwriting* (New York: Putnam's, 1949), 364; and Beranger, *Writing for the Screen*, 52–55.

In the era of the package unit system (1950/60s to the present), circumstances contrived to create conditions in some ways similar to those of the early period. Studios changed from being highly stratified entities controlling every aspect of production into operations providing contracted-out services for package-led productions. A single producer organised a film project by securing the finance, hiring the studio and outsourcing employment, including that of writers.[13] Writers were no longer on contract or being trained in-house by studio story departments and freelance writers once again had a toehold in the industry.

This shift in organisation triggered an increase in the level of activity of screenwriting teachers, which resembled that of the early period. Again, the general public was drawn in and a similar level of interest resulted – a level of interest that remains in place today. Although this phase of screenwriting history is not the primary focus of this study, it may be possible to draw out some parallels and comparisons, which may further elucidate the overall role and contribution of early screenwriting teachers to the Hollywood film industry, and throw some light on the current activity of those who have come to be known as 'screenwriting gurus'. As Allen and Gomery suggest:

> The historian's study of the past seeks to explain why a particular set of historical circumstances came about and with what consequences. The historian's interest in the past stems directly or indirectly from the belief that an understanding of the past is useful in understanding the present.[14]

By the late 1970s, a spate of manuals had been published. The most significant was Syd Field's *Screenplay: The Foundations of Screenwriting* (1979) with its focus on three-act structure.[15] Although not a new concept in this period, since Constance Nash and Virginia Oakey diagrammatically represent their 'script divisions' in this way in *The Screenwriter's Handbook* (1974),[16] Field brought it to the fore with his structural 'paradigm'. As a consequence, it popularised:

> a much more specific formulation of a 'three-act structure' […that] has become enormously influential among screenwriters, studio heads, and employees alike – so much so that the book is sometimes referred to as the 'Bible' of screenwriters.[17]

The term 'screenwriting guru' has become common parlance in the screenwriting community as a term that describes the screenwriting teachers who have been active since the 1970s. Today it continues to denote the increasing myriad of so-called experts

---

13   Bordwell, Staiger and Thompson, *Classical Hollywood Cinema*, 330 and 367.

14   Allen and Gomery, *Film History*, 6.

15   Syd Field, *Screenplay: The Foundations of Screenwriting* (New York: Dell, 1979).

16   Constance Nash and Virginia Oakey, *The Screenwriter's Handbook* (New York: Harper Perennial, 1974), 2–3.

17   Thompson, *Storytelling in the New Hollywood*, 22.

who pepper the writers' conference circuit, explaining their particular 'take' on how to write the successful screenplay. The steady publication of new manuals became a flood by the 1990s and the level of activity has still not abated. Field was soon joined by others, such as Robert McKee and Christopher Vogler (see Figure 74), who also wrote their manuals from first-hand experience as studio story analysts.[18] Their roles in this industry gave them the advantage of knowing exactly what was required, in a similar way to the studio editors of the early period.

Figure 74: Syd Field (1935–2013), Robert McKee (1941–) and Christopher Vogler (1949–)
Source: Left and right: Supplied by Aviva Field and Christopher Vogler (published with permission). Middle: *elartedepresentar.wordpress.com/tag/libros/page/3*.

The ranks have been swelled by many others, such as Lewis Hunter, Richard Walter, Linda Aronson, John Truby, Michael Hauge and Linda Seger to name but a few.

Figure 75: John Truby (1952–), Michael Hauge (1947–) and Linda Seger (1945–)
Source: Supplied by John Truby, Michael Hauge and Linda Seger (published with permission).

The demand for 'original' stories, characteristic of the early period when 'scenario fever' produced dozens of how-to books, contests and privately run screenwriting schools, had returned. As Decherney observes, 'The legacy of this culture, in which everyone

---

18 'Guru' is a term academics regularly apply to screenwriting teachers in the modern period. For example, Bordwell calls Field, McKee and Vogler, 'script gurus'. See Bordwell, *The Way Hollywood Tells it*, 28.

has a screenplay, is still with us.'[19] Dubbed by Stempel as the 'Return of the Son of Scenario Fever', it smacks of the early period, with its proliferation of manuals and private correspondence courses and the rapid rise to almost celebrity status of a number of screenwriting gurus:

> not only were there screenwriting courses in colleges and privately run schools, there were also series of weekend seminars taught by such well-known screenwriting teachers as Robert McKee and Richard Walter.[20]

The demand for the kind of services that screenwriting gurus offered may have also been fuelled by the wider cultural currency, notion or fantasy of the desire for celebrity status. The sheer pervasiveness of film and media in modern Western society and the draw of being famous for creating it cannot be overestimated. As Cooper Lawrence argues, the widespread fascination with celebrity is more than likely associated with 'our need to form bonds and social connections' in an increasingly busy and socially fragmented society.[21]

On the surface, the early period does appear to bear some likeness to what is happening today. Film had become the main entertainment medium by the late teens of the twentieth century; working in the film industry appeared glamorous and many people wanted to enter it. However, the wider social reasons that might explain this fascination with stardom might be different from those of today. As pointed out earlier, Morey puts this fascination down to a desire for personal development. She suggests this may have been stimulated by a sense of disenfranchisement on the part of those individuals who felt excluded from the dominant culture of American society.[22] Success in the film industry would provide an individual with the social capital to improve their status in this society.

The manuals of recent screenwriting gurus are written to gain the widest possible public appeal in order to sell more copies, regardless of how many readers could really write saleable scripts. Nevertheless, there is always the draw that a successful screenwriting career does pay extremely well. With this prospect, the slick presentation skills and easy-to-follow steps of the screenwriting guru explaining how to write a potential 'Hollywood blockbuster' play into that rather nebulous and evasive notion of the 'American dream'; this again is not too dissimilar to the early period, with its prospect of sudden success and wealth as America emerged as an entrepreneurial and industrial power.

---

19 Decherney, *Hollywood and the Culture Elite*, 43–44.

20 Stempel, *Framework*, 256.

21 Cooper Lawrence, *The Cult of Celebrity: What Our Fascination with Stars Reveals about Us* (Connecticut: Globe Pequot, 2009), 236–237.

22 See 19–20 and 122.

The modern screenwriting guru is a controversial figure, often viewed from a negative perspective. The very epithet 'guru' has quasi-religious connotations. Various dictionaries define a 'guru' as anything from a 'revered mentor' or 'influential teacher' to a guide in 'intellectual', 'spiritual' or 'philosophical' matters.[23] The idea of the 'guru' has enjoyed a certain cultural resonance since the 1960s when Westerners, such as the Beatles, dallied with religious mysticism. For the convinced religious adherent of some philosophies or creeds, it implied devotion to, or the following of, a particular body of instruction, and in some cases the elevation of the 'guru' to near-cult status.

The term has since been applied to other areas of knowledge and used to refer to experts in areas such as popular psychology, business practice, the 'life skills' movement and screenwriting. Such populist speakers and writers distil apparently complex notions into straightforward steps for the general public to consume. These kinds of gurus resist the idea that there are enclaves of knowledge to which only the truly initiated and trained expert has right of entry. As Tony Keily points out:

> [the] flavour comes from a whole generation of American self-help and pop psychology bestsellers. The ones that tell you, you can. You can. Stop smoking, lose weight, stop losing money on stocks, speed read, use more than 10% of your brain, be confident, swing that club like a pro, get fit, get fucked. Oh, and why not? Screenwrite.[24]

According to Kathryn Millard, screenwriting gurus and their books fit the notion of the self-styled guru and parallel many of the features of their counterparts in other fields:

> words like 'success,' 'tips' and 'techniques' all feature strongly in screenwriting books, and the language of both religion and pop psychology abounds in both screenwriting texts and seminars [...]. In a seminar that I attended in Sydney in the early 1990's, Christopher Vogler, author of *The Writer's Journey*, even advised participants to 'take the template and go out into the world. See the changes it will make in your life.' It is not that big a leap then, to view many of the (mostly North American) screenwriting books as having most value as contributions to the literature of the self-help movement.[25]

To support her contention that most screenwriting manuals strongly relate stipulated actions to particular outcomes, Millard draws on the work of psychologist Steven Starker:

---

23   For dictionary definitions, see *Oxford Dictionary* online, *Cambridge Dictionary* online, *Collins Dictionary* online, Dictionary.com and *The Free Dictionary* online.

24   Tony Keily, 'Gurus Methods Teachers'. *Film Ireland* August/September, 2001.

25   Kathryn Millard, 'Writing for the Screen: Beyond the Gospel of Story', *Journal of Media Arts Culture*, June 2006, accessed October 13, 2013, http //scan.net.au/scan/journal/display.php?journal_id=77

> The prescribed behaviours usually are linked with the presumed utility of the work by way of a simple promise: 'do this and you will get that.' Failure to achieve the desired results usually suggests that the prescribed behaviours have not been followed faithfully.[26]

Leaving aside the dubious claims that have developed alongside the self-help movement, the self-improvement culture of the early period does actually bear some resemblance to its modern-day manifestation and resonates with it. Liepa neatly draws out this connection:

> The legacy of amateur film writing, in fact, continues to loom large today with the profusion of screenplay manuals, romantic success stories of screenwriters who 'made it,' and screenwriting courses offered in colleges around the country, still promising to divine market demands and convey them to eager novices.[27]

As already noted, Morey has also demonstrated that a similar desire for self-improvement was a major theme in the handbook culture of the early period.[28] Fan press literature carried many advertisements about how to achieve success through personal development, public speaking and career progression in virtually every area, including the creative industries (see Figure 76).[29] Screenwriting advertisements were similar in their appeal, containing strong claims and promising successful outcomes (see Figures 77 and 78).[30]

The legitimate early screenwriting teachers (those recognised and accredited by the industry) had salutary remarks at the ready to prepare their prospective followers for the possibility of failure. For those who thought only of making money, Wright cautions, 'You will have to look on scenario writing as a diversion, an interesting pastime, something you can afford to entertain yourself with'.[31] Furthermore, the writing process could:

---

26   See Steven Starker, *Oracle at the Supermarket: the American Preoccupation with Self Help Books* (London: Transaction, 1989) 9–10; cited in Millard, 'Writing for the Screen', *Journal of Media Arts Culture*, June 2006.

27   Liepa, 'Entertaining the Public Option' in *Analyzing the Screenplay*, ed. Nelmes, 20.

28   Morey, *Hollywood Outsiders,* 4–22.

29   See advertisements, 'The Intense Life, The Better Life – Swoboda System of Conscious Evolution', 6–7, 'Modern Eloquence' by Geo. L. Shuman, 10, 'Become a Lawyer: We train you by Mail' – La Salle Extension University, 159 in April, 1915, *Photoplay* and 'Practical Art: You can make good at it' – Rosing School of Lettering and Design, 5, 'Travelling Men Earn Larger Salaries Than Any Other Class Of Men', National Saleman's Training Assn, 165, 'Improve your Face by Making Faces' by Professor Anthony Barker, 168 in *MPM*, August 1915.

30   See advertisements '$500 in Cash for Motion Picture Plots – How to Write Photoplays' by Elbert Moore in *Photoplay*, February 1915, 186 and 'The Art of Selling a Photoplay' – Photoplay Clearing House, in *MPM*, September 1915, 151.

31   Wright, *Photoplay Writing*, 7.

mold you and make you as no other agency will. Knowledge will come, and power will grow for you, and with knowledge and power will come a sense of responsibility for others.[32]

Strong parallels appear in Hauge's claim in 1991 that 'as long as you find the process of writing screenplays personally fulfilling, then you should keep at it'.[33] In an echo of Vogler's words (cited above), Hauge also asserted, at a seminar in 2011, that writing screenplays might even prove to be a life-changing experience, irrespective of any monetary gain.[34]

Figure 76: Some of the many fan press advertisements offering paths to self-improvement
Source: *Photoplay*, April 1915, 159 and *MPM*, August 1915, 168.

---

32 Wright, *Motion Picture Story*, 226.

33 Michael Hauge, *Writing Screenplays that Sell* (New York: Harper Collins, 1991), xx.

34 *Screenwriters' Summit* in Toronto, 2011. I attended Hauge's presentation, which ended with this message. See Toronto Screenwriters' Summit 2011 held on March 28, 2011, Hollywood University Blog, http://hollywoodu.net/2011/03/28/screenwriters-summit-2011-toronto/

Figure 77: Manual advertisement highlighting
scenario writing as a money-making venture
Source: *Photoplay*, February 1915, 186.

THE ART OF SELLING A PHOTOPLAY

A THING MORE DIFFICULT TO ACQUIRE THAN THE KNACK OF WRITING ONE

The Photoplay Clearing House Acts as Advisor, Friend and Agent in Setting You on the Right Road to Successful Scenario Writing

Established for over two years, with a record of hundreds of sales over 13,000 manuscripts reviewed, criticized and placed upon the market, the Photoplay Clearing House has become the one authoritative and reliable agent for the handling of authors' product in the Moving Picture industry. We have received over 5,000 testimonial letters; we are under the supervision of the MOTION PICTURE MAGAZINE; our business is in intimate personal touch with all of the leading photoplay manufacturers, and our staff of editors, who personally pass upon all material, consists of the following well-known photoplaywrights: Edwin M. La Roche, Henry Albert Phillips, L. Case Russell, William Lord Wright, Courtney Ryley Cooper, Dorothy Donnell, Russell E. Ball, Gladys Hall and others. In order to qualify for our reading staff of editors, it is necessary that an editor be a successful scenario writer, a fair and able critic, and a good judge of market conditions and values.

The Photoplay Clearing House was established to aid and counsel authors and to sell their wares. We believe we have given more definite help to the discouraged, have furnished more practical criticism, and have sold more photoplays at a higher price than all other similar institutions combined.

We tell you: How to Go About it, Where to Market Your Product, How to Revise and Cure its Weak Points, The Kind of Photoplays Wanted, and a hundred other details of making and selling a finished scenario.

Recent Letters from Patrons and Studios—5,000 Others on File.

Dear La Roche:
For the benefit of your readers who are scenario writers, would like to give you an idea of our needs here. Would be pleased to have submitted to me detailed synopses of any ideas you may have that would make four- or five-reel photoplays. Am particularly looking for strong material suitable for Mary Pickford, Marguerite Clark, Hazel Dawn or John Barrymore. Quick decisions will be given and payment made immediately on acceptance.

FAMOUS PLAYERS FILM CO.,
Russell E. Smith, Scenario Editor.

Photoplay Clearing House:
I beg to acknowledge herewith your check for $35.80 in full payment for my script, "Scared o' Women," sold by you to the Vitagraph Co. Please accept thanks.
You are aware that I have been for a long time much interested in the work of writing scripts, not as a vocation, nor for the check, but as a real pleasure. I shall continue to send them in to you from time to time, and assure you that I am much gratified by your very cordial treatment.

Barton, Vt. F. H. PILLSBURY.

Photoplay Clearing House:
Regarding my manuscript, "The Half Eagles," which you recently sold for me to the Biograph Co., I appreciate your work in this matter most highly, for I was about to give up in despair, until I noticed your ad in the "Motion Picture Magazine."
I fully realize that it is more difficult to sell a script than write one, because the same script was turned down by a number of companies. Also, your revision helped to land the bacon.

CHESTER B. STROBEL.
799 Lehigh St., Wilkes-Barre, Pa.

The Photoplay Clearing House:
We enclose check for $75.00 for manuscript entitled "What Happened on the Barbuda," by Willis C. Pratt, 479 W. 152d St., New York, as per contract on file.

THOMAS A. EDISON, Inc.

Photoplay Clearing House:
Your check ($31.10) for my photoplay, "The Light in the Window," sold to the Mutual Film Corporation, just received. The greatest praise I can make is to say that your ability is only equaled by your promptness. I am sending you more scenarios shortly.

Yours sincerely,
Hotel Van Nuys, SYDNEY K. RUSSELL.
Los Angeles, Cal.

Photoplay Clearing House:
We are more than busy here now, turning out some good stuff, tho material is as scarce as ever. Trusting that everything is well with the Clearing House, and hoping to have the pleasure of considering more scripts therefrom in the very near future, I am

DORIS M. SCHROEDER,
Editor, the Vitagraph Co., Western Studio.

Photoplay Clearing House:
Briefly, my object was to avoid mistakes in the future rather than negotiate sales of the plays in question. On this point your work has been of decided help to me, and I feel that the fee has brought its return already, for I have a small market, tho not a howling demand, for my work.
I hope within the near future to revise the three plays you recommend and will send them to you as soon as completed. Pray accept my thanks and appreciation.

41 Broad St., N. Y. A. L. STILLMAN.

Dear Sirs:
We are enclosing herewith the release slips for the two scenarios entitled "The Proof," by S. Y. Cooke, Elmwood Hotel, Halifax, N. S., and "Weeds," by H. F. Jamison, Alexander, Ark., made out to the amount of twenty-five dollars ($25.00) each. As per your request, we will mail the checks to you immediately upon return of these slips.

UNIVERSAL FILM MANUFACTURING COMPANY,
Scenario Dept.

THE PLAN OF THE PHOTOPLAY CLEARING HOUSE.

We are intimately connected with the Motion Picture business and in close touch with the manufacturers. We are advised of all their advance releases, their requirements and the kind of scripts they want. As suitable ones come to us, in salable shape, they are immediately sent to the proper studio. No stale, imperfect or copied plots are submitted.

All photoplaywrights are invited to send their Plays to this company, advising as to what manufacturers they have been previously submitted, if any. Every Play will be treated thus:

It will be read by competent photoplay editors, numbered, classified and filed. If it is, in our opinion, in perfect condition, we shall at once proceed to market it, and when we are paid for it, we will pay the writer 90% of the amount we receive, less postage expended. If the Scenario is not in marketable shape, we will so advise the author, stating our objections in detail, offering to return it at once, or to revise, typewrite and try to market it. IF THE MANUSCRIPT IS HOPELESS, WE SHALL SO STATE, and in some cases advise a course of instruction, naming various books, experts and schools to select from.

Fee for reading, detailed, general criticism and filing, $1.00 (multiple reels, 50c. per reel extra). For typewriting, a charge of $1.00 for each Play will be made, provided it does not run over 10 pages. 10c. a page for extra pages. The fee for revising will vary according to work required, and will be arranged in advance. No Scenarios will be placed by us unless they are properly typewritten. Payment in advance is expected in all cases. RETURN POSTAGE SHOULD BE INCLUDED, and foreign contributors should allow for U. S. exchange. Enclose P.O. order, stamps, checks, or money with manuscripts. 1c. stamps accepted.

PHOTOPLAY CLEARING HOUSE, 175 Duffield Street, Brooklyn, N. Y.

Figure 78: Clearing house advertisement highlighting scenario writing as a money-making venture
Source: *MPM*, September 1915, 151.

The work of modern screenwriting gurus is often dismissed by industry figures, including working screenwriters, as irrelevant. A number of successful screenwriters have been highly critical of screenwriting gurus and rarely admit to owing any of their understanding or craft to them. The rather jaundiced view of the highly successful Lee Hall, writer of *Billy Elliot* (2000) and *Gabriel and Me* (2001), is typical of many:

> I spent about six months [...] reading all those 'How to Write a Screenplay' books [...]. They're both useful and complete rubbish. All they actually say is a screenplay should have a beginning, a middle and an end – in that order. The rest is filler, really.[35]

Further criticism comes from Scott Myers, whose credits include *K-9* (1989), *Alaska* (1996) and *K-9: P.I.* (2002). Screenwriting gurus' emphasis on structure over other storytelling elements, he claims, has led to formulaic stories, thinly drawn characters, and narratives without emotional resonance. For him, becoming a screenwriter means:

> striving to learn the craft day in and day out [...;] it takes time, it takes work, it takes immersing oneself in the world of cinema, it takes reading hundreds of scripts, watching thousands of movies.[36]

Although his list of activities sounds very similar to those that the early key screenwriting teachers advocated as a means of learning the craft, Myers remains negative about modern screenwriting gurus. He quotes Frank Darabont, writer of *The Shawshank Redemption* (1994) and *The Green Mile* (1999), who he claims crystallises his thoughts on this:

> Everybody wants to hear, 'I can teach you a three-act structure. I can give you a formula, and you'll be selling screenplays within six months.' Bullshit. And what's really funny is, these guys in the business of being screenwriting gurus, they don't ever write screenplays. I have never seen one of these guys' names on a screen credit.[37]

Such comments indicate that these screenwriters have at least accessed or referred to these books during their careers, even though they are so critical of them. We can speculate that inexperienced writers may initially seek out as much help as they can get; however, once they have achieved success, it is not inconceivable that they may be less willing to give any credit or acknowledgement to anything or anyone that may have aided them along the way. After all, it may make them appear less creative and kill the commonly held myth that such abilities cannot be taught. Perhaps it may lead to a loss of respect and admiration for their own work.

---

35   Cited in Alistair Owen, ed., *Story and Character – Interviews with British Screenwriters* (London: Bloomsbury, 2003), 40–41.

36   Cited in Christopher Boone, 'How I Really Feel About Screenwriting Gurus: Courtesy of Frank Darabont and Scott Myers', *No Film School*, July 23, 2012, http://nofilmschool.com/2012/07/screenwriting-gurus-frank-darabont-scott-myers

37   Ibid.

In discussing his screenwriting career with the late William Froug, Dan O'Bannon, whose credits include *Alien* (1979) and *Total Recall* (1990), joins the criticism of screenwriting gurus: 'What there is out there is usually how to do the format. Most of what is written about how to write a screenplay is written by people who don't know how.'[38] Ironically, Froug was regarded as a screenwriting guru himself and had given many seminars and written extensively on how to write screenplays.[39] For his part, however, Froug tended to play down this role and highlight his standing as an industry insider and Emmy-nominated screenwriter instead.[40] His seminars and writings indicate that he did not wish to be categorised with other screenwriting gurus, was dismissive of them and regarded them with suspicion. This was because either he genuinely believed that most of them had never had any significant success as screenwriters or he thought it might damage his own status as a screenwriter.[41]

This brings me to a vital point. Although it is probably true that some modern screenwriting gurus have never written a successful screenplay, or worked effectively as professionals in the film industry, this is certainly not the whole story. Modern screenwriting gurus have no pedigree in common. A number have come from the ranks of story editors and analysts, creative producers and, most importantly, writers, some of whom do have impressive screenwriting credits.[42] This bears some resemblance to the early period, in which the key screenwriting teachers generally had an impressive industry track record, but those on the periphery were more mixed in their levels of experience and industry recognition.

Many successful writers admit that, at some point, they have signed up to a screenwriting seminar or read a 'how to' book. The gurus cite many endorsements from named writers,

---

38   Cited in William Froug, *The New Screenwriter Looks at the New Screenwriter* (Los Angeles: Silman-James, 1992), 59. Froug could be dubbed as a 'guru' as his book sold well and his screenwriting seminars were well attended.

39   See Froug, *Screenwriting Tricks of the Trade* (Los Angeles: Silman-James, 1993). The hyperbolic claims on the book jacket confirm his status in the community of screenwriting gurus. Hunter (himself a 'script guru') gushes praise in claiming Froug is 'THE premiere screenwriting teacher in the history of motion pictures'.

40   Froug is best known for his TV series *The Twilight Zone* (1959–64) and *Bewitched* (1964–72), which was Emmy-nominated in 1967. See 'William Froug', *IMDbPro*: https://pro-labs.imdb.com/name/nm0296618/?ref_=sch_int

41   Froug, 'Screenwriting Tricks of the Trade – The Workshop', *Writers Audio Shop* (Allen: Timberwolf Press, 1993).

42   Many of the current screenwriting gurus such as Hunter, Vogler, McKee and Field have impressive screenwriting, producing or acting credits. However, Truby, who was a story analyst and wrote *The Anatomy of Story* (London: Faber and Faber, 2007), has only one writer/director screen credit, *All American Boy* (2003), as does Hauge for *Hoops & Yoyo's Haunted Halloween* (2012). See *IMDbPro*: https://pro-labs.imdb.com

who each claim they have been helped by a particular guru's 'take' on screenwriting.[43] For many, it seems to have become a 'rite of passage' to attend the three-day 'Story' seminar led by McKee, whose profile as a screenwriting guru is illustrated by his presence as a character in the Oscar-winning film *Adaptation* (2002) written by Charlie Kaufman. Many of the same prospective writers will be found at a whole barrage of conferences led by leading gurus as they tour the main European and American cities.[44] Their manuals have sold extremely well too; Field's *Screenplay* tops the list, with over half a million copies sold over four editions.[45]

In contrast to those discussed so far, some contemporary successful screenwriters do acknowledge the contributions of screenwriting gurus. For example, Jim Sheridan, whose credits include *My Left Foot* (1989), *In the Name of the Father* (1993) and *The Boxer* (1997), observes:

> Film is a time medium and the job of the writer is to create emotions which the audience responds to in a time structure. People like Syd Field […] have examined this structure, showing how Hollywood movies tend to follow the traditional three acts […]. It works with audiences because they are used to the pattern and they feel safe with it […]. A writer must manipulate the story within the conventional structure while trying to make it seem unconventional and unexpected to the audience.[46]

Out of all this discussion, one thing is clear: the presence of screenwriting gurus as an adjunct to Hollywood and the views they hold provoke a wide range of reactions. Screenwriting gurus have been variously associated with encouraging formulaic output from Hollywood and offering simplistic writing solutions. It may well be asked whether, having inspired such ire, a significant number of them are simply opportunists, out to

---

43 McKee is endorsed by two-time Oscar winner William Goldman and by Ed Saxon, Oscar-winning producer of *Silence of the Lambs* (1991). See *Robert McKee* website, http://mckeestory.com. Truby is endorsed by Jeff Arch, who was Oscar-nominated for *Sleepless in Seattle* (1993), and by the five times Emmy-nominated Richard Kramer. See *John Truby* website, 'Endorsements', *The Anatomy of Story Master Class*, http://trubywriting.com/node/10. Hauge is endorsed by Shane Black, whose credits include *Lethal Weapon* (1987, 1989 and 1992), and by Terry Rossio, whose credits include *Shrek* (2001 and 2004) and *Pirates of the Caribbean* (2003, 2006, 2007 and 2017). See Michael Hauge, *Story Mastery*, http://www.storymastery.com. Vogler is endorsed by Darren Aronofsky, Oscar-nominated for *Black Swan* (2010), and by Bruce Joel Rubin, who won the Oscar for *Ghost* (1990). See Christopher Vogler, *The Essence of Storytelling*, http://www.christophervogler.com

44 The Screenwriters Summit features leading screenwriting gurus such as Truby, Vogler, Hauge and Seger in joint conferences in many cities across the world; see Final Draft Newsletter for 2014 conference, http://newsletter.finaldraft.com/newsletter-20140123_WritersSummit.html. I have attended conferences led by Field, Truby and McKee and met many of the same writers trawling the conference circuit.

45 McKee, *Story* is in its 19th US and 14th UK printing; Vogler, *The Writer's Journey* has sold 200,000 copies over two US editions and Seger, *Making a Good Script Great* had sold 250,000 copies by 2006. See Conor, *Screenwriting: Creative Labor and Professional Practice*, 132.

46 Declan McGrath and Felim MacDermott, *Screencraft – Screenwriting* (Switzerland: RotoVision, 2003), 54.

make money from desperate 'wannabees' unlikely to ever write a successful screenplay, or they are in large part professional teachers who are making a significant contribution to the screenwriting community. Despite the controversy around their work, they remain well known and their popular appeal has not waned.

In contrast, and unjustifiably, the early key screenwriting teachers have become a footnote in screenwriting history, although this book is part of my effort to rectify their status. Their virtual omission from the historical record is certainly not deserved, as these screenwriting teachers came from the writing community and were highly regarded in their day. Admittedly, the many correspondence schools and clearing houses were generally run by charlatans, but these were vilified by the industry, including by the people we might term the 'genuine' teachers. Successful screenwriter Jeanie Macpherson writes positively about the contribution of screenwriting teachers in 1922:

> The fundamentals of screen technique, though not the creative 'spark,' can be learned from books and competent teachers – and the best way in the world to learn to apply these principles is by learning to write salable screen stories.[47]

However, by this time the fate of the early screenwriting teacher had been sealed. Peacocke states in his regular column for *Photoplay* that 'it is difficult to predict what the future of the moving picture industry is going to bring forth'.[48] Recognising himself as a man of his time, he acknowledges that, as the film industry was constantly changing, it was difficult to know what would happen next. Nevertheless, he remains optimistic about the future:

> There will shortly be a wild scramble for original photoplays [read screenplays] written especially for the screen by writers who are thoroughly capable and who have a virile imagination.[49]

His forecasts about the prospects for the freelance writer at that time did not come true once the studio system was established. With the reduced need for instruction came not only the disappearance of the key screenwriting teachers from the scene, but also their virtual obliteration from the historical record. Ironically, the rise of independent production, decades later, has made Peacocke's predictions sound strangely modern, as today's freelance writers also buy into a probably mythic bonanza of writing opportunities.

Similarly the issue of whether screenwriting gurus are teaching an art or a craft continues to permeate the debate today, because the dichotomised intellectual constructs of 'art' and 'craft' that Shiner identified are still in play. Interestingly, Truby responds to Darabont's criticisms (cited above) about screenwriting gurus in an interview:

---

47   Macpherson, 'Functions of the Continuity Writer' in *Opportunities in the Motion Picture Industry*, 33.

48   Peacocke, 'The Scenario Writer and the Director', *Photoplay*, May 1917, 112.

49   Peacocke, 'Hints on Photoplay Writing', *Photoplay*, January 1916, 124.

> I'm not teaching them the art of writing, nobody can teach them that [...] [W]hat I'm trying to do is teach all these craft elements, these techniques which are very useful. [referring to Darabont ...] What they don't admit or tell you is that they have quite a background of craft technique that they know [possibly due to] natural storytelling ability and through the practice of writing they have developed these techniques.[50]

The art–craft issue is the crux of the continual debate over whether these individuals' work is worthwhile. Truby's attempt to negotiate this issue in his answer is a strong example of the continuity between the early screenwriting teachers and today's screenwriting gurus in trying to articulate how far screenwriting can be taught, if it is not exclusively a lofty gift. As Conor points out, these continued tensions play into a 'wider battle for legitimacy that dominates the subsequent discourse about screenwriting as a new but marginal literary form'. As screenwriters sit between the worlds of literature/theatre and filmmaking, it has led to 'wider debates on familiar polarizing terrain: art versus commerce, craft versus creativity, artist versus hack'.[51] Screenwriting teachers of the past and their modern counterparts, the screenwriting gurus, will continue to be embroiled in these controversies.

The modern freelance writer seeks practical instruction in a similar way to the amateur writers of the early period. While the contextual differences are significant, many of the maxims and concerns of those early screenwriting teachers still resonate in the platitudes and advice of the modern screenwriting gurus. This guidance presents an interesting connection between today's screenwriting gurus and the screenwriting teachers of the past in terms of their activity and role. Early screenwriting teachers coached prospective writers on how to train for, write for and sell to the industry – three concerns that form the basis of instruction of modern screenwriting gurus.

Training for the Industry

Modern screenwriting gurus encourage prospective screenwriters to read and study successful screenplays, which are widely available in book form and on the Internet. They also stipulate that writers should watch as many films as possible to analyse their content and structure. These gurus regularly lead seminars and speak at conferences and festivals for the uninitiated.[52] In addition, a great deal of information is now available on

---

50 Truby, 'Thoughts on Screenwriting Gurus' on *YouTube*, https://www.youtube.com/watch?v=k267ReHztF4

51 Conor, *Screenwriting*, 19.

52 For example, most of the seminars at the London Screenwriters Festival in 2010, 2011, 2013 and 2014 (at which I was a delegate) focused particularly on how to successfully write, promote and sell your screenplay. This event has grown to be the largest screenwriting festival in the world. See http://www.londonscreenwritersfestival.com

the Internet.[53] Web-based instruction has also become highly popular.[54] Hauge's advice has a similar ring to that of early screenwriting teachers, as he encourages his followers to 'establish a writing regimen', 'immerse [themselves] in the movies' and 'join a writer's group'.[55]

The key early screenwriting teachers likewise encouraged their followers to spend time at the cinema and to analyse films. They recommended their own manuals and columns in the fan and trade press as the main source of screenwriting guidance. Lecture-style public instruction was generally only given in the college context, in which Phillips was certainly involved.[56] The key screenwriting teachers, Sargent in particular, described the process of film production in great detail – from the acquisition of a scenario right through to the final exhibition of the product – because public knowledge about how films were made was more limited in the early period.[57]

Writing for the Industry

The best known of the recent screenwriting gurus is probably the late Syd Field, who is widely known for his 'script paradigm'. Correspondingly, Sargent was certainly the most prominent of the screenwriting teachers of the early period and is frequently referred to in past and present academic discourse. A straight comparison of their descriptions of the nature of the screenplay may seem simplistic, but it is rather revealing. Field states:

> A screenplay is a story told with pictures, in dialogue and description, and placed within the context of dramatic structure.[58]

---

53   For example, Kathie Fong Yoneda offers step-by-step information on essentials such as creating log lines, compelling pitches and effective marketing techniques through her seminars and her best-selling book, *The Script-selling Game* (Los Angeles: Michael Wiese, 2002), http://www.kathiefongyoneda.com. Two successful Hollywood screenwriters, Robin U. Russin and William Missouri Downs, offer advice from experience on how to write and market scripts in *Screenplay: Writing the Picture* (Los Angeles: Silman-James, 2003), Preface.

54   Advertisement for a 'webinar' with Corey Mandell, who teaches at UCLA, called 'The Insider View: How the Pros Rewrite with Corey Mandell' Sept 25, 2012. 'Screenwriter Corey Mandell reveals the secrets the pros use to rewrite their scripts'. He begins, 'Professional writers know how to rewrite while most amateurs do not. Too many writers rewrite their scripts over and over without really improving it.' Advertised through *Final Draft*, http://www.finaldraft.com and http://coreymandell.net

55   Hauge, *Writing Screenplays that Sell*, 269–272.

56   Sargent, 'The Photoplaywright', *MPW*, March 25, 1916, 2001.

57   Azlant, 'Theory, History and Practice of Screenwriting', 218–219.

58   Field, *Screenplay*, 19–20.

Peculiarly, this language is reminiscent of Sargent's comment that:

> A story is the narration of events in words. Done into dialogue and actions, it becomes a drama. [...] The photoplay then, becomes a story told in actions and therefore it is written in action instead of dialogue or polished phrase.[59]

While the structural similarity of this prose may be entirely coincidental, or may arise because the two authors are discussing the same core aspect of the medium, it is not beyond the realm of possibility that Field actually read Sargent's book. Sadly, it is too late to establish definitively whether he did.

As well as being criticised by academics and some industry professionals for the formulaic content of their teaching, modern screenwriting gurus are noted for drawing heavily upon, in Thompson's words, 'the basic techniques of classical storytelling – or at least what Hollywood practitioners think those techniques are'.[60] Leaving aside the question of whether modern gurus follow these 'techniques' precisely, both Bordwell and Thompson agree that these principles, which they view as core components of 'classical Hollywood cinema', were set down by the late teens of last century.[61] However, as previous chapters have demonstrated, what scholars seem to have overlooked is that the key screenwriting teachers made a significant contribution to refining, solidifying and confirming these principles during the early period. This perspective puts a new light on comments by academics, such as Nannicelli, about how contemporary practice follows these principles, indicating that these particular teachers were among the significant parties actually involved in achieving this connection:

> contemporary Hollywood screenwriting practice largely adheres to the fundamental narrative principles regarding causality, clarity, coherence and unity, as well as more specific standards with respect to plot structure, conflict and character development.[62]

Similarly, if we examine Bordwell's points about the fine-tuning process that occurred to produce these industry norms, it should be recognised that these key screenwriting teachers contributed at least in part to that process, rather than only 'Hollywood filmmakers':

> As feature films became standardized, *Hollywood filmmakers* established firmer guidelines for creating intelligible plots. These guidelines have changed little

---

59   Sargent, 'Technique of the Photoplay', *MPW*, July 22, 1911, 108.

60   Thompson, *Storytelling in the New Hollywood*, 11.

61   Bordwell and Thompson, *Film History,* 32.

62   Nannicelli, *Philosophy of the Screenplay*, 106.

since then. Hollywood plots consist of clear chains of causes and effects, and most of these involve character psychology (as opposed to social or natural forces) [emphasis added].[63]

The key screenwriting teachers gave detailed advice on plotting and character development, as previous chapters have confirmed, and placed great stress on the importance of continuity:

> Modern continuity editing, on which the classical Hollywood system was based (and which still predominates today), began when they realized that action could be made to seem continuous from shot to shot.[64]

Chapter 6 has set out how the manuals of the key screenwriting teachers describe in great detail this shot-to-shot process through the use of 'busts', 'close-ups', 'cut-backs' and 'leaders' in order to achieve an unbroken narrative that cumulatively builds towards a satisfying climax and resolution. This series of events usually focuses on a single character with a specific and defined goal, while all other characters are meant to be completely understandable and distinct. In her manual, Patterson advises that only characters with 'pre-eminent cinematic qualities should be chosen',[65] which, for silent cinema, meant that they were not defined by dialogue but by their visual attributes. As writers mentally visualise the story, Sargent states, they 'do not have to write all the action [they] see, but only the action that helps to tell the story'.[66] In this schema, an 'inciting incident' must start the action and everything will revolve around a single conflict that is integrally linked to this incident. It is crucial that the writer can express the 'plot of action' in plain and understandable language. Simplifying the plot of the single reel, Ball considers that it can be summed up as 'one line of action' that the central character must follow,[67] but this has become true of the feature too.

The parallel is evident in Hauge's argument that every story can be reduced to a single sentence: 'It is a story about [character] who wants to [action or goal].'[68] Likewise, Bordwell and Thompson's summing up of the modern screenwriting gurus' 'take' on plot and character is almost identical to that of the key early screenwriting teachers:

> Each major character is given a set of comprehensible consistent traits. The Hollywood protagonist is typically goal-oriented, trying to achieve success in work, sports, or some other activity. The hero's goal conflicts with the desires of

---

63   Bordwell and Thompson, *Film History*, 59.

64   Cook, *History of Narrative Film*, 22.

65   Patterson, *Cinema Craftsmanship*, 2nd ed. (New York: Harcourt and Brace, 1921), 68.

66   Sargent, *Technique of the Photoplay* 2nd ed., 81.

67   Ball, *Art of the Photoplay*, 35.

68   Hauge, *Writing Screenplays that Sell*, 25.

other characters, creating a struggle that is resolved only at the end – which is typically a happy one. Hollywood films usually intensify interest by presenting two interdependent plot lines. Almost inevitably one these involves romance, which gets woven in with the protagonist's quest to achieve a goal. The plot also arouses suspense through deadlines, escalating conflicts, and last minute rescues.[69]

Compare the above statements with Phillips's observations, which have a contemporary ring to them:

> The hero sets out to reach his goal, but pressure from the sidelines hampers his progress at every step. The pressure increases as he nears the apex, near where it is so great that something must break in order that he may reach his goal. As the moment of the inevitable Big Collision approaches, our suspense increases. We call the Collision, the Climax.[70]

If what Phillips calls melodramatic is added, romance is introduced into the mix:

> [And] what a handsome, virtuous Hero he is and what blood-curdling perils he has gone through single-handed to woo and win the woman he loves.[71]

The connection between early screenwriting teachers and modern screenwriting gurus is clear from Bordwell's ready acknowledgement that the content of modern screenwriting manuals is a 'consolidation of studio-era principles [which] nicely exemplif[y] how modern American moviemaking pays its tribute to tradition'.[72] What he does not go on to recognise is that this tradition was probably in large part established, disseminated and refined by the key screenwriting teachers of the early period. This study contends that the contribution of these key screenwriting teachers should now be emphatically acknowledged and plainly stated. The adjustment to the discourse may be subtle, but omitting it skews the argument and fails to give the key early screenwriting teachers the place in screenwriting history that is justified by the evidence presented here.

Another important connection not generally acknowledged by the screenwriting gurus of today is that, as Nannicelli points out, 'classical Hollywood screenwriting practice has its roots in late-nineteenth and early-twentieth century playwriting practice'.[73] Although Dallas contends that the current manual writers have distanced themselves from former dramatic theorists such as Freytag and Archer, he picks up on this point – but for the wrong reason. Modern gurus ignore these theorists, he argues, because the early screenwriting teachers/theorists had spurned them too:

---

69   Bordwell and Thompson, *Film History*, 59.

70   Phillips, *Feature Photoplay*, 115.

71   Ibid., 70.

72   Bordwell, *The Way Hollywood Tells It*, 27.

73   Nannicelli, *Philosophy of the Screenplay*, 106.

> The fact that the photoplay theorists [presumably, he also means teachers] moved away from academic sources and even suggested that academic training was not required to write the photoplay could be why scholars like Archer and Freytag disappeared from the discussion and debate of dramatic principles.[74]

Certainly it is an important point that the modern screenwriting gurus may be disassociating themselves from the academic community and dramatic theorists of the past. However, as previous chapters have shown, the early manual writers regularly referred to Archer and other play theorists. Moreover, screenwriting teachers like Sargent and Wright also had strong links with academic film theorists of the time, such as Freeburg and Münsterberg, and recommended their works as part of the library of the scenario writer. On the other hand, Dallas makes a pertinent point about how the modern screenwriting gurus are fixated with Aristotle as their main inspiration:

> They all cite Aristotle's *Poetics* as their source for the dramatic principles essential to script development, but fail to credit any other theorists for establishing any rules for dramatic writing over the last 2500 years. These theorists suggest they have merely taken Aristotle's fundamental principles and adapted and expanded them for the cinema.[75]

The key early screenwriting teachers understood the connections between scenario writing and playwriting and were involved in adapting stage technique and the conventions of the playwright to film writing. Perhaps if modern screenwriting gurus acknowledged that they also draw on this broader theatrical tradition, rather than just continually citing Aristotle as their source, they would attract more respect. This link was certainly understood by manual writers in the studio era, such as Lane, Vale and Herman, all of whom acknowledge their debt to the stage play as a form. The first part of Lawson's manual on playwriting forms the foundation for his understanding of screenwriting. Vale also refers to Aristotle's ideas as the mainstay of dramatic construction, and Beranger quotes Aristotle on 'Unity of Action'.[76] In addition, however, Beranger cites Freytag in support of her views about conflict driving the action to the point of 'crisis' and how this is 'diagrammed as a pyramid'; and she quotes Archer as an authority on more than one occasion.[77] The dependency of today's screenwriting practice on a playwriting tradition that extends far beyond the bounds of Aristotle seems to be entirely lost on recent screenwriting gurus, even though studio-era screenwriting teachers clearly acknowledged it.

---

74 Dallas, 'Play, Photoplay, and Screenplay Structure', 75.

75 Ibid., 1.

76 Lane, *New Technique of Screen Writing*, 22; Vale, *Technique of Screenplay Writing*, 95–99; Herman, *Practical Manual of Screen Playwriting for Theatre and Television Films*, 7–8; Lawson, *Theory and Technique of Playwriting and Screenwriting*, 1–302; and Beranger, *Writing for the Screen*, 69 and 100.

77 Beranger, *Writing for the Screen*, 105, 108 and 113–114.

Dallas correctly points out that modern 'instruction manuals are a valuable resource for tracing dramatic principles'.[78] However, it is important not to assume that the use of principles proves a source or connection. A short survey of the views of modern screenwriting gurus on principles such as 'unity of action', 'probability of action' and three-act structure may indicate how indebted they are to this playwriting tradition, especially as expressed in Freytag's codification. Such connections may also help link them with the key early screenwriting teachers, who helped to re-order these dramatic principles for the film medium for the first time.

With regard to 'unity of action', Freytag states that:

> the action must move forward with uniform consistency. This internal consistency is produced by representing an event which follows another, as an effect of which that other is the evident cause [...]. Through the motives [of the characters], the elements of the action are bound into an artistic, connected whole.[79]

Field echoes this advice:

> You've got to be on track every step of the way; every scene, every fragment, must be taking you somewhere, moving you forward in terms of story development.[80]

On 'probability of action', Freytag also requires that in the drama, 'all the accessory inventions, are conceived as probable and credible motives of the represented events'.[81] Similarly Hauge states, 'In order to maintain maximum emotional involvement by your reader, your story must be logical and believable with its own set of rules.'[82]

How similar Field's paradigm and Hauge's diagram are to Freytag's pyramidal structure on three-act structure (Figure 79) is striking, as the following three figures illustrate.

---

78 Dallas 'Play, Photoplay, and Screenplay Structure', 72.

79 Freytag, *Technique of the Drama*, 29.

80 Field, *The Screenwriter's Workbook* (New York: Dell Publishing, 1984), 12.

81 Freytag, *Technique of the Drama*, 49–50.

82 Hauge, *Writing Screenplays that Sell*, 99.

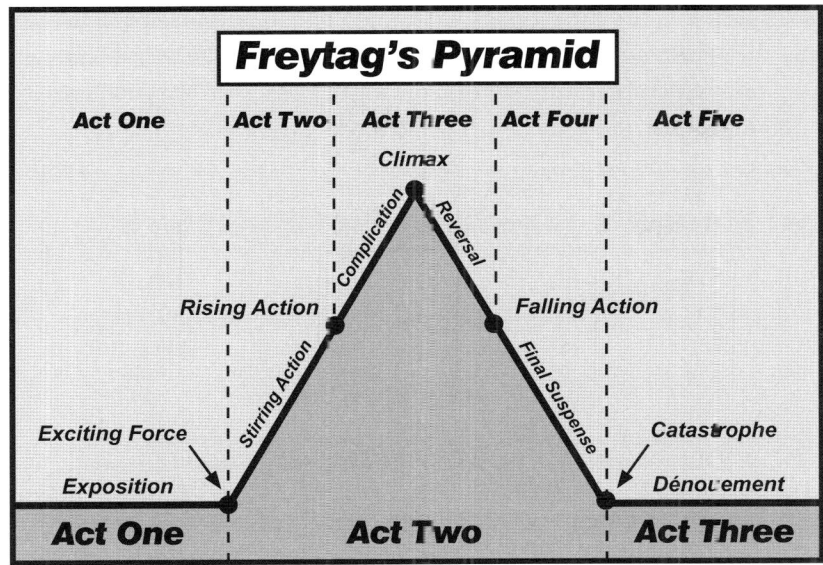

Figure 79: Comparing early and modern plot structures: Freytag's pyramid
Source: Adapted from *archive.org/details/freytagtechniqu00frey/page/115.*

Field's paradigm (Figure 80) matches Freytag's three crises (Figure 79): the 'Exciting Force' is the inciting incident or plot point 1; the 'Tragic Moment' is the midpoint or plot point 2; and the 'Force of Final Suspense' is plot point 3.[83]

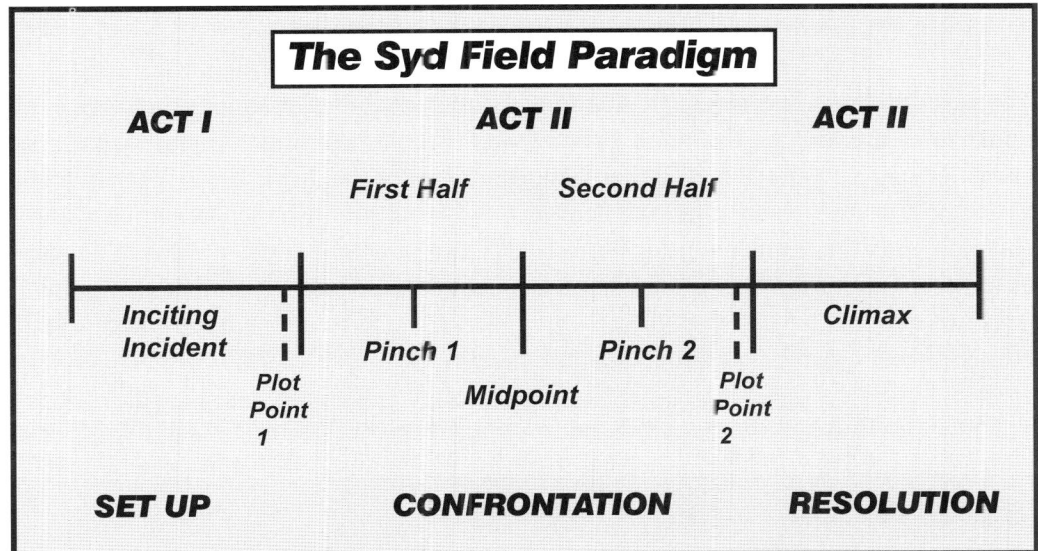

Figure 80: Comparing early and modern plot structures: Field's paradigm
Source: Adapted from *commons.wikimedia.org/wiki/File:Outline_the_Syd_Field_Paradigm.jpg.*

---

83 Chris Huntley, 'How and Why Dramatica is Different from Six Other Story Paradigms (revised July 2007)'. See Dramatica, accessed April 6, 2014, http://dramatica.com/articles/how-and-why-dramatica-is-different-from-six-other-story-paradigms

In Hauge's diagram (Figure 81), the three crises are termed turning points – specifically the 'Change of Plans,' the 'Point of No Return' and the 'Major Setback'. Despite having two additional turning points, 'Opportunity' in first act and 'Climax' in the final act, the overall structure is fundamentally the same.[84]

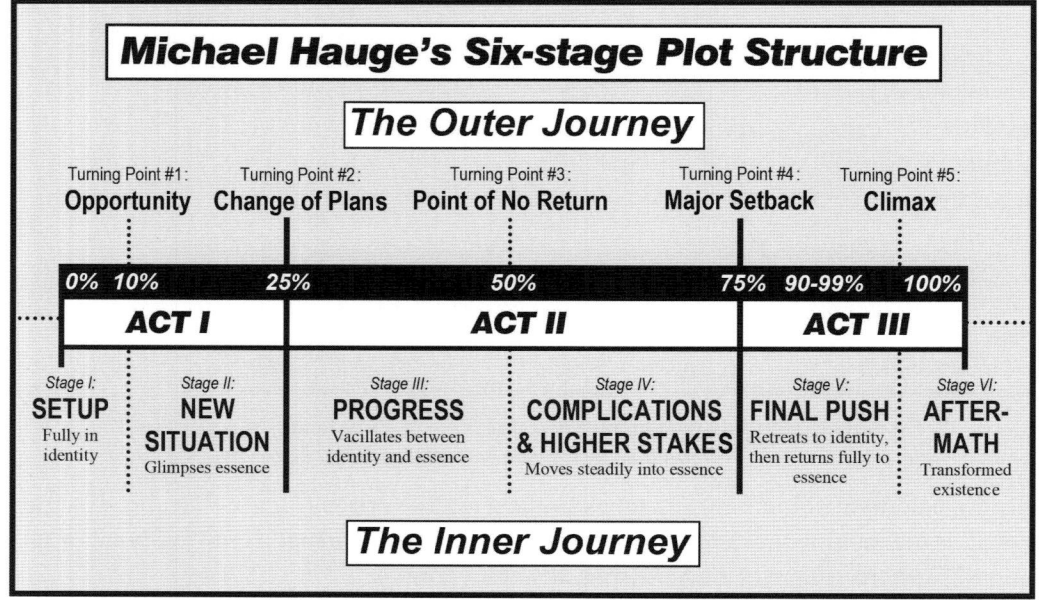

Figure 81: Comparing early and modern plot structures: Hauge's diagram
Source: *Published with permission*, Michael Hauge *storymastery.com*.

The descriptions of the three acts that Field, Hauge and other prominent screenwriting gurus offer are also in line with Freytag's. In the introduction, Freytag defines the characters and situations. In a similar vein, Hunter states the 'beginning, is the situation. The idea.'[85] Hauge claims that 'the goal of Act 1 is to establish the setting, characters, situation and outer motivation for the hero'.[86] This motivation, which Freytag refers to as the 'exciting force',[87] is what Field connects to the end of Act One or plot point 1. According to Field, 'a plot point [is] – an incident, episode, or event that "hooks" into the action and spins it around into another direction'.[88]

Just as in Freytag's pyramid, Hauge explains, 'the goal of Act 2 is to build the hurdles, obstacles, conflicts, suspense, pace, humor, character development, and character

---

84 Ibid.

85 Lew Hunter, *Screenwriting 434* (New York: Perigree, 1993), 20.

86 Hauge, *Writing Screenplays that Sell*, 86.

87 Freytag, *Technique of the Drama*, 121.

88 Field, *Screenwriter's Workbook*, 31.

revelations'.'[89] To Hunter, this act comprises simply 'the complications'.[90] Both Field and Hauge, like Freytag, break the second act into two parts at the midpoint. As Field describes it, 'The midpoint is a link in the chain of dramatic action, it connects the first half of Act II with the second half.'[91] He further claims that he found the midpoint on his own by reading thousands of screenplays. This is possible but, as Dallas points out, he seems to have merely 'rediscovered what Freytag identified more than a hundred years before Field's book was published'.[92]

Moving on to Act Three, Freytag's characterisation of it as the 'Catastrophe' finds a similar idea in Field's questions about the climax: 'What happens to your main character? Does he live or die? Succeed or fail?'[93] Other echoes of early theorists are in Hauge's succinct description that 'the goal of Act 3 is to resolve everything, particularly the outer motivation and the conflict for the hero'[94] and in Hunter's terms: the 'conclusion' or 'catharsis' or 'wrap up'.[95]

One possible reason why current screenwriting gurus fail to mention the richness of the playwriting tradition and earlier theorists, such as Freytag, is that twentieth-century theatre built up a degree of hostility towards Freytag's codified structures and the Aristotelian model. Traces of this attitude appear in Archer's advocacy of a more organic approach to structure:

> the modern tendency to take lightly Aristotle's demand that the drama should have a 'beginning, a middle, and an end' arises from the nature of things, and implies, not […] a decline in craftsmanship, but a new intimacy of relation to life, and a new sincerity of artistic conscience.[96]

Considering that Freytag applied rigid rules, Archer rejected his 'five-act dogma [where] each act was supposed to have its special and pre-ordained function' in favour of a more experimental and exploratory approach.[97] As theatre abandoned more codified approaches, at the same time screenwriting teachers began to see screenwriting as a separate art form with its own dramatic rules. In 1937 Marion writes, 'Though any form of dramatics may be an art rather than a science, at present the film story comes nearer

---

89 Hauge, *Writing Screenplays that Sell*, 36.

90 Hunter, *Screenwriting 434*, 20.

91 Field, *Screenwriter's Workbook*, 139.

92 Dallas, 'Play, Photoplay, and Screenplay Structure', 62.

93 Field, *Screenwriter's Workbook*, 177.

94 Hauge, *Writing Screenplays that Sell*, 36.

95 Hunter, *Screenwriting 434*, 20.

96 Archer, *Play-making*, 246–247.

97 Ibid., 145.

to being written to formula than does any other type of writing.'[98] At this point, Marion seems to cling to a more formulaic approach reminiscent of earlier theatrical forms, as do other studio-era teachers who mention Aristotle and Freytag in their writings. More recent screenwriting gurus also appear to adhere to a more formulaic theatrical approach to screenplay structure, as noted above, but have dropped any mention of the historical connection.

One minor exception is perhaps the continual reference to Lajos Egri (1888–1967), a playwright and teacher who wrote *The Art of Dramatic Writing* (1948). According to Hunter, this text is the 'second Holy Treatise'.[99] Egri's detailed treatment of character, which he – like Aristotle – does not regard as secondary to plot, is reminiscent of Archer's objection to Aristotle's elevation of plot over character.[100] However, the deeper reasons for severing the theatrical connection can only be noted, as a full investigation of this subject is beyond the scope of this study.

Whatever the reasons, this approach obscures how recent screenwriting gurus actually stand in a clear and unbroken dramatic and theatrical tradition. Notably, however, it is not a tradition of theatre in the modern era: most plays from the twentieth century onwards appear to break into two parts as designated by the interval and it is not always easy to detect three acts. The Hollywood film industry appears to have appropriated a nineteenth-century model and continued with it while modern theatre branched off into more experimental forms. Recent screenwriting gurus do not acknowledge this connection, but only appear to have rediscovered Aristotle in the spirit of some kind of modern classical renaissance.

They have another important connection with the playwriting tradition of the past. Those who wrote playwriting manuals were very aware of the importance of emotionally engaging the audience, as Archer confirms: 'the dramatic quality of an incident is proportionate to the variety and intensity of the emotions involved in it'.[101] Price also draws attention to the requirement for it to lead to emotional conflict:

> The heart of the dramatic is emotion and that action which springs from or leads to a clash of personal interests that by incertitude of incident proceeds to a final result. [102]

Across a century of writing for film, screenwriting teachers have recognised that the cinematic experience has the power to absorb and involve the viewer in a unique visual

---

98   Marion, *How to Write and Sell Film Stories,* 22–23.

99   Hunter, *Screenwriting 434*, 7.

100   Lajos Egri, *The Art of Dramatic Writing* (New York: Simon and Schuster, 1946), 32–124.

101   Archer, *Play-making*, 76.

102   Price, *Technique of the Drama*, 5.

form of storytelling. In a darkened space, the viewer can feel involved, as they are drawn into the story by identifying with the main character in a seamless flow of action in conflict with the opponent. Hence, for the modern screenwriting guru, it is crucial that the viewer experiences emotions. Hauge sums this up as the main purpose of a screenplay:

> All filmmakers, therefore have a single goal: to elicit emotion in an audience [… and] when the movie creates that emotion in an audience it is successful; when it doesn't, it fails.[103]

He also emphasises the centrality of emotion in the script when he links it to conflict: 'I don't think I have ever said that emotion IS conflict. But I repeatedly preach that emotion *grows out of* conflict.'[104] As stories are normally based around one central conflict, this again confirms the importance of the emotional journey for the audience.

This focus on the emotional power of cinema was well understood by the key early screenwriting teachers. Phillips articulates this cogently:

> the reader, the listener, the participant in a work of art, must concentrate all the attention of his body, mind and soul upon the *emotional message* it contains, regardless of the artificial mediums employed in giving it material existence [emphasis added].[105]

In this statement, Phillips has clearly recognised that, for a photoplay to succeed, it must essentially achieve the same result as it is claimed all 'art' sets out to do. It must move us. Putting this in the strongest possible terms in relation to film as a silent medium, he also hints at the melodramatic:

> Perfect visualization, then, demands an exquisite command of language capable of nicely interpreting the finest shades of pathos, the deepest wells of passion, the most delicate waves of emotion, and a thousand grades of feeling.[106]

This also raises the question as to whether remnants of melodrama found in the sentiments of early screenwriting teachers have some echo or resonance in their modern counterparts.

Selling to the Industry

The screenplay manuals form part of the help offered to writers trying to make their scripts appeal to story analysts or readers. The screenwriting gurus of today have just as much to advise about marketing the screenplay as the key screenwriting teachers of

---

103   Hauge, *Writing Screenplays that Sell*, 3.

104   Hauge, *StoryMastery*, http://www.storymastery.com

105   Phillips, *Photodrama*, 28.

106   Ibid., 69.

the early period. The difference is that they provide this advice through their websites and specialised manuals rather than through columns.[107] Examples of modern manuals focused on marketing include Field's *Selling a Screenplay* (1989) and Hauge's *Selling Your Story in 60 Seconds* (2006). Detailed information on the specific requirements of various studios is advertised in trade journals, such as *Variety*. The ideal for a modern screenwriter is to sell their screenplay as part of a package of a one-off production, with a director and star usually attached.[108]

For the inexperienced outsider, just finding an agent, or having the opportunity to pitch an original or adapted screenplay to an independent producer, is difficult enough. The limited few who are successful could even find they are involved in direct negotiations with a producer or studio.[109] The professionalism of the script and its presentation is vital, as it will only impress the 'gatekeepers' or development staff if it arrives in a specifically developed form. Screenwriting gurus such as Seger, Hauge, Aronson and Vogler use their own industry experience, along with their long association with the studios as script consultants and story analysts, as a basis for their work with individual screenwriters in the development process.[110] Trading on this insider knowledge of how the industry works, they give detailed advice on all aspects of the industry. This advice ranges from how to create log lines and write compelling pitches to how to negotiate and network, self-agent (if necessary) and set up effective meetings with the gatekeepers.[111] Hauge encourages writers to describe their film by using 'commercially attractive categories' or 'genres',[112] although what Altman observes of many critics could also be applied to screenwriting gurus; that they rarely feel the need to 'reflect openly on the assumptions' that genres 'reside in a pre-existing pattern'.[113] That is, they tend to reinforce a more traditional understanding of genre, rather than seeing that the term

---

107   Hauge runs 'Coaching for Marketers', in Hauge, *Story Mastery*, http://www.storymastery.com/coaching/coaching-marketing/

108   Bordwell, *The Way Hollywood Tells It*, 27.

109   Stempel points out that, where previously agents had an important role, they became crucial to the business. Negotiation became a part of the process of getting a film made and screenwriters often found themselves spending more time at meetings than writing. See Stempel, *Framework*, 184.

110   All these screenwriting gurus have sophisticated script development services. See *Linda Seger Script Consultant*, http://www.lindaseger.com/script-consultant/, Linda Aronson Script Consultant, http://www.lindaaronson.com/consultant-teacher.html and Christopher Vogler, *Storytech Literary Consulting*, http://www.thewritersjourney.com

111   Ashley Scott Meyers, 'How to Sell Your Screenplay (in a Nutshell)', in *sellingyourscreenplay.com*, http://www.sellingyourscreenplay.com/how-Mito-sell-your-screenplay/how-to-sell-your-screenplay-in-a-nutshell/ and Michael Hauge on pitching – Screen Australia Industry Lecture on *YouTube*, https://www.youtube.com/watch?v=KZrvgU10hA0

112   Hauge, *Writing Screenplays that Sell*, 227.

113   Rick Altman, *Film/Genre* (London: BFI, 1999), 12 and 216.

has different meanings for different groups and that the understanding of various categories has shifted over time.

The screenwriting gurus encourage their students to aim to sell at a particular price and stick to it, in the hope they might enter a bidding war. When the market was buoyant, those who managed to sell 'spec scripts' could sell them for anything from the hundreds of thousands to over a million dollars.[114] However, since the 2008 recession the industry has tended to rely even more on franchise films with guaranteed sales, rather than take risks on untested original ideas. Screenwriting competitions have also proliferated in the last decade, with their organisers promising the winners recognition and marketing assistance.[115] Screenwriting gurus collaborate with and support a number of these competitions.[116]

As Chapter 6 has described, the key early screenwriting teachers provided detailed information on how to market scenarios through their manuals. Their columns and articles regularly updated writers on the latest developments and what studios were looking for. Unlike recent screenwriting gurus, they tended to discourage taking part in competitions and told their readers to stay away from film exchanges or schools that promised to market their work. Direct contact with the studios was the best route available at the time, as few agents and managers were operating. As already noted, the key screenwriting teachers constantly discussed the market price of scenarios in their fan and trade press columns. Given many screenwriting teachers were also editors in film companies, they actually functioned as the 'gatekeepers' too, and what they had written in their manuals expressed the current standards of entry.

This raises another interesting historical connection – namely the informal regulatory function of those offering screenwriting instruction. In focusing on this issue, Maras argues that the manuals helped to establish a kind of hierarchy among writers. Screenwriting teachers were in a position to speak with authority about the industry, to define what was considered legitimate and to modify these definitions, in order to control access to

---

114   In 1984 *Lethal Weapon* went for $250,000, and by 2004 *Déjà Vu* had sold for $5 million. The spec market has declined since 2008. In 1995, 173 specs were sold but by 2010 the number was only 55. See Margaret Heidenry, 'When the Spec Script Was King', *Vanity Fair*, March 2013, http://www.vanityfair.com/hollywood/2013/03/will-spec-script-screenwriters-rise-again

115   See http://www.moviebytes.com. This website lists all reputable screenwriting competitions in the USA and gives them a rating. At any one time, it lists over 70 competitions.

116   Hauge provided script-pitch consultation advice to the winner of the Grand Prize Award in 2014. See 'The CWA Blog', *Creative World Awards*, http://www.creativeworldawards.com. McKee endorses the Scriptapalooza screenwriting competition. See Mark Andrushko, 'Scriptapalooza interviews Screenwriting Guru Robert McKee' in *Screenwriting Contests and Markets Online*, April 29, 2004, *Moviebytes* website, http://www.moviebytes.com/contestDetail.cfm?tab=tab3&ContestNumber=123&StoryID=1876.   Field became an adjudicator for the Final Draft screenwriting contest. See 'Syd Field Joins Big Break! Judges Panel' in *Film Industry News*, June 30, 2004, http://www.filmmakers.com/news/contests/article_159.shtml

production.[117] As Maras indicates, because it involves providing a script, screenwriting is the space where 'industry, practitioners and lay-people' interact and 'where stories and industrial processes intersect'.[118] Teaching people how to write scripts thus acts as a filtering process:

> The fact that the majority of script books speak to novices is particularly important here; the bulk of 'how-to books' are, after all, primers to screenwriting that define writing for the screen, and access to it in a particular way.[119]

This tendency towards 'particularism' is as true now as it was a century ago, as aspirant screenwriters attempt to negotiate entry into the industry. As Conor comments:

> the how-to genre concretizes and regulates the profession through a particular set of hegemonic codes and conventions – structure, characters, conflict, entrepreneurialism and precariousness.[120]

In 1922 Macpherson refers to the high level of skill demanded for continuity writing and the role of the staff writer, and readily talks of 'insiders' and 'outsiders', indicating how much the role had professionalised by this point:

> So don't waste your time and vital energy envying and criticizing the staff writer. Get busy! REMEMBER THAT HE WAS ONCE AN OUTSIDER JUST AS YOU ARE NOW – and that he became an insider by the very method I am explaining to you![121]

Eugene W. Presbrey, also writing in 1922, sets a high ideal for any freelance writer – they must be experienced, acquainted and appreciative of all the arts, '[c]ultured by education and travel, [… and be a] product of many environments' – before he finally admits, 'the freelance writer is usually a staff writer out of a job'.[122] A specific emphasis on technique, due to the increased complexity of the scripts and the terminology of filmmaking, gave impetus to the formalisation of writing for the screen and the virtual exclusion of outsiders. The bar was set high and has remained so ever since.

Film censorship is not dealt with in more recent manuals, as it seems that the general parameters of acceptability are understood. For modern screenwriting gurus, the focus

---

117 Maras, *Screenwriting*, 25.

118 Ibid.

119 Ibid.

120 Conor, *Screenwriting*, 12.

121 Macpherson, 'Functions of the Continuity Writer' in *Opportunities in the Motion Picture Industry*, 33.

122 Eugene W. Presbrey, 'The Free Lance Writer' in *Opportunities in the Motion Picture* Industry, 45–46. Presbrey was secretary to the Screen Writers' Guild, the Authors' League of America and The Writers' Club. He also lectured at the American Academy of Dramatic Arts, New York and was an author, painter, actor and playwright.

has shifted to another question – namely the target audience – and, to address it, writers need to understand the important issue of film ratings.[123] As Chapter 6 has specified, early screenwriting teachers continually addressed the matter of censorship and gave cogent and detailed advice on avoiding the censor's knife. These screenwriting teachers, particularly Wright as a strong campaigner against unnecessary censorship, fired the first shots in a long and arduous struggle that led the industry to where it is today.

To recent screenwriting gurus, copyright is not a significant issue, because screenplays have the same protection as all other artistic works; although most writers in the USA still use the script registration service offered by the Writers' Guild of America to prove ownership.[124] In contrast, with the matter of copyright unsettled at the time when the key screenwriting teachers were operating, they played an important part in achieving the protection that writers are now afforded. The Photoplay Author's League, of which Sargent and Wright were prominent members, was formed in part to achieve copyright protection for authors. Incorporated in 1914, it aimed to get the same results as the Authors' League of America Inc., which offered protection to its members' work in print.[125] In 1917 Sargent endorsed the Authors' League and recommended that scenario writers register their scripts with it, even though it afforded no protection in law for the present.[126] However, the Photoplay Authors' League failed to achieve its aim and ceased to exist in 1919. The Authors' League of America joined with the Screen Writers' Guild in 1921, eventually becoming what we know today as the Writers' Guild of America.[127]

Having campaigned through his work with Congress to achieve copyright protection for photoplay authors since 1914 (see Figure 82),[128] in 1921 Wright finally recorded that a bill had been approved by the state legislature in California to give copyright protection for screenwriters (see Figure 83), but there was still no national legislation.[129] The Photoplay Authors' League and the key screenwriting teachers who were involved in it were true forerunners of the Writers' Guild of America, which exists for the protection of screenwriters in the USA today.

---

123 The Motion Picture Association of America categorises film using five ratings: G – General, PG – Parental Guidance, PG-13 – Parents Strongly Cautioned, R – Restricted, NC17 – No one 17 and under admitted; *MPAA*: http://www.mpaa.org/film-ratings/

124 See 'WGA West Registry', https://www.wgawregistry.org/webrss/

125 'Film Flashes', *Variety*, March 20, 1914, 23.

126 Sargent, 'The Photoplaywright', *MPW*, July 7, 1917, 94.

127 Louis B. Perry and Richard S. Perry, *A History of the Los Angeles Labor Movement, 1911–1941* (London: University of California, 1963), 354.

128 'Scenario Copyright Law in View', *MPN*, April 4, 1914, 22.

129 Wright, 'Hints for Scenario Writers', *Picture-Play Magazine*, July 1921, 10.

SCENARIO COPYRIGHT LAW IN VIEW

Congressman Frank B. Willis, of Ohio, last Friday notified Congress that he had in preparation a measure to secure copyright protection to motion picture manuscripts and that he would introduce his bill within a few days. William Lord Wright, the photoplaywright and special writer, conferred with Congressman Willis recently, and the legislation begins as a result.

There is no intention to interfere with motion picture legislation in any way, it is said, but to secure protection to photoplay authors and endeavor to check all crys of "plot stealing" that are prevalent, but not merited. It is believed the manufacturers will not object to this bill, for it relieves them of much responsibility.

Figure 82: Part of Wright's campaign for copyright protection: 'Scenario Copyright Law in View' article
Source: *MPN*, April 4, 1914, 22.

A Scenario Bill

At Sacramento, California, in March, the final State legislative approval was given a bill to protect the rights of scenario writers. The bill provides that scenarios or stories may be filed with the secretary of state and thereafter be used as prima-facie evidence in actions wherein theft of plots for motion pictures is charged.

Figure 83: California provides copyright protection for screenwriters, as Wright reported in 'Hints for Scenario Writers'
Source: *Picture-Play Magazine*, July 1921, 10.

9. Evolution of the Screenplay

In today's industry, a 'step outline' (or a 'scene-by-scene', 'beat sheet' or 'extended treatment'), describing what happens in each scene and normally worked out prior to writing the script, may be requested before an agent, manager or studio reader reads the full screenplay.[1] If the step outline is accepted, a development deal will be struck and the long process of developing the script will commence. Ultimately, a 'shooting script' will be achieved and filming will start. The script format that is currently in use first emerged in the studio period, and must still be followed exactly.[2]

Although scholars have searched for the earliest form of script, it has been a futile exercise that has led nowhere, as Raynauld confirms.[3] The consensus of scholars is that:

> The history of the screenplay is notoriously difficult to trace, due both to a problem of language (the word 'screenplay' itself does not come into common usage until the 1940s) and to the fact that its earliest antecedents are private industrial documents, many of which have been lost to time.[4]

This study indeed corroborates that during the early period the scenario had no set format, and screenwriting teachers were addressing an industry in a state of flux. As Chapter 6 has reported, Sargent himself recommends a variety of formats in the appendix of his own manual.[5] What the key screenwriting teachers generally confirm is that submissions consisted of a series of documents, such as a synopsis, scene plot, cast of characters and scenario ('plot of action' or later 'the continuity'), although variations were possible. Kevin Boon suggests:

> All four are still in use today in slightly different forms. The synopsis is comparable to a contemporary film treatment, the cast of characters, and the scene plot are similar to documents used to facilitate production; and the continuity is much like the contemporary screenplay.[6]

---

1 Danny Stack, 'Screenwriting Bullet 14: Step Outline', March 8, 2013, *Scriptwriting in the UK*, http://dannystack.blogspot.co.uk/2012/09/screenwriting-bullet-14-step-outline.html

2 Lewis Ward, 'Structure and Breaking In: An Interview with Syd Field', *Script Magazine*, April 10, 2013, http://www.scriptmag.com/features/structure-and-breaking-in-an-interview-with-syd-field; Hauge, 'Composing Effective Query Letters', http://www.storymastery.com/selling-your-story/composing-effective-query-letters https://www.storymastery.com/coaching/109-consultation-submission-checklist

3 Isabelle Raynauld, 'Written Scenarios of Early French Cinema: Screenwriting Practices in the First Twenty Years', *Film History 9*, 3, (1997): 257–268.

4 Andrew Kenneth Gay, 'History of Scripting and the Screenplay' in *Screenplayology: An Online Centre for Screenplay Studies*, http://www.screenplayology.com/content-sections/screenplay-style-use/1-1/

5 Sargent, *Technique of the Photoplay*, 3rd ed., 99–100 and 373–398.

6 Kevin Alexander Boon, *Script Culture and the American Screenplay* (Detroit: Wayne State University, 2008), 7.

This could be viewed as an over-simplification, however, since Gay links the continuity to the modern shooting script and traces the emergence of the master scene format as a separate form. Such differences indicate how complex the process of standardisation actually was, and its exact timing is imprecise:

> Something curious happens in the period between the collapse of the studio system and the 1970s. The continuity script becomes the *shooting script*, in which shot-by-shot scene writing is reserved for the director after a script has been greenlit for production, while the master scene format emerges as the new standard for writers' drafts.[7]

However they are viewed, all the components identified by the key early screenwriting teachers remain present in some form.

What was also clear by end of the teens was that the script had become an important tool in controlling production costs, which meant that it had to be of high quality in whatever format it appeared. Decherney confidently asserts, 'Instruction manuals and professional script technicians standardized a script style – the continuity script – complete with descriptions of camera placement, mise-en-scène, and performance.'[8] Supported by evidence from his close study of Sargent's discourse, Azlant confirms:

> the centrality of the scenario in communicating a design intention to all the personnel creating a fiction film and, at the very same, its tentative provisional nature within the normal procedures of this collaborative and compounded medium.[9]

By indicating that the 'screenplay functions as a document of design in the creation of the fictional narrative film', Azlant was suggesting that the script was effectively a 'blueprint' for the film.[10] In response to Azlant's views, Maras cautions us not to read back our modern understanding of the screenplay into previous complex and multifarious documents. Nevertheless, Maras concludes that Sargent's:

> emphasis on writing in photoplay form underpins some now common aspects of writing for the screen. [… It] foregrounds the importance of photoplay form and writing in form through plotting.[11]

As this study has shown, this assertion should probably be broadened to include the other key screenwriting teachers.

---

7   Gay, 'History of Scripting and the Screenplay' in *Screenplayology*, http://www.screenplayology.com/content-sections/screenplay-style-use/1-1/

8   Decherney, *Hollywood and the Culture Elite*, 43.

9   Azlant, 'Theory, History and Practice of Screenwriting', 215.

10   Ibid.,5

11   Maras, *Screenwriting,* 148–149.

Another crucial connection that recurs is the importance of 'the read', meaning the manner in which a script reader envisages the film. The modern screenwriter must convey, through language, a visual experience for the reader of the screenplay. To do so, they use economy of language and make description active and visual. As Hauge puts it, any reader must see the movie 'projecting' in their head as they read.[12] Chapter 6 has described how all the key screenwriting teachers strongly advocated developing the ability to visualise the story as they told it. For example, Peacocke advises, 'Do not attempt to be "literary"', adding that the reader 'cares nothing about literary style' and looks at things with a 'camera eye'.[13] The theorist Freeburg emphasises this skill: 'The scenario writer must not only imagine his pictures but he must learn to imagine them in terms of the screen.'[14] These views were also widely held by screenwriting teachers on the periphery. Esenwein and Leeds told authors that they needed to:

> Cultivate the picturing eye [...] so that by being able to visualize each scene as you
> plan it in your mind you cannot fail to produce in your scenario a series of scenes
> whose action is logically connected and essentially natural and unforced.[15]

Screenwriting discourse had always been concerned with 'the read'. In picking up on this point, Maras highlights the emphasis that Sargent – and by association we can say the other key screenwriting teachers – place on '"the read" of the script, [that] function[s] as the movie before the mind's eye', which we also recognise in the modern context.[16]

---

12 Hauge, *Writing Screenplays that Sell*, 113.

13 Peacocke, *Hints on Photoplay Writing*, 20 and 40.

14 Freeburg, *Art of Photoplay Writing*, 29

15 Esenwein and Leeds, *Writing the Photoplay*, 97.

16 Maras, *Screenwriting*, 149.

10. Education of the Screenwriter

The means by which screenwriters acquire their skills is another area that connects the modern screenwriting guru with the key screenwriting teachers of the past. Towards the end of the studio period, newly created university and film school courses in film studies and screenwriting were receiving thousands of applications and had come to be seen as academically respectable.[1] Stempel points out that:

> Screenwriters in American film have traditionally come from a great variety of backgrounds, but it was not until the sixties that screenwriters came straight out of film schools. […]. Los Angeles was, and is, crawling with screenwriting courses at colleges and universities as well as privately run screenwriting schools.[2]

Evidence indicates substantial cross-fertilisation occurred between the work of recent screenwriting gurus and those who teach screenwriting in an academic context. Since the 1990s university screenwriting courses have expanded on a large scale, and writing a full-length screenplay usually forms the final project of a Master of Arts course, as well as of some undergraduate degrees.[3] Some professors involved in leading these courses openly endorse material from the screenwriting gurus in addition to their own literature. For example, as a respected academic, Hunter is Professor Emeritus in Screenwriting at the University of California, Los Angeles (UCLA), but he is also regarded as a screenwriting guru due to the many short courses on screenwriting he runs.[4] His active support of the work of other screenwriting gurus is evident in his advice to prospective screenwriters:

> Forgo writing exercises when you're learning to write screenplays. Read the books by Bill Froug, Richard Walter, Bill Goldman, Syd Field, Linda Seger, Whitcomb, Hauge, Dorethea Brande, and Sol Saks for instruction.[5]

Notably, among this list of gurus, the late Field was also a member of the University of Southern California (USC) faculty and taught on its Master of Professional Writing programme; Froug was a professor at UCLA and had reorganised its whole screenwriting

---

1   See Donald H. Johnston, ed., *Encyclopedia of International Media and Communications*, vol. 4 (San Diego: Academic Press, 2003), 498; and Fereydoun Hoveyda, *The Hidden Meaning of Mass Communications: Cinema, Books, and Television in the Age of Computers* (Westport: Praeger, 2000), 55.

2   Stempel, *Framework*, 197.

3   A number of leading American universities offer specialised Master of Fine Arts programmes in screenwriting, including the American Film Institute, UCLA, USC and NYU. Some schools also offer non-degree programmes, such as the year-long UCLA Professional Program in Screenwriting, which can also be taken online. See websites of these universities for more detail.

4   For Hunter's academic, writing and producing background and the screenwriting courses he runs, see Lew Hunter's Screenwriting 434 Colony, http://lewhunter.com/index.html

5   Hunter, *Screenwriting 434*, 53.

programme, which Walter now chairs; and Seger has taught on the UCLA and USC extension programmes.[6]

The sheer proliferation of such courses may well have helped to popularise writing for the screen and provide a further incentive for public instruction. Beyond the USA, the number of screenwriting courses has grown hugely in the United Kingdom too.[7] One of the most successful courses is the Screenwriting Master of Arts at the University of the Arts (formerly the London College of Communication), founded by Philip Parker, a respected academic and producer as well as a leading UK screenwriting teacher. A number of his graduates have gone on to win major film awards such as the Palme d'Or and have been Oscar-nominated. In the appendix of *The Art & Science of Screenwriting*, Parker also recommends as further reading many of the same screenwriting gurus as Hunter.[8]

The early period also spawned academic courses that had links to screenwriting teachers of the day. The teacher of the first of these courses, Freeburg, had strong connections with key screenwriting teachers, such as Sargent. Patterson succeeded Freeburg and developed the courses further. The content of Patterson's two manuals are representative of instruction, as far as it had developed to that point. As Polan observes, 'the photoplay composition courses that began at Columbia University in the mid-1910s represent [...] the first academic offerings on film in the United States'.[9] In response, Jan-Christopher Horak claims that Polan wants to portray '"the moment of self-invention," when the field's identity was yet unformed'. Given that Columbia's 1915 course was the start of a trend and was followed by courses at USC in 1929 and New York University (NYU) in 1933, Polan can indeed lay claim to documenting the birth of film studies.[10] It is evident too that what was taught by the first key screenwriting teachers is strongly connected to

---

6 Biographical information: for Field, see 'About Syd Field', http://sydfield.com/about/; for Seger, see 'About Linda Seger Script Consultant', http://www.lindaseger.com/script-consultant-screenplay-coach/; for Froug, see Alex Stedman, 'Writer-Producer William Froug dies at 91', *Variety*, September 5, 2013, http://variety.com/2013/tv/news/writer-producer-william-froug-dies-at-91-1200600523/; and for Walter, see 'About Richard Walter', http://richardwalter.com/about-richard/

7 Janet Murray of the *Guardian* confirms the huge growth in writing courses in the UK over the last decade. See Murray, 'Can You Teach Creative Writing?' *Guardian*, May 10, 2011, http://www.theguardian.com/education/2011/may/10/creative-writing-courses. The Undergraduate Courses at University and College (UCAS) lists 47 universities that provided courses with 'screenwriting' in the UK for 2016. Most of these courses are either completely devoted to screenwriting or contain a screenwriting option; see UCAS, http://www.ucas.com

8 Philip Parker, *The Art & Science of Screenwriting* (Bristol: Intellect Books, 2006), 214–215.

9 Polan, *Scenes of Instruction,* 37.

10 Jan-Christopher Horak, 'Review of Dana Polan, Scenes of Instruction: The Beginnings of the U.S. Study of Film' in *Screening the Past*, http://tlweb.latrobe.edu.au/humanities/screeningthepast/22/scenes-instruction.html

the first academic writing programmes, so perhaps their genesis is more complex. The institutions that delivered these first courses have continued this unbroken connection by providing screenwriting programmes ever since, and 'Columbia, USC and NYU represent top-tiered academic film programmes today'.[11]

11 Ibid.

CONCLUSION

CONCLUSION

This book has assessed the contribution that early screenwriting teachers made to the film industry. First, to contextualise their work, it traced their origins; second, it examined in detail the contribution of key screenwriting teachers; and third, it considered their possible legacy by briefly examining their links with today's screenwriting gurus.

A survey of the academic literature confirmed that this area of film history had been neglected and had only been considered as part of other lines of enquiry, rather than being the subject of close and detailed examination in its own right.

Investigating the origins of screenwriting teachers involved embracing the literary and theatrical sources from which early screenwriting teachers drew. Also pertinent were the economic conditions that led to the script becoming a controlling factor in production and the circumstances that sparked 'scenario fever', which in turn prompted the emergence of screenwriting teachers.

An assessment of the contribution of the early screenwriting teachers entailed, first, reviewing when and how the first screenwriting teachers appeared and establishing a set of criteria to distinguish between those screenwriting teachers who were peripheral and those who were more significant to the industry. These criteria were then applied to eliminate the more peripheral screenwriting teachers from the main study and to identify five key screenwriting teachers whose contribution merited detailed interrogation. The next stage consisted of a thorough and comprehensive investigation of how the work of Sargent, Wright, Peacocke, Ball and Phillips contributed to the screenwriting discourse in three major ways: showing prospective writers how to train for, write for and sell to the industry. Part of this investigation was to assess the probable overall contribution of these screenwriting teachers by considering how they helped to adapt playwriting technique and theatrical understanding into a powerful form of visual storytelling, as well as to create a coherent film language that was eventually encapsulated in the scenario and continuity script.

The potential legacy of these key screenwriting teachers was then briefly examined by considering their equivalence with modern screenwriting gurus whose work may indicate how freelance writers train for, write for and sell to the industry today. Other issues addressed were what they might have contributed to the evolution of the modern-day screenplay and how they may have influenced the recent education of the screenwriter.

What emerges is that modern screenwriting gurus clearly stand on the shoulders of the early screenwriting teachers, as they reiterate principles set down in the early period. However, their indebtedness to these early teachers is rarely, if ever, acknowledged. Although early screenwriting manuals did not always speak with a consistent or unified voice, I argue that their discourse was the grist that provided the industry with the opportunity to impose shape and definition on the storytelling process, before the studio system was fully operative. Due to the central position the key screenwriting teachers held, the processes and standards they insisted upon more than likely played a significant role in the professionalisation of writing for the screen, of which all the present-day screenwriting gurus and screenwriters are beneficiaries.

By tracing the history of the emergence of key screenwriting teachers in American cinema, I believe I have demonstrated that they were central to the development of both the screenwriting process and the filmmaking industry. Much of the primary data upon which this study has been based had not previously been consulted or accessed. Close examination of the trade and fan press literature, in particular, has indicated the industry did see the key screenwriting teachers as important. It is not my intention to discount in any way the excellent work of many revisionist historians who have researched the development of early cinema using a more context-based approach, rather than relying upon a teleological and deterministic conception of cinema change. On the contrary, I hope my analysis of the role early key screenwriting teachers have played will contribute to this body of knowledge, enrich it and draw much-needed attention to a part of the discourse that has hitherto been virtually ignored.

The evidence suggests that the key screenwriting teachers were highly involved in, and interacted with, the industry during this early period. As motion pictures adopted the fictional narrative mode and films grew to feature length, a host of identifiable screenwriting teachers, from various backgrounds, were likely to have attended and aided this evolution. This supposition has never been postulated before: that these key early screenwriting teachers were integral to and central to this development in the industry rather than simply an adjunct to it; that as scenario editors, writers and directors, columnists, manual writers and influential people in the business of film, they made a significant and lasting contribution to the discourse on screenwriting. For these reasons, I contend that they should no longer be regarded as marginal to the industry, but as important agents of change, and contributors to the development of a cinema that has increasingly integrated narrative. As the film industry adjusted to the complexity and changes spurred by phenomenal growth, censorship, the studio and star systems, copyright law and large-scale production, the key screenwriting teachers played a role in making these accommodations, as evidenced by their own testimony through the various columns they wrote, the testimony of others who wrote about them and confirmed their involvement, and the body of work contained in their surviving manuals.

I have suggested that these screenwriting teachers helped to tailor and modify theatrical techniques to the medium of film writing. Although this knowledge was not materially new, its translation to the medium of film was. They embraced Aristotle's *Poetics* and Freytag's recalibration of these ideas, as well as much of the advice contained in contemporary playwriting manuals, and absorbed into their teaching some prevailing melodramatic influences. They were also aware of film theorists, such as Münsterberg and Freeburg, who were making significant comment and familiarised themselves with this work. Their columns and manuals represent a codification and summation of screenwriting, as it was understood up to this point. In this respect, I propose that their contribution to the discourse on screenwriting was potentially considerable. Among the key screenwriting teachers, Sargent was the most significant, because he produced a highly detailed and exhaustive manual and his columns contained an on-going commentary on screenwriting discourse. However, Phillips and Wright were both prolific and they too provided an impressive and weighty body of instruction, for which they have been given hardly any recognition or credit. The significant contributions of both Ball and Peacocke also deserve note. Together, these key screenwriting teachers produced the most significant body of instruction on writing for film between the years 1910 and 1922 and, as the evidence suggests, it is likely that they were influential in shaping the discourse and playing an important role in the professionalisation of writing for the screen during this period.

My examination of the contribution of the screenwriting teachers of the early period is incomplete. Much more remains to be done. This study has in fact opened up a number of other interesting lines of enquiry, which require much further investigation and research. For the purposes of the study, a distinction was made between the peripheral and key screenwriting teachers; however, a number of the former teachers deserve closer attention. For example, the contribution of significant women screenwriting teachers, especially Loos and Patterson, although it was not as important as that of the key teachers identified in this study, merits closer scrutiny. Other screenwriting teachers, such as Esenwein and Leeds, Dimick and Nelson, wrote noteworthy manuals as well, which could form the basis of further investigation. This study has also opened up discussion about how the content of early playwriting manuals and other literary sources is related to the instruction offered by early screenwriting teachers.

The activity and role of screenwriting teachers during the studio period emerges as another topic that requires examination. Did the manual writers of that period only service the internal needs of the industry? If not, who were these manuals really for? Were they written for hopeful amateurs who still regarded them as a means of training for, and entering the industry? A more detailed and cogent survey of this period beckons.

In addition, while not its main focus, this study has begun to examine the correlation between the instruction offered by early screenwriting teachers and the advice of contemporary screenwriting gurus. Further investigation into this area may provide a better framework for evaluating the current screenwriting gurus' relationship with, and contribution to, the last 40 or so years of package-led production, and to the twenty-first century Hollywood film industry as it currently operates.

By way of summary, I restate what has been proposed by this study. I do this with reference to the late Edward Azlant, whose own unpublished dissertation on the early

history of screenwriting itself deserves more recognition. Namely, Azlant claims that
through:

> the appearance of various forms of public instruction in screenwriting, including
> textbooks and manuals, and the strong qualifications of many of the authors of such
> materials, we possess much authoritative description of the craft of screenwriting
> for the early silent film.[1]

Azlant's final assertion that we 'possess much authoritative description of the craft of
screenwriting' in the materials that have been handed down to us has needed rigorous
examination but, from the evidence, it seems that this is likely to be true. It is a body of
instruction that has required systematic analysis and interrogation, and this study has gone
some way towards addressing this. What has emerged is a relatively detailed historical
sense of the filmic instruction relayed to screenwriters by key early screenwriting
teachers. Their views appear to have produced a rich discussion of the various techniques
of screenwriting in the early period and seem to be indicative of the high level to which
the craft had evolved by 1922. If this is the case, it means that the key early screenwriting
teachers helped take the materials of story, character, setting and leaders and apply them
through the dynamics of probability, logic, chronology, dramaturgy, convention and
aesthetics to create the motion picture plot. Evidenced in the scenario of yesterday, it
appears likely that this contribution still reverberates through the screenplay of today.

---

1   Azlant, 'Theory, History and Practice of Screenwriting', 337.

BIBLIOGRAPHY

BIBLIOGRAPHY

Primary Sources

Books

Andrews, Charlton. *The Technique of Play Writing*. 1915; repr., Michigan: University of Michigan, 2013.

Archer, William. *Play-making: A Manual of Craftsmanship*. 1912: repr., London: Forgotten Books, 2012.

Aristotle. *Poetics*. Translated by Malcolm Heath. London: Penguin Books, 1996.

Badger, Clarence G. *The Point of Attack or How to Start the Photoplay*. Los Angeles: Palmer Photoplay Corporation, 1920.

Ball, Eustace Hale. *The Art of the Photoplay*. 1913; repr., London: Forgotten Books, 2012.

------. *Photoplay Scenarios: How to Write and Sell Them*. 1915; repr., Eastbourne: Wildside Books, 2013.

Barry, John Francis and Sargent, Epes Winthrop. *Building Theatre Patronage: Management and Merchandising*. New York: Chalmers, 1927.

Beranger, Clara. *Writing for the Screen*. Iowa: Brown, 1950.

Buren-Powell, Ardon Van. *The Photoplay Synopsis*. 1919; repr., Memphis: General Books, 2013.

Caine, Clarence J. *How to Write Photo-plays*. Philadelphia: McKay, 1915.

Carr, Catherine. *The Art of Photoplay Writing*. 1914; repr., Charleston: Nabu Press, 2013.

Charlton, Carl. *How to Write Photoplays*. 1916; repr., Philadelphia: BiblioBazaar, 2012.

Dimick, Howard T. *Photoplay Making*. New Jersey: Editor Company, 1915.

------. *Modern Photoplay Writing: Its Craftmanship*. Ohio: James Knapp Reeve, 1922.

Egri, Lajos. *The Art of Dramatic Writing*. New York: Simon and Schuster, 1946.

Emerson, John and Loos, Anita. *How to Write Photoplays*. Philadelphia: Jacobs, George W. Jacobs & Co, 1920.

Esenwein, J. Berg and Leeds, Arthur. *Writing the Photoplay*. 1913; repr., London: Dodo Press, 2007.

Field, Syd. *Screenplay: The Foundations of Screenwriting.* New York: Bantam Dell, 1979.

------. *The Screenwriter's Workbook.* New York: Dell Publishing, 1984.

Fox, Charles Donald. *The Fox Plan of Photoplay Writing.* 1922; repr., Whitefish, MA: Kessinger Legacy, 2013.

Freeburg, Victor Oscar. *The Art of Photoplay Making.* 1918; repr., London: Forgotten Books, 2012.

Freytag, Gustav. *Technique of the Drama.* 1895: repr., London: Forgotten Books, 2014.

Froug, William. *Screenwriting Tricks of the Trade.* Los Angeles: Silman-James, 1993.

------. *The New Screenwriter Looks at the New Screenwriter.* Los Angeles: Silman-James, 1992.

Gordon, William Lewis. *How to Write Moving Picture Plays ...* 1914: repr., New York: Nabu, 2013.

Grau, Robert. *The Theatre of Science: The Volume of Progress and Achievement in the Motion Picture Industry.* New York: Broadway, 1914.

Hannon, William Morgan. *The Photodrama: Its Place Among the Fine Arts.* 1915; repr., Charleston: BiblioBazaar, 2013.

Harrison, Louis Reeves. *Screencraft.* 1916: repr., Memphis: General Books, 2012.

Hauge, Michael. *Writing Screenplays that Sell.* New York: Harper Collins, 1991.

Herman, Lewis, *Practical Manual of Screen Playwriting for Theatre and Television Films.* 1952; repr., New York: Meridian, 1974.

Hoagland, Herbert Case. *How to Write a Photoplay.*1912: repr., New York: Nabu, 2012.

Hunter, Lew. *Screenwriting 434.* New York: Perigree, 1993.

Irving, James. *The Irving System: A New Easy Method of Story and Photoplay Writing.* 1919; repr., Memphis: General Books, 2012.

Lane, Tamar. *The New Technique of Screen Writing.* New York: Whittlesey House, 1936.

Lawson, John Howard. *Theory and Technique of Playwriting and Screenwriting.* New York: Putnam's, 1949.

Lindsay, Vachel. *The Art of the Moving Picture.* 2nd ed.1922; repr., London: Forgotten Books, 2012.

Lytton, Grace. *Scenario Writing Today*. 1921; repr., Miami: Hard Press, 2013.

Marion, Frances. *How to Write and Sell Film Stories*. New York: Covici Friede, 1937.

Matthews, Brander. *The Principles of Playmaking*. New York: Charles Scribner's Sons, 1919.

Moore, Elbert. *Elbert Moore's Textbook on Writing the Photoplay*. 1915; repr., Memphis: General Books, 2012.

Motion Picture Studio Directory and Trade Annual. 1916, 134; April 12, 1917, 144 and 1918, 188.

Motion Picture Studio Directory and Trade Annual. New York, Motion Picture News, 1916.

Münsterberg, Hugo. *The Photoplay: A Psychological Study*. 1916; repr., Charleston: BiblioBazaar, 2007.

Nash, Constance and Oakey, Virginia. *The Screenwriter's Handbook*. New York: Harper Perennial, 1974.

Palmer, Frederick. *Palmer Plan Handbook*. ... 1921; repr., BiblioBazaar, 2013.

------. *Photoplay Plot Encyclopedia*. Los Angeles: Palmer Photoplay Corporation, 1922.

------. *Technique of the Photoplay*. Los Angeles: Palmer Institute of Authorship, 1924.

Parsons, Louella Oettinger. *How to Write for the 'Movies ...* 1916; repr., New York: Nabu, 2012.

Patterson, Frances Taylor. *Cinema Craftsmanship: A Book for Photoplaywrights*. 1920; repr., Charleston: Bibliolife, 2013.

------. *Cinema Craftsmanship*. 2nd ed. New York: Harcourt and Brace, 1921.

Peacocke, Leslie Tufnell. *Hints on Photoplay Writing*. 1916; repr., Charleston: BiblioBazaar, 2012.

Phillips, Henry Albert. *Art in Short Story Narration*. 1913; repr., London: Forgotten Books, 2012.

------. *The Photodrama*. 1914; repr., Charleston: Bibliolife, 2013.

------. *The Universal Plot Catalogue*. 1920; repr., New York: Nabu, 2013.

------. *The Feature Photoplay*. Springfield: Home Correspondence School, 1921.

------. *The Art of Writing Photoplays*. Cincinnati: Writer's Digest, 1922.

Price, William T. *The Technique of the Drama*. 1892; repr., Miami, Hard Press, 2013.

Radnor, Leona. *The Photoplay Writer*. 1913; repr., New York: Nabu, 2013.

Ross, Ernest N. *Scenario Writing*. Philadelphia: Penn Association, 1912.

Sargent, Epes Winthrop. *Picture Theatre Advertising*. New York: Chalmers, 1915.

------. *The Technique of the Photoplay*. 1st ed. New York: MPW, 1912.

------. *The Technique of the Photoplay*. 2nd ed. 1913; repr., BiblioBazaar, 2012.

------. *The Technique of the Photoplay*. 3rd ed. New York: MPW, 1916.

Slevin, James. *On Picture-play Writing: A Handbook of Workmanship.* 1912; repr., BiblioBazaar, 2013.

Stoddard, Ralph Perkins. *The Photoplay: A Book of Valuable Information for Those Who Would Enter A Field of Unlimited Endeavor. ...* 1911; repr., Whitefish, MA: Kessinger Legacy, 2013.

Talbot, Frederick. *Moving Pictures: How They are Made and Worked.* 1912; repr., Whitefish, MA: Kessinger Publishing, 2013.

Taylor, James A. *The Photoplay.* Washington: Washington DC Printing, 1914.

Thomas, Arthur W. *How to Write a Photoplay*. Chicago: Photoplaywrights' Association of America, 1914, accessed December 2, 2013, http://www.oocities.org/emruf1/photoplay.html

Truby, John. *The Anatomy of Story*. London: Faber and Faber, 2007.

Vale, Eugene. *The Technique of Screenplay Writing*. 1944; repr., London: Souvenir Press, 1973.

Winkopp, C. G. *How to Write a Photoplay*. 1915; repr., Whitefish, MA: Kessinger Legacy, 2013.

Wright, William Lord. *The Motion Picture Story*. Chicago: Cloud Publishing, 1914.

------. *Photoplay Writing*. 1922; repr., New York: Nabu, 2012.

Trade and Fan Press Columns of Key Screenwriting Teachers

Peacocke, 'Hints for Photoplay Writers', in *Photoplay*, 1915–1917.

Phillips, 'The Photodrama' and 'Photodrama in the Making', in *MPSM and MPM*, 1917–1918.

Sargent, 'Technique of the Photoplay', 'The Scenario Writer' and 'The Photoplaywright', in *MPW*, 1911–1919.

------.'Thinks and Things' in *The Photoplay Author*, 1914–1915,

Wright, William Lord, 'William Lord Wright's Page' and 'For Those Who Worry O'er Plots and Plays' in *MPN*, 1911–1914;.

------. 'For Photoplay Authors, Real and Near' in *NYDM*, 1914–1917.

------. 'Hints For Scenario Writers' in *Picture-Play Magazine*, 1917–1921.

Trade and Fan Press, Journal, Anthology and Periodical Sources

Ball. Eustace Hale. 'Ten Things I Would Tell a Beginner', *Fhotoplaywright*, July 1912, 5.

------. 'The Scenario Writer, the Director and the Censor', *MPN*, December 26, 1914, 36.

Barrett, Ada. 'The Plea for the Photoplay', *MPSM*, July 1911, 115–116.

Bedding, Thomas. 'The Dramatic Moment', *MPW*, March 12, 1910, 372.

Craw, George Rockhill. 'Technique of the Picture Play', *MPW*, January 21, 1911, 126–127; January 28, 1911, 178–180; and February 4, 1911, 229.

Emar. 'Concerning Scenarios', *MPW*, July 7, 1910, 76.

Fox, William. 'The Scenario Makes the Picture', *Motography*, May 20, 1916, 1155.

Grau, Robert. 'The Potency of the Motion Picture', *MPSM*, November 1911, 118–119.

------. 'The Picture Play', *MPN*, December 30, 1911, 9.

Hamilton, Clayton. 'The Art of the Moving Picture', *Nickelodeon*, January 14, 1911, 50–52.

------. 'Mr. Hamilton on Photoplays', *The Nickelodeon*, January 14, 1911, 41–42.

Hanson, W. 'A Few Particular Points', *The Photoplaywright*, November 1912, 4.

Harrison, Louis Reeves. 'Five Reels', *MPW*, February 7, 1914, 652.

------. 'Theatrical Plots', *MPW*, October 23, 1915, 586.

------. 'Stealing Plays', *MPW*, June 24, 1916, 2208.

------. 'The Law of the Drama', *MPW*, January 25, 1919, 485–486.

Hermit, The. 'The Photoplaywright's Earnings', *Motography*, May 1911, 93.

Katterjohn, Monte M. 'The Photoplay Dramatist', *MPSM*, June 1912, 145–147.

------. 'Captain Leslie T. Peacocke: And What He Thinks Is in Store for the Picture Play', *Movie Pictorial*, August 15, 1914, 16–17 and 32.

Key, Pierre V. R. 'Continuity is Important Factor', *Motography*, November 17, 1917, 1033–1034.

Leeds, Arthur. 'So You'll Know Them Better – XVI. Henry Albert Phillips – An Idealist with a Punch', *The Photoplay Author*, September 1914, 69–74.

Macpherson, Jeanie. 'Functions of the Continuity Writer', *Opportunities in the Motion Picture Industry*, 25–35.

Manker, Roy L. 'The New Way to Enter Motion Pictures', *Opportunities in the Motion Picture Industry*. 1922; repr., Los Angeles: Nabu, 2013, 5–8.

McElravy, Robert L. 'The Voice on the Wire', *MPW*, March 24, 1917, 1948.

O'Neill, James. 'Technique and the Tale', *MPW*, November 18, 1911, 541.

Palmer, Frederick. 'Today and Tomorrow', *The Story World and the Photodramatist*, September 1923, 70–71.

Patterson, Frances Taylor. 'University Training at Home', *Photoplay*, December 1920, 126.

Peacocke, Leslie Tuffnell. 'The Scenario Writer and the Director', May 1917, 111–114.

------. 'Studio Conditions as I Know Them', *Photoplay*, June 1917, 127–130.

------. 'Original Photoplays – versus Adaptations', *Photoplay*, July 1917, 127–130.

------. 'The Story's the Thing', *Motography*, March 31, 1917, 687.

------. 'Knowledge of the Camera Essential to Successful Photoplay Writing',

Photoplay, October 1917, 108 and 118.

Phillips, Henry Albert. 'Visualisation', *The Photoplay Author*, August 1914, 35–38.

------. 'The New Literary Profession', *MPM*, October 1914, 81–82.

------. 'Where to Get Photoplay Plots', *MPM*, February 1915, 101–105.

------. 'Literary Construction – Its Art and Technique', *The Photoplay Author*, March 1915, 67–69.

Porter, Edwin S. 'The Great Train Robbery', *Screenplays for You*, accessed March 8, 2013, http://sfy.ru/?script=great_train_robbery_1903

Presbrey, Eugene W. 'The Free Lance Writer' in *Opportunities in the Motion Picture Industry*, 45–48.

R.V.S., 'Scenario Construction', *MPW*, February 11, 1911, 294.

Sargent, Epes Winthrop. 'The Earmark on the Film', *MPW*, August 26, 1911, 521.

------. 'Handling the Kalem Release', *MPW*, October 19, 1912, 233.

------. 'Progress in Photoplay Writing', in *Motion Picture Annual and Yearbook for 1912*. New York: MPW, 1913.

------. 'The Literary Side of Pictures', *MPW*, July 11, 1914, 199–202.

------. 'Another Censorship Angle', *MPW*, October 30, 1915, 806.

------. 'Necessity of Encouraging the Author', *MPW*, July 22, 1916, 623.

------. 'Münsterberg on the Photoplay', *MPW*, July 15, 1916, 436–437.

------. 'Wanted – A Museum', *MPW*, September 9, 1916, 1704.

------. 'Photoplay Writing, Then and Now', *MPW*, March 10, 1917, 1491–92.

------. 'What Is Photoplay?' *MPW*, July 21, 1917, 369–370.

Smith, Frederick James. 'The Evolution of the Motion Picture – VII. From the Standpoint of the Photoplaywright. An Interview with Captain Leslie T. Peacocke, *NYDM,* July 23, 1913, 25 and 31.

Spencer, Richard. 'Fifty Dollar Scenarios', *Photo Playwright*, November–October 1912, 5.

Sylvester, Richard. 'The New Art of the Photoplay-dramatist', *The Drama*, February 1918, 96–102.

Thomas, Arthur W. 'The Photoplaywright and His Art', *Photoplay*, August 1914, 85–88.

Wickes, E.M. 'So You'll Know Them Better – Catherine Carr, Editor of Kinetophote Company', *The Photoplay Author*, November 1914, 134–138.

Wright, William Lord. 'The Idea is the Thing', *Photo Playwright*, September/October 1912, 11–13

------. 'The Spark of Genius', *MPSM*, September 1912, 135–136.

------. 'The Successful Plot', *Photo Playwright*, October/November 1912, 9.

------. 'The Tremolo Touch', December 1912, 130 in *MPSM*.

------. 'Censors a Costly Luxury for Ohio', *MPN*, May 30, 1914, 25–26.

------. 'Looking Over the Field', *The Photoplay Author*, October 1914, 117–119.

Miscellaneous Trade and Fan Press Articles

'Associated M. P. Schools' in *MPN*, September 30, 1911, 20 and 34.

'Better Treatment for the Story Writer', *Motography*, September 29, 1917, 651–652.

'Photoplay Authors' League', *MPW*, July 10, 1915, 268.

'Scenario Copyright Law in View', *MPN*, April 4, 1914, 22.

'Scenario School Advertising Barred by Photoplay Magazine', *Photoplay*, April 1915, 114-117.

Video and Audio Sources

Black Beauty (Vitagraph, 1921) at http://www.movies.msn.com. The seven-reel original survives in fragments of two and half reels from a 1929 re-release and can be accessed at http://www.harpodeon.com

Froug, William. 'Screenwriting Tricks of the Trade – The Workshop', *Writers Audio Shop*. Allen: Timberwolf Press, 1993.

Hauge, Michael. On pitching – Screen Australia Industry Lecture on *YouTube*, accessed March 25, 2014, https://www.youtube.com/watch?v=KZrvgU10hA0

Truby, John. 'Thoughts on Screenwriting Gurus.' *YouTube*, accessed July 15, 2014, https://www.youtube.com/watch?v=k267ReHztF4

Secondary Sources

Books and Theses

Abel, Richard. *The Red Rooster Scare: Making Cinema American, 1900–1910*. Berkeley: University of California, 1999.

Allen, Robert C. 'Vaudeville and Film 1895-1915: A Study in Media Interaction.' PhD diss., University of Iowa, 1977. ProQuest (UMI 7728428).

Allen, Robert C. and Gomery, Douglas. *Film History: Theory and Practice*. New York: McGraw-Hill, 1985.

Altman, Rick. *Film/Genre*. London: BFI, 1999.

Azlant, Edward. 'The Theory, History and Practice of Screenwriting, 1897–1920.' PhD diss., Wisconsin University, 1980. ProQuest (UMI 8111443).

Black, Gregory D. *Hollywood Censored: Morality Codes, Catholics and the Movies.* Cambridge: CUP, 1994.

Boon, Kevin Alexander. *Script Culture and the American Screenplay*. Detroit: Wayne State University, 2008.

Bordwell, David, Staiger, Janet and Thompson, Kristin. *The Classical Hollywood Cinema: Film Style and Mode of Production to 1960.* New York: Columbia, 1985.

Bordwell, David. *The Way Hollywood Tells It: Story and Style in Modern Movies.* London: University of California Press, 2006.

Bowser, Eileen. *The Transformation of Cinema: 1907–1915.* London: University of California Press, 1990.

Bradley, Patricia. *Making American Culture: A Social History, 1900–1920.* New York: Palgrave Macmillan, 2009.

Brewster, Ben and Jacobs, Lea. *Theatre to Cinema: Stage Pictorialism and the Early Film.* Oxford: Oxford University Press, 1997.

Brownlow, Kevin *The Parade's Gone By.* London: Columbus, 1968.

Carson, Marvin. *Theories of the Theatre: A Historical and Critical Survey from the Greeks to the Present.* London: Cornell University Press, 1984.

Ceplair, Larry and Englund, Steven. *The Inquisition in Hollywood: Politics in the Film Community, 1930–1960.* Chicago, University of Illinois Press, 2003.

Chapman, James, Glancy, Mark and Harper, Sue. eds. *The New Film History: Sources, Methods and Approaches.* Basingstoke: Palgrave MacMillan, 2007.

Conor, Bridget. *Screenwriting: Creative Labor and Professional Practice.* Oxon: Routledge, 2014.

Cook, David A. *A History of Narrative Film.* New York: Norton, 1981.

Dallas, Colonel Barnaby. 'Play, Photoplay, and Screenplay Structure: Dramatic Principles from Theater to Cinema.' MA Diss., Jan Hose State University, 2000. ProQuest (UMI 1399789).

Decherney, Peter. *Hollywood and the Culture Elite: How the Movies Became American.* New York: Columbia University Press, 2005.

de Mille, William. *Hollywood Saga.* New York: E. P. Dutton, 1939.

Eagan, Daniel. *America's Film Legacy: The Authoritative Guide to the Landmark Movies in the National Film Registry*. New York, Continuum International, 2010.

Fell, John. *Film and the Narrative Tradition*. Oklahoma: University of Oklahoma Press, 1974.

Francke, Lizzie. *Script Girls: Women Screenwriters in Hollywood*. London: BFI, 1994.

Gauntier, Gene, 'Blazing the Trail', unpublished manuscript. MOMA Archives, New York, 1928.

Goddard, Charles W. and Ball, Eustace Hale. *The Mysteries of Myra* (Stedman, 2010). For details, see http://www.mysteriesofmyra.com

Gunning, Tom. *D.W. Griffith and the Origins of Narrative Film: The Early Years at Biograph*. Chicago: University of Illinois Press, 1994.

Hamilton, Ian. *Writers in Hollywood: 1915–16*. New York: Harper-Collins, 1990.

Hampton, Benjamin B. *History of the American Film Industry from its Beginnings to 1931*. 1931; repr., New York, Dover, 1970.

Higham, Charles. *Cecil B. DeMille*. New York: Da Capo Press, 1973.

Hoveyda, Fereydoun. *The Hidden Meaning of Mass Communications: Cinema, Books, and Television in the Age of Computers*. Westport: Praeger, 2000.

Jacobs, Lewis *The Rise of the American Film: A Critical History*. 1939: repr., New York: Teachers College Press, 1967.

Johnston, Donald H. ed. *Encyclopedia of International Media and Communications*, vol. 4. San Diego: Academic Press, 2003.

Kiel, Charlie. *Early American Cinema in Transition: Story, Style, and Filmmaking 1907-1913*. London: University of Wisconsin Press, 2001.

Kleber, J. E. ed. *The Encyclopedia of Louisville*. Kentucky: University of Kentucky Press, 2001.

Koszarski, Richard. *An Evening's Entertainment: The Age of the Silent Feature Picture, 1915–1928*. London: University of California Press, 1994.

Lawrence, Cooper *The Cult of Celebrity: What Our Fascination with Stars Reveals About Us*. Connecticut: Globe Pequot, 2009.

Liepa, Torey. 'Figures of Silent Speech: Silent Film Dialogue and the American Vernacular, 1909–1916.' PhD diss., New York University, 2008. ProQuest (UMI 3320809).

Lowe, N. J. *The Classical Plot and the Invention of Western Narrative*. Cambridge: CUP, 2000.

Macgowan, Kenneth. *Behind the Screen: The History and Technique of the Motion Picture*. New York: Delacorte, 1965.

Maher, Karen Ward. *Women Filmmakers in Early Hollywood*. Baltimore: John Hopkins University Press, 2006.

Manchel, Frank. *Film Study: An Analytical Bibliography Vol. 1*. London: Associated University Press, 1990.

Maras, Steven. *Screenwriting: History, Theory and Practice*. London: Wallflower Press, 2009.

Marks, Martin Miller *Music and the Silent Film: Context and Case Studies, 1895–1924*. Oxford: OUP, 1997.

McGrath, Declan and MacDermott, Felim. *Screencraft – Screenwriting*. Switzerland: RotoVision, 2003.

Morey, Anne. *Hollywood Outsiders: The Adaptation of the Film Industry 1913–1934*. Minneapolis: University of Minnesota Press, 2003.

Mott, Frank L. *A History of American Magazines, 1865–1885 Vol. 3*. London: OUP, 1938.

Musser, Charles. *Before the Nickelodeon: Edwin S. Porter and the Edison Manufacturing Company*. Berkeley: University of California Press, 1991.

------. *The Emergence of Cinema*: *The American Screen to 1907*. London: University of California Press, 1994.

Nannicelli, Ted. *The Philosophy of the Screenplay*. London: Routledge, 2013.

Neale, Steve. *Genre and Hollywood*. London: Routledge, 2000.

Norman, Marc. *What Happens Next: A History of American Screenwriting*. London: Aurum, 2008.

Owen, Alistair. ed. *Story and Character – Interviews with British Screenwriters*. London: Bloomsbury, 2003.

Parker, Philip. *The Art & Science of Screenwriting*. Bristol: Intellect Books, 2006.

Perry, Louis B. and Perry, Richard S. *A History of the Los Angeles Labor Movement, 1911–1941*. London: University of California, 1963.

Polan, Dana. *Scenes of Instruction: The Beginnings of the U.S. Study of Film*. London: University of California Press, 2007.

Price, Steven. *A History of the Screenplay*. Basingstoke: Palgrave Macmillan, 2013.

Ramsaye, Terry. *A Million and One Nights: A History of the Motion Picture through 1925*. New York: Simon and Schuster, 1926.

Rice, Elmer. *Minority Report: An Autobiography*. New York: Simon & Schuster, 1963.

Robinson, David. *The History of World Cinema*. New York: Stein and Day, 1974.

Ross, Steven J. *Working-class Hollywood*. New Jersey: Princeton University Press, 1999.

Russin, Robin U. and Downs, William Missouri. *Screenplay: Writing the Picture*. Los Angeles: Silman-James, 2003.

Sanderson, Richard Arlo. 'A Historical Study of the Development of American Motion Picture Content and Techniques Prior to 1904.' PhD diss., University of Southern California, 1961. ProQuest (UMI 6102538).

Schoch, Richard. ed. *Great Shakespeareans: Macready, Booth, Irving, Terry*. London: Continuum, 2011.

Sennett, Mack. *The King of Comedy*. 1954: repr., iuniverse.com, 2000.

Shiner, Larry. *The Invention of Art: A Cultural History*. London: University of Chicago, 2001.

Singer, Ben. *Melodrama and Modernity: Early Sensational Cinema and Its Contexts*. New York, Columbia University Press, 2001.

Slide, Anthony. *The New Dictionary of the American Film Industry*. Maryland: Scarecrow Press, 1998.

Soister, John T. *American Silent Horror, Science Fiction and Fantasy Feature Films*. North Carolina: McFarland, 2012.

Staiger, Janet. *Interpreting Films: Studies in the Historical Reception of American Cinema*. New Jersey: Princeton University Press, 1992.

Stamp, Shelley. *Movie Struck Girls: Women and Motion Picture Culture after the Nickelodeon*. New Jersey: Princeton University, 2000.

Starker, Steven. *Oracle at the Supermarket: the American Preoccupation with Self Help Books*. London: Transaction, 1989.

Stempel, Tom. *Framework: A History of Screenwriting in the American Film*. 3rd ed. New York: Syracuse, 2000.

Thompson, Kristin. *Storytelling in the New Hollywood: Understanding Classical Narrative Technique*. London: Harvard University Press, 1999.

Thompson, Kristin and Bordwell, David. *Film History: An Introduction*. 3rd ed. New York: McGraw Hill, 2010.

Thorpe, James Ernest. *Henry Edwards Huntington: A Biography*. Los Angeles: University of California, 1994.

Tibbetts, John. 'The Stage/Screen Exchange: Patterns of Imitation in Art: 1896–1930.' PhD diss., Kansas University, 1982. ProQuest (UMI 8301749).

------. *The American Theatrical Film*. Ohio: Bowling Green State University, 1985.

Vardac, A. Nicholas. *Stage to Screen: Theatrical Method from Garrick to Griffith*. Cambridge, Harvard University Press, 1949.

Vincent, Carl, Redi, Ricardo and Venturini, Franco. eds. *General Bibliography of the Motion Pictures*. 1953; rep., New York: Arno, 1972.

Waters, Malcolm. *Modern Sociological Theory*. London: Sage, 1994.

Yorke, John. *Into the Woods: A Five Act Journey into Story*. London: Penguin Books, 2013.

Article, Journal, Anthology and Periodical Sources

Aberdeen, J. A. 'The Edison Movie Monopoly: The Motion Picture Patents Company vs. the Independent Outlaws', *Hollywood Renegades Archive – SIMPP Research Database*, accessed January 3, 2013, http://www.cobbles.com/simpp_archive/edison_trust.htm

Aitken, Harry and Aitken, Roy. 'The Continuity Script and the Rationalization of Film Production', *Wisconsin Center for Film & Television Research*, accessed January 20, 2014, http://old.wcftr.commarts.wisc.edu/collections/featured/aitken/continuity/

Altman, Rick. 'Dickens, Griffith, and Film Theory Today' in *Classical Hollywood Narrative: The Paradigm Wars*, ed. Jane Gaines. Durham: Duke University Press, 1992. 9–47.

Andrushko, Mark, 'Scriptapalooza Interviews Screenwriting Guru Robert McKee' in *Screenwriting Contests and Markets Online*, April 29, 2004, *Moviebytes* website accessed November 28, 2014, http://www.moviebytes.com/contestDetail.cfm?tab=tab3&ContestNumber=123&StoryID=1876.

Aristotle. *The Poetics*, Chapter 7; 'The Plot Must Be a Whole'; Chapter 8, 'The Plot Must a Unity'; and Chapter 9, 'Dramatic Unity', accessed March 14, 2014, http://www.identitytheory.com/etexts/poetics.html

Azlant, Edward. 'Screenwriting for the Early Silent Film: Forgotten Pioneers, 1897–1911', *Film History* 9 (1997): 228–256.

Birch, Anthony. 'Aristotle's Elements of Drama', accessed March 13, 2014, http://www.mindtools.net/MindFilms/aristot.shtml

Boone, Christopher. 'How I Really Feel about Screenwriting Gurus: Courtesy of Frank Darabont and Scott Myers', *No Film School*, July 23, 2012, accessed June 16, 2014, http://nofilmschool.com/2012/07/screenwriting-gurus-frank-darabont-scott-myers

Bratton, Jacky, Cook, Jim and Gledhill, Christine. 'Introduction' in *Melodrama: Stage, Picture, Screen*, eds. Bratton, Cook and Gledhill. London: BFI, 1994. 1–8.

Brewster, Ben. 'Traffic in Souls: An Experiment in Feature-length Narrative Construction' in *Cinema Journal* 31, no.1 (1991): 37–56.

Brower, Jordon and Glick, Josh. 'The Art and Craft of the Screen: Louis Reeves Harrison and the Moving Picture World' in *Historical Journal of Film, Radio and Television* 33, no. 4 (2013): 533–551, accessed January 15, 2014, http://dx.doi.org/10.1080/01439685.2013.847652.

Butsch, Richard. 'The Making of American Audiences: From Stage to Television, 1750–1990' in *Movies and American Society*, ed. Steven J. Ross. Oxford: Blackwell, 2002. 14–31.

Cardwell, Douglas. 'The Well-made Play of Eugène Scribe', *The French Review 56*, May 1983, 876–884, accessed February 21, 2014, https://ibenglish2011.wikispaces.com/file/view/The+Well-Made+Play+of+Eugene+Scribe.pdf

Chiarulli, Raffaele. 'Strong Curtains and Dramatic Punches: The Legacy of Playwriting and the Debate on the Three-act Model in the Screenwriting Manuals of the Studio Era', Screenwriting Research Network Conference, October 16–19, 2014, Potsdam, Berlin.

Dirks, Tim. 'The History of Film – The Pre-1920s' in *Early Cinematic Origins and the Infancy of Film 3*, accessed January 3, 2013, http://www.filmsite.org/pre20sintro3.html

------ 'The History of Film', in *Early Cinematic Origins and the Infancy of Film 4*, accessed January 3, 2013, http://www.filmsite.org/pre20sintro4.html

Dodds, George. *Beyond the Banyans* (A short story by Epes Winthrop Sargent), accessed June 8, 2013, http://www.erbzine.com/mag18/banyans.htm

Donaldson, Peter. Film Editing Terms from *Film Lexicon*, accessed February 2, 2014, http://art3idea.psu.edu/locus/film_terms.pdf

Elsaesser, Thomas, 'Tales of Sound and Fury: Observations on the Family Melodrama' in *Home Is Where the Heart Is: Studies in Melodrama and the Women's Film*, ed. E. A Kaplan. London: BFI, 1987.

Field, Syd, 'About Syd Field' (biographical information), accessed November 5, 2014, http://sydfield.com/about/

Final Draft, 'Syd Field Joins Big Break! Judges Panel' in *Film Industry News*, June 30, 2004, accessed November 28, 2014, http://www.filmmakers.com/news/contests/article_159.shtml - all accessed November 28, 2014.

Gay, Andrew Kenneth. 'History of Scripting and the Screenplay' in *Screenplayology: An Online Centre for Screenplay Studies*, accessed June 28, 2014, http://www.screenplayology.com/content-sections/screenplay-style-use/1-1/

Gerstner, David A. 'The Practices of Authorship' in *Authorship and Film*, eds. Gerstner and Staiger. London: Routledge, 2003. 4–25.

Grieveson, Lee and Krämer, Peter. eds. 'Classical Hollywood Cinema' in *The Silent Cinema Reader*. London: Routledge, 2004.

Gunning, Tom. 'The Cinema of Attractions: Early Film, Its Spectator, and the Avant-Garde' in *Theatre and Film: A Comparative Anthology*, ed. Robert Knopf. London: Yale University Press, 2005. 37–45.

Haddock, G. W, 'The Art of the Photoplay', *Publishers' comments*, New York: G. W. Dillingham, 1913, accessed March 20, 2014, http://tera-3.ul.cs.cmu.edu/NASD/4dcb85c3-9fee-4c83-9e6d-fe6ce5522b59/China/disk2/20050318-062/31004109/HTML/00000004.htm

Hartley, George. 'Analyzing a Story's Plot: Freytag's Pyramid' in *English 250 Unit: Freytag's Pyramid*, Ohio University, accessed February 10, 2014, http://www.ohio.edu/people/hartleyg/ref/fiction/freytag.html

Hauge, Michael. 'Composing Effective Query Letters', accessed January 16, 2014, http://www.storymastery.com/selling-your-story/composing-effective-query-letters and https://www.storymastery.com/coaching/109-consultation-submission-checklist

Heidenry, Margaret, 'When the Spec Script Was King', *Vanity Fair*, March 2013, accessed March 12, 2014, http://www.vanityfair.com/hollywood/2013/03/will-spec-script-screenwriters-rise-again

Hidalgo, Santiago. 'Early American Film Publications' in *A Companion to Early Cinema*, eds. Andre Gaudreault, Nicholas Dulac and Santiago Hidalgo. Chichester: Wiley-Blackwell, 2012. 202–223.

Horak, Jan-Christopher. 'Review of Dana Polan, Scenes of Instruction: The Beginnings of the U.S. Study of Film' in *Screening the Past*, accessed July 14, 2013, http://tlweb. latrobe.edu.au/humanities/screeningthepast/22/scenes-instruction.html

Huntley, Chris, 'How and Why Dramatica is Different from Six Other Story Paradigms (revised July 2007).' See *Dramatica*, accessed April 6, 2014, http://dramatica.com/ articles/how-and-why-dramatica-is-different-from-six-other-story-paradigms

Keeting, Patrick. 'Prologue: Emotional Curves and Linear Narratives' in *The Classical Hollywood Reader*, ed. Steven Neale. Oxen: Routledge, 2012. 6-20.

Keily, Tony. 'Gurus Methods Teachers', *Film Ireland,* August/September, 2001.

Knopf, Robert .'Introduction' in *Theater and Film: A Comparative Anthology*, ed. Robert Knopf. London, Yale University Press, 2005. 1–20.

Kosman, Aryeh. 'Acting: Drama as the Mimesis of Praxis' in *Essays on Aristotle's Poetics*, ed. Amélie Oksenberg Rorty. Princeton: Princeton University Press, 1992. 51–72.

Langdale, Allan. ed. 'The Stimulation of the Mind: The Film Theory of Hugo Münsterberg' in *Hugo Münsterberg on Film – The Photoplay: A Psychological Study and Other Writings*. New York: Routledge, 2002. 1–41.

Lanouette, Jennine. 'A History of Three-act Structure' in *Screentakes: Studies in Screenwriting for Writers, Directors and Creative Professionals*, December 24, 2012, accessed October 10, 2014, http://www.screentakes.com/an-evolutionary-study-of-the-three-act-structure-model-in-drama/

Liepa, Torey. 'The Sound of Silents: Representations of Speech in Silent Film', MiT4: The Work of Stories, New York University, May 7, 2005, 1–15, *Learning Ace*, accessed March 3, 2014, http://www.learningace.com/doc/68479/ d904421577ff2a31aba0874760e184fb/liepa

------. 'Entertaining the Public Option: The Popular Film Writing Movement and the Emergence of Writing for the American Silent Cinema' in *Analyzing the Screenplay*, ed. Jill Nelmes. Oxon: Routledge, 2011. 7–23.

Loughney, Patrick G. 'In the Beginning Was the Word: Six Pre-Griffith Motion Picture Scenarios' in *Early Cinema: Space, Frame, Narrative*, eds. Thomas Elsaesser and Adam Barker. London: BFI, 1990. 211–219.

Macdonald, Ian W. 'Forming the Craft: Play-wrighting and Photoplay-writing in Britain in the 1910s' in *Early Popular Visual Culture* 8, no. 1 (2010): 75–89.

McManus, Barbara F. 'Outline of Aristotle's Theory of Tragedy in the Poetics', *CLS 267 Topics Page*, November 1999, accessed March 12, 2014, http://www2.cnr.edu/home/bmcmanus/poetics.html

Meyers, Ashley Scott. 'How to Sell Your Screenplay (in a Nutshell)' in *sellingyourscreenplay. com*, accessed February 5, 2014, http://www.sellingyourscreenplay.com/how-Mito-sell-your-screenplay/how-to-sell-your-screenplay-in-a-nutshell/

Millard, Kathryn. 'Writing for the Screen: Beyond the Gospel of Story', *Journal of Media Arts Culture*, June 2006, accessed October 13, 2013, http://scan.net.au/scan/journal/display.php?journal_id=77

Mitchell, George. 'The Movies and Münsterberg', *Jump Cut*, no. 27, July 1982, 57–60, accessed May 30, 2013, http://www.ejumpcut.org/archive/onlinessays/JC27folder/Munsterberg.html

Morey, Anne. '"Have You the Power?" The Palmer Photoplay Corporation and the Film Viewer/Author in the 1920s', *Film History* 9 (1997): 300–319.

Murray, Janet. 'Can You Teach Creative Writing?' *Guardian*, May 10, 2011, accessed August 10, 2014, http://www.theguardian.com/education/2011/may/10/creative-writing-courses

Musser, Charles. 'The Early Cinema of Edwin S. Porter' in *The Wiley-Blackwell History of American Film*, eds. Cynthia Lucia, Roy Grundmann and Art Simon. Malden: Wiley-Blackwell, 2012. 39–86.

Nyyssonen, Passi. 'Film Theory at the Turning Point of Modernity' in *Film-Philosophy Electronic Salon*, October 17 (1998), 2. 1–17, accessed September 1, 2014, http://www.film-philosophy.com/vol2-1998/n31nyyssonen

Panofsky, Erwin. 'Style and Medium in the Motion Pictures (1934)', in *Film Theory and Criticism*, 4th ed., eds. Gerald Mast, Marshall Cohen and Leo Braudy. Oxford: OUP, 1992. 233–248.

Pascal, Ernest, 'The Author of the Piece', *The Screen Guilds' Magazine* 2, August 8, 1935.

Pratt, Judith Stevens. 'The Vaudeville Criticism of Epes Winthrop Sargent 1896–1910 (abstract).' PhD diss., Nebraska University, 1985. ProQuest (UMI 303387823), accessed June 12, 2014, http://search.proquest.com//docview/303387323

Princi, Lorenzo. 'Review of Shoot! By Luigi Pirandello', *Blurb Hack*, August 21, 2010, accessed August 12, 2014, http://blurbhack.com/reviews/review.php?recordID=80&type=book&code=shoot

Raynauld, Isabelle. 'Written Scenarios of Early French Cinema: Screenwriting Practices in the First Twenty Years', *Film History 9*, no. 3 (1997): 257–268.

Roche, Mark W. 'Introduction to Hegel's Theory of Tragedy', accessed April 15, 2014, http://aplangandcomp.blogs.rsu1.org/files/2011/03/hegelontragedy.pdf

Seger, Linda. 'About Linda Seger, Script Consultant' (biographical information), accessed November 5, 2014, http://www.lindaseger.com/script-consultant-screenplay-coach/

Singer, Ben. 'Fiction tie-ins and narrative intelligibility 1911–1918', *Film History* 5, (1993): 489–504.

Sontag, Susan. 'Film and Theatre' in *Film Theory and Criticism*, eds. Gerald Mast, Marshall Cohen, Leo Braudy. 362–374.

Stack, Danny, 'Screenwriting Bullet 14: Step Outline', March 8, 2013, *Scriptwriting in the UK*, accessed January 12, 2014, http://dannystack.blogspot.co.uk/2012/09/screenwriting-bullet-14-step-outline.html

Staiger, Janet. 'Blueprints for Feature Films: Hollywood's Continuity Scripts' in *The American Film Industry*, ed. Tino Ballo. Madison: University of Wisconsin, 1985.173–194.

Stedman, Alex. 'Writer-Producer William Froug dies at 91', *Variety*, September 5, 2013, accessed November 5, 2014, http://variety.com/2013/tv/news/writer-producer-william-froug-dies-at-91-1200600523/

Thompson, Kristin. 'Narrative Structure in Early Classical Cinema' in *Celebrating 1895: The Centenary of Cinema*, ed. John Fullerton. Sydney: John Libbey & Co, 1998. 225–238.

Urbanora. 'The Theatre of Science', August 29, 2007 in *The Bioscope*, accessed July 10, 2013, http://thebioscope.net/2007/08/29/the-theatre-of-science/

Walter, Richard. 'About Richard Walter', (biographical information), accessed November 5, 2014, http://richardwalter.com/about-richard/

Ward, Lewis. 'Structure and Breaking In: An Interview with Syd Field', *Script Magazine*, April 10, 2013, accessed August 13, 2014, http://www.scriptmag.com/features/structure-and-breaking-in-an-interview-with-syd-field.

Wiles, David. 'Aristotle's Poetics and Ancient Dramatic Theory' in *The Cambridge Companion to Greek and Roman Theatre*, eds. Marianne McDonald and J. Michael Walton. Cambridge: CUP, 2007. 92–107.

Yoneda, Kathie Fong. *The Script-Selling Game*. Los Angeles: Michael Wiese, 2002, accessed June 12, 2014, http://www.kathiefongyoneda.com

Other Miscellaneous Sources

Biograph Story Department Logbook. MOMA Archives, New York, 1910–15.

Pamphlet on 'How to Write Motion Picture Plays.' New York, MOMA, 1912.

Screenwriters' Summit in Toronto, 2011. See Toronto Screenwriters' Summit 2011 held on March 28, 2011, Hollywood University Blog, http://hollywoodu.net/2011/03/28/screenwriters-summit-2011-toronto/

The London Screenwriters Festival, http://www.londonscreenwritersfestival.com

The Motion Picture Association of America (MPAA), http://www.mpaa.org/film-ratings/

'WGA West Registry, https://www.wgawregistry.org/webrss/

Access to Online Sources

Cambridge Dictionary online: http://www.dictionary.cambridge.org

Creative World Awards, http://www.creativeworldawards.com

'Inflation Calculator' in *DaveManuel.com*, accessed May 20, 2014, http://www.davemanuel.com/inflation-calculator.php

Mandell, Corey seminar advertisement, accessed March 10, 2014, See http://www.eventbrite.com/e/the-insider-view-how-the-pros-rewrite-with-corey-mandell-tickets-4158070902 and http://coreymandell.net

FictionMags Index lists American published short stories from 1880 to the present, accessed June 8, 2015, http://www.philsp.com/homeville/FMI/0start.htm#TOC

Final Draft Newsletter for 2014 Screenwriters' Summit conference, accessed August 21, 2014, http://newsletter.finaldraft.com/newsletter-20140123_WritersSummit.html

Hauge, Michael, *Story Mastery*, accessed May 14, 2014, http://www.storymastery.com.

Hunter, Lewis, *Lew Hunter's Screenwriting 434 Colony* website, accessed December 12, 2014, http://lewhunter.com/index.html

Internet Movie Database (IMDbPro) sources were accessed from January–June 2014, https://pro-labs.imdb.com

McKee, Robert website, accessed May 14, 2014, http://mckeestory.com.

Moviebytes lists all reputable screenwriting competitions in the USA, http://www.moviebytes.com

Newspapers.com for historical newspapers from the 1700s to 2000s, accessed September 17, 2013, http://www.newspapers.com

New York Public Library, Manuscript and Archives Division, accessed December 10, 2013, http://www.nypl.org/about/divisions/manuscripts-division

Oxford Dictionary Online: http://www.oxforddictionaries.com

Script Consultancy Services. See *Seger, Linda Script Consultant*, http://www.lindaseger.com/script-consultant/, Aronson, Linda Script Consultant, http://www.lindaaronson.com/consultant-teacher.html and Vogler, Christopher, *Storytech Literary Consulting,* http://www.thewritersjourney.com all accessed April 20, 2014.

Truby, John website, 'Endorsements', *The Anatomy of Story Master Class*, accessed May 14, 2014, http://trubywriting.com/node/10.

Undergraduate Courses at University and College (UCAS), accessed February 21, 2015, http://www.ucas.com

Vogler, Christopher website, *The Essence of Storytelling*, accessed May 14, 2014, http://www.christophervogler.com.

Women Film Pioneers Project at Columbia University sources were accessed between January-June 2014, https://wfpp.cdrs.columbia.edu.

WorldCat OCLC, accessed between January-June 2014, https://www.worldcat.org

Wikipedia: 'List of Lost Silent Films (1915–19)', accessed April 10, 2013, http://en.wikipedia.org/wiki/List_of_lost_silent_films_(1915–19)

Ways Trade and Fan Press Were Accessed

Media History Digital Library, sources were accessed from January–June 2014, http://mediahistoryproject.org

Fulton History (Historic Newspapers) All Fulton Newspaper sources were accessed from January–June 2014, http://fultonhistory.com/Fulton.html

Trade Press

MPW – Moving Picture World

MPN – Moving Picture News and Motion Picture News

NYDM – New York Dramatic Mirror

The Photoplay Author

Variety

Fan Press

Photoplay

MPSM – The Motion Picture Story Magazine

MPM – Motion Picture Magazine

Picture-Play Magazine

Screenland.

APPENDIX ONE

Example of Synopsis,
Cast of Characters, Scene Plot and Scenario

By

Eustace Hale Ball

"THE CHAP FROM BROADWAY."

An Original Drama for Photoplay.

Synopsis.

HENRY ALLEN, a hustling New Yorker, goes to the timber regions of Tennessee to make some big purchases of land for a rich syndicate. He goes to see old Ezekial Burrows, the biggest landholder of the neighborhood, whose pretty daughter Betsy, makes a conquest at sight. Betsy is beloved by a rough, handsome and unscrupulous mountain fellow, named Clay Nash, who intends to gain the girl for a wife and the old man's timber lands for himself. The arrival of the stranger enrages Clay, who determines to "show up" the city fellow by frightening him, and driving him back to the city in disgrace. Henry Allen puts up such a resistance, never lacking his sense of humor, that Clay is driven to desperation and with some of his mountaineer clansmen he tries to murder the visitor. They are told that Allen is a deputy for Uncle Sam, searching for illicit stills, and they swear to

kill the city chap. While Allen is inspecting
timber lands with old Burrows he is captured by a treacherous ruse and taken to the
gang headquarters, an old mountain farm-
house. Betsy has learned of their trickery
and comes to the house to beg Clay for his
release. Allen hears her talking with Clay
as he slips away, and believes that she is
really in love with the mountaineer. He
escapes through a window, jumping to a tree
nearby, and mounts his horse, galloping back
to Burrows' home where he has been stop-
ping. He signs the agreement to purchase
the old man's holding, and is starting away
on his long ride to the railroad with her
father to guide him, when Betsy rides up
breathlessly to warn them that the gangsters
are after them. They barricade the house,
awaiting the mountaineers. Clay enters,
leaving his men outside on guard. Clay accuses Allen of stealing his sweetheart, but
Betsy blushingly declares that she loves not
him, but the city man. Clay staggers, and
starts to walk out, realizing his defeat. As
he turns to look at them, in the doorway, the
city man offers his hand and Clay's manly
instincts conquer, and he acknowledges his
defeat with his good wishes, promising to
send his men away and to leave the new-

comer undisturbed. Old Burrows, his daughter and Allen follow Clay to the gate. As the happy lovers wave farewell, he starts on up the mountain road, head hanging and dragging his gun, as he leads his horse with the others. The last view shows a silhouette against the sunset sky as Clay ascends a high peak of the mountain to gaze sadly into the valley below, where he has lost his happiness, but gained the great lesson of manliness.

CAST OF CHARACTERS.

PARTS:

Henry Allen, the city chap, clever young New York business man.

Ezekial Burrows, old Tennessean, rich landowner.

Betsy, his pretty daughter.

Clay Nash, a handsome and dissolute mountaineer.

EXTRAS:

Burrows' hired man.

First mountaineer.

Second mountaineer.

Third mountaineer.

Fourth mountaineer.

Director of Syndicate, a New York business man.

Second director.
Third director.

SCENE PLOT.

Interiors:

Office in New York—1.
Burrows' living room—5-7-9-16-18-35-39.
Mountaineers' saloon—24-26-29.
Small attic room—25-30.

Exteriors:

All photographed around Palisades district.
30 scenes (either snow or bare).

THE ACTION.

Scene 1.
Interior: Office.

Henry leaving his office and bidding farewell to directors of big syndicate, on his way to buy land in Tennessee. They wish him luck.

Scene 2.
Exterior: Station.

Henry arrives at mountain station of railroad. Met by Ezekial Burrows' hired man. Rides away with him.

SCENE 3.

Exterior: Mountain scene.

Riding along mountainous country stretch with heavy timber. Man and Allen talking about the timber.

SCENE 4.

Exterior: Burrows' house.

Arrival at house. Greeted by old man at front porch.

SCENE 5.

Interior: Burrows' house.

Allen meets pretty Betsy and falls in love at sight. He gets down to business with the old man, who insists on making him comfortable at first. Log fire, big chimney, etc. Betsy gets good things for him to eat. Henry lays out proposal of the syndicate. Old man tells fears of the mountaineer gang led by Clay Nash.

SCENE 6.

Exterior: Burrows' house as in 4.

Clay Nash arrives with two other horsemen. Inquires from hired man about purpose of stranger. Goes up steps, listens at door and then enters.

SCENE 7.

Interior: Burrows' house as in 5.

Clay enters and breaks up conference. Clay very insulting to the stranger, while Allen is diplomatic and "kids" him along. Quarrel between Clay and Betsy there, and Clay exits threatening the stranger, and daring him to come outside.

SCENE 8.

Exterior: Burrows' house as in 4.

Clay comes outside, and gives orders to his two men to wait in ambush for the stranger.

SCENE 9.

Interior: Burrows' house as in 5.

Allen talks a minute with the old man and his daughter, who warns him. He laughs, pulls out his revolver, and throws it on the table, to show them that he has a different method.

SCENE 10.

Exterior: Burrows' house as in 4.

Allen on porch, he laughs at Clay, and walks down steps with him.

Scene 11.

Exterior: From window.

Ten-foot flash of girl and old man at window, watching fearfully.

Scene 12.

Exterior: Burrows' house as in 4.

Allen and Clay walking along, and Allen asking the other to help him buy up timber lands. Clay denounces Allen as a revenue spy. Allen laughs, and Clay, seeing a good chance, takes off his hat, and steps to one side. It is a signal, and two gun shots come from a clump of nearby bushes. Allen drops low, and is unhurt. Instantly he springs up, grabs Clay by the neck and gives him some jiu-jitsu, holding him between the two hidden marksmen and himself. He beats up Clay, gets his gun away from him, holds it at his stomach and commands the two men to come forth, or he will kill their leader. They grudgingly do so.

Scene 13.

Exterior: Flash.

Flash of old man and Betsy on porch with rifles in hand.

Scene 14.

Exterior: Burrows' house as in 4.

Allen gives Clay a blow, knocks him down and kicks him, and then hands him his gun back, telling him to get out. The two men glare at each other, but Clay's face falls and he looks down. The mountaineers sneak away.

Scene 15.

Exterior: Porch again as before.

Allen joining the two. Betsy now weeping as though her heart was broken. Allen thinks she loves Clay, and he hesitates, then thanks the father and daughter. He sadly goes inside, with Betsy and her father following.

Scene 16.

Interior: Burrows' house as in 5.

Old man and Allen, smoking before big fireplace. Betsy bids them good night, leaving them to talk over plans of timber sale. Betsy comes back and looks at Allen, without his knowing it, and unseen by him, slips his fur cap from the hook on the wall, kisses it, and takes it to bed with her. (Fade out.)

SCENE 17.

Exterior: Moonlight. Old Farm House.

Clay and his gangsters drawn up before an old farm house, planning deviltry against the newcomer.

SCENE 18.

Interior: Burrows' house as in 5.

NEXT MORNING.

Betsy, tidying up living room, and setting breakfast table. She takes down a photograph of Clay, which she looks at and cries over. Allen enters unseen, and looks over her shoulder, sees the picture and turns away believing that she loves Clay. He leaves the room, and then misses seeing her tear up the picture scornfully, as she realizes that the old love was not worth while—and that Clay is a bad man. Allen re-enters the room with the old man, and they start at breakfast. He is very downcast, however, and cannot eat, despite the attention of the girl.

SCENE 19.

Exterior: Burrows' house as in 4.

Allen and old man, coming down porch steps and mounting horses, to go out and see

the timber.   Allen and the girl wave good-
bye.

SCENE 20.

Exterior: Burrows' lands.

Out in the woods, Ezekial showing his
possessions.

SCENE 21.

Exterior: Another woods scene.

Clay and men following in the woods.

SCENE 22.

Exterior: Woods scene.

Allen and Ezekial met by two horsemen,
who tell Ezekial some cock-and-bull story,
and get them separated.   Clay and his men
close in on the city fellow as soon as Ezekial
is out of the way, and bind him, at the point
of guns.

SCENE 23.

Exterior: Old farm house as in 17.

Clay's   headquarters.   Mountaineers
around.   They hurriedly roll barrels out of
sight, as Clay rides up with prisoners, but
Allen notices this.   Prisoner taken inside.

SCENE 24.

Interior: Saloon, "blind tiger."

In the farm house, regular speak-easy, with sanded floor, tables, etc. The men crowd around Clay and his prisoner, who is made to write a letter to old Burrows, demanding money for his ransom. The prisoner is roughly treated, cursed and insulted by the mountaineers. He is led upstairs to a little prison on the loft.

SCENE 25.

Interior: Attic room, rough walls.

Clay leads in Allen, bound. Leaves him with threat of death, after lashing him across face, leaving welt.

SCENE 26.

Interior: Saloon as in 42.

The mountaineers getting rougher and rougher. More drink. Clay tells them that their prisoner is a revenue spy, and they want to lynch him. But he tells them to get a rope, and wait until the messenger has taken the demand for money to old Burrows.

SCENE 27.

Exterior: Burrows' home as in 4.

Betsy leaving home, worried about the absence of her father and visitor.

SCENE 28.

Exterior: Woods scene.

Betsy meets her father racing back on horseback, and he tells her of the disappearance of Allen. She tells him to ride for home, and she will search in a certain place. He wants to accompany her, but she tells him to do as she bids, scorns fear, and insists that she has a plan to save Allen. Betsy rides along toward Clay's house.

SCENE 29.

Interior: Saloon as in 24.

Clay decides to leave and attend to the ransom matter himself. He exits.

SCENE 30.

Interior: Attic as in 25.

Allen is working himself loose from ropes. He succeeds, and hurries to window, where he slips out.

SCENE 31.

Exterior: Roof of house, showing slanting roof.

Allen slides down from window and then jumps to tree. Before getting down, he sees Betsy coming.

SCENE 32.

Exterior: Showing Allen up in tree and farm house.

A few feet back Allen is seen up in tree. Clay comes out of house, just about to mount his horse. Betsy approaches and intercedes for Allen. Allen thinks it is a rendezvous, instead, and broken-hearted he turns away and under cover of their talking makes his escape. He cuts his horse from the hitching post in the rear, and rides off through the country. Clay, meanwhile, refuses to help the girl unless she marries him. She refuses. He tries to kiss her, and Betsy lashes him severely with her riding whip, taking his gun from him, and making him apologize on his knees for his insult. She mounts and rides home. Clay goes inside, wiping blood from his face and swearing vengeance.

SCENE 33.

Exterior: Woods scene.

Flash.   Allen riding through woods.

SCENE 34.

Exterior: Burrows' house as in 4.

Allen dashes up and rushes inside, where the old man is waiting.

SCENE 35.

Interior: Burrows' house as in 5.

They draw up the papers, Allen delivers the check, obtains the deeds, etc., and then starts away.   The old man agrees to take him to the railroad.   Allen is very sad, and asks the old man to give him a picture of Betsy, which he does.

SCENE 36.

Exterior: Burrows' house as in 4.

They are starting away with their horses, when Betsy gallops up.   She warns them of Clay's pursuit, which she has heard.   They hurry into the house to barricade it.

SCENE 37.

Exterior: Woods scene.

Clay and gangsters riding rapidly for revenge and a lynching party.

SCENE 38.

Exterior: Burrows' house as in 4.

The gangsters remain on their horses at Clay's command to guard the house. Clay, swearing vengeance, knocks on door and is admitted.

SCENE 39.

Interior: Burrows' house as in 5.

Inside, Clay is covered by the weapons of Ezekial, his daughter and Allen. He accuses Allen of stealing his sweetheart, but Betsy, blushing, declares her love for the Chap from Broadway. Clay drops his head and turns to go, but Allen offers his hand. Clay braces up and takes it like a man, saying that he will no longer contend, and will order his men away. He wishes the successful rival luck. Betsy impetuously offers her hand to him. Clay leaves, dragging his rifle. They all follow him out.

SCENE 40.

Exterior: Burrows' house as in 4.

Clay comes down steps and bruskly orders his men to go back to headquarters and leave him alone—forbidding them to persecute Burrows and Allen further. Astounded, the men gallop away. Clay stumbles awkwardly, blinded by tears, as he approaches his own horse, which he takes by the bridle. Ezekial, Betsy and Allen follow and wave good-bye to him, as he dejectedly starts up the rocky trail above, leading his steed, and dragging his gun.

SCENE 41.

Exterior: High cliff on the mountain.

Clay ascends to the edge of the precipice, leading his horse, and looks over the valley beneath him. He takes off his hat and stands there, silhouetted against the sunlight (orange colored film), and the picture fades out into blackness.

APPENDIX TWO

Example of Synopsis,
How the full synopsis became the standard submission

By

Henry Albert Phillips

The Synopsis is a Photoplay's Soul, Created and Athrob with all the Potentialities of a Complete Cycle of Life ready to take its place among the Prime Experiences of a Generation the Moment a Body is made for it in which to step out of the Realm of the Imagination into the World's Playhouse.

CHAPTER XXII

An Accepted Synopsis

"Pierre Le Grand"

THE following complete Synopsis is printed just as it was written and accepted. With few exceptions, it will be found as a model for the foregoing discussion and examples. It is suggested that it be studied and reviewed as an exemplification of every paragraph of the text. Herein we find an example of the fully extended script. Every thought in the play has been given full reign to leave no room for misunderstanding.

A seven-Part example has been chosen in preference to a five-part, because it is possible to demonstrate the Feature Photoplay and its superior construction more fully by taking an

AN ACCEPTED SYNOPSIS

example that includes the five-Part play and adds two more Parts. We thus illustrate the principle of Part-building when applied to more than five Parts. So we solve *additional* problems in a practical, commercial demonstration.

"Pierre Le Grand" was produced under the title of "Heart Strings," with William Farnum in the title role. The play was emasculated, however, of all virility by eliminating its sterner aspects and substituting sentimentality. The result therefore could scarcely be said to be the play the author wrote.

(EXAMPLE 132.)

Henry Albert Phillips   All Fiction and Dramatic
The Lambs Club   Rights Reserved
New York City, N. Y.   By the Author

PIERRE LE GRAND
An Emotional Drama with Pathos and Comedy—
In Seven Parts

BY HENRY ALBERT PHILLIPS

THE MOTIF: There are Great Hearts—like Fixed Stars—which though storms may rage that cloud the Horizon and threaten their very Existence, shine and smile ever on, guiding Weaker Mortals in their Upward Climb.

CHARACTERS

PIERRE FONTANELLE.....A Grand Figure among the simpler French people of Old Quebec;

THE FEATURE PHOTOPLAY

he is a potential Musician and Composer of rare
ability, with a cherished Dream of Musical Fame
in the Secret Garden of his heart; but he is Dreamer rather than Doer, and has none of the harsher
traits of commercial Ambition; yet he is the sub-
limer Doer when it comes to Sacrifice for others—
especially his little sister, Gabriele; he is emotional
and always ready to dream his Dream but needs a
force to push him on to action; he is gentleness
personified, and part of his creed is an abhorrence
to violence and combat, which makes his enemy
think him a coward; withal, he is intensely human
and, baited beyond endurance, turns upon his tor-
mentor with a ferocity such as only the long-suf-
fering are capable of.

OLD LA TOUCHE.....A Doer with other
men's Dreams; Pierre's best friend and "discover-
er"; a mass of ceaseless energy, gesticulations,
harmless ferocity and big-heartedness; he is all for
business; he sees a chance to become famous by
making another man famous; he is an eternal bore
and domineering "manager" of everything he comes
in contact with; yet he is impressive, and actually
makes people do the things he intends them to do
and they don't intend to do; he is bombastic and
blustery and is always ready to take the foreground
and settle the affairs of the fishmonger or the nation; yet in the last analysis his affairs seem to
bungle, though he is not conscious of his failure
and lives on the glory of conquest.

GABRIELE.....Pierre's weak little sister; while
she loves her brother, her devotion to Le Boeuf
amounts to an obsession that will carry her any
lengths; Le Boeuf controls and compels every
thought and act in her early life.

AN ACCEPTED SYNOPSIS

LE BOEUF.....A big handsome reprobate; he has little heart or soul; while his feeling for Gabriele is real in the beginning, his desire for money is always greater and he uses her as a tool or a stepping stone to pelf.

ALVA BLASHFIELD.....A typical New York society girl who is drifting with the tide of her caste; she has her pronounced tastes, chief among which is music; she is ready to marry Blake, who is very wealthy and years older than herself, if he will let her and her tastes alone; she holds herself aloof from all things and submits to all cold conventions until she meets Pierre; he then becomes part of the inner life that will never die and which Blake can never touch or comprehend.

BLAKE.....A phlegmatic society man, well along in years, who is annoyed by anything unconventional; he looks upon Alva as a chattel and resents the invasion of Pierre.

AN OUTLINE OF THE PARTS OF THE PLAY

Part I.—A Dream of Youth
Part II.—The Beautiful Lie
Part III.—The Dread Spectre
Part IV.—The Blessed Demoiselle
Part V.—The Sublime Sacrifice
Part VI.—The Supreme Struggle
Part VII.—The Embers of a Dream

Part I.—THE DREAM OF YOUTH

We first meet Pierre playing in a field where country people have come out for a holiday and to dance. They are dancing a quaint folk dance

THE FEATURE PHOTOPLAY

that has been long ago imported to French-Canada from their dear France. On Pierre's face is that wonderful smile that is known all over the Province, but in his eyes we can see a faraway Dream that he is living that moment. Occasionally someone drops a coin in the hat by his side, or children come and caress his arm, and then he directs that sunny smile on them for an instant only.

La Touche is coming along the road in a queer cart known to Quebec, loaded with merchandise. He stops his horse and looks on a moment, and then recognizes Pierre, and his face lights up and he gets down, adjusts himself for a dignified entry among the yokels whom he literally pushes aside, and makes a swath straight for Pierre, at once becoming per force and audacity the central figure. The playing is stopped and consequently the dance. They greet with mutual effusion: "MON DIEU, DREAMER, YOU STILL PLAY TO THE YOKELS OF THE PROVINCE WHEN YOU HAVE PROMISED ME YOU WOULD GO TO PARIS AND LEARN TO ENTHRALL THE WORLD!" La Touche thus reproves Pierre, who regards him with a look of pain, and then proceeds to explain, and La Touche deliberately takes him away with him in his little cart.

Gabriele at home is pleading with her lover Le Boeuf to take her with him, but he tells her he cannot yet. Suddenly she espies Pierre coming down the road with La Touche, and fearfully hustles Le Boeuf from the house, he smiling cynically at her thought of danger to him.

Pierre enters, now thoroughly inflamed with the vision that La Touche is branding on his soul. He catches Gabriele joyously to him: "AND HERE IS

AN ACCEPTED SYNOPSIS

MA PETITE GABRIELE—SHE IS THE BEST
PART OF MY LIFE—WHEN I GO TO PARIS
SHE MUST COME TOO." La Touche signifies,
of course.   Gabriele gives a frightened look and
goes pensively to a corner while the men continue
to plan.   Pierre empties his pockets of coins, giving
the largest to Gabriele.   La Touche counts them.
Pierre lifts the tile in front of the fireplace and
takes out a bag of gold and together he and La
Touche count it.   "LET US SAY, IN A MONTH
FROM TODAY THE FUND I HAVE BEEN
SAVING FOR FIVE YEARS WILL BE COM-
PLETE, AND THEN I WILL BE READY TO
GO!"

We see Le Boeuf being put out of his uncle's
house.   He is telling the servant: "MY NEPHEW
IS A RASCAL—YOU WILL SEE THAT HE
NEVER ENTERS MY HOUSE AGAIN."   Le
Boeuf leaves with his ever-cynical smile, and we
see him enter a gambling place and produce a thick
roll of bills and join the game.

The Day marking the end of the month when
Pierre said he would have his Five-Year Fund
complete we find him about to be totally surprised
through the efforts of La Touche who has gathered
all his neighbors and friends for miles around.
Gabriele is in on this secret and has invited Le
Boeuf, who comes with his cynical smile.

Pierre's attention is attracted elsewhere and La
Touche forms the people outside like a procession
and then they suddenly burst in with all the simple
joy of their type.   La Touche the practical and
commercial takes a bowl and puts it on the table
and makes each one put a coin in.   In fact, he is
busy in every part of the room marshalling, com-

THE FEATURE PHOTOPLAY

manding, interfering, reprimanding, and letting no one have a thought of their own in the matter. He pulls a piece of paper from his pocket on which he has jotted the program he has arranged. First the ladies through a dumpy spokeswoman present a typical Frenchy artificial bouquet. In the midst of her speech La Touche yanks her away and takes the floor, but not before she has embraced the shy Pierre. Then follows a quartet of four over-dressed yokels whom La Touche attempts to lead in vain. The result is a startling exhibition that makes La Touche perspire freely. Pierre is frightened and pained at the so-called music.

La Touche now steps forward to make a presentation Speech which he has written down and has great difficulty in reading. Pierre awkwardly listens and then is soon immersed, as all are, in the vivid presentment of the things he is going to do, La Touche acting out how he will play, how the audiences will respond, and taking in turn the parts of all the episodes of his Fame Period. But the speech is so long that old ladies sleep, children play, and the youths gape in vain, though all remain in agonized solemnity.

Le Boeuf stands regarding the whole adventure with wearied contemptuousness, most of all Pierre, whom he considers a big softy. Gabriele has sought his side and endeavors to cling to him. The other guests regard him with dislike.

At last comes the Presentation of the gold-mounted Baton: "..... WITH WHICH SOME DAY MON AMI PIERRE—FONTANELLE LE GRAND THEY SHALL CALL HIM—WILL LEAD THE ORCHESTRA AS IT PLAYS ONE OF HIS OWN COMPOSITIONS!" There is

AN ACCEPTED SYNOPSIS

loud applause that rudely awakens the sleepers in
alarm and Pierre the Dreamer takes the baton
tremulously in his hand. He cannot speak, but his
smile tells them what is in his full heart. At length
he says: "WHEN I RETURN FROM PARIS—
WHERE I SHALL STUDY UNDER THE FA-
MOUS MAITRE DUPRE—IT IS FOR YOU—
FIRST OF ALL—I SHALL PLAY MY COMPO-
SITIONS!" Then he plays for them and stirs
their souls.

Formalities over, La Touche again seizes the
reins and proposes a toast and all raise glasses.
Pierre has seen Gabriele intimately standing by
Le Boeuf for the first time and calls her. She tries
in vain to have Le Boeuf come with her. La
Touche stands on a chair and all raise their glasses
enthusiastically except Le Boeuf. Pierre says to
Gabriele: "THIS IS THE LAST TIME YOU
AND I SHALL SEE OUR DEAR FRIENDS, SO
LET US SAY FAREWELL TOGETHER!" Sev-
eral times he glances uneasily at the handsome big
fellow with the curled lip.

La Touche cries: "TO THE COMING
GREAT MASTER OF MUSIC—FONTANELLE
LE GRAND!" All are about to drink when several policemen appear at the exits with Le Boeuf's
uncle. The company put down glasses that are
never drunk. Le Boeuf attempts to slink away,
when he is pointed out and seized. A sigh of relief
goes up, which is dispelled the next moment by
Gabriele, who breaks from her brother's side and
throws her arms about Le Boeuf.

Pierre in soul agony over the terrible truth behind it all, demands of Le Boeuf an explanation.
Le Boeuf smiles defiantly and tells them to ask

THE FEATURE PHOTOPLAY

Gabriele. But Gabriele has swooned. Pierre, tragedy and determination in his eyes, tells them to bring the prisoner and tenderly carries Gabriele into another room.

La Touche disperses the crowd just after a physician is called from among them. The uncle is telling Pierre the story: "THE RASCAL MUST GO TO PRISON UNLESS HE PAYS BACK THE THREE THOUSAND DOLLARS HE HAS STOLEN FROM MY SAFE!" Pierre is called in the next room by the doctor. "SHE IS VERY ILL—HER LIFE HANGS ON A THREAD—SHE IS ABOUT TO BECOME A MOTHER!"

Pierre is struck to the heart. He staggers to the dividing curtain and approaches Le Boeuf with a look that for a moment gives him misgivings. He goes up as though to throttle Le Boeuf, just as Gabriele's cry of fear arrests Pierre. She has come to and seen this. Then Le Boeuf hastens to explain: "IS IT THEN A CRIME THAT MY WIFE SHOULD BECOME A MOTHER?" All are skeptical, and Le Boeuf with his evil smile again produces his wedding certificate from his inner pocket.

Le Boeuf is then yanked away by the officers and Pierre is left standing there. It is Gabriele's weak little voice that reawakens him to her peril. He puts his ear down: "IF THEY SEND HIM TO PRISON I SHALL DIE!" Pierre turns a startled look. Then suddenly the smile breaks on his face He goes to the fireplace and gets out the bag and shows it to her. She understands. He empties the cash into his pockets and hurries out.

Pierre arrives at the police court just as the

AN ACCEPTED SYNOPSIS

magistrate is about to send Le Boeuf to jail.
Pierre gives the astonished uncle the money. They
count it and give him back a few pieces. Le Boeuf
is discharged, laughing loudly as he exits uncom-
prehendingly and thinking Pierre did it out of fear
of him.   The money that was to have bought a
Dream has saved the Life of his Beloved and let
loose a Devil destined to destroy most of the Precious things to come—but not all.

PART II.—THE BEAUTIFUL LIE

Pierre returns to the cottage to find Gabriele a
premature Mother and seemingly dying. They
make a great fight for her life. They take Pierre
out.   Then in the agonized hours of the night that
follows he prays and what he prays he plays and
so composes his wonderful "Prayer Sonata."

Neighbors open their windows and listen with
clasped hands. Passersby pause and sigh. Pierre
concludes in a return to belief in a Great God and
His goodness with the tears streaming down his
face.

Gabriele, too, vaguely senses it and feebly keeps
time.   Doctor tells him to come and say goodbye,
but when they arrive there is a turn for the better.

Gabriele gets slowly better. And something new
enters Pierre's life—it is little Pierre, the mite that
Gabriele has mothered. Pierre in his sister's hour
of trial and in his big-hearted childish efforts to
divert her, puts aside his own Great Sorrow completely, and is Pierre of the Sweet Smile again.
Little, tender, and over-delicate Pierre he plays with
and croons to hours at a time, and so the little
thing comes to nestle in his heart and bring him
true joy.

THE FEATURE PHOTOPLAY

Old La Touche meets him again and asks in surprise why it is that he has not gone to Paris: Pierre says: "ASK MECHANTE GABRIELE—A LITTLE HAPPINESS OF HERS HAS DETAINED US A LITTLE."

Gabriele is wan and impatient and does nothing but yearn for Le Boeuf, the father of her child, and it stabs Pierre to the heart to think that she still yearns for him with her brother and her child by her side. She spends most of her time at the window watching and waiting. At length she cannot any longer resist Pierre's big-hearted appeals and they become a gloriously happy group. He is again Pierre the Light-hearted and begins again to build a Paris Fund.

Le Boeuf has become a downright crook. A conference among him and some of his thieving companions has brought out the fact that they need to protect themselves and their pelf through having a woman about as a "fence." Le Boeuf then thinks of his Gabriele: "WHAT WE NEED IS A WOMAN ABOUT AS A 'FENCE' FOR OUR OPERATIONS—I'LL HAVE HER HERE TOMORROW."

Gabriele is startled into ecstasy when Le Boeuf appears. He is half agreeable and she is sickeningly adoring. He tells her that he has provided a home for her. She brings their child, which sets him aghast and perplexes him for a moment. She wants to wait for Pierre, but Le Boeuf is insistent and makes a feint to leave and then she quickly writes a note: "MY LE BOEUF HAS COME FOR ME AS HE PROMISED.....COME TO SEE US OFTEN, MON GRAND FRERE.....I AM SO HAPPY....."

AN ACCEPTED SYNOPSIS

Pierre too has spent a happy day. He comes home singing and with an armful of gifts for his darlings. He thinks at first that they are playing hide and seek. Then he finds the note. His big heart is shaken as he walks the floor, futilely whispering: "MON PETIT PIERRE! MA PETITE GABRIELE!" Then he seizes a little sock that has dropped, which he holds to his breast. Again he plays his Prayer Sonata.

La Touche has dropped in to drink with some friends in the Quarter whom he treats liberally, having made himself a great man by having made another man famous. He remarks: "WHO KNOWS—PERHAPS MY BELOVED PIERRE IS ALREADY FONTANELLE LE GRAND!" At which moment the inimitable strains of Pierre's melody reaches their ears. The company laughs at La Touche, who scowls and stalks out. He appears before Pierre in a stormy mood. "TIENS! WHY DO YOU NOT HURRY AND BECOME FAMOUS AS I HAVE PROMISED—YOU MAKE ME RIDICULOUS!"

It is always La Touche that gives balm to Pierre's wounds and brings him back within the thrall of his dear Dream again. His sweet smile reappears, though a curtain of sadness has been lowered behind it. He gets a bottle of wine and soon they are immersed in a new plan for the dream of Fame. La Touche picks up the little sock when Pierre is out of the room. It gives him some annoyance as he thinks he smells a rat: "CHERCHEZ LA FEMME! YET SHE SHALL NOT ROB US OF FAME." As he is leaving Pierre promises: "SOON MA PETITE GABRIELE WILL RETURN—THEN I SHALL BE VERY HAPPY

THE FEATURE PHOTOPLAY

AND VOILA! AT ONCE WE SHALL ALL GO!"
But Gabriele does not return, for she still wor-
ships and clings to the handsome brute who alternately pets and maltreats her. Each week Pierre
sorrowfully though smilingly goes to visit her and,
seeing her want, leaves money. He sees that to
interfere will mean inevitable tragedy.

Le Boeuf sees in Pierre's non-interference only
cowardliness. At length on one of his visits Pierre
finds the little frail Pierre dead in his mother's
arms. This time Le Boeuf drives him from the
house, when he would turn on him, and it is Gabriele who interferes and beseeches him to go.

The secret Police visit Gabriele and make a search
of the place and find a large quantity of pelf. They
then set a trap for Le Boeuf, who eludes them and
gets in and learns the truth. He is mad with rage
and flings the cowering Gabriele out of the door
where she stumbles and falls down the rickety
stairs. Le Boeuf finds her a mass of inert flesh.
She seems to be dead, and with real fear written
on his face he slinks away in the darkness just as
the watching policeman comes up.

Pierre is sent for and he comes to find his little
Gabriele with her hip badly broken. We see something new in Pierre for the first time, that resembles
a wild lion of vengeance. Instead of a smiling, sen-
timental musician, he becomes a scowling, blood-
thirsty brute. But to no avail, he cannot find Le
Boeuf.

Gabriele does not die, but instead emerges from
it a helpless cripple. The smile slowly returns. But
Gabriele has seen Pierre's strange look. Her first
anxious thought has been for Le Boeuf and she
calls Pierre and asks: "OH, PIERRE, YOU DID

AN ACCEPTED SYNOPSIS

NOT HURT HIM—YOU DID NOT—" Again
and with a twinge of pain he sees how things lie
and he has to promise Gabriele that he never will
hurt him: "THEN, MY GABRIELE, WE MUST
LEAVE QUEBEC—CANADA—RUN AWAY
FROM HIM—ELSE I CANNOT KEEP MY
HANDS FROM—FROM—" He goes through the
motions of throttling, but Gabriele's horrified look
stops him.   He smiles piteously and kneels con-
tritely, asking her to forgive him.   Their predica-
ment is critical, for Gabriele's expenses have exhausted all their funds.   Then the bright hope of
his life "LA TOUCHE!" flashes through his mind
and he writes him.

La Touche, with a gingham apron on, is bossing
everyone within half a mile of his confiserie in
Papineauville when he receives Pierre's letter.   At
once he is blusteringly angry and doffs his apron
and starts down to give Pierre a piece of his mind.
He blusters in: "MON DIEU! YOU ARE YET
HERE!   MUST I BECOME A CLOWN FOR
THE PEOPLE BECAUSE YOU ARE A SNAIL!"
On seeing the plight of poor Gabriele he is at once
softened.   When told the truth he cannot under-
stand all, but asks him why he does not sell his
precious violin: "NON, MON AMI, THIS IS
WORTH MORE THAN A MAN'S LIFE TO
ME—FOR A CENTURY MY FAMILY HAS
SACRIFICED ALL BUT LIFE ITSELF TO
PASS IT ON."

They puzzle over the problem and then La
Touche gets the brilliant idea: "VOILA, I HAVE
IT—OUR FAME IS ASSURED!   I SHALL BE-
COME YOUR IMPRESARIO!   YOU WILL GO
TO NEW YORK!   I WILL SELL MY CON-

THE FEATURE PHOTOPLAY

FISERIE AND JOIN YOU!" He then gives Pierre funds and their plan is ready to begin at least.

PART III.—THE DREAD SPECTRE

Thus Pierre and Gabriele come to New York and by chance land in the artist colony in Greenwich Village. They are assisted in getting to rights by several of the frayed-out types who dwell in the converted mansion they take two rooms in. Pierre protests especially when an old Dreamer who has dreamed in vain actually brings them in victuals, and he tells them prophetically: "I HAVE BEEN HERE SEEKING FAME THIRTY YEARS—MY POCKETS WILL BE EMPTY AGAIN TO-MORROW, THEN YOU WILL HELP ME." Thus we show the spiritual and mutual aid and poverty among the Clan of the High Art—always hopeful; up today, down tomorrow; gambling on Fame; seizing at straws; spending sleepless nights, but their days peopled with glorious Dreams or dire Want. But nothing can now seem to dampen Pierre's vision of Fame. He is sure that he is very near to it now.

Pierre starts out with a high heart and boldly assaults the highest musical centers. He seeks a try-out at the Metropolitan Opera, the famous orchestras, the theaters, the palatial photoplay houses —all in vain. One tells him: "FOR GOD'S SAKE GIT OUT O' HERE AND GIVE OUR NEW OR-CHESTRION A CHANCE TO PLAY, WILL YOU?" So they bully him and throw him out.

Gabriele is very morose and Pierre has the double task of lying to her and pretending.

AN ACCEPTED SYNOPSIS

At length all the money is gone. Then Pierre tries playing on the streets, is passed coldly by, and finally he is roughly arrested by a policeman who nearly throttles him for not having a license to beg and showing no disposition to hand out graft. Each night he throws the supposed proceeds of the day into Gabriele's lap. Each day the pile grows smaller, for his little Gabriele must live and live well for she is so delicate and unhappy. He eats next to nothing and daily grows weaker from hunger.

The old Artist drops in again one day and reads the truth in Pierre's emaciated face: "DON'T BE DISCOURAGED—FAME IS JUST PLAYING YOU ONE OF HER TRICKS—I'VE BEEN SPEAKING TO A FRIEND OF MINE WHO NEEDS A MUSICIAN."

The whole complexion of affairs is at once changed for the emotional Pierre. He informs Gabriele that he is now about to achieve fame in truth tomorrow, and he buys a bottle of wine with his last penny and invites the old Artist to share it with him and the two of them cross the portal of Dreams, and one would think that they had their Desire. He plays and soon others drop in to join them and Gabriele too takes on something of the Myth.

But the Job proves to be a miserable affair. It is a "red ink joint" in a dingy basement where the old Artist comes to tipple because of its cheapness. Here Pierre has to play in accompaniment to a blowsy woman pianist and a sour piccolo player whose music saws his artistic soul raw. They have no idea of how to play well and blame their mistakes on Pierre. Between all these circumstances

THE FEATURE PHOTOPLAY

Pierre's life is made truly miserable. He gets a dollar a night and "keep" for the poor job of playing to a questionable gathering from 9 P. M. to 3 A. M.

Gabriele is always awake and waiting for him, and then so weary and heartsore that he can barely stand he must tell of the wonderful success he is and describe the bright lights, the dazzling life and the beautiful women, and offer new excuses why he cannot take Gabriele to hear him—yet. He shows her how he appears at the encores and gives vivid descriptions that are *visioned*. He brings home a discarded bouquet and describes how it was given to *him*. Then his playing and pantomime is interrupted by several indignant fellow tenants pouncing down: "SAY—IF YOU *MUST* PLAY— GO DOWN TO THE RIVERFRONT!" Thus poor Pierre's soul is tortured beyond endurance, though there is only a momentary glimpse of pain— then the *smile*.

Then one night Pierre sees a Dread Spectre that threatens to envelop his little Gabriele and so destroy *all* happiness.

It is Le Boeuf and two companions, who take a table and are carousing when suddenly Le Boeuf pauses in terror as though he saw the gallows. Simultaneously Pierre's bow sags and his hands clinch. He loosens his collar from the passionate emotion.

Le Boeuf sneaks out. Pierre's anger slowly fades in the thought of Gabriele, whom he has promised not to kill this Le Boeuf. Poor Gabriele! He must hasten to her—she is his Life.

Meantime all eyes are directed upon Pierre, for the music has stopped dead. The accompanists are berating him. But the proprietor likes him and the

AN ACCEPTED SYNOPSIS

patrons like his music after all. Pierre cannot go on. The Boss is solicitous: "HERE, FOUNTAIN, YOU AIN'T WELL—HERE'S FIVE DOLLARS WHICH I'M RAISIN' YOU EVERY WEEK— OUR KIND LIKES YOUR PLAYIN'—BE SURE TO BE ON TIME TOMORROW."

Outside Le Boeuf is telling his companions: "I'VE GOT TO GET RID OF THAT BIG BOOBY BEFORE HE SQUEALS ON ME." One of the men hands him a blackjack and Le Boeuf starts out trailing Pierre and waiting his opportunity to strike.

But Pierre has cooled off. He can think of but *one thing*—this big brute owns his little Gabriele body and soul. Again he must *hide*. He stops in a little dry goods shop and with the five dollars buys Gabriele a pretty frock. This will please her and the new ordeal may be easier.

Le Boeuf sees the dress and at once his fears vanish and he laughs as he sees ahead of him a good living without work. Gabriele is *alive!* He follows Pierre home and gets their number.

Gabriele is surprised at Pierre's early return and overjoyed with the frock. Then Pierre suddenly clasps her protectingly in his big arms and holds her, rocking her to sleep like a child, a look of futile agony on his face.

Pierre is afraid to go back to the cafe and thus loses the only job he has had. Again they are flotsam and jetsam in the Great City of Few Dreams.

Back in Papineauville we have seen La Touche trying almost in vain to sell out his confiserie. This shocks his vanity, as he had thought that everyone who heard of it would rush to him with an

THE FEATURE PHOTOPLAY

offer.   At length strangers who are not in the
least prepossessing consent to take the business for
six months with the option of purchase.   This is
a bad bargain, but La Touche consents because he
is many weeks overdue with his dear Pierre, whose
Fame he has solemnly promised to make.

Affairs have reached their very worst with Pierre
when who should blow in like a gale of Southern
wind but La Touche.   The whole house is aroused
by the noise and fuss he makes and come in to see
what it is all about.   La Touche is arrayed regardless.   He wears silk hat, cane, frock coat, fierce
moustaches and all that goes with it.   He enters like
a brass band and with an irresistible air of importance, enthusiasm and bombastic energy.   He introduces himself to the somewhat astounded assembly:
"I AM LA TOUCHE, THE IMPRESARIO—I
HAVE COME A LONG WAY TO MAKE HIM
FAMOUS!"

At once all is changed, temperamentally and liter-
ally.   Pierre forgets all things in the flood of op-
timism that La Touche lets loose in their hearts.
"HOW IS IT? ARE YOU NOT RICH? I WILL
SHOW THESE STUPID AMERICANS WHAT
CLEVER ONES WE ARE! TIENS!"

So next day La Touche and Pierre go out.
Pierre is rigged up like a Continental musician.   La
Touche goes directly to the swellest restaurant.
He makes his way through all barriers.   His nerve
is superior to the nerviest city people.   They take
him at first for a buffoon, then he turns on them
and bowls them over.   He sends in a pompous card
to the Proprietor: JEAN BAPTISTE MARIE
ALENCON   LA   TOUCHE—SOUS-CAPORAL
DANS   LA   GRAND   ARMEE—IMPRESARIO-

AN ACCEPTED SYNOPSIS

SUPERIEUR DE FONTANELLE-LE-GRAND—
PREMIER VIOLIN ET COMPOSER—(CONFI-
SEUR A PAPINEAUVILLE, P. Q.). This card
is too much for the proprietor's curiosity and afraid
of missing something worth while, though understanding not a word of it, he has La Touche
brought in.

La Touche enters like an emperor, the shy Pierre
following. La Touche out-bullies the proprietor
when he gets on his high horse, and finally brings
him into submission. He informs him: "FONTA-
NELLE-LE-GRAND EES ON HEES VAY TO
PAREE BUT HE VEEL PLAY FOR YOU BY
MY SPECIALE PERMISSION." The proprietor
thanks him. A fine contract is made.

The two walk out in a maze after Pierre has
played entirely to satisfaction. To Pierre this *is*
Fame.

At home, however, Le Boeuf has stolen in and
has taken Gabriele in his arms. He pretends to be
repentant and promises to take Gabriele with him
soon if she will do *everything* he asks. It is quite
obvious that she will. She promises not to tell of
his visit.

Pierre in his great happiness does not see that
hers is a thing apart.

PART IV.—THE BLESSED DEMOISELLE

We find Pierre's name emblazoned outside the
famous restaurant alongside that of La Touche the
great impresario. Here it is discovered by Ignatz
the Leader of the orchestra, who is both jealous
and outraged at not having been consulted. His
nose is thus put out of joint. He protests in vain

THE FEATURE PHOTOPLAY

to the proprietor and then swears vengeance by bringing the Union down on him.

But a period of blessed prosperity ensues. Daily Pierre comes home laden with gifts for Gabriele and she is happy though oblivious. All she can remember is that Le Boeuf took her in his arms.

Pierre plays at the restaurant in a mood of sheer dazzling joy that delights the diners and makes Ignatz hotter with jealousy. Then comes the night of nights when Alva Blashfield, Blake and their party visit the restaurant. Pierre plays and his music enters Alva's heart like a refreshing draft. Pierre is not conscious of her or the impression he has made until the encore, when her enthusiasm shows no bounds, much to Blake's disgust.

Then Pierre and Alva look into each other's eyes, yes, very souls. Then Pierre plays again, not for the throng, but for her. He *knows* and she *knows* Blake is annoyed and shows his displeasure in vain. Pierre plays for the first time his Prayer Sonata, for HER, to her. The gayety stops and an air of depression in accord with the music takes its place. Many of the guests leave with almost conscience-stricken faces as though they had come face to face for the first time with their wicked selves. The proprietor is alarmed and hurries to Ignatz: "FOR GOD'S SAKE, CUT OUT THE FUNERAL MARCH—THESE TIRED BUSINESS MEN WANT NOTHING PUT RAGTIME—GET ME!" Ignatz points to Pierre as the one responsible for this number.

Blake especially has complained of the Sonata. He returns sullenly to the table to find Alva gone.

Alva has approached Pierre, who turns and is blinded by the new emotion that envelops his be-

AN ACCEPTED SYNOPSIS

ing as she whispers: "OH, IT WAS SO WON-
DERFUL—*Y O U* WERE WONDERFUL! I
SHALL COME AGAIN!"

Ignatz has been joined by the Walking Delegate
of the Musicians' Union, who now comes to the
proprietor threateningly. Ignatz introduces the delegate triumphantly, who announces: "THIS GUY
IS A SCAB—AND UNLESS YOU FIRE HIM
NOW THE UNION SAYS YOU'LL GET NO
MORE MUSIC IN THIS JOINT—SEE!" The
proprietor argues in vain, then pleads, with the result that Pierre is discharged.

Pierre goes home hovering between heaven and
hell. An angel has descended at his feet with the
annunciation that he is wonderful—and he always
will be wonderful after that, because she has said
it. But just now he had been thrown out of
heaven!

La Touche receives the news and is furious be-
yond description: "THIS IS NOT POSSIBLE!
I SHALL SHOW THIS MONSIEUR UNION
WHO LA TOUCHE IS! I SHALL PULL HIS
NOSE!"

In his impractical way Pierre keeps his money as
of old in a vase where Gabriele can hobble to it
and get coins for their daily needs. The contract
had brought a large number of small bills and to
the impractical Pierre they were rich again.

The old Artist enters and finds Pierre once
more downcast: "AH, I SEE THAT YOU
PLUCKED ONLY A TAIL FEATHER OF THE
BIRD OF FAME—THERE IS A WAY TO FOR-
GET, HAVE SOME?" At which he produces a
bottle of liquor, which Pierre refuses. He goes
out and Pierre strums a few notes that show the

THE FEATURE PHOTOPLAY

color of his amorous soul and his dawning Love.
Gabriele in the next room looks up as though someone had called. She lays her hand with a sigh on
her breast and asks him to play it over and over
again.

La Touche goes out in the evening to the restaurant bent on reprisal and justice to his protege.
The proprietor will not see him, and he paces up
and down in front of the orchestra until Ignatz
appears, bowing and smiling, whereupon La Touche
pulls his nose soundly: "YOU SHALL NOT
NAME MY PIERRE A SCAB—A PIECE OF
DEAD SKIN—HE IS FONTANELLE-LE-
GRAND!" The proprietor orders him put out
forthwith and he puts up a noise and a fight that
can be heard a block away.

Alva has come again tonight to hear Pierre, and
it is she, much to Blake's disgust, who brings the
melee to a halt by touching the irate La Touche
on the arm and signaling the others away. She
asks where Fontanelle is. La Touche seeing commercial possibilities is calmed instantly: "AH, MA-
DAME, YOU VEEL VANT FONTANELLE-LE-
GRAND TO PLAY AT A MUSICALE—N'EST
C' PAS?" Alva had not thought of this, but the
idea is not bad and offers an excuse. She nods,
takes down the address. La Touche now walks
slowly out with unwonted dignity.

PART V.—THE SUBLIME SACRIFICE

To Pierre the news of Alva's visit means that
heaven is full upon him. He is in a constant
flutter of happiness that knows no bounds.

La Touche, too, is in a fever of preparation for
madame's promised visit, and as in all things he

AN ACCEPTED SYNOPSIS

purposes to make it one of the most theatrical events in his career. He will stage the whole thing with becoming atmosphere. He gets his idea from the print of "The Beethoven Sonata" hanging on the wall, which he intends to reproduce exactly. He hires the services of people he picks up here and there to furnish figures for the composition, and he rehearses them with harsh severity. They are all bad actors and need him constantly gesticulating in the foreground to maintain anything like a semblance of the desired effect.

The day upon which Alva is expected sees the tableau arranged with sweating difficulty by La Touche. Pierre is posed at the piano with his violin. The others are supposed to listen, enthralled by the air. Most of them go to sleep or center their frail attentiveness on less artistic things, and others cannot keep their eyes off the jumping La Touche, who as she enters takes his position behind Alva, engaged in wildly directing the affair almost in vain.

When all is a la Beethoven Sonata, La Touche beckons for Alva to be ushered in. All seemingly ignore her, though in reality they are looking cross-eyed in their efforts to look two ways at one time. La Touche asks her politely to wait for a moment. He, behind her back, holds the tableau, trying with difficulty to appear enraptured, while really shaking his fists at the fishlike postures.

Alva is truly impressed. Yet strangely it is Gabriele with her eyes upon her whom Alva notices first, and goes straight to her with a smile and outstretched hands. Alva touches the girl's heart as she approaches the wheel chair and speaks with her in French.

THE FEATURE PHOTOPLAY

Pierre is impressed beyond words by this action of Alva's. He says simply with his open smile showing like a window into his heart: "I THANK YOU FOR THIS HAPPINESS YOU GIVE MY LITTLE SISTER—THAT IS THE GREATEST DESIRE IN MY LIFE." Alva looks at him with a deep sympathetic understanding. Gabriele is entranced by the kind lady who has completely won her heart.

La Touche hustles the supers out of the room and manages it so that Alva and Pierre are left alone in the room. He peeps from behind an adjoining portiere.

Thus Pierre and Alva spend a wonderful Hour together, an hour that neither of them will ever forget, and in which each is irresistibly attracted. Pierre now plays, now ingenuously discloses his Dream of going to Paris to meet Maitre Dupre, now becomes shy under the pressure of circumstance, now emotionally enthusiastic.

La Touche at length not being able to hear what they say and seeing an hour has passed is too impatient to stand it longer approaches, obviously trying not to interrupt by his coughing and so on. "PERHAPS MADAME AND FONTANELLE-LE-GRAND HAVE MADE ALL ARRANGE-MENTS FOR THE MUSICALE?" They had not even mentioned it and show they are embarrassed.

Alva insists on giving them a check for five hundred dollars in advance. She kisses Gabriele and tells her she is coming again to see her only, and leaves them all in the clouds, La Touche with the big check, Gabriele with the tangible Sympathy, Pierre with a Love that will never die. The musicale is to be given within a week.

AN ACCEPTED SYNOPSIS

Le Boeuf calls, in the men's absence, obviously down and out. Gabriele is sorry for him and discloses the secret of the money vase and he helps himself to nearly all of the contents, Gabriele turning painfully away so that she will not see. Just then there comes a knock at the door. In consternation Le Boeuf runs to seek a hiding place in the next room.

Alva enters, followed by a footman bearing an armful of potted plants and cut flowers. Alva kisses Gabriele again and asks her to go out for a ride in the car in vain. As she is leaving she says: "NOW, ON THE DAY OF THE MUSICALE, I AM GOING TO COME FOR YOU EARLY IN THE MORNING TO SPEND THE WHOLE DAY LONG."

Gabriele, overjoyed, has forgotten all about Le Boeuf until he appears all excitement. For Alva had removed her coat and disclosed a wonderful pearl neckband. Le Boeuf sees a way out of all things. He tells Gabriele that she must get that necklace for him—*steal it*. Gabriele recoils, and then Le Boeuf wheedles, threatens, and finally promises that this will enable him to come for her and take her away with him. At last she consents to his wishes.

Pierre and La Touche come home laden with gifts and goodies for their darling, but she is only sad and morose. Pierre says he has spent all their change and goes to their vase "bank" and finds it practically *empty*. He turns to Gabriele startled with fear of the serpent.

Gabriele looks guilty, but when he asks her if she knows she shakes her head, no, and he will not pain her, but is stabbed to the heart with appre-

THE FEATURE PHOTOPLAY

hension. La Touche comes in with a diagram on paper for the musicale and Pierre is taken away from the subject. He throws off the care with a smile, though it will persist in coming back.

Then the wonderful day of the musicale arrives, and with it Alva for Gabriele with a new frock and all. Gabriele goes with her, her heart sore with the weight of the coming treachery.

Blake wants to know, "YOU MAY TRUST THESE CANUCKS WITH THINGS OF VALUE, BUT I DON'T."

Alva tells him later when he continues to annoy her: "I AM SORRY YOU DO NOT LIKE THIS MUSICIAN—I WOULD BE AFRAID TO TELL YOU WHAT I THOUGHT OF HIM."

Evening approaches and La Touche personally attends to Pierre's make-up. Then he sends him to the musicale alone. "YOU MUST TELL THEM YOU CANNOT PLAY WITHOUT MY PER- MISSION, AND I, LA TOUCHE, SHALL AP- PEAR WHEN THEY ARE BEGINNING TO FEAR THEY WILL NOT HEAR YOU."

Gabriele is being amused by Alva as the latter dresses for the evening. At length Gabriele gets hold of Alva's jewel case and amongst its contents finds the neckband. There is an agonized moment of indecision, then the opportunity comes and Ga- briele slips the pearls into a wrist bag that Alva has given her.

Alva has just come back, and noting Gabriele has put down the case, hurries to it and puts on her rings. Then she misses the pearls. Looks around hastily. An early guest is announced and finally in despair she shrugs her shoulders, gives an order about Gabriele, and hurries out.

AN ACCEPTED SYNOPSIS

Pierre arrives, shy and retiring. Then all present must wait interminably. Alva comes and asks Pierre to play. He says, no, he cannot without La Touches permission. Then Alva has a surprise for Pierre. She brings forward a big Frenchman: "PERMIT ME TO PRESENT TO YOU FONTA-NELLE-LE-GRAND, M. DUPRE, THE GREAT FRENCH MASTER OF MUSIC YOU WANTED TO STUDY WITH!" Pierre is overwhelmed and the two chat until the arrival of La Touche is announced.

Blake has noted his fiancee's missing neckband of pearls from the first: "SINCE IT WAS I WHO GAVE YOU THAT BAND OF PEARLS I DO NOT THINK IT AMISS TO ASK WHERE THEY ARE." Alva implores him to wait. He agrees.

Then the footman reads La Touche's card to the mingled amusement and amazement of the impatient guests. Then Sous-Caporal La Touche appears in the full dress uniform of a Turco of the Franco-Prussian War, blouse, bagged trousers, sword and all, gold lace and a broad riband across his breast, and numerous medals. All are astounded, but are finally impressed as he lengthily introduces Pierre, who shyly retreats to the shadow of the curtain while La Touche struts up and down in front of the assembly.

Then Pierre plays to and for Alva alone, and Alva is with him in spirit and truth.

Dupre is enthusiastic and with Alva makes an appointment for five o'clock the next day, promising him all that he has ever dreamed. Pierre kisses his hand.

Pierre is directed to the room where Gabriele is

waiting for him. It is Alva's room, and he emerges
from it carrying Gabriele as Blake and Alva come
along the hall, Alva having promised to come up
and convince him that the necklace is not lost.
Blake registers his suspicions as Pierre and his
sister pass on.

They search in vain for the pearls. Blake questions the maids and learns that Pierre and his sister
and Alva have been the only persons in the room
since the necklace was last seen. Blake bids Alva
goodnight, registering in his look news that will be
bad for her. Alva is very uneasy.

Blake goes outside and telephones the police.
"THERE HAS BEEN A VALUABLE NECK-
LACE OF PEARLS STOLEN AND I WANT
YOU TO SEND TWO MEN WITH ME TO AR-
REST THE THIEF!"

PART VI.—THE SUPREME STRUGGLE

Pierre's ecstatic mood is somewhat dimmed by
Gabriele, who is solemnly sad. The two hold each
other in arms a minute when La Touche bursts in
with copies of the evening papers. He dispels their
gloom by undignified conduct in his exuberance.
Then they all sit about and talk. They are interrupted by a knock on the door. Gabriele starts and
trembles. Pierre notices this and goes to the outer
door, where he finds Blake and two policemen.

Blake at once points Pierre out as the man.
Pierre shakes his head vehemently. Then Blake
says: "WELL, IT WAS EITHER YOU OR YOUR
SISTER!" Pierre staggers as though struck a
blow. At once he changes, and after a flash of
pain sembles a confession. Asks a moment to say

AN ACCEPTED SYNOPSIS

goodbye. He pitifully tries to think up something to say and then comes the idea. He puts that dear sweet smile of delusion on his lips and comes in apparently overjoyed: "I HAVE GREAT NEWS —MAITRE DUPRE HAS SENT FOR ME— PERHAPS WE SHALL GO TO PARIS YET— I DON'T KNOW HOW LONG I SHALL BE GONE. LA TOUCHE, LOOK AFTER MA PE- TITE." Then he kisses Gabriele and leaves them discussing the great news wildly.

Thus Pierre is taken to jail broken hearted. He has confessed to stealing from her who had become the foremost angel in his Greater Dream.

In the morning Blake calls on Alva and tells her what has happened. She protests it never could be. He smiles and says it is because Pierre has con- fessed. She then turns on him and commands him to leave her. She then thinks and thinks, until finally she recalls having come in the room for her jewel box which Gabriele was toying with when she put something in her wrist bag. She will go to Ga- briele.

Gabriele is being entertained by La Touche, who has bought *all* the morning papers, which have col- umns about the musicale and wonderful things to say about Pierre. The photographs of La Touche and Pierre appear in several of the papers, La Touche having sent them to all. La Touche is walking up and down in his dressing gown with his thumbs in his arm pits, gesticulating and panto- miming what he intends doing.

Alva comes and Gabriele is conscience stricken at the sight of her. She throws off La Touche, who tells her the latest news about Pierre having gone to M. Dupre. In the next room she takes Gabriele,

THE FEATURE PHOTOPLAY

who is filled with remorse, and soon Alva sees her Pierre's release. Gabriele still denies the truth, however, and then Alva goes straight to the bag and takes the neckband from it.

Gabriele is ashamed and mortified. But Alva realizes the grand man her brother is and hugs her and lets her weep on her shoulder, then hurries away after telling her that she will buy a splendid necklace for her very own.

La Touche has had a little excitement of his own in receiving a telegram: YOUR TENANTS HAVE RUN AWAY, TAKING WITH THEM EVERYTHING THEY COULD LAY HANDS ON IN THE CONFISERIE—YOU HAD BETTER COME AT ONCE. There remains but one thing to do, and that is to hasten back to Papineauville at once and wring the neck of everyone in sight. Thus La Touche leaves Gabriele, saying her brother will soon return. Yet taking with him a Dream that has come true of his dear Pierre.

Alva, with something new shining in her eyes, hurries away to the police station and demands Pierre's release, explaining that she has found the missing jewels and has them with her.

Pierre is brought out of the cell silent, and his pain and shame are very great when he sees who it is. Alva goes straight to him and takes his two hands in hers and he lifts his head which he has hung till now. "AH, I SHALL NEVER THINK OF YOU AS FONTANELLE AGAIN, BUT AS PIERRE-LE-GRAND! REMEMBER, TOMORROW I BRING MAITRE DUPRE TO YOU, AND THEN—"

Pierre stands for a long time where she has left him. Looking at the hands she has held and bask-

AN ACCEPTED SYNOPSIS

ing in the realization that SHE is his Dream made flesh. The police rudely wake him up and tell him to get out while the going's good.

Le Boeuf sneaks in in a fever of happy expectation. At once he demands of Gabriele, "Where is it?" She looks at him speechless and piteously. She sees him for what he is for the first time. She is a stricken doe with the fierce hound at her throat. There is murder in his eye. "SO YOU LET THE SWAG SLIP THROUGH YOUR FINGERS, EH? WELL, I'M GOING TO KILL YOU THIS TIME, YOU—"

Pierre the Emotional has climbed to the skies again in which his Sun seems shining with new lustre. He comes home aglow and happy in the thought that Gabriele did not take the jewels, as he believed. He has bought flowers and knick-knacks for her, and he tiptoes in, expecting to surprise her. He listens at the door of the next room and opens it only a crack.

Le Boeuf at this moment has just given the poor clinging Gabriele a shove from him that has sent her sprawling on the floor. She lies there quivering and helpless and waiting face down for the final blow.

Pierre droops like a flower in a cold blast. The happiness fades from his face and gives place to a carnal look. He has heard, and he realizes the whole truth. With a silent commanding jerk of the hand he beckons Le Boeuf from the inner room.

Le Boeuf, strangely impelled, comes out. Pierre locks Gabriele's door. Then, like a crouching tiger, and with working hands, Pierre approaches Le Boeuf. Le Boeuf looks behind quickly, espies Pierre's precious violin where it has lain uncased

THE FEATURE PHOTOPLAY

since the night before. He backs to the table until his hands come in contact with the instrument. This is his one opportunity. He raises the violin above his head. The onrushing Pierre cringes at the sight. Le Boeuf does not hesitate a second but lets Pierre have it full over the head. The priceless violin flies into a thousand pieces!

Pierre sinks down with a moan as though struck a vital blow. Gathering up some of the fragments with trembling hands he presses them in mental anguish to his lips and heart. Gradually his eyes take on a murderous gleam, his jaws set, his nails dig into his working hands. He is a tiger now, and only the heart's blood of his victim will compensate, he is mad with the wrongs that for years have been piled up on his breaking heart, he is wild because of the personal insults and injuries that his darling Gabriele has endured, and reason vanishes at the sight of his precious violin destroyed!

Le Boeuf is about to descend when he hears a group of tenants ascending. He sees that will not do and turns to the roof. He is delayed getting the hatch off. He is barely outside on the roof when Pierre is seen coming. He closes the hatch and fastens it.

Gabriele has raised herself and listens, now for the first time in positive revolt and revulsion against the brute Le Boeuf. She wants herself to kill him. She cannot get out, and fears for her Pierre now.

Pierre has come to the fastened door and with an unguessed strength in his madness fairly rips it from its fastening and appears like a rapacious beast emerging from the hole.

Le Boeuf has discovered to his horror that the building is connected with no other and projects it-

AN ACCEPTED SYNOPSIS

self alone into the sky. Either he or Pierre—perhaps both—must conquer or perish. Pierre is deliberately refastening the hatch. It is Pierre who discovers a sort of iron ladder scarcely visible which he wrenches from its moorings and flings over the side. Then panting like a beast and crouching in his movements, Pierre goes after Le Boeuf. He is more like a gorilla than a man as he chases Le Boeuf from point to point about the roof.

Pierre finally gets hold of the now terrified Le Boeuf. Le Boeuf's one move is to try to hurl Pierre over the ledge. Pierre wants nothing but to keep his victim on the roof and gradually beat and tear him to pieces. Le Boeuf defends himself with the strength of a man fighting for his life. Pierre fights with the brutal gratification of a beast of prey mauling his victim. He laughs mirthlessly at every blow.

The men seem evenly matched at first, and the fight is herculean, and sometimes they are actually hanging over the edge of the roof. But nothing can withstand the mad unfeeling fury of Pierre's strength. He is literally beating Le Boeuf to a pulp. Both men are torn in body and raiment and covered with blood.

Le Boeuf's only hope is the pile of fallen bricks that the chimney has become because of their fighting about it. He manoeuvers the fighting nearer and nearer to this pile of bricks. His hand at length gets close enough to seize one and then he smashes Pierre on the head, nearly braining him. Pierre releases his hold and Le Boeuf breaks away.

Pierre shakes himself and with the blood running into his eyes he groggily gropes his way toward

THE FEATURE PHOTOPLAY

Le Boeuf who, still afraid, has moved with an armful of bricks to a wide ledge or coping. Here he waits for Pierre to get within range, a brick in each hand. When Pierre is within ten feet he lets one fly and it grazes Pierre's head and he goes down on his knees. But again he rises with even less strength and decision. Now Le Boeuf takes deliberate aim and Pierre draws nearer, seemingly unconscious of his certain peril. Le Boeuf raises the missile high, steps back and—the whole coping gives way and over he goes!

Pierre creeps to the edge and looks over, and gradually the mist of madness clears, and with it comes to him the worst of all his ordeals. *He has killed a man!* Or if not, he tried to. He has killed that which Gabriele loves more than any other thing. He will go down and try to put life into the body himself. Muttering and lifting his eyes to God for forgiveness, he creeps to the hatch, and fumbles weakly.

Finally he gets or falls down the stairs to his floor. There he is about to go down further when he hears excitement below. One of the tenants has just found the body and he hears her tell the policeman: "A MAN HAS JUST BEEN MUR-DERED—HIS BODY IS LYING OUTSIDE MY WINDOW!" So this is the end then!

From this instant Pierre becomes in fancy, if not in truth, a fugitive from justice. He must ever flee the heavy hand of the law. He sneaks into their room and lets the terrified Gabriele out.

Gabriele is the one who is changed now. Her joy is half complete on seeing her brother alive. He says nothing, but she *understands* and by her manner approves. She is now the protector of her

AN ACCEPTED SYNOPSIS

poor Pierre who has given up *all things* that were his for her. She tenderly bathes him, binds his wounds and soothes him. "AH, MY GABRIELE, IT IS TERRIBLE! YOU KNOW I COULD NEVER KILL EVEN THE SPIDER THAT BITES ME!" He breaks down and sobs in her lap like a child, as he picks up a piece of his dear violin. Every moment he starts up and tries to appear composed, as though the police were entering now. He is waiting for them to come and get him.

The police have examined the body and identify it: "OH, JUST ANOTHER GANG MURDER—THIS IS 'JULES THE CANUCK' AND YOU CAN SEE HE HAS BEEN KILLED BY ONE OF HIS PALS IN A FIGHT." So they dismiss the matter.

But not so with Pierre. He has packed a few things and they are ready to steal away under cover of darkness. He has just finished a letter to Alva, which he leaves as a blind to the police on the table. Then he carries Gabriele tenderly but in terror down the stairs. Then the wheel chair and they are off into oblivion, leaving the Fair City of Dreams-Almost-Come-True.

Alva comes with Dupre the next day, having made all plans herself to see to it that Pierre got all things on the ladder of Fame. She finds only the letter: WHEN YOU RECEIVE THIS YOU WILL *KNOW* WHY WE CAN NEVER MEET AGAIN—THOUGH YOU SHALL NEVER BE ABSENT FROM ME. AS A LAST FAVOR I ASK YOU TO INFORM M. LA TOUCHE THAT I AM GOING TO PARIS, WHICH WAS HIS DEAREST WISH, AND SHALL BE ALWAYS GRATEFUL. PIERRE.

THE FEATURE PHOTOPLAY

And "Somewhere in Canada" we see Pierre and Gabriele in her wheel chair skulking along a highway. Gabriele is so tired, but she is so solicitous of Pierre, and the two are bound together now with a Golden String of memory. He kisses her tenderly. "I WOULD HAVE FACED THEM AND TOLD THEM THE TRUTH BUT FOR THEE, MY POOR LITTLE SISTER—THOU HAST SUFFERED SO!" Then they resume their journey, looking fearfully about from right to left for strangers from whom to hide, Pierre's big returned smile illumining the way for weary Gabriele.

PART VII.—THE EMBERS OF A DREAM

Several years have elapsed.

We meet La Touche, considerably aged, a little lame and half blind. That memory of the Fame of Fontanelle-le-Grand which he created has become an obsession. Anyone who will listen he tells about the wonder of it. He has had a medal cast which he wears pinned to his breast for that great service to "Art and Humanity."

One day he is passing through the Lower Town of Quebec and he hears the notes of a violin. They strike a cord of memory, and he approaches toward the street fiddler playing to a group of children. His hat is at his feet, into which a few pennies have been tossed.

This is our Pierre. He has grown a beard, his glance is shifty, his clothes ragged. He plays on, but he neither sees nor hears. His eyes are set on an Invisible Star. When he "comes to" it is with a start of fear.

AN ACCEPTED SYNOPSIS

La Touche hobbles up and sees *something* familiar in his half turned figure. He touches him on
the arm, his face filled with hopeful anticipation.

Pierre cringes under the touch and turns a face
filled with terror, that at last the law is upon him.
Pierre is shaken to the foundations of his tender
soul at the sight of La Touche, whom he at length
identifies. He is torn between many emotions—pity,
gratitude, sorrow, fear. He is almost ready to confess his identity when his lips form the word "Gabriele" and he shakes his head and closes his lips
tightly.

La Touche shakes his head disappointedly:
"FOR A MOMENT I THOUGHT YOU WERE
FONTANELLE-LE-GRAND—IT WAS I WHO
MADE HIM FAMOUS, YOU KNOW—HE IS
IN EUROPE NOW—PROBABLY PLAYING
BEFORE CROWNED HEADS—" La Touche
has called attention to his medal and rattles on.

At the mention of his name, Pierre is filled with
fear that someone may hear, and hustles La Touche
into a nearby wineshop in a secluded corner.

La Touche takes a great mass of brown and
worn clippings from his pocket, which he tenderly
handles as he reads them to Pierre, who sits with
knit brows and listens: "FONTANELLE-LE-
GRAND A TREMENDOUS SUCCESS! PRO-
TEGE OF MISS ALVA BLASHFIELD WITH
LA TOUCHE THE FAMOUS CANADIAN IM-
PRESARIO ACCLAIMED BY SOCIETY!" La
Touche rambles on and on. Pierre, keeping him
from making too much noise, sits there shaking his
head.

Pierre finally tells him that Fontanelle-le-Grand
is dead. La Touche, angry and ready to fight him:

THE FEATURE PHOTOPLAY

"FONTANELLE-LE-GRAND DEAD, YOU SAY? THAT IS IMPOSSIBLE—FONTANELLE-LE-GRAND CAN NEVER DIE!" The two are ordered out for making so much noise, and La Touche leaves Pierre standing there, repeating his words as he goes away talking vehemently to himself.

Pierre returns to Gabriele in their neat but ill furnished little place that supposedly guards their identity. Gabriele has changed. She it is whose every thought is for Pierre, whom she guards and comforts. He is so immersed in reflection that she cannot rouse him, until suddenly his face illumines with his old smile as he repeats almost fiercely triumphant: "IT IS TRUE—FONTANELLE-LE-GRAND CAN NEVER DIE!" Gabriele nods, but tells him to speak that name more softly.

Pierre and she are very happy again as he dumps the coins from his pocket on the table. He finds a bank note for $100. Tears come in his eyes as he thinks and then knows it was the dear old La Touche: "AH, MA PETITE, I AM HAPPY AGAIN! FOR NOW WE SHALL BUY MANY PRETTY NEW THINGS FOR THEE!"

Next we see Alva and her decrepit husband Blake arriving at the hotel in Quebec. Blake has aged and has more than one foot in the grave. Alva has matured into a beautiful woman.

Blake tells her querulously: "FOR THE LIFE OF ME I CANNOT SEE WHY YOU HAVE COME TO THIS RAT-HOLE OF A PLACE!" She smiles reminiscently. She puts on a heavy veil and tells him despite his protests that she is going to look around the Lower City. She means to visit every corner of HIS dear town.

She is coming back to the hotel that night when

AN ACCEPTED SYNOPSIS

she hears certain notes from a violin that transfix her. The music comes from a dirty little wine shop. She enters, much to the amusement of the patrons. She goes into a secluded private drinking room where she can see in a half-dark corner Pierre playing his "Prayer Sonata." He stands oblivious to all things else. His eyes are again fixed on the Invisible Star, a half smile on his lips.

Alva is struck deep with pity and sobs. She too had thought he was playing to Royalty abroad! Then she is happy in the thought that this is he. Pierre passes around the hat, still enthralled and unseeing. Alva lays her hand on his and whispers, "PIERRE!"

He is frightened at first. Can scarcely believe it is she. Then breaks the real smile that wipes away five years' bitterness from his soul. She has risen. They read the truth in each other's eyes and then by a common impulse are in each other's arms.

Then follows their Wonderful Hour that will make all the suffering in the world endurable, that will keep his heart forever green and his smile sweet for all the days to come. She orders wine and the waiter looks on skeptically.

They then review his night of triumph long ago. Pierre mimics La Touche and how amusing he was. Alva acts the applause and the shyness of Pierre. They laugh and weep alternately and forget all things. Pierre takes Alva's hands and kisses them: "AND ALL THE YEARS THOU HAST BEEN MY INVISIBLE STAR TO WHOM I HAVE PLAYED AND SUNG AND SMILED!" She takes his brow and pushes back the hair and kisses him. Oh, the joy of telling each other their great love!

THE FEATURE PHOTOPLAY

Back at the hotel the hours have passed petulantly for Blake. He has tickets for the midnight express. Worried and annoyed he at length gets the police and insists on going with them and making a search of the Lower City.

Gabriele at home is distracted with anxiety.

But for Pierre and Alva there are neither time nor things, all is eternal love. Pierre is saying: "AH, MY ANGEL! THIS NIGHT SHALL BE MY ETERNITY, COLORING ALL TIME THAT HAS BEEN OR SHALL BE!" They drink deeply to their love.

Then it is that in a hopeless digression the police come to this joint and find them. Blake is horrified, outraged.

Pierre for a moment is roused to horror at the sight of the police, but it is Alva who in a look gives him strength and he is resolute to stand the supposed ordeal. Alva remarks: "I DID NOT TELL YOU—BUT WHAT DOES IT MATTER TO US!—HE IS NOW MY HUSBAND!" Pierre smiles that nothing can dim his happiness. Blake in his rage at Pierre, who does not move when he shakes his fist under his nose, tumbles over in exhaustion, plainly showing that he is not good for many more years. They revive him with whisky. Pierre's smile seems chiseled in his heart as she says: "AU REVOIR, MY PIERRE-LE-GRAND! UNTIL SOME DAY—YOU UNDERSTAND, MY LOVE—AU REVOIR!"

Pierre stands with clasped hands as though he saw a vision, and then marches away like one inspired, saying to himself: "YOU, MY LOVE, AND TONIGHT, CAN NEVER LEAVE ME!" He takes the tearful Gabriele in his arms and together

AN ACCEPTED SYNOPSIS

they watch the lights of an express train passing
by: "TONIGHT! TONIGHT, MA PETITE, MY
FAIREST DREAM CAME TRUE! YES, AND
TOMORROW—TOMORROW—P E R H A P S—"
And we know that She will return tomorrow—
one day—and all that he has Dreamed will live!

THE END OF THE PLAY.

INDEX OF SUBJECTS AND NAMES

Index of Subjects and Names

L

M

Y

INDEX OF FILM TITLES

Index of Film Titles

A

B

C

T

Tarzan of the Apes (1912) 116n

Ten Commandments, The (1923) 267

They Looked Alike (1915) 117

Total Recall (1990) 285

Traffic in Souls (1913) 137–138, 143

Twilight Zone, The (1959–1964) (TV series) 285n

U

Untamed, The (1917) 138n

V

Voice on the Wire (1917) 144–145

W

What Happened to Mary? (1912) 76–77

Wonderful Eye, The (1911) 138